SCHOLASTIC READ XL®

Acknowledgments and credits appear on pages 358-360, which constitutes an extension of this copyright page.

ISBN 0-439-19865-8

18 14 09 08 07

CONTENTS

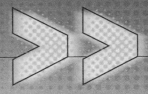

CONTENTS

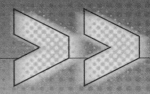

FOR PETE'S SNAKE

Will is home alone — in the dark and during a thunderstorm — but that's not his biggest problem. He's agreed to watch his sister's pet, and it's slithering around in the house with him!

BY ELLEN CONFORD

The last, tearful words my sister, Petra, said to me as they drove her off to the hospital were, "Please, Will, take care of my Coily!"

It was Saturday evening, on the Fourth of July weekend. My parents didn't know how long they'd have to wait in the emergency room. But they were used to it. This was not the first time Pete had fallen out of a tree. Or off the roof. Or off her skateboard.

Pete is a major klutz. She breaks things. Mostly her bones. Whenever anyone asks my father for a credit card, he says, "Visa, American Express, or County General?"

So there was really nothing new about Pete being carried off to the hospital again.

Except that this time I had promised to baby-sit a boa constrictor.

Well, I hadn't really promised. But I had nodded. I'm her brother, what else could I do? The kid was in pain, in tears, and in the car. If I'd said no, she might have jumped out of the car and tried to take Coily with her to the hospital. Then my mother and father would probably have argued over who would get to shoot me.

And besides, I thought, as I sat down on the front steps, it's a snake, not a baby. It's not as if I'd have to pick him up, or rock him, or burp him or anything.

As Pete told my mother when she begged to adopt the beast, "They're really no trouble at all. You don't have to walk them, and you only have to feed them every two weeks. And they eat mice."

"We don't have any mice," my mother had pointed out.

"So we'll get some," Pete said.

The sky was beginning to turn a coppery color, and I could see hard-edged dark clouds on the horizon. The air was heavy and still. I hoped we weren't going to have a thunderstorm.

It's not that I'm really afraid of storms. It's just that when I was five, I wandered away from our tent during a family camping trip. I got lost, and this monster thunderstorm came up—

Well, ever since then I've been a little tense about thunder and lightning.

Except for the occasional sound of a distant firecracker, the neighborhood was unnaturally quiet. A lot of people were away for the holiday weekend, and the others were at Waterside Park, waiting for the fireworks display.

Which is where we were planning to go before Petra fell out of the tree.

I can go anyway, I realized. After all, it wasn't as if I had to do anything for Coily. Mostly he lay on the flat rock in his tank, or wrapped himself around the tree branch in there, or hid inside the copper water pipe Pete had found for him.

"They like to hide," Pete explained. "Where they can't be seen."

"Great," I'd told her. "The less I see him, the better."

Not that I'm afraid of snakes—but, hey, even Indiana Jones thinks they're **repulsive.** So I'd just look in on Coily—very briefly—and then go off to see the fireworks. If I could find someone to drive me.

I went into the house, flipping on light switches as I made my way to the kitchen. It was getting pretty dark. The fireworks would probably begin in about an hour.

I phoned my friend Josh, hoping he was home.

"Hey, Will!" he shouted. "Boy, am I glad to hear somebody who doesn't sound like Popeye the Sailor Man."

"Excuse me?"

"There's a six-hour Popeye **marathon** on cable. We're into the fourth hour here."

"Then you'll be glad to know why I'm calling," I said. "Though it does involve water." I explained about Pete and the hospital, and about how I wanted to go down to Waterside Park.

"That would be great," he said.

"Okay, come over and pick me up and—"

"Except that I have to sit with Steffie." Steffie is Josh's five-year-old sister.

"Bring her along," I said.

"She's got a strep throat," Josh said. "I can't take her anywhere."

"It's hot out," I said. "It wouldn't hurt her to just lie on a blanket and watch—"

"She's got a hundred-and-one fever," he said. "Hey, I have to go. I think I hear her croaking for something. Enjoy the fireworks."

"How can I—" But he'd already hung up. How can I enjoy the fireworks, I'd been about to ask, with no one to drive me there? The park is four miles away.

Shelly! I thought. My friend Shelly had a brand-new driver's license and was always looking for an excuse to drive somewhere.

I heard a lot of noise in the background when Mrs. Getz answered the phone. Kid noise. Like a bunch of preteenies squealing and giggling.

"Hi, Mrs. Getz. It's Will. May I speak to Shelly?"

"She's sort of tied up at the moment," said Mrs. Getz. "Can she call you back?"

"What's going on there?" I asked. "Is that Shelly screaming?"

"I think so," Mrs. Getz answered. "She's supposed to be running Carol's birthday party."

Carol is Shelly's eleven-year-old sister.

"I forgot about the party," I said glumly. "I guess she'll be tied up for a while then."

"She will until I go untie her," said Mrs. Getz. "I believe they're playing Joan of Arc."

WORDS. WORDS. WORDS

repulsive: distasteful or disgusting
marathon: any long contest or event
defensively: feeling and acting as if you have been criticized

"I do *not* have a thing about thunderstorms."

"Boy," I said, thinking of Pete and Steffie, "kids can sure be a pain sometimes."

Mrs. Getz snorted. "Tell me about it," she said, and hung up.

I dropped the phone back on the hook. I peered out the window over the kitchen sink. It was only seven thirty, but the darkness was closing in fast.

I called three other friends. Two weren't home. Chip, the third, had to shout over the sound of an electric guitar, and some horrible wailing.

"Family reunion!" he yelled. "That's my cousin Dennis."

"What's he doing?"

"Elvis Presley. Why don't you come over? We're barbecuing."

"Dennis, I hope," I muttered.

"What? I can't hear you."

"I said, great, I'll be right there." It was only half a mile to Chip's, and even if I'd have to listen to Dennis, it was better than sitting alone in the house with a boa constrictor.

And then I heard a distant rumble.

"Was that thunder?" I asked.

"I can't hear a thing," Chip shouted. "Dennis is doing 'Hound Dog.' "

Another rumble. Closer.

"I think it's starting to rain," Chip said. "It doesn't matter. Come on over."

"Well, maybe not," I said. "I mean, if it's raining."

"That's okay. We'll go inside. Whoo, there goes the lightning."

"I'd better stay here," I said. "My folks might try to call."

"Oh, yeah," Chip said. "You have this thing about thunderstorms."

"I do *not* have a thing about thunderstorms," I said **defensively.** "I just don't feel like walking half a mile in a downpour, that's all." With lightning striking all around me.

"Suit yourself," Chip said. "I'd better help Dennis get his amp inside before he's electrocuted."

"Right." I slammed the phone down. Okay. Fine. I'll stay home. I'll read. I'll watch TV. I'll listen to music. I'll worry about my sister.

I'll be alone in the house with a boa constrictor.

Big deal. It doesn't scare me. All he ever does is lie on his rock. Or curl up inside his pipe. I won't bother him, he won't bother me. I'm not really afraid of snakes anyway. I just happen to find them repulsive, disgusting, and evil looking.

But I'm not afraid of them.

And I'm certainly not afraid of being alone in the house. And even though it's starting to thunder, I'm perfectly safe, as long as I don't talk on the telephone, stick my toe in a light socket, or stand under a tree.

So there's nothing to be afraid of. Even if it is getting so dark that the light over the kitchen table is barely making a dent in the gloom.

So don't stay in the kitchen, dummy, I told myself. There's a whole, brightly lit house to wander around in. I'll just go check the stupid snake, I thought, then settle down in front of the TV. There's nothing like a Popeye festival to calm your nerves.

ASK YOURSELF

- What does Will do to avoid being alone after his parents and his sister leave?

Think about what you've read so far.

I turned on the light in the hallway and headed toward Pete's room.

One quick look into the glass tank and I could say that I'd kept my promise. Coily will be curled up on his rock, and I'll go curl up with Popeye and Olive. The rumbles of thunder that had seemed so far away a moment ago were louder now. The storm was coming closer.

That's okay, I told myself. The closest thing to a tree in this house was Coily's branch, and I would hardly climb into the tank and wedge myself under it, so there was nothing to worry about.

The door to Pete's room was wide open. This was a major **violation** of rules. Ever since she'd gotten the boa, Pete had strict orders to keep her door closed. That way, in case Coily ever managed to escape from his tank, he'd be confined to Petra's room and be reasonably easy to recapture.

Not that any of us, except Pete, would ever try to recapture him. My father said, "If that thing gets loose, I'm moving to a motel and putting the house up for sale."

So far the only time the snake had been out of Pete's room was when she would occasionally drape Coily around her shoulders and parade around the house so we could admire his **exotic** markings and alleged tameness.

When Pete "walked" her scaly pet, the rest of us found urgent business to attend to in rooms with doors that locked.

Anyway, it disturbed me that Pete's door was wide open, but I figured that in her hurry to get to the yard and climb a tree so she could fall out of it, she'd forgotten the rule.

I reached inside the room and flicked the light on. From the entrance I peered at the snake tank. It was a large, glass rectangle with gravel on the bottom and plastic mesh screening over the top. Pete had taped a little sign on the side that said COILY'S CORNER.

I couldn't see the beast at first, but that didn't throw me. As Pete had said, snakes like to hide, so I figured Coily was scrunched inside his copper pipe.

I moved into the room. A clap of thunder made me jump, but it wasn't too bad, and I didn't see any lightning flash.

"Miles away," I reassured myself. "Just get the stupid snake check over with and go watch something dumb on the tube."

Okay. I cleared my throat so Coily would know I was coming and not feel he had to rear up and do anything dramatic to protect his territory. I know snakes can't hear. But why take chances?

I edged closer to the tank. I could see it all, the whole thing. But I couldn't see Coily. Inside the pipe, I reminded myself. Just squat down, look inside the pipe, barf, run out of the room, and shut the door.

The lights flickered with another burst of thunder. Lights flicker in a storm, I reminded myself. No need to panic. I squatted down and looked into the copper pipe. I could see clear through it to the other side. There was nothing inside it but air.

"Yikes!" I straightened up, and as I did, I noticed that the plastic mesh screening on top of the tank had a jagged rip in one corner.

As if something—something with fangs—had gnawed right through it.

"Yikes!" I was repeating myself, but this was no time to worry about being clever. I raced out of Pete's room and slammed the door. I leaned against the wall, panting, even though I'd only sprinted ten feet.

What a narrow escape. I could have been standing—or squatting—right there in front of the tank, with the boa lurking under a chair just waiting to slink up and constrict me.

WORDS. WORDS. WORDS

violation: the breaking of a rule
exotic: strange and fascinating
instinctively: thinking or feeling something without being told about it
ironic: when a situation is unexpected and not what you thought it would be

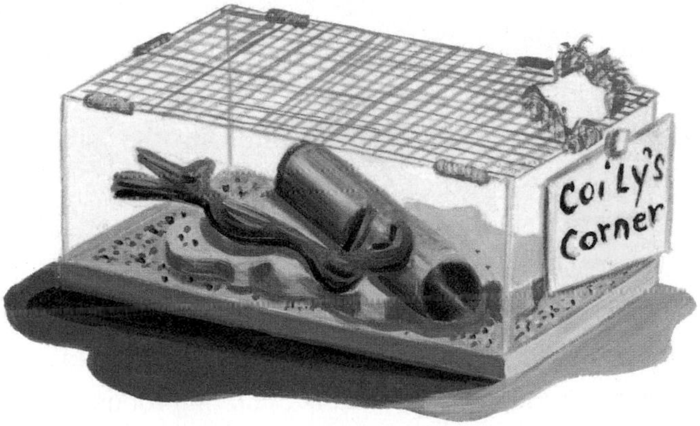
Coi Ly's
Corner

And then it hit me.

Pete's door had been open when I went into her room. It had been open for almost an hour. The snake might not be in there at all. In fact it could be anywhere in the house by this time.

I hugged the wall, wanting to climb up it. If I could hang from the light fixture on the ceiling, chances were the creature couldn't reach me.

Don't lose it, Will, I told myself. This is stupid. I could see all the way up and down the hall, and the boa was nowhere in sight.

There are seven rooms in this house, I reminded myself. Plus the hall. The odds are eight to one that I won't be in the same place as the snake. As long as I keep my eyes open—

Two deafening bursts of thunder, one right on top of the other. **Instinctively** I shut my eyes and clapped my hands over my ears. Then I thought of the twelve-foot-long snake slithering along the hall toward me. I snapped my eyes open and did a 360 to make sure I was still alone.

Another clap of thunder. The lights went out.

"No!" I yelled. *"No!* Don't let the electricity go off!"

The lights came back on.

"Thank you."

A drenching rain began to pound the house. It sounded as if I were standing in the middle of Niagara Falls.

Flashlight! I thought. Candles. Quick, while I could still find them.

I ran for the kitchen. I opened the utility cabinet, next to the refrigerator. Something smacked against the window. It was probably a branch of the mimosa tree, driven by a sudden, howling wind that had seemed to come from nowhere.

"Just the tree," I told myself. "It happens all the time when it's windy."

As I turned around to make sure it was nothing more sinister than the tree branch, the room went black.

ASK YOURSELF

- How would you feel if you were in Will's place?

Think about a time when you were scared.

Another flicker. I tried to keep calm. The electricity would come back on in a moment.

But it didn't.

"Aw, no!" I begged. "Not the lights. A boa constrictor and a thunderstorm aren't enough for one night?"

As if in **ironic** answer, a flash of lightning—very close, *extremely* close—illuminated the room with a harsh, chalky light. For three seconds I could see as clearly as if it were daytime. The mimosa tree, the sink, the white curtains at the window . . .

And the giant brown reptile twined around the curtain rod flicking his forked tongue at me.

I screamed and jumped backward, crashing against the open door of the utility cabinet. Shrieking, I stumbled out of the kitchen, flailing my arms in front of me to keep from banging into anything else.

Which didn't work. I tripped over the stepladder, bounced off a wall, and staggered into the dining room, where I met the china cabinet head-on. Every dish on the shelves clattered as I careened into it and landed on the floor. I moaned, and wondered which part of my body hurt the most.

I sat huddled there for a moment, dazed and whimpering. Now, accompanying the torrential rain, there was a loud, rattling sound, as if someone were hurling handfuls of gravel against the windows. Hail, I thought. You sometimes get hail with severe thunderstorms. And tornadoes.

Great. A tornado. Just what I need. Thunder and lightning and hail and total darkness and a wandering boa constrictor and a tornado.

Mommy!

ASK YOURSELF

- What has happened to make a bad situation worse?

Review the events that have taken place since Will discovered the empty cage.

The hail and rain were making so much noise that I could hardly hear myself think. If you could call what I was doing thinking. If I can't hear myself think, I realized, I can't hear the brown **monstrosity** unwind himself from the curtain rod.

I can't hear him slip down off the sink, and across the floor, and out of the kitchen, and into the dining room, where I'm curled up here on the floor like a sitting—

"Ayiee!"

I leaped to my feet—or at least I crawled to my knees and stood up as quickly as I could with an entirely black-and-blue body. *Think, Will,* I ordered myself. *Just shut the kitchen door, and—*

Good idea. Except we don't have a kitchen door, only an archway that separates the kitchen from the dining room. At this very moment Coily could be slithering past the refrigerator, heading for the dining room.

I'll go to my room. I'll go to my room and shut the door. No problem. Just grope around the table, through the living room, down the hall, and into my room. I can certainly move faster than a snake can slither—at least I can when the lights are on.

Of course there is another archway that leads from the kitchen and into the hall. The snake could be creeping out that way and into the hall just as I—

Don't even think about it.

Move.

I moved. As fast as I could, in the dark, with only an occasional flash of lightning to help me around the maze of furniture that clutters the living room.

"Why is this room so crammed?" I wondered, as I banged my shin against a footstool. "Does anyone really need this much furniture?"

I flung my arm against a plant stand. A flowerpot crashed to my feet.

"Please don't let it be my mother's African violet that didn't bloom for three years up until last week," I prayed.

I made it to my room without further damage to myself or to our overfurnished house. I slammed the door behind me. I was sure the snake couldn't have gotten to my room before I did.

Well, I was pretty sure.

Call Josh, I thought. *Maybe his parents are home by now. Maybe he can come over with a flashlight, find the boa, and put him back in his tank.*

The phone next to my bed has a lighted keypad, which is **convenient** if you have to call the police in the middle of the night, or if a boa constrictor gets loose in the dark.

When Josh picked up his phone, I didn't even say hello. I just shrieked.

"You have to come over and help me! I don't know where Coily is!"

"Did you check with Larry and Moe?" he asked.

"What?"

"A Three Stooges joke," he explained. "You know Larry, Moe, and—"

"Just what I need. Thunder and lightning and hail and total darkness and a wandering boa constrictor and a tornado."

"This is no time for jokes!" I yelled. "I'm alone in the house with a rampaging boa constrictor, and the lights are off, and—"

"I can't take my sister out in this storm," he cut in.

"When will your parents be home?" I asked desperately

"Monday," he answered.

"ARRGGHH!" I slammed down the phone.

There was only one thing to do. Only one intelligent, mature way of coping with the situation.

I dived into bed and pulled the covers over my head.

The snake couldn't be in my room. He just couldn't be. I'd be perfectly safe here under the covers. If I didn't pass out from the heat or smother myself.

I **cowered** there, sweating and shaking, waiting for my parents to come home. Once in a while I'd think I'd heard a car door slam. Then I'd poke my head out and listen. And gasp for air. But the only sounds were the rain—softer now—and distant rumbles of thunder.

I don't know how long I stayed there, trying to breathe, feeling my clothes getting wetter and wetter with sweat, telling myself that there was no snake in my room and that even if there was, he preferred curtain rods to beds.

And then I felt something soft graze my leg.

For a moment I froze. I couldn't breathe, couldn't even scream, which is what I really wanted to do.

It can't be a twelve-foot boa constrictor, I told myself. *It's just a beetle or a mosquito or something.* But it didn't feel like a beetle or a mosquito.

It felt like a wet strand of spaghetti crawling up my leg.

I threw the covers off, howling. Just as I did, the electricity came back on. My room blazed with light. I blinked, and like a kid waking up from a nightmare, clutched my pillow to my chest. I forced myself to look down, down toward the end of the bed, where I had flung off the covers.

And saw a **procession** of brown, foot-long snakes writhing up my sheet, heads darting, tongues flicking, coming straight at me.

Screaming uncontrollably, I threw myself out of bed. I could still feel something on my leg. When I looked down, I saw that one of the creatures was hanging from my ankle like a loose boot strap.

"NO! *NO!*" I shook my leg violently, and the snake fell to the floor. I felt as if there were snakes crawling all over my body. I twisted around frantically, smacking my pillow against my legs, my arms, my chest.

What if they're in my shorts?

I screamed even louder, dropped my pillow, and scrambled out of my cutoffs. Through my screaming I heard feet pounding down the hall.

"Will! *Will!*" My father threw my door open and grabbed me by the shoulders.

"Snakes! Snakes!" I screamed. "In my pants! In my bed!"

My mother was right behind him. Dimly, through a haze of terror, I saw Pete peer into my room. She had a splint on one arm and a boa constrictor wrapped around the other.

"How come you're running around in your under—" She looked over at my bed.

WORDS, WORDS, WORDS

monstrosity: a horrible or frightening thing
convenient: useful or easy to use
cowered: crouched in fear
procession: a number of persons or things moving in an orderly manner

"Coily!" she cried delightedly. "You're a girl!"

Maybe the biggest surprise was that my hair did *not* turn completely white. Although I was afraid to look in a mirror for two days.

Coily has been adopted by one of my sister's weird friends. My mother put her foot down. She told Pete, "Look, your brother cannot live in the same house with that snake."

"So let him move," Pete said.

They think they found all the babies. But since no one knows how many snakes Coily actually gave birth to, no one is positive they're really all gone. Pete says if there are any left, they ought to come out pretty soon, because they'll be hungry.

In the meantime they could be anywhere. In the pipes under the toilet, in the back of a closet, behind the refrigerator.

So I did move. I'm staying at Josh's house for a while. My parents have been very understanding about my traumatic experience. Especially my father.

He's checked into a motel for two weeks. ●

What Are You Afraid Of?

PHOBIA. It's a fancy word for something that really freaks you out.

No doubt about it. Will had a phobia about snakes. What is a phobia? It's an extreme or unreasonable fear of something. About one in ten people have some kind of phobia.

So, what causes phobias? There are many causes, but here's a common scenario. Let's say a dog bites you when you're a little kid. You might get over it. But you might fear dogs—even friendly, harmless ones—for the rest of your life. Now you've got a phobia.

WHEN PHOBIA STRIKES

Your brain says you're being silly, but your body says otherwise. How do you know when your fear has reached phobic proportions? Here's how a phobia might feel—from mild to severe symptoms.

mild You feel like you just ran a road race. Your body is shaking, you're panting, and your heart is beating faster and faster.

moderate You're getting really scared now. You're dizzy, your palms are sweating, and you feel like you're having a heart attack.

severe Now you're really freaking out. You can't move and you feel like you might die! ●

TOP 10 PHOBIAS

You may have noticed that phobias have funny-sounding names, like *arachnophobia*. That's because the word *phobia* is Greek for "fear." So when experts name a phobia, they usually give it a Greek name. For instance, *arachnophobia* means "fear of *arachnids*." That's Greek for "spiders." Hundreds of different phobias have been reported. Here are ten of the most common.

- **Acrophobia** fear of heights
- **Aviophobia** fear of flying
- **Claustrophobia** fear of cramped spaces
- **Cynophobia** fear of dogs
- **Dentophobia** fear of dentists
- **Entomophobia** fear of insects
- **Hydrophobia** fear of water
- **Herpetophobia** fear of reptiles or of creepy, crawly things
- **Musophobia** fear of mice
- **Nyctophobia** fear of the dark

Does something on this list creep *you* out? Don't worry. You're not alone. Millions of people share these ten phobias.

Wrap-Up

TALK ABOUT IT

Now that you've read "For Pete's Snake" and "What Are You Afraid Of?" what do you have to say about these questions?

- If you made a list of scary things, would snakes and thunderstorms be on it? Why or why not?
- Why do you think some people enjoy scary movies and scary rides?

COMPREHENSION CHECK

Write your answers to the questions below. Use information from the story and the article to support your answers.

1. How did Will end up home alone, watching his sister's pet snake?
2. How do you think Coily escaped the tank?
3. Why do you think the snake ended up in Will's bed?
4. What are two ways that your body might react to fear?
5. What did Will say caused his phobia of thunderstorms?

Coily's Corner

VOCABULARY CHECK

Complete each sentence starter below. Before you answer, think about the meaning of the vocabulary word in bold.

1. One smell that I find really **repulsive** is . . .
2. Sometimes people act **defensively** because . . .
3. I thought it was **ironic** when . . .
4. If I was scared, I would **instinctively** . . .
5. A serious fashion **violation** might be . . .

WRITE ABOUT IT

Choose one of the writing prompts below.

- Think of a scary situation, like getting lost. Write a list of at least five safety tips that might help someone get through this situation.
- Most scary stories have a spooky setting. What's the scariest setting you can think of? Describe it using a lot of details.
- Which was your favorite part of "For Pete's Snake?" Make a cartoon of that part of the story. Include speech bubbles that show what the characters say.

About the AUTHOR

Ellen Conford has written more than thirty books for children and young adults. Her books are so full of humor, even the titles are funny. And that's a good thing, since Conford says, "I want to make them laugh."

Conford lives in Great Neck, New York, with her husband. In her spare time, she likes to read, watch old movies, collect cookbooks, and compete in Scrabble and crossword-puzzle tournaments. She especially enjoys reading mysteries.

More Books by Ellen Conford

- *Dear Lovey Hart, I Am Desperate*
- *Seven Days to a Brand New Me*
- *We Interrupt This Semester for an Important Bulletin*
- *If This Is Love, I'll Take Spaghetti*

Interpreting Survey Results

Surveys can be a great way to learn about people's opinions and habits. But when you read the results of a survey, there are some details you should check. Who took the survey? Who was surveyed? What questions were asked?

Check out the survey below. Read all about it. Can you figure out the results?

Read survey graphs carefully. Notice that the top level on this graph is 40%, not 100%.

What Teens Spend Their Money On

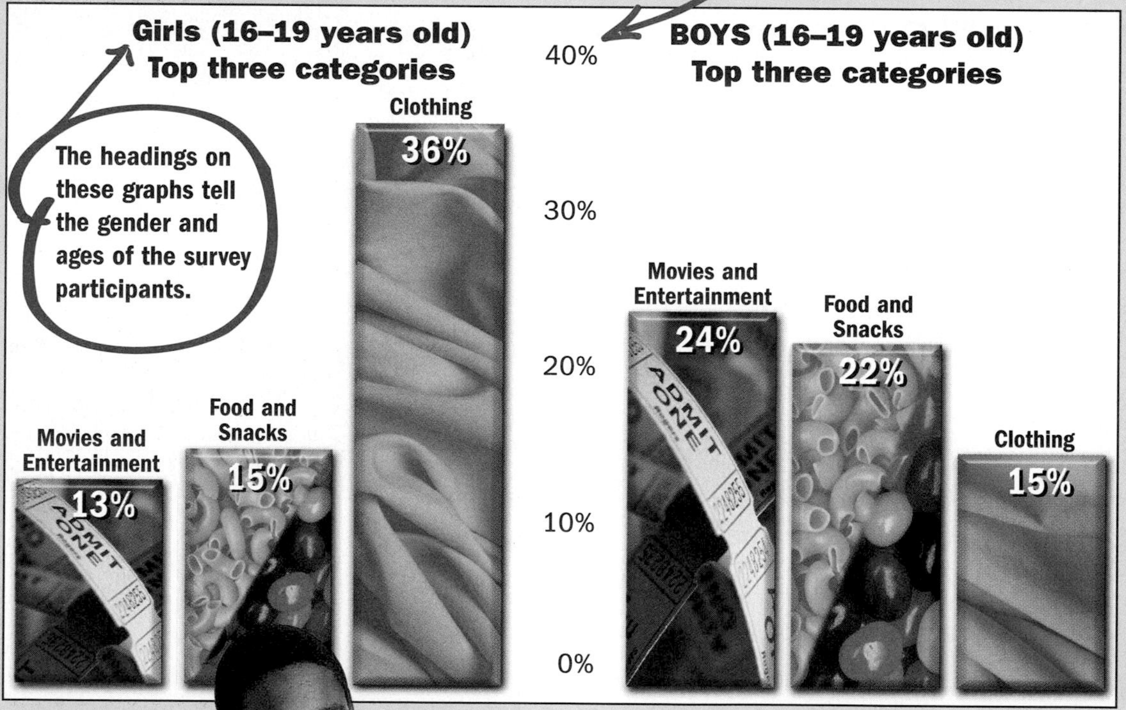
Girls (16–19 years old)
Top three categories
The headings on these graphs tell the gender and ages of the survey participants.
Movies and Entertainment
13%
Food and Snacks
15%
Clothing
36%
40%
30%
20%
10%
0%
BOYS (16–19 years old)
Top three categories
Movies and Entertainment
24%
Food and Snacks
22%
Clothing
15%

Poll based on representative sample of 1,000 teenagers in major U.S. cities.

"Notice that the percentages do not add up to 100. That's because this bar graph shows only the top three answers kids chose."

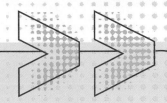

Survey Says . . .

We've got a few questions for you to answer. No, it's not a survey. But the questions are about surveys. Reread the bar graph and the tips that go with it. Then use the graph and tips to answer the questions below. Write your answers on your own paper.

1. On what do girls spend 13% of their money?
   a. food and snacks
   b. movies and entertainment
   c. clothing
   d. none of the above

2. Which of the following is **not** a true statement about these survey results?
   a. Boys spend more money on movies and entertainment than girls do on clothing.
   b. Girls spend as much on food and snacks as boys spend on clothing.
   c. Boys spend the most on movies and entertainment, and girls spend the most on clothing.

3. How many teens were included in this survey?

4. Write about it. How might the results be different if younger kids were surveyed? How might they be different if adults were surveyed?

5. What types of companies might be interested in the results of this survey? How could they use the results?

Survey Search

Look for survey results in newspapers and magazines. (They are often shown as bar graphs or pie graphs.) Choose one and then write down one thing you learned from it.

Take a Poll

Ask ten classmates where they spend most of their money. Record the top three answers on a graph like the one in this lesson.

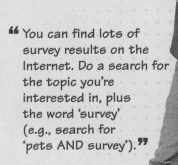

"You can find lots of survey results on the Internet. Do a search for the topic you're interested in, plus the word 'survey' (e.g., search for 'pets AND survey')."

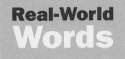

Real-World Words

survey: a report, study, or poll on people's opinions or activities
results: answers, findings

the science behind EXTREME SPORTS

Speed, thrills, danger —and science— that's what extreme sports are all about.

Jump from an airplane and do a back flip. "Sled" down steep asphalt at 80 mph, with just a few inches between you and a really bad road rash. Do extreme sports like this sound like nightmares—or dreams of a lifetime? Find out how they work, and then decide for yourself.

GOING EXTREME

Speed. Thrills. Danger. That's what extreme athletes want. They'll work hard—way hard—to find it, too.

There's no dictionary definition for "extreme sport." It is a daredevil competition in which athletes push themselves to the limit. Athletes may even risk their lives.

Pedaling a mountain bike around your neighborhood wouldn't qualify, for example. But if someone was to race the same bike down a steep, rocky, tree-filled slope—they've gone extreme.

Many of these sports started with small groups of athletes. They invented new and daring ways to test their skills. Now, extreme games are drawing huge crowds. The sports television network ESPN began running X Games in 1995. Then it began to air separate summer and winter games. By the year 2000, the summer games were in more than 200 million living rooms in more than 190 countries. About 200,000 fans showed up to catch the action live.

Extreme sports may seem like wild stunts. But in fact, it takes a lot of science to get each stunt off the ground—and to let the athlete finish in one piece. Take a look inside some of the most extreme sports of all.

GRUNDIG
124
DIESEL
KASTLE
Giro

An extreme mountain biker—not just a ride around the block.

SURF THE FRIENDLY SKIES

Imagine this: You're in an airplane, flying at 14,000 feet—about 1/4 mile—in the air. Below, all you see is a blur of green. You pick up something that looks like a skateboard with no wheels. You strap this *skyboard* onto your feet and step out of the window. What would you do next? If you answered a roll, flip, or spin, then you are thinking extreme!

Skysurfing is probably the only sport **inspired** by a comic book. In 1987, a group of French skydivers **imitated** the moves of superhero Silver Surfer. Skyboarding was born.

Skysurfers "swim" through the air to do their tricks. But they also need help from *air resistance*—the force of air pushing on something. (If you've ever put your hand out the window of a moving car, you've felt strong air resistance.)

Skysurfers fall at about 100 mph. That means air is pushing up on them at 100 mph. If the surfer keeps the board flat, air shoves against the whole bottom of the board. This air resistance slows the fall slightly.

Science at work: A skysurfer at ESPN's X Games.

If a skysurfer wants to dive, she just has to dip the board so the tip is facing down. Now, air is pushing against a smaller surface—the board's tip. This lowers air resistance, speeding up the fall.

To spin, surfers angle the board so air pushes hardest on one part. This unequal push sends the surfer spinning.

Air resistance also keeps skysurfers from going "splat!" on the ground. When the ground gets close, surfers open parachutes. Parachutes spread out to catch a huge chunk of air. This creates a large amount of air resistance, which slows the fall enough for surfers to land.

In the X Games, an airborne "camera flyer" films each skysurfer. Judges watch the film to score each jumper on **technical** skill and style.

ASK yourself

- How does air resistance help a skysurfer do tricks?

Reread the details slowly to be sure you understand.

Words, Words, Words

inspired: influenced by something or someone
imitated: copied
technical: having to do with the way an athlete performs certain moves and positions

AIRWALK

AIRWALK

SUPER SLEDDING

If you think sledding is kid stuff, check out an X Games sport called *street luge*. This sport is modeled after an Olympic event called luge. Ordinary luge **involves** sledding at top speeds down a track of ice. Street luge riders cruise down curvy asphalt hills. The tracks may be up to 13 miles long. The world speed record: 87 mph.

A street luge, however, is not a sled. It's basically a three-inch-wide piece of **aluminum** on wheels. Riders sit on a seat, then lie back. To stay on, lugers jam their feet into footholds in the front. They also hold on tight to handlebars.

To steer, riders use their bodies. Leaning to the left will apply a *force* (a push or pull) to the luge. That force will turn the luge to the left.

In this sport, riders want to avoid air resistance. This is because air pushing against the luge slows it down. So lugers lie flat and wear tight uniforms. That way, wind has less of a surface to push against.

Lying low also helps keep riders from tipping over—a very good thing when you're rolling at 80 mph. Objects balance best when they have a low *center of gravity* (an object's central point, by weight). In other words, stable objects have most of their weight near the bottom. That's why it's easier to tip over a tall, thin ketchup bottle than a short, fat mustard jar, for example.

A street luge is only a few inches off the ground. As riders bend around turns, their skulls may be just an inch or two away from a major headache. Good thing they wear strong helmets!

Words, Words, Words

involves: includes something
aluminum: a light, silver-colored metal
principle: a rule or law of a certain subject

RAD BOARDING

If you've seen the X Games, you've seen skateboarders fling themselves off of a tall *halfpipe* (a u-shaped concrete ramp). Riders roll down one steep wall and then up the other. But they don't stop at the top. Freestylers may fly up to nine feet above the halfpipe. When they catch air, they can try a twist, flip, handplant, or maybe a combination of tricks.

How does a trick like a handplant work? The athlete starts on top of the halfpipe. The force of gravity pulls him down the first side. Then a physics **principle** called *inertia* gets him up the other half.

The law of inertia says this—a moving object will keep moving unless a force acts on it. Once the board gets going, inertia keeps it in motion.

When the rider gets to the top, he kicks his feet up. Then he plants one hand on the *coping* (the pipe on top of the ramp). For a few seconds, he rests his weight on his hand. The other hand holds the board to his feet. Then he lowers his feet and board back onto the ramp.

Of course, gravity doesn't always help skateboarders. It can also pull them down for a major wipeout. But here, physics can lessen the pain. How?

It takes a lot of force to stop a fast-moving object. That's why speeding skateboarders hit the ground hard. If the force hits all at once—SMACK!—it hurts a lot. So skateboarders learn to spread the force out over a distance. They can do this with a *knee slide*—dropping to their knee pads and skidding along the ground. If they fall backwards, they can use a *body roll*—rolling their bodies over and over from shoulder to hip.

One of the keys to successful skateboarding, and all balance sports, is keeping the knees bent. Bent knees help balance by lowering the center of gravity. They also allow boarders to shift their weight more easily. As the board twists and turns, a rider needs to keep her center of gravity on top of it. Otherwise: Wipeout!

ASK yourself

- How does science relate to skateboarding?

Think about the effects of gravity and inertia.

Extreme sliding on a mountain: It's a long way down!

SNOW AND SAND SLIDING

Like skateboarders, extreme snowboarders show their stuff on halfpipes. The X Games include a "Big Air" jumping competition. Snowboarders speed down a ramp and fly as far as they can. Judges score them on distance, height, and landing style.

The faster snowboarders fly down the ramp, the farther they'll fly in the air. Gravity helps them pick up speed. But there's also a force that's putting on the brakes: *friction* (rubbing) between the board and the snow.

Slippery surfaces have less friction. So snowboards are coated with slick wax.

But boarders have other ways to **reduce** friction. If less of the snowboard touches the snow, there will be less friction. That's why racers *carve their turns:* They lean into turns so the board tips. Only the edge of the board carves through the snow.

What if you long to snowboard but live in a part of the country where snow falls only on TV? There's a **solution,** and it's called *sand*boarding! Riders glide down hills of sand—hills with plenty of ramps to catch air and try out tricks. Sand creates more friction than slick snow, though. So sandboards are made of super-slippery *formica,* the material that covers many kitchen counters. The only problem? There are no lifts to carry riders to the top!

Words, Words, Words

reduce: to make something smaller or less
solution: the answer to a problem
intense: using a lot of effort and energy

EXTREME DANGER

Millions of TV viewers tune in to extreme programs like the X Games. Can you guess which age group is most likely to watch these sports? The answer: Young people, ages 12 to 18.

TV shows how cool extreme sports are. But you rarely see how dangerous they are. You may have seen the beverage commercials featuring skysurfers, for example. But did you know that Rob Harris, a practiced skysurfer, died while filming one spot?

Injuries are common for X Game competitors. But injuries rarely cramp their style. Take trick bicyclist Dennis McCoy, for example. Dennis has broken several bones, suffered a wrist injury that needed surgery, and had a few concussions. And he is still riding.

High-speed sports often lead to extreme injuries. Extreme athletes are more likely than other athletes to suffer serious injuries such as broken necks or backs.

One thing keeps the injury rate from skyrocketing: **intense** training. The pros on TV may make it look easy. But they've worked very hard to get where they are. Experts say the easiest way to get hurt is to try tricks that are too difficult for your skill level.

Before going extreme, it's important to have safety gear such as helmets and pads. It's also important to know which muscles to train. Some people only build their legs for mountain biking, for example. But upper body strength helps a rider stay upright on bumpy ground, avoiding bad spills.

ASK yourself

- What do extreme sports athletes do to avoid getting hurt?

List the details that tell you how they stay safe.

What Do You Think?

Extreme sports shows are heavily marketed to teens. Do you think that could lead to danger? If so, what could be done to make the situation safer?

Extreme bikers know the dangers involved with going airborne.

ANOTHER EXTREME: Swimming With the Sharks

Though swimming hasn't made it to the X Games, there are athletes who have taken it to the extreme. Some people have accomplished super-long swims, sleeping in a boat at night. In 1998, a man named Ben Lecomte swam across the Atlantic Ocean! He swam from Massachusetts to France in 80 days.

Swimmer Susie Maroney has set records for her non-stop swims. As a young child, Susie suffered from *asthma*—a disease that affects breathing ability. To strengthen her lungs she learned to swim. She must have learned it well. In 1997, Susie managed something that 50 people had tried and failed. After 24 1/2 hours, Susie swam from Cuba to Florida.

Susie swam inside a shark cage pulled by a boat. And that move saved her life. A ten foot hammerhead shark trailed her. Other sharks battered the cage. Jellyfish slipped between the bars and dotted her body with stings.

Susie's only rest was to tread water for a while every hour, during which she downed sports drinks and ate yogurt and bananas. Before the swim, she built strength and *stamina* (staying power) by swimming six hours a day. That training built up many of Susie's muscles—including her heart.

A stronger heart can pump more blood. Blood *circulates* (moves in a loop) around the body. It picks up oxygen gas from the lungs and *nutrients* (healthy material) from food. The blood delivers the oxygen and nutrients to the muscles. And that "food" keeps muscles pumping!

Now you know the science scoop behind some extreme sports. They may look like just fun and games, but as you can see, there's a lot more involved with these sports than meets the eye. A healthy heart and body, lots of training, and the basic principles of science are all forces that make extreme sports possible.

Super Athlete Susie Maroney

Muscles on the Move

The muscles Susie uses the most are:

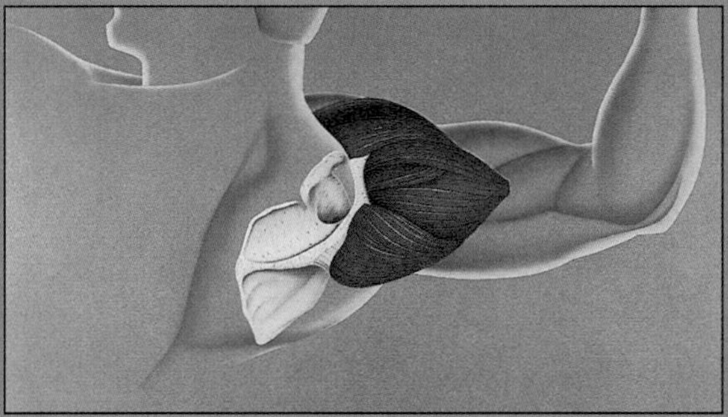

deltoid (DELL-toyd) muscles in Susie's shoulders lift her arms when she swims the crawl.

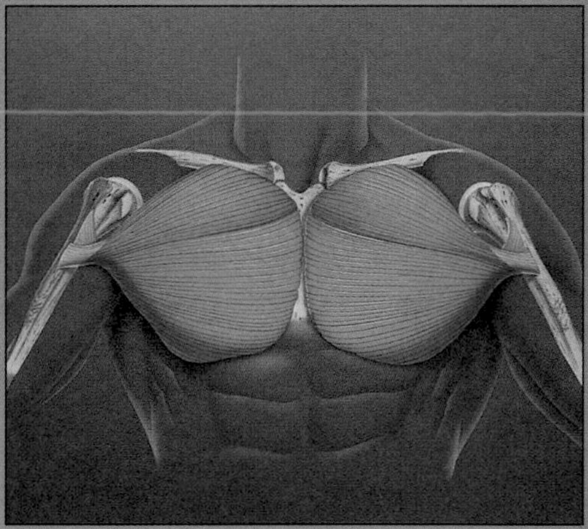

pectoralis (pek-tor-AH-lis) muscles in Susie's chest pull her arms through the water.

sternocleidomastoid (STUR-no-kly-doh-MASS-toyd) muscles in her neck rotate Susie's head when she breathes.

Take the Balance Challenge

Extreme athletes use their centers of gravity to gain a winning edge. You can use yours to trick your friends!

BACKGROUND for Tricks

1. Stand naturally. Then shift your weight to your left leg.
2. **Predict:** If you lean as far as you can to the left without falling over, what will happen to your right leg?
3. **Try it:** Lean to the left as far as you can. Keep your body straight—don't bend at the waist! What does your right leg do?

Explanation: Like every object, your body has a *center of gravity*—the central point of your body, by weight. For you to stay balanced, your center of gravity must be over your feet. When you lean to the left, your center of gravity moves left. So your right leg moves to the right to even things out. That keeps your center of gravity over your feet, so you don't topple over.

Trick One: Leg of Lead

1. Try this trick on yourself, then spring it on a friend.
2. **Say this to a friend:** "Without touching you, I am going to make it impossible for you to lift your right leg."
3. Have your friend stand with his or her left side against a wall. Make sure the side of his foot and hip are touching the wall.
4. **Say:** "Now your right leg is made of lead. You can't move it, can you?"

Explanation: Lifting your right leg shifts your center of gravity to the right. You need to shift some weight left to even things out. But you can't because the wall is in the way. So you can't lift the leg.

Trick Two: Unbendable Friend

1. Now have your friend stand with her back to wall. Make sure both her heels touch a wall.
2. **Say:** "Pretend someone dropped a $100 bill on the floor by your feet. Without moving your feet, lean forward and pick it up."
3. As you watch your friend struggle, try to answer this question: Why can't she bend forward in this position?

Wrap-Up

Talk About It

Now that you've read "The Science Behind Extreme Sports" and "Take the Balance Challenge," what do you have to say about these questions?

- Should extreme sports be included in the general Olympic games? Why or why not?
- What do you think about people who take big risks for fun? Give reasons for why you feel this way.

Comprehension Check

Write your answers to the questions below. Use information from the article and the activity to support your answers.

1. Give two examples of an extreme sport.
2. How would you define what an extreme sport is?
3. Why are young people more likely to be interested in extreme sports?
4. When you shift your weight to one side, why does the other side of your body move?
5. How can understanding the idea of balance help people who do extreme sports?

Vocabulary Check

solution **inspired** **technical**
imitated **intense**

Complete each sentence with the correct vocabulary word.

1. My best friend was angry when I _______ her walk.
2. I stared and stared at the math problem, but I couldn't come up with the _______.
3. After reading the lyrics, I was _______ to try to write a song myself.
4. My sister is a good basketball player, but she still needs work on her _______ skills.
5. Taking a test requires _______ concentration.

Write About It

Choose one of the three writing prompts below.

- Write a letter to the Olympic committee asking that an extreme sport be included in the next Olympics. Name the sport you think should be included and give at least two reasons why.
- Imagine that a friend ended up in the hospital after trying an extreme sport. What would you say to him or her? Write a letter to this friend explaining what you think about the accident.
- Write a news story about Susie Maroney's swim from Cuba to Florida. Use details from the article as well as some from your imagination.

Fact FILE

Want to be extreme?

Take some lessons from the pros and play it safe.

1. **Do your homework before you run out to buy those new bikes, boards, or blades. Consider taking lessons. The local sporting goods store might be able to recommend an instructor. You might even be able to rent equipment and try it out before you buy.**
2. **Use your head and always wear a helmet. Every year, people without helmets suffer serious, and sometimes deadly, head injuries. Bike helmets work fine for skateboarding and blading, too.**
3. **Wear the right gear. If you're skateboarding or blading, a helmet isn't going to be enough. You'll also need to wear wrist guards and pads on your elbows and knees.**
4. **Pay attention. The best athletes are the ones who focus on what they're doing. So leave the headphones at home.**

Using a Road Map

You and your family are driving from your home in Atlanta, Georgia, to the White House in Washington, D.C. The last thing you want to do is get lost. You need to use a highway map.

Check out the map below. Then get ready to hit the road.

Interstate Highway Map

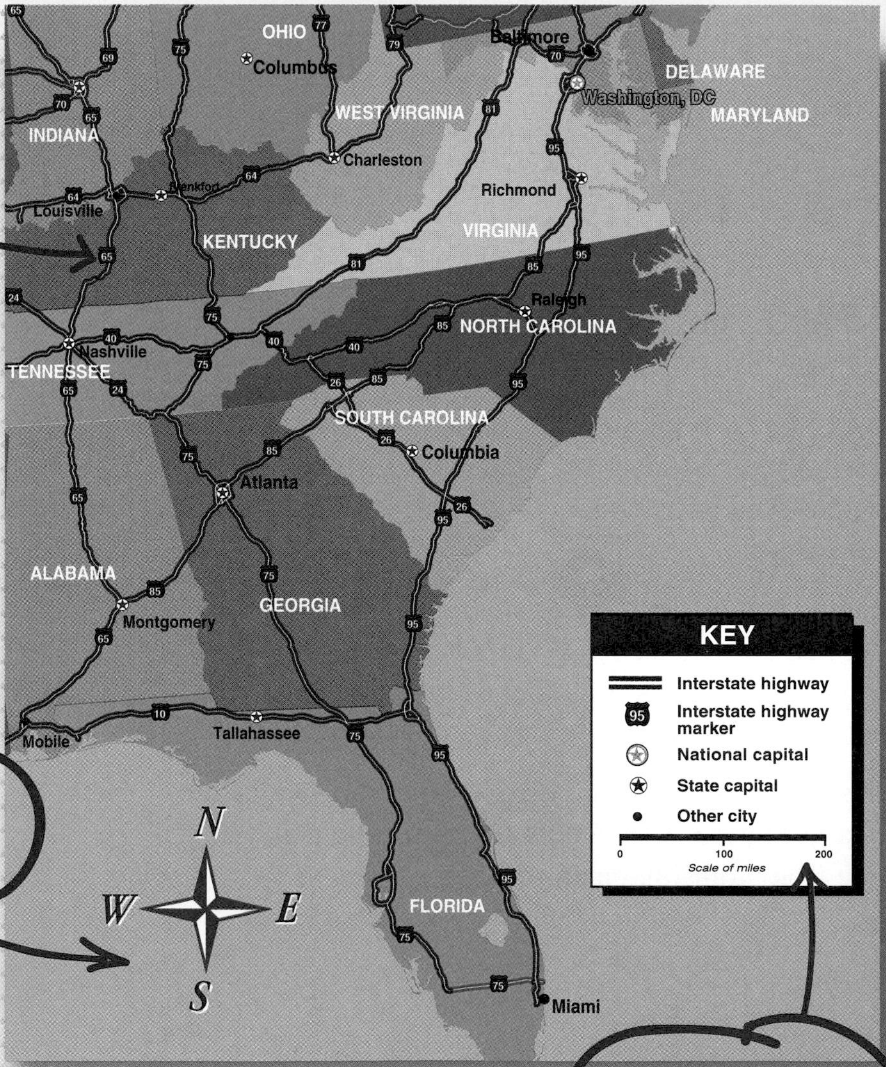
OHIO
Columbus
Baltimore
DELAWARE
Washington, DC
MARYLAND
WEST VIRGINIA
Charleston
INDIANA
Frankfort
Louisville
Richmond
KENTUCKY
VIRGINIA
Raleigh
NORTH CAROLINA
Nashville
TENNESSEE
SOUTH CAROLINA
Columbia
Atlanta
ALABAMA
Montgomery
GEORGIA
Mobile
Tallahassee
FLORIDA
Miami
N
W
E
S
KEY
Interstate highway
Interstate highway marker
National capital
State capital
Other city
0
100
200
Scale of miles

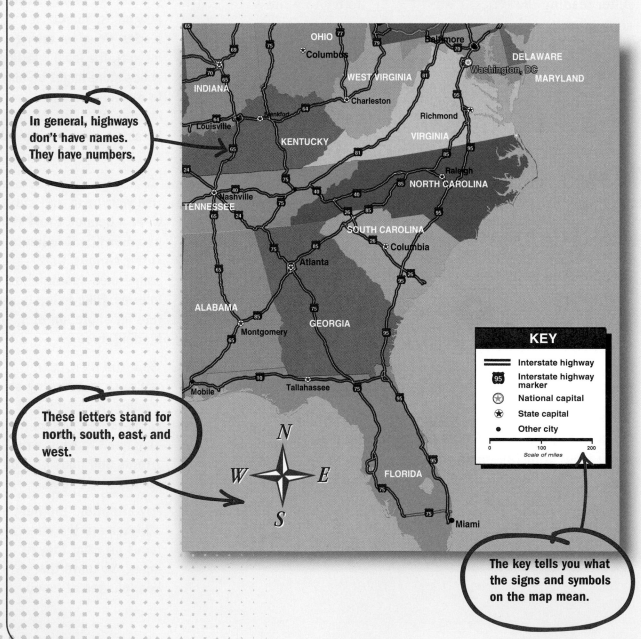

In general, highways don't have names. They have numbers.

These letters stand for north, south, east, and west.

The key tells you what the signs and symbols on the map mean.

Test Your Road Map Skills

Are you ready to hit the road? Review the map and the tips that go with it. Then use them to answer the questions below. Write your answers on your own paper.

1. Plan the shortest route from Atlanta, Georgia, to Washington, D.C. What is the first highway you would take? In which direction would you be traveling?

2. What is the second highway you would take on this trip? In what direction would you be traveling?

3. Which state capital would you pass through on your way from Atlanta to Washington, D.C.?
   a. Frankfort, Kentucky
   b. Columbus, Ohio
   c. Raleigh, North Carolina
   d. Richmond, Virginia

4. About how far is it from Louisville, Kentucky, to Charleston, West Virginia?
   a. 50 miles **c.** 200 miles
   b. 75 miles **d.** 400 miles

5. You're in Nashville, Tennessee. You drive south on Highway 65 until you reach Highway 10. You take 10 east until you reach a state capital. Which state capital is it?

Figure It Out

Let's say you're traveling from Miami, Florida, to Baltimore, Maryland. You're going to drive 200 miles each day. Plan out a schedule that shows which state you'll stay in each night.

Write About It

You live in Frankfort, Kentucky. You want to visit three state capitals on this map. Choose the capitals. List the order in which you'd visit each capital. Then write a description of your route.

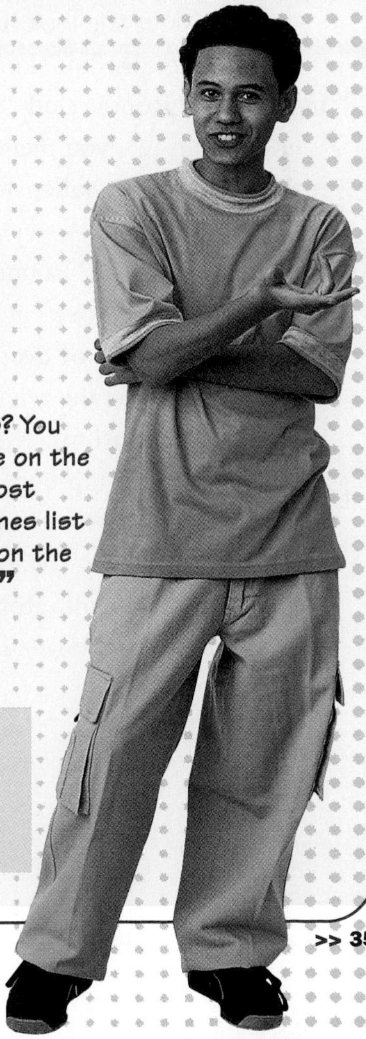

"Need a map? You can find one on the Internet. Most search engines list them right on the home page."

Real-World Words

interstate highways: roads that connect two or more states
key: an explanation of the symbols on a map
route: the roads that you follow to get from one place to another

82501202

What do a mask, a goldfish, and a jigsaw puzzle have in common? Read these three stories and try to figure it out!

MASQUERADE

Ronnie has met a great girl.
Everything should end up happily ever after, right?
So, what's the problem?

by Phyllis Fair Cowell

Ronnie leaned back in his chair, closed his eyes, and sighed. "She was an angel!" he breathed.

Todd smiled and rolled his eyes. "You've said that before." Ronnie sat up straight. "No," he said, "I mean she really *was* an angel. At least, she was dressed like one last night."

"What does she look like?" Todd asked.

"Well, I really don't know, because she was wearing a mask," Ronnie said. "It was a costume party."

"Hmmm . . . you met a girl who was wearing a mask, *and* you've fallen for her. Interesting," Todd said.

"Yes. That, too," Ronnie went on excitedly. "She knows all about hockey and basketball, and she can tell you the names of every Indy 500 winner since 1970, and tell you the winners of the last ten World Series Championships. We like the same kind of music—rock and hip-hop. And man, can she move on the dance floor!"

Todd was happy for Ronnie, but he was getting bored with all this talk. Ronnie kept going.

"She's totally the first girl I can even talk to!" he explained.

"Then talk to *her!*" Todd insisted.

Ronnie continued. "Wait until I tell the guys about her!"

"Everyone is at the skating rink," Todd said.

"Let's go!" Ronnie yelled, as he ran out the door.

All the way to the rink, Todd had to listen to every single detail about this amazing girl that Ronnie had met at a costume party. He pretended to be annoyed, but actually, Todd was happy for Ronnie. Especially since Ronnie wasn't known to give many girls a chance. He usually blew them off, saying something was wrong with the girl. Perfection . . . that's what Ronnie wanted, and now it seemed he had found it.

"I didn't wear a costume!" he said. "But the other guys will give me a hard time if they knew I went to a costume party. Don't tell them about the party. Okay? Just the girl."

The skating rink was unusually packed for a Thursday afternoon. When Ronnie saw his other friends, however, he charged right in. "You're not going to believe it, but I met this great girl last weekend!" he said.

"What does she look like?" was the first thing Craig asked.

"She's uhh . . ." Ronnie didn't know what to say.

"Ronnie told me that she's a real angel!" Todd

"Ronnie told me that she's a real angel."

jumped in quickly to save his buddy. Ronnie gave him a quick look to acknowledge his appreciation for the save.

Just then, one of the guys made a face at a girl skating by. "Ugly," he said as he turned to Ronnie. "So when are you bringing this angel around for all of us to meet?"

"I'm meeting her tomorrow at her school," Ronnie said proudly. "If we're not *too* busy, I'll bring her to the rink."

Ronnie thought of nothing but his "angel" the next day. At three o'clock, he was standing outside her school. Todd, who wouldn't miss this moment for anything, stood right next to him.

"I've heard so much about this girl, even I'm getting nervous," he whispered to Ronnie. "Which one is she?"

Ronnie looked totally confused. "I . . . I don't know, I told you, she was wearing a mask."

Todd laughed at his friend's predicament. "Let's hope she sees you."

Ronnie jumped out in front of every pretty girl. Some looked at him like he was crazy. Some just kept walking by. One tried to knock him over.

Finally, someone called his name. A girl came running toward him. The smile faded from Ronnie's face.

"She's not . . . not that great-looking," Ronnie mumbled.

Todd thought the girl was ordinary-looking, but he also thought she seemed pretty nice.

"I wasn't sure you would be here," she said. "Want to go hang out someplace?"

"Um . . . no," Ronnie stalled. "I just came by to say hi. I have some homework to do and then I have to go . . . to practice."

They didn't talk long. But the girl stood, staring after the boys as they walked away.

After they walked for a while without talking, Todd suddenly turned to Ronnie. "Take off your mask!" he demanded.

"What do you mean?" asked a confused Ronnie. "She's the one who was wearing a mask. I never wore one."

"Oh yeah?" Todd said. "Just think about what you've been saying for the last two days. You wear a mask all the time. And underneath it, you're a hypocrite . . . a real phony!"

The Fish Story

Ernie was really surprised when Mrs. Benson offered him a summer job. That was just the first of his surprises!

by Mary Lou Brooks

I know what I'm going to be when I grow up—**unemployed.** "Face it, Ernie," my dad always says. "The way you mess up every job, you have a great future—as a bum."

He's probably right. My first summer job was cutting the neighbor's lawn. The mower got away from me and ate ten tomato plants. Another time, I forgot to close the windows when I washed Mr. Hammer's car. The weeds I pulled out of Mrs. Miller's garden turned out to be flowers.

So I was really surprised when the Bensons asked me to look after their house while they were away on vacation. The Bensons are new on the block. I guess they hadn't heard about me yet.

"We're leaving on Monday," explained Mrs. Benson. "You'll start on Tuesday. Just bring in the newspapers and the mail." That didn't sound too hard. Even *I* could probably handle this job.

"And feed Jaws once a day," Mrs. Benson added.

"Jaws?" I gulped. Did they have a pet shark or something?

Mrs. Benson laughed. "That's what the twins named their goldfish."

On Tuesday, I had baseball practice. So I was late getting to the Bensons'. I put the mail and the newspaper on the hall table. Then I headed for the fishbowl. Jaws was floating on top of the water.

I moaned. My first day on the job, and I killed the dumb fish! Not even the Army would want me now. That's what my dad would say—after he stopped yelling.

Now wait a minute, Ernie, I said to myself. This little fellow *could* still be alive. His eyes are open. He could be in a coma. I bent down very close to the water.

"Jaws!" I yelled. "It's me, Ernie, your babysitter. If you can hear me, blink once." He didn't.

I touched him with my finger. He was cold, stiff, and very slimy. "Face it, Ernie," I said out loud. "This is one dead fish you have here."

That night, I lay awake a long time trying to figure out why that dumb fish died. I didn't overfeed him. I never had a chance to feed him at all.

When I finally fell asleep, I had a nightmare. The shark from *Jaws* was chasing me. He was wearing a six-shooter. "You bumped off my kinfolk," he yelled. "Draw!"

Words, Words, Words

unemployed: without a job
glared: looked at someone in an angry way
dreading: being afraid of doing something
responsible: sensible and trustworthy

I didn't tell my parents about Jaws. Every day, I went over to the Bensons' as though nothing was wrong. I had until Sunday. That's when the Bensons were coming home. Why rush things?

On Saturday, I remembered that Jaws was still in the fishbowl. I was about to toss him into the garbage. Suddenly, I had a great idea. I slipped Jaws into a baggie and ran to the nearest pet store.

"I'd like another goldfish exactly like this one," I told the owner. Then I held up the baggie.

The owner **glared** at me. Half an hour later, he was still glaring. That's how long it took to find a perfect match. I paid the owner and headed back to the Bensons' house.

My first day on the job, and I killed the dumb fish!

When I got there, I cleaned the fishbowl and added fresh water. Soon, Jaws II was in his new home. But instead of swimming around, he just stared at me.

"What you did was wrong," those tiny black eyes seemed to say.

The Bensons arrived home at 1:55 Sunday afternoon. I watched from my bedroom window as they piled out of their car. At 2:13, my mom called up the stairs.

"Ernie," she said, "Mrs. Benson is here." Caught! I trudged down the stairs to face the music.

Mrs. Benson was sitting at the kitchen table with my parents. "Here's the boy behind the Great Goldfish Switch," she said.

I felt like running. But Mrs. Benson put her arm around my shoulder.

"That was very thoughtful, Ernie," she said. "Monday was so crazy I didn't have time to pick up another fish. I've been **dreading** telling the twins that Jaws died. Thanks to you, I won't have to."

She handed me money in an envelope. "This is for house-sitting," she said. "There's something extra for the new Jaws. You hear so many wild stories about kids these days. It's nice to know one who is **responsible**."

ASK yourself

- Why does Mrs. Benson's reaction surprise Ernie?

Think about the problem Ernie thought he had.

Mom looked so proud I thought she might cry. But Dad had a funny look on his face. I think he was trying not to laugh.

THE Jigsaw Puzzle

BY J.B. STAMPER

Jigsaw puzzles are fun to put together. But when the results are more than just a picture, watch out. . . .

It was on the top shelf of an old bookcase, covered with dust and barely visible. Lisa decided she had to find out what it was. Of all the things in the old junk shop, it aroused her curiosity most. She had looked through old books, prints, and postcards for hours. Nothing had caught her interest. Now the old box, high and out of reach, intrigued her.

She looked around for the old man who ran the store, but he had gone into the back room. She saw a stepladder across the room and brought it over to the bookcase. It shook on the uneven floorboards as she climbed to the top step.

Lisa patted her hand along the surface of the top shelf, trying to find the box. The dirt was thick and gritty on the board. Then she touched the box—it was made of cardboard. The cardboard was cold and soft from being in the damp room for such a long time. She lifted the box down slowly, trying to steady her balance on the stepladder.

As the side of the box reached her eye level, she could read the words: 500 PIECES.

She sat the box down on top of the stepladder and climbed down a few steps. Then she blew away some of the dust that had accumulated on the lid. It billowed up around her with a musty, dead odor. But now she could make out a few more words on top of the box:

THE STRANGEST
JIGSAW PUZZLE
IN THE WORLD

There were other words underneath that, but they had been rubbed off the cardboard lid. The big picture on the cover had been curiously damaged. Lisa could make out areas of light and dark, and it looked as though the scene might be in a room. But most of the picture had been scratched off the card-

MORRIS

"How strange could a jigsaw puzzle be?"

board box, probably by a sharp instrument.

The mysterious nature of the jigsaw puzzle made it even more appealing to Lisa. She decided she would buy it. The lid was taped down securely; that probably meant that all the pieces would be there. As she carefully climbed down the stepladder, holding the box in both hands, Lisa smiled to herself. It was quite a find, just the sort of thing she had always hoped to discover while rummaging through secondhand stores.

Mr. Tuborg, the owner of the store, came out of the back room as she was walking up to his sales desk. He looked curiously at the box when Lisa set it down.

"And where did you find that?" he asked her.

Lisa pointed to where she had set up the stepladder. "It was on top of that bookcase. You could barely see it from the floor."

"Well, I've never seen it before, that's for sure," Mr. Tuborg said. "I can't imagine how you found it."

Lisa was more pleased than ever about her find. She felt as though the puzzle had been hiding up there, waiting for her to discover it. She paid Mr. Tuborg the twenty-five cents he asked for the puzzle and then wrapped it carefully in the newspapers he gave her to take it home in.

It was late on a Saturday afternoon. Lisa lived alone in a small room in an old apartment house. She had no plans for Saturday night and now she decided to spend the whole evening working on the puzzle. She stopped at a delicatessen and bought some meat, bread, and cheese for sandwiches. She would eat while she put the puzzle together.

As soon as she had climbed the flight of stairs to her room and put away the groceries, Lisa cleaned off the big table in the center of the room. She set the box down on it.

THE STRANGEST JIGSAW PUZZLE IN THE WORLD

Lisa read the words again. She wondered what they could mean. How strange could a jigsaw puzzle be?

The tape that held the lid down was still strong. Lisa got out a kitchen knife to slice through it. When she lifted the cover off the box, a musty smell came from inside, but the jigsaw pieces all looked in good condition. Lisa picked one up. The color was faded, but the picture was clear. She could see the shape of a finger in the piece. It looked like a woman's finger.

Lisa sat down and started to lay out the pieces,

Words, Words, Words

texture: the look and feel of something
incredible: amazing
coincidence: a chance happening
resemblance: the state of looking like something else

top side up, on the large table. As she took them from the box, she sorted out the flat-edged pieces from the inside pieces. Every so often, she would recognize something in one of the pieces. She saw some blonde hair, a window pane, and a small vase. There was a lot of wood **texture** in the pieces, plus what looked like wallpaper. Lisa noticed that the wallpaper in the puzzle looked a lot like the wallpaper in her own room. She wondered if her wallpaper was as old as the jigsaw puzzle. It would be an **incredible coincidence,** but it could be the same.

By the time Lisa had all of the pieces laid out on the table, it was 6:30. She got up and made herself a sandwich. Already, her back was beginning to hurt a little from leaning over the table, but she couldn't stay away from the puzzle. She went back to the table and set her sandwich down beside her. It was always like that when she did jigsaws. Once she started, she couldn't stop until the puzzle was all put together.

She began to sort out the pieces according to their coloring. There were dark brown pieces, whitish pieces, the wallpaper pieces, and some pieces that seemed to be like glass—perhaps a window. As she slowly ate her sandwich, Lisa pieced together the border. When she was finished, she knew she had been right about the setting of the picture when she had first seen the puzzle. It was a room. One side of the border was wallpaper. Lisa decided to fill that in first. She was curious about its **resemblance** to her own wallpaper.

She gathered all the pieces together that had the blue and lilac flowered design. As she fit the pieces together, it became clear that the wallpaper in the puzzle was identical to the wallpaper in her room. Lisa glanced back and forth between the puzzle and her wall. It was an exact match.

ASK Yourself

- What do you think this puzzle will turn out to be?

Think about what you've read and the kind of story this is.

By now it was 8:30. Lisa leaned back in her chair. Her back was stiff. She looked over at her window. The night was black outside. Lisa got up and walked over to the window. Suddenly, she felt uneasy, alone in the apartment. She pulled the white shade over the window.

She paced around the room once, trying to think of something else she might do instead of finishing the puzzle. But nothing else interested her. She went back and sat down at the table.

Next she started to fill in the lower right-hand corner. There was a rug and then a chair. This part of the puzzle was very dark. Lisa noticed uneasily that the chair was the same shape as one sitting in the corner of her room, but the colors didn't seem exactly the same. Her chair was maroon. The one in the puzzle was in the shadows and seemed almost black.

Lisa continued to fill in the border toward the middle. There was more wallpaper to finish on top. The left-hand side did turn out to be a window. Through it, a half moon hung in a dark sky. But it was the bottom of the puzzle that began to bother Lisa. As the pieces fell into place, she saw a picture of a pair of legs, crossed underneath a table. They were the legs of a young woman. Lisa reached

down and ran her hand along one of her legs. Suddenly, she felt as though something was crawling up it, but it must have been her imagination.

She stared down at the puzzle. It was almost three-quarters done. Only the middle remained. Lisa glanced at the lid of the puzzle box:

THE STRANGEST
JIGSAW...

She **shuddered.**

Lisa leaned back in her chair again. Her back ached. Her neck muscles were tense and strained. She thought about quitting the puzzle. It scared her now.

She stood up and stretched. Then she looked down at the puzzle on the table. It looked different from the higher angle. Lisa was shocked by what she saw. Her body began to tremble all over.

It was **unmistakable**—the picture in the puzzle was of her own room. The window was placed correctly in relation to the table. The bookcase stood in its exact spot against the wall. Even the carved table legs were the same. . . .

Lisa raised her hand to knock the pieces of the puzzle apart. She didn't want to finish the strangest jigsaw puzzle in the world; she didn't want to find out what the hole in the middle of the puzzle might turn out to be.

But then she lowered her hand. Perhaps it was worse not to know. Perhaps it was worse to wait and wonder.

ASK Yourself

- What problem is Lisa having with this puzzle?

Think about how the strangest jigsaw puzzle in the world is making her feel.

Lisa sank back down into the chair at the table. She fought off the fear that crept into the sore muscles of her back. **Deliberately,** piece by piece, she began to fill in the hole in the puzzle. She put together a picture of a table, on which lay a jigsaw puzzle. This puzzle inside the puzzle was finished. But Lisa couldn't make out what it showed. She pieced together the young woman who was sitting at the table—the young woman who was herself. As she filled in the picture, her own body slowly filled with horror and dread. It was all there in the picture . . . the vase filled with blue cornflowers, her red cardigan sweater, the wild look of fear on her own face.

The jigsaw puzzle lay before her—finished except for two **adjoining** pieces. They were dark pieces, ones she hadn't been able to fit into the area of the window. Lisa looked behind her. The white blind was drawn over her window. With relief, she realized that the puzzle picture was not exactly like her room. The puzzle showed the black night behind the window and a moon shining in the sky.

With trembling hands, Lisa reached for the second to last piece. She dropped it into one of the empty spaces. It seemed to be half a face, but not a human face. She reached for the last piece. She pressed it into the small hole left in the picture.

The face was complete—the face in the window. It was more horrible than anything she had ever seen, or dreamed. Lisa looked at the picture of herself in the puzzle and then back to that face.

Then she whirled around. The blind was no longer over her window. The night showed black through the window pane. A half moon hung low in the sky.

Lisa screamed . . . the face . . . it was there, too.

Words, Words, Words

shuddered: shook violently from fear
unmistakable: very obvious
deliberately: purposely
adjoining: connecting

With trembling hands,
Lisa reached for the second to last piece.
She dropped it into one of the empty spaces.
It seemed to be a face . . .

Wrap-UP

Talk About It

Now that you've read "Masquerade," "The Fish Story," and "The Jigsaw Puzzle," what do you have to say about these questions?

- Have you ever had a strange experience when things weren't what they seemed? What happened?
- Do you think it's always better to face your fears rather than to run from them or cover them up? Explain.

Comprehension Check

Write your answers to the questions below. Use information from the three stories to support your answers.

1. Why does Ernie buy a new goldfish?
2. How do you think Todd feels about his friend Ronnie by the end of the story?
3. What would you have done in Ronnie's place?
4. How do you think the jigsaw puzzle might have gotten onto the top shelf of the store?
5. Neither Ernie nor Todd were being completely honest, so why do you think Ernie gets rewarded?

Vocabulary Check

Answer each question below with a complete sentence. Before you answer, think about the meaning of the vocabulary word in bold.

1. What would you do if you were **unemployed?**
2. If you were **dreading** a test, what could you do?
3. How would you show your parents you are **responsible** enough to own a pet?
4. If a stranger **glared** at you on the street, what would you do?
5. What **coincidence** has happened to you?

Write About It

Choose one of the three writing prompts below.

- Whose face is it in Lisa's window? Continue that story for one more paragraph.
- Write a letter from Ronnie to the "angel," apologizing for how he acted when he met her outside of school.
- Write a diary entry as if you were Ernie. Say how you felt after the Bensons returned.

More to READ

If you enjoyed these stories, here are some other books that will give you the chance to figure things out.

You Be the Jury
by Marvin Miller

You the reader decides on the guilt or innocence of the accused in these ten exciting minute mysteries, presented in a courtroom format. And if you really like this book, you can also check out *You Be the Jury: Courtroom II.*

Surprising Stories by Saki: 22 Tales with Twists
by Hector Hugh Munro

These stories are famous for their unexpected twists and their humor. For example, experience the drama of two enemies trapped together beneath a fallen tree in "The Interlopers." Saki is the pen name of the author H. H. Munro. Munro was born in 1870 and grew up in England. If you really like his stories, check out two of the books he loved best when he was young, *Alice in Wonderland* and *Robinson Crusoe.*

Reading a Schedule

You've just landed a great part-time job. How will you know when you're supposed to work? You need to get a copy of the employee schedule. It shows when each worker should be on the job.

Read the employee schedule below. Can you figure it out?

Employee Schedule

The workdays are listed at the top of the schedule. The times appear on the side. Notice that Joe's does not open until 4 P.M., Monday through Friday.

Joe's Pizza
Employee Schedule 11/5–11/11

	Monday	Tuesday	Wednesday	Thursday	Friday	Saturday	Sunday
12 P.M.	CLOSED	CLOSED	CLOSED	CLOSED	CLOSED		
1 P.M.						Felipe	Amir
2 P.M.							
3 P.M.							
4 P.M.	Damon	Damon	Michelle	Lisa			Felipe
5 P.M.					Damon	Amir	
6 P.M.	Kim	Lisa	Kim				
7 P.M.				Michelle	Kim		Kim
8 P.M.							

Employees

Name	Phone	Available
Damon Jones	555-0996	M–F 4–9/Sat. anytime
Kim Lee	555-2517	M, W, F, Sun. 6–9
Amir Toor	555-2773	Sat. 4–9/Sun. anytime
Felipe Cruz	555-0677	Sat., Sun. 12–5
Lisa Cardella	555-9020	T, Th, 4–9/Sun. anytime
Michelle Meyers	555-6948	W, Th 4–9

Damon's shift starts at 4 P.M. The arrow goes to the bottom of the 6 P.M. box. That means Damon has to work until 7 P.M.

Notice that these shifts overlap? That guarantees that Lisa will be around if Michelle is late.

"Many schedules include employees' phone numbers and available times. Copy this information so you can find a substitute if you are ill or have an emergency."

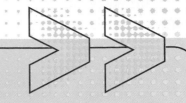

Shift Change

Don't want to be late for work? Learn to read an employee schedule. Use the schedule from Joe's Pizza and the tips that go with it to answer these questions. Write your answers on your own paper.

1. Who will be working Thursday at 5 P.M.? Who will be working the first shift on Saturday?

2. Damon wants to buy tickets for a basketball game. He must work at least eight hours this week to pay for them. Will he work enough hours this week to afford the game?

3. It's Sunday afternoon and Felipe is sick. Kim can't come in early. Who can substitute?
a. No one else is available.
b. Lisa is the only one available.
c. Lisa and Amir are both available.

4. Felipe has this Friday off from school. He would like to trade his Saturday shift for the same shift on Friday. Who should he call to arrange this trade?
a. Amir; he can work Saturdays.
b. Kim; she is available Fridays.
c. No one; this is an impossible plan.

5. Lisa needs to go shopping with her family on Thursday afternoon. Who can cover for her?
a. Michelle or Damon
b. Damon only
c. Michelle only

Work It Out

You just got a job at Joe's. Take another look at the schedule. Think about your other activities. Which shifts could you work at Joe's? List the shifts on your own paper.

Manage It!

Now you're the manager of a cable channel. Your channel is on the air Monday–Friday, from 9 A.M. to 5 P.M. Make a list of the shows you'd put on your channel. Then make a schedule for one day.

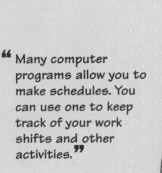

"Many computer programs allow you to make schedules. You can use one to keep track of your work shifts and other activities."

Real-World Words

manager: a person who supervises a team of workers
overlap: to cover part of something
shift: a scheduled period of work

play

BEARST

Adapted from the Award-Winning Novel by Will Hobbs

Cast of CHARACTERS

Narrator 1*

Narrator 2*

Cloyd, a 14-year-old Native American boy*

Nurse

Susan, Cloyd's housemother

Walter, an old farmer*

Rusty, a hunting guide*

Grandmother, Cloyd's grandmother

Brother, Rusty's brother

Game Warden

Delivery Man

*starred characters are major roles

scene ONE

Narrator 1: When Cloyd was born, his mother died. Soon after, his father disappeared. Cloyd lived on the Ute reservation with his grandmother. As he got older, he got into trouble. His grandmother loved him, but she couldn't handle him. Eventually, the tribe sent him away to live in a group home.

Narrator 2: Cloyd wasn't happy there. His dream was to find his real father. His father would understand him, Cloyd thought, and together they would be a family. Cloyd ran away to find him. He found out that his father was in a hospital in Arizona.

Narrator 1: At the hospital, Cloyd sneaked past the nurse's station and into his father's room. The man inside didn't even look human. He was a mummy attached to a bunch of tubes. Could this be his father?

Cloyd *(frightened):* What's the matter with him?

Nurse *(walking into the room):* Have you heard the expression "brain dead"? He's a very sick man.

Cloyd *(upset):* How did this happen?

Nurse: He was in a car accident four years ago.

Narrator 1: Cloyd took one more look at the wrinkled, shrunken shell of a human being. How could this be his father? Inside Cloyd, a dream died.

scene TWO

Narrator 2: Cloyd caught a ride back to the group home. When he got back, his housemother had a plan. She wanted him to spend the summer helping an old farmer; he had been alone since his wife died. She drove Cloyd to the man's farm in the Colorado mountains.

Susan: Would you open the gate, Cloyd? Just look at that lovely peach orchard.

Narrator 1: Cloyd did as she asked. Then he bolted into the trees. He would run away to his real home on the reservation, he decided. Maybe his grandmother would take him back.

Susan: Cloyd! You come back here!

Narrator 2: He hid on top of a boulder and listened to Susan talk to the old man.

ONE

Cloyd was in trouble. Could an old man and an ancient stone make any difference?

Walter: So he's run off, has he? Does he do that often?

Susan: Only once before. I thought working with you might be good for him. School has been a disaster for him.

Walter: I wasn't so good at school myself.

Susan: He failed all seven of his classes this year. Before that, he missed four years.

Walter: Four years?! Where was he?

Susan: Out in the canyons, herding his grandmother's goats.

Walter *(chuckling):* Isn't that something?

Susan: How have you been doing?

Walter: Not worth a darn. Since Maude passed away, I haven't even put up hay.

Susan: But look at these beautiful peaches. You're taking care of the orchard.

Walter: It's for her—for Maude. You know how she loved peaches.

Narrator 1: As he listened, Cloyd realized he liked the farmer. Maybe he would stay for a while, but first he wanted to explore.

Narrator 2: High on the mountainside above the farm, he tip-toed along a ledge. It led to a cave. Inside he found a crumbling blanket and a human skeleton. It was an infant, an Ancient One.

Narrator 1: He also found a small piece of turquoise made in the shape of a bear. Bears were **sacred** to the Utes. Cloyd decided to keep the bearstone. The smooth, blue stone in his pocket made him feel new and powerful.

Cloyd: I'll take a secret name. My grandmother told me that's what our people used to do. I don't need a father—or anyone else. I'll name myself Lone Bear after this stone.

scene THREE

Narrator 2: It was getting dark. Cloyd climbed down from the canyon. He went into the farmhouse to meet the old man.

Walter: I've got supper here. Like pork chops?

Cloyd: O.K., I guess. I'm hungry.

Walter: I'm hungry, too.

Narrator 1: The two ate dinner in silence.

Walter *(proudly):* I've got something special for dessert.

Narrator 2: He came back with peaches and ice cream.

Walter: Fresh from the farm. *(after a moment)* So did you have a look around today?

Cloyd: I climbed up above the cliff.

Walter: That's one of my favorite places around the farm.

Cloyd: How come you call this ranch a farm?

Walter: My wife always said a ranch was like a house, but a farm was a home.

Narrator 1: Cloyd looked around. This was a good place, Walter's farm.

Narrator 2: Walter and Cloyd got up early the next day.

Walter: I've got something I'd like to show you.

Narrator 1: Walter took Cloyd to a tack room full of saddles and bridles.

Walter: If you'd like to ride, you can have your pick of horses.

Narrator 2: Cloyd dreamed of going to the mountains. His grandmother had told him that these mountains were the ancient home of the Utes.

Cloyd: Do you go to the mountains?

Walter: I have a gold mine there, the Pride of the West. I loved it, but my wife made me give up mining. She was scared to death I'd get caught in a cave-in.

Narrator 1: Walter and Cloyd found the horses along the river. Cloyd knew **immediately** which horse he wanted: the blue roan.

Cloyd *(calling):* Hey-a, hey-a.

Narrator 2: The horse came toward him. Cloyd let him eat from the feed bag. Then he slipped the halter over his head.

Walter: Very nice. You made that look easy.

Narrator 1: Cloyd climbed on the roan.

Walter: He's really taking a shine to you.

Cloyd: Does he have a name?

Walter: I never gave him one.

Cloyd: I'll call him Blueboy. *(to the horse, whispering)* You and me, Blue. We'll go to the mountains.

ASK yourself

- What has happened to Cloyd so far?

Retell the important events that you've read about.

scene FOUR

Narrator 2: The next morning, Cloyd asked what his job on the farm would be.

Walter: I need a fence built.

Cloyd: Show me. I can do it.

Narrator 1: Cloyd worked on the fence all through June. He was **determined** to finish. Then he would ask Walter if he could ride Blueboy into the mountains. He started to work so hard that he and Walter hardly even talked.

Walter: You might want to give that fence a rest. Take more time with the horse.

Cloyd: I don't want to.

Narrator 2: Cloyd felt that he had to prove himself. A few days later, he finished the post holes.

Cloyd: Now I can start cutting the posts.

Walter: Wait and let me do that. I'm worried about the chain saw. Have you used one?

Cloyd: You can show me.

Walter: I believe you can do anything you set your mind to.

Narrator 1: Cloyd started cutting posts. He was working so hard that Walter worried about him.

scene FIVE

Narrator 2: One day in July, three pickups pulled into the farm. Six men in orange vests got out.

Narrator 1: Walter was friends with their leader. He called Cloyd over to meet him.

Walter: Cloyd, this is Rusty. He's the best hunting guide I know. More than likely he'll scare up a bear. Rusty, this is Cloyd.

Rusty *(mocking):* Cloyd, is it? Never heard a name like that.

Narrator 2: Cloyd didn't like the big red-haired man. The guide looked at him with disrespect.

Walter: Cloyd's good with horses. The roan has really taken to him.

Rusty *(laughing):* Is that so? Well, a horse ain't a dog, Cloyd. It could care less about you. All it cares about is getting fed.

Narrator 1: Cloyd was furious. He knew now that he didn't mean anything to Walter. The big man—a man who hunted sacred bears—was the old man's real friend.

Narrator 2: Cloyd was supposed to help Walter bale the hay. But he ran off instead. He didn't care any more about the fence. The old man would never let him go to the mountains anyway.

Words, Words, Words

sacred: very important and deserving great respect
immediately: right now or at once
determined: decided or settled on an idea

scene SIX

Narrator 1: The next day Walter acted as though nothing had happened.

Walter: Got anything in mind today, Cloyd? Maybe you'd like to take that roan . . .

Cloyd *(cutting him off)*: I'll make some more fence posts, I guess.

Narrator 2: Cloyd went out to work in the blazing hot sun. He was sick of the fence. If he wasn't going to get to go into the mountains, he wanted to go back home to his grandmother. He was homesick.

Narrator 1: An hour into his work, he saw the hunters returning. A dead black bear was heaped on top of one of their horses.

Rusty *(to one of the hunters)*: A bearskin for your den! And good sausage for Walter.

Narrator 2: Sausage! Cloyd felt sick. Had he been eating bear meat every morning? Anger rushed through him. He hated the red-haired guide, and he hated Walter too. Walter didn't really care about him. He only cared about his stupid fence—and the bear hunters.

Cloyd *(to himself)*: Laughs-with-Bear Hunters should be the old man's secret name.

Narrator 1: A plan of terrible revenge came into Cloyd's mind. He found the chainsaw and ran to the orchard. He sawed into the nearest peachtree. He ran from one to the next, hollering. He cut each one most of the way through. He wanted them to die slowly. He didn't know why he had ever liked Walter.

Cloyd handed Walter the Bearstone. He knew he deserved to be punished.

Narrator 2: The old man found him later.

Walter *(shaking Cloyd)*: What's the matter with you? Who are you to come ruin our peaches? You knew what they meant to me!

Narrator 1: Cloyd felt awful. He remembered that he had liked the old man once. He remembered the sweet taste of the peaches and that they had belonged to Walter's wife. Now he had spoiled everything.

Walter *(angry)*: Give me that little blue rock.

Cloyd *(concerned)*: What rock?

Walter: I've seen you sneaking it in and out of your hand. C'mon. Give it!

Narrator 2: Sadly, Cloyd handed him the bearstone. He knew he deserved to be punished.

Walter: You care about this little rock, eh? C'mon, I want to teach you something.

Narrator 1: Cloyd followed Walter into the machine shop. Walter reached for his sledgehammer.

Walter: A dose of your own medicine!

Narrator 2: Walter paused with the hammer in midair.

Walter: What the heck is this thing?

Cloyd: A bear.

Narrator 2: The old man picked the stone up in his hand and **examined** it.

Walter: A bear?

Narrator 1: Cloyd remained silent and looked at the ground.

Walter: You care about this quite a bit, don't you? *(after a pause)* Oh, to heck with it. Keep it. But go get your stuff. I just want you to leave.

ASK yourself

- Why does Cloyd destroy Walter's peach trees?

Think about how Cloyd was feeling before he did it.

scene SEVEN

Narrator 2: Cloyd packed up, and Walter started driving him back to the group home.

Walter: I wonder if you'd mind if I looked over that turquoise piece of yours again.

Cloyd *(handing it over):* OK.

Walter: It's a sure-enough bear. Could even be a grizzly from the shape of it. *(realizing something)* You cut those peaches right after those fellows came in from their bear hunt. Isn't that right?

Narrator 1: Cloyd **grimaced**.

Walter *(understanding):* Well, that helps some. It sure does.

Cloyd: Here it is—the group home.

Narrator 2: Walter didn't like the look of it. He drove right past it.

Cloyd: Where are you going?

Walter: Susan told me you'd rather go home to your grandmother than anything else. Is that right?

Cloyd: The tribe won't let me. *(after a pause)* Where are you driving me?

Walter: To your home on the reservation.

Cloyd: Why?

Walter: You're not going to do any good at the group home, are you? I'll wait a week before I tell Susan where you are. You'll have some time at home.

Narrator 1: At the reservation, Cloyd got out of Walter's truck. He didn't know what to say.

Walter: Good luck. And no hard feelings.

Narrator 2: As the truck drove away, Cloyd realized he'd lost a priceless friend. He waved hard as the truck disappeared. Then he found his grandmother.

Grandmother: This man you work for, he lives in a good way?

Cloyd *(realizing):* He's the best man I ever knew. He's old. His wife died so he's all alone.

Narrator 1: Suddenly Cloyd knew what he wanted to do.

Cloyd: I can't stay with you long. I have to go back tomorrow. He needs me to help him.

Narrator 2: The next day Walter was in his field, thinking about what had happened. He wished he'd done better by the boy. He wished he hadn't let him work so hard. Then suddenly, he saw Cloyd coming through the ruined peach trees.

Cloyd *(nervous):* I want to try again. Please, I'll do better.

Walter: Of course you can. Maybe I can too.

Cloyd: I'm sorry about the trees.

Walter: I see you are. Both of us were hurt. I like to think that the hurt you get over makes you stronger.

Narrator 1: Cloyd smiled at Walter **wearily**. Then they walked back up to the house.

Walter: Cloyd, I've been thinking up a storm today. I'm old and I don't have that much time left. I'm tired of farming. Remember my old mine?

Cloyd: The Pride of the West?

Walter: I figure now is the time to reopen it. And I remember you were always asking about the mountains. Let's go up into that high country. How would that suit you?

Cloyd: Will we take the horses?

Walter: Of course. You can take Blueboy!

Cloyd: When can we go?

Walter: It will take us a while to get ready. I figure in about three weeks.

scene EIGHT

Narrator 2: In late July, Cloyd and Walter rode into the mountains. Feeling close to Walter, Cloyd took out his stone.

Cloyd: I found this with one of the Ancient Ones—a baby—up above your farm. Bears are very special for Ute people. They bring strength and good luck.

Walter: This here's a real treasure. Its forehead is dished out like a

Words, Words, Words

examined: looked at carefully
grimaced: made a facial expression that shows unhappiness or pain
wearily: in a tired or worn-out way

grizzly. Used to be a lot of them around here.

Cloyd: Grizzlies? Are there any left?

Walter: Probably not. If there are, they're **endangered.**

Cloyd: When I found this stone, I gave myself a new name. Utes used to do that. They kept the name secret and only told one other person. You're the only one I'll ever tell. My secret name is Lone Bear.

Walter *(moved):* Thanks for telling me, Cloyd. You know, that piece might just bring us good luck.

Narrator 1: At the mine, Cloyd and Walter worked hard. First they'd drill. Then they'd blast with dynamite. They weren't finding any gold. Days went by without Cloyd seeing the peaks. By mid-August, Walter began to feel guilty.

Walter: Didn't you want to climb those mountains? The air's too thin for me up there. But you take Blueboy and go. Just stay off those peaks in bad weather.

Cloyd: I'll be careful.

Narrator 2: Cloyd and Blueboy climbed into the high mountains where the Utes used to live. As Cloyd tried to cross a muddy slope on a steep slide, Blueboy fell. Cloyd jumped free of the saddle, but then got pinned in the mud. Blueboy tensed and got ready to kick to keep his balance. If he did kick, he would crush Cloyd's skull.

Narrator 1: Their eyes met. The horse didn't kick. He tumbled down the mountain instead. Then Cloyd knew what Rusty had said was wrong. Horses could care about people, at least this one could. Cloyd ran down to see the horse. He was breathing. He was still alive, but how badly was he hurt?

Cloyd: Maybe you're OK. You've got to get up Blueboy!

Narrator 2: Miraculously, the horse stood up.

Narrator 1: Cloyd climbed on foot to the top of the highest mountain he saw. He took the bearstone in his hand. In **gratitude**, he offered it in turn to the Four Directions—north, south, east, and west—and then to the Earth and Sky.

Narrator 2: On the way back, a dark shape moved at the meadow's edge. It was a huge brown bear. That had to be good luck. Cloyd couldn't wait to get back to tell Walter what he had seen.

ASK yourself

- What news is Cloyd excited to share with Walter?

Recall what happened to Cloyd up in the mountains.

scene NINE

Narrator 1: When Cloyd got back to camp, his heart sank. Rusty was there with Walter.

Walter: Did you climb the Rio Grande Pyramid?

Cloyd *(half-heartedly):* Yes.

Rusty: See any wildlife?

Cloyd: Some elk. And a bear.

Rusty: What kind?

Cloyd: A brown bear.

Rusty: No grizzlies are around anymore. It must have been a black bear in a cinnamon phase. How big was it?

Cloyd: Bigger than you, standing up.

Rusty: Where was it?

Cloyd: Rincon Meadow.

Rusty: Walter, would Cloyd let his imagination get away from him?

Walter: No. Cloyd's got an eye for detail.

Rusty: No hard feelings, kid. I believe you.

Narrator 2: The red-haired man left. Cloyd turned to Walter.

Cloyd: Why did he keep asking me about the bear? Didn't he believe me?

Walter: He believed you. That's why he left so fast. He wanted to

Words, Words, Words

endangered: in danger of not being alive anymore
gratitude: a feeling of being thankful
illegal: against the law

get started after that bear. Rusty's having a hunting contest with his brothers. They use bows and arrows to make it more of a challenge.

Cloyd: But it's not bear-hunting season!

Walter *(with a smirk on his face):* Open season on bears, Cloyd.

Narrator 1: Cloyd felt horrible that he'd given the bear away. Somehow he had to keep Rusty from killing it. He slipped away and followed Rusty as the man tracked the bear. Finally, Cloyd saw the bear far below him. Rusty saw it too.

Narrator 2: Rusty sneaked along the edge of the brush, until he got a clear look at the bear. Sensing that something was wrong, the bear stood up. Cloyd yelled with all his might, trying to warn the bear. But he was too far away, and the wind was against him.

Narrator 1: Rusty pulled back his bow and shot the bear, once, twice. It fell dead. He circled it and then examined it closely. As he did, his brothers joined him. Cloyd crept closer. He could hear them talking.

Brother: Biggest bear I ever saw.

Rusty *(worried):* Look at the forehead. It's dished out. See the hump on its back?

Brother: So?

Rusty: Look at the claws. It's a grizzly.

Brother: You've got yourself a real trophy!

Rusty: It's **illegal** to kill a grizzly.

Brother: You didn't know what it was.

Rusty: It crossed my mind, but it charged me. I had to defend myself.

Narrator 2: Cloyd knew that was a lie.

Rusty: I could lose my guide's license over this. Even if a grizzly's found dead, you have to report it so that the scientists can study it.

Brother: We'll pack it out. Nobody will know.

Rusty: We'd have to leave the carcass. Backpackers would report us. No, I'll call the game warden. He'll send a helicopter to take it out before it spoils. He'll just have to believe it was self-defense.

scene TEN

Narrator 2: Cloyd was grief-stricken about the bear. When he got back to camp, he looked everywhere for Walter. He finally found him in a mine tunnel—under a lot of rubble. The old man was badly hurt. Walter must have had an accident trying to blast without Cloyd.

Narrator 1: Cloyd tried not to panic. He dragged Walter out of the tunnel. The old man's leg was broken, and he was bleeding badly. Suddenly Cloyd realized that he had just one chance to get Walter to a hospital in time: A helicopter was coming to get the bear. Cloyd jumped on Blueboy.

Narrator 2: Cloyd reached Rusty as the game warden's helicopter was about to take off with the bear carcass.

Cloyd *(shouting):* Wait! Walter's hurt! You've got to help get him to the hospital!

Narrator 1: The warden stopped. He and the other men dragged the bear out of the helicopter.

Warden: Get in with me. We'll go get Walter.

Brother: How did you know about this helicopter? How did you know to come up here?

Rusty *(with concern):* You did good, boy. However you knew to come here, you did real good. Tell Walter I'll bring all his horses and stuff out for him. Tell him not to worry about anything.

Narrator 2: The copter rose into the air.

Warden: How did you know I was coming? Did you know something about the bear?

Narrator 2: Cloyd knew that Rusty must have lied to the warden. It was his chance to get back at him. Then Cloyd remembered the peach trees and his awful revenge. He said nothing.

Narrator 1: For a week or two, Walter got better in the hospital. Then he just stayed the same. Cloyd tried to cheer him up.

Cloyd: I want you to have my bearstone.

Walter: Now wait a minute.

Narrator 2: Cloyd wanted the old man to know how much he meant to him.

Cloyd: I want you to keep it.

Walter *(grateful):* I'll always treasure this piece. I'll think of you each time I see it.

Narrator 1: Then it was September and Cloyd had to go to school. He lived in the group home and came to see Walter every afternoon. Walter really needed company. He was getting worse again. One day he seemed really sad.

Walter: They're going to put me in a nursing home. I'm going to have to sell the farm to pay my room and board.

Narrator 2: Then Cloyd thought of a plan. He'd live on the farm and help Walter while he went to school. He checked, and the school bus went out as far as Walter's farm. But there was a surprise for Cloyd at the group home.

Susan: I've got good news! The tribe says you can come home now. You've been trying so hard and doing so well. You can live with your grandmother again.

Cloyd *(to himself):* This is what I've been hoping for, but . . . *(to Susan)* I can't go now. Maybe I'll go next spring. Walter needs me. He can't handle the farm without me.

Susan: But he's going to the nursing home.

Cloyd: He'll die there. He's starting to die already. He needs the farm.

Narrator 2: Cloyd remembered standing in his father's hospital room. He remembered finding the bearstone and killing the peach trees. He saw himself standing on the mountain and knew a father had come into his life after all.

Narrator 1: He remembered the bear. He'd never forget the bear. The hurt you get over makes you stronger, Walter had said. Then Cloyd knew what he would do. He would stay with Walter and learn to live in a good way.

scene ELEVEN

Narrator 2: By the end of September, Walter and Cloyd were back at the house. One day, a truck pulled up.

Walter *(surprised):* Durango Nursery? He must be lost.

Narrator 1: The driver walked up and gave Walter a receipt.

Delivery Man: The seedlings are in the back of the truck.

Walter *(confused):* Seedlings?

Delivery Man: All paid for. Twenty-two peach trees. You are Cloyd Atcitty, aren't you?

Cloyd: I'm Cloyd. I bought them. *(gesturing toward Walter)* It was a surprise.

Delivery Man: I never heard of anybody growing peaches up here. Too cold, isn't it?

Walter *(winking at Cloyd):* I suppose it is. But we'll sure give it a try! ●

Will Hobbs

Will Hobbs knows better than to mess with Mother Nature. His stories reflect his respect for the outdoors.

Will Hobbs loves to write about outdoor adventures, like Cloyd's trips into the mountains. Hobbs doesn't just write about adventures, though—he lives them. Along with reading and writing, Hobbs's favorite activities are hiking, backpacking, and whitewater rafting. He even lives on a mountain, in a rock house that he built himself. But for Hobbs, the great outdoors is more than just a place to find excitement. Like Cloyd did, Hobbs feels that people can draw strength from nature and "get a sense of where we all fit into the much bigger picture."

How did you get the idea for *Bearstone*? Do bears have special meaning to you, like they did to Cloyd?

The starting point for *Bearstone* was a friend who owned a gold mine. Like Walter, my friend was always talking about reopening his mine. I couldn't see that happening in real life, but I decided to make it happen in a story. First, I relocated the mine to the upper Pine River—a very special place to me. I based the ranching work on my own experiences helping my friend on his ranch. I thought Walter should have a helper, so I created a Ute Boy named Cloyd. I wanted to show that Cloyd loves and respects nature. So I gave him his bearstone and his love for bears, because bears are sacred to the Ute people.

Are your other books based on real-life experiences with nature?

Yes, definitely. For instance, turtles were my first love in the world of nature. I'll never forget holding a turtle in my hand when I was four. So my first novel, *Changes in Latitudes,* was about endangered sea turtles. Later in life, I fell in love with moving water. I've rafted the Grand Canyon ten times. Two of my novels—the whitewater-rafting adventures *Downriver* and *River Thunder*—are based on my Grand Canyon experiences.

Whitewater rafting sounds exciting. Have you been doing it for a long time?

Whitewater rafting *is* exciting! My wife and I began rafting about 25 years ago, and it's become a big part of our lives. We love to go through the Grand Canyon with a few friends. It takes 18 days to go all the way through the Canyon and there are 160 rapids to run. You've got to do a lot of planning to make the trip successful. ●

Other Books by Will Hobbs

Bearstone

BEARSTONE

You may want to read the original novel, *Bearstone.* Get the whole story of what happens to Cloyd and Walter.

Downriver

Seven kids run away from a rafting trip on a quiet river and head for the wild rapids of the Grand Canyon.

Wrap-UP

Talk About It

Now that you've read *Bearstone* and the author profile, what do you have to say about these questions?

- Do you think taking revenge on someone makes you feel better or worse? Explain.
- Have you, or anyone you know, ever followed a dream, only to be disappointed in the end? Describe the situation.

Comprehension Check

Write your answers to the questions below. Use information from the play and the profile to support your answers.

1. Why was the bearstone important to Cloyd?
2. Why doesn't Cloyd just come out and ask Walter if he can go to the mountains?
3. Do you think that a good luck charm like the bearstone can really make a difference in someone's life? Explain.
4. Where did Will Hobbs get the idea for *Bearstone*?
5. If Rusty were a real person, do you think Will Hobbs would be friends with this bear hunter? Why or why not?

Vocabulary Check

sacred **illegal** **immediately**
examined **determined**

Complete each sentence below with the correct vocabulary word.

1. We were _______ to make it to the campgrounds before it got dark.
2. But we stopped when we saw the _______ burial grounds.
3. I picked up a small stone figure and _______ it.
4. "Put that down!" yelled my friend. "It's _______ to take anything from a burial ground."
5. I _______ put it back where I found it, and we went on our way.

Write About It

Choose one of the writing prompts below.

- Make a get-well card for Walter. Inside, write a personal message from Cloyd, telling Walter how he feels about him.
- Write a thank-you letter to Cloyd from Walter for the new peach trees. In the letter, explain how Walter feels about Cloyd.
- Using Cloyd's voice, write an e-mail message home to Grandmother. Have Cloyd explain to her why he decided to stay at Walter's ranch.

Fact FILE

SACRED ANIMALS

The Utes were not the only people who believed an animal to be sacred.

- In ancient Egypt, many animals were considered sacred, including cats. Some of these animals were made into mummies.
- Hindus regard the cow as sacred. Cows are allowed to wander the busy city streets in India.
- In addition to bears, the eagle, horse, wolf and raven are sacred to many Native American people.

Chief Dan George described why animals are so valued by many Native American tribes:

If you talk to the animals
they will talk with you
and you will know each other.
If you do not talk to them
you will not know them,
and what you do not know
you will fear.
What one fears
one destroys.

Using the Yellow Pages

You want to buy a bike. But you don't know where to shop. Check out the Yellow Pages. That's a phone book that lists businesses by *type* of business. To find a bike store, for example, just look under "Bicycles."

A Page From the Yellow Pages

The categories are in alphabetical order. Use the guide words at the top of each page to find out which categories are on that page.

Want to buy a yacht? Try "Yachts." Or think of the kind of business you need. Want some flowers? Try "Florists."

675 WOODWORKING—YOGA

▶ Woodworking

ABC CABINET MAKERS
62 State 555-6050
Valley Design and Restoration
5 Stanton 555-6000

▶ Work Clothing-Retail

FRANK'S SPORT SHOP
Outdoor Apparel
12 Main 555-2920
JAY'S ARMY & NAVY, *uniforms*
Rt. 3 555-3467

▶ Woven Wood Products

See "Bamboo and Woven Wood Products"

▶ X-Ray Laboratories–Medical & Dental

DC Imaging, *dental X-rays*
44 Sutton 555-3498
Med-Time X-Rays, *medical & dental*
14 Sutton 555-6120
REGENCY ASSOC. MEDICAL X-RAYS
244 Fulton 555-8709

▶ Yachts

Lots of Yachts Co., *wholesale*
9 Riverway 555-2109
Ultramarine Yachts, *retail & rentals*
678 Pearl 555-4572

▶ Yarn–Retail

KNITS INCREDIBLE *knitting classes*
129 Front 555-9349
Yarn & Beyond, *wall hangings, rugs*
62 Walden 555-1830

▶ Yoga Instruction

Best Health Club
229 Fulton 555-2109
Yoga Zone 77 Main St. 555-6643

Yoga Zone
Rated "Top Yoga Studio"
Yoga and Pilates
Beginner to Advanced
77 Main St. 555-6643

Found the category you need? Keep reading, and you'll see an alphabetical list of businesses that provide this product or service.

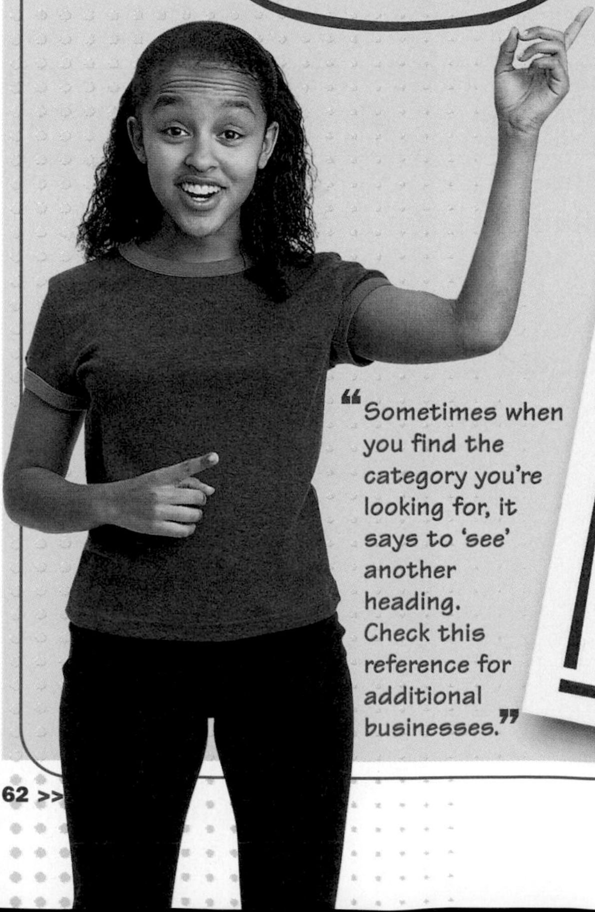

"Sometimes when you find the category you're looking for, it says to 'see' another heading. Check this reference for additional businesses."

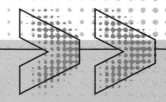

Let's Search

Review the sample page from the Yellow Pages and the tips that go with it. Then use them to answer the questions. Write your answers on your own paper.

1. You are fixing up your kitchen and need some new storage space. Which business might you call?
   a. Jay's Army & Navy
   b. Yarn & Beyond
   c. DC Imaging
   d. ABC Cabinet Makers

2. You hurt your wrist at the Best Health Club on Fulton Street. Your doctor says you can get an X-Ray right down the street. Where do you go?
   a. DC Imaging
   b. Med-Time X-Rays
   c. Regency Assoc.
   d. There's no laboratory nearby.

3. Your parents are planning a vacation. They want to go on a cruise. Under which heading on this page of the Yellow Pages should they look?

4. You want to sign up for a class at the Yoga Zone. What is the Yoga Zone's phone number?

5. You want to buy a new CD player. What heading should you look under in the Yellow Pages?
   a. "Electronic Equipment"
   b. "Music"
   c. "Entertainers"
   d. "Recording Studios"

Shop Till You Drop

It's time to buy gifts: hiking boots for your sister, an army jacket for your brother, and a wall hanging for your parents. Use the Yellow Pages entries on page 62. List the name and address of each store you'll visit.

Sell It

You own a business. Create an ad to go in the Yellow Pages. Use the Yoga Zone ad as a model. List your business name, address, and phone number. Include a brief description of the products or services your business provides.

"You can also find Yellow Pages on the Internet. Most search engines list them right on their home pages."

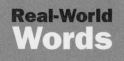

Real-World Words

category: a group of things that has something in common
retail: relating to the sale of goods directly to consumers
wholesale: relating to the sale of goods to buyers for resale

novel

SLAM!

SLAM!

By
Walter
Dean Myers

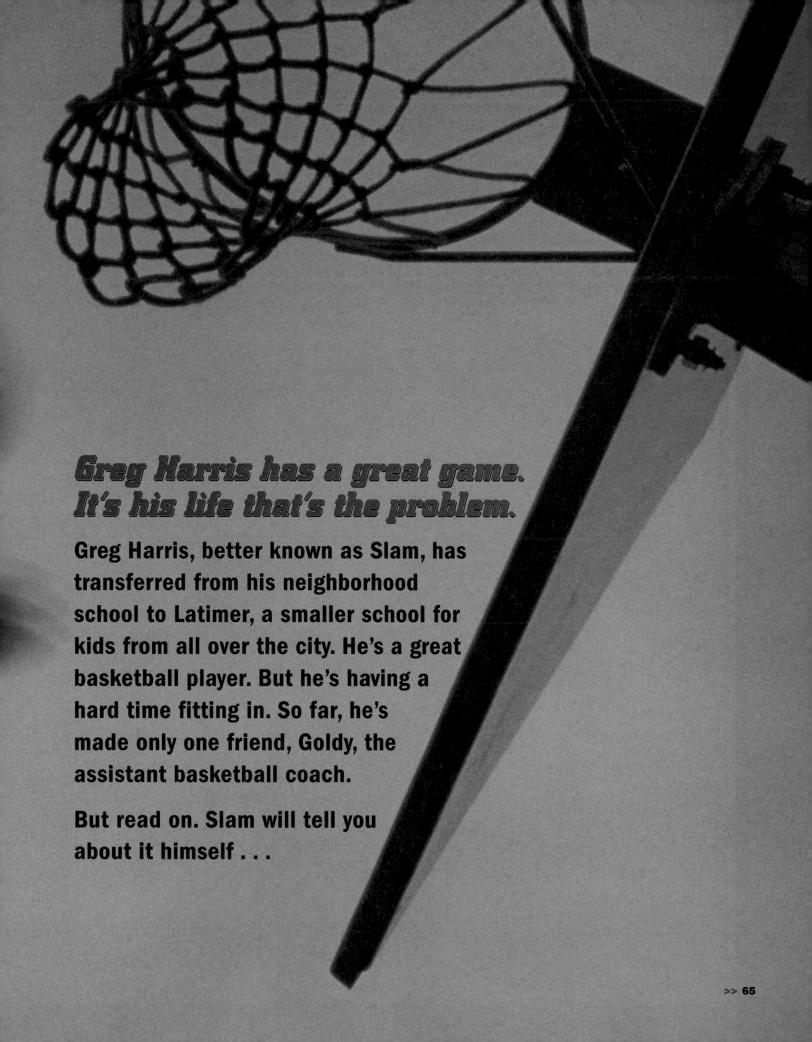

Greg Harris has a great game. It's his life that's the problem.

Greg Harris, better known as Slam, has transferred from his neighborhood school to Latimer, a smaller school for kids from all over the city. He's a great basketball player. But he's having a hard time fitting in. So far, he's made only one friend, Goldy, the assistant basketball coach.

But read on. Slam will tell you about it himself . . .

Basketball is my thing. I can hoop. Case closed. I'm six four and I got the moves, the eye, and the heart. You can take my game to the bank and wait around for the interest. With me it's not like playing a game; it's like the only time I'm being for real. Bringing the ball down the court makes me feel like a bird that just learned to fly. I see my guys moving down in front of me, and everything feels and looks right. Patterns come up and a small buzz comes into my head that starts to build up and I know it won't end until the ball swishes through the net. If somebody starts messing with my game, it's like they're getting into my head. But if I've got the ball, it's okay, because I can take care of the **situation.** That's the word and I know it the same way I know my tag, Slam. Yeah, that's it, Slam. But without the ball, without the floorboards under my feet, without the mid-court line that takes me halfway home, you can get to me.

So when Mr. Tate, the principal at my new school, started talking about me laying low for the season until I got my grades together, I was like seriously turned out. No way was I going for that. I couldn't stand walking away from basketball.

So, I stayed on the team. But things didn't get much better. The worst day was when I got into a fight with my English teacher, Mr. Parrish. Well, not really a fight. Here's what went down.

When I got to school, it was like everybody had a chip on their shoulder. We had a paper due in English and Mr. Parrish collected them. I remembered that we had the paper due some time soon, but I forgot just when. Mr. Parrish is the kind of guy who always thinks somebody is dissing him because they don't do their homework. Like, you're supposed to give him his propers by going home and working on what he wants you to work on. Then if you show late, he cops this nasty **attitude** and puts his mouth on you.

> **"The only difference between on the court and off the court is that everybody is in the game off the court. You will play and you will win or lose."**

"So, Mr. Harris, just why are you taking up classroom space?" He was standing over me. "Why don't you just go out to your neighborhood and find a corner to stand on? That's what you want from life, isn't it?"

"Don't be standing over me, man," I said.

"Don't *be* standing over me?" He raised his voice. He was making fun of me and I didn't like it.

As I got up, I knew I was wrong. And I knew that what I had in mind was to rock his jaw. I pulled my fist back and felt somebody grab my arm. It was little Karen, this white girl in my class. By the time I had turned and pushed her away, Mr. Parrish had backed away and was headed toward the door.

"Forget him!" Karen was yelling at me. "He's wrong. Forget him!"

My books were on my desk, and I reached for them and knocked them to the floor. I left them there and walked on out of the classroom. Mr. Parrish was already all the way down the hall, headed toward the principal's office. The door leading outside was in the other direction and I headed that way.

It was cold as it wanted to be. The hawk was biting and there were snow flurries in the air. There was a little restaurant down the street and I went into it and ordered a cup of soup.

The soup was barley bean, which I don't dig that tough but it was hot and the restaurant was warm. I kept having flashes of scenes go off in my mind. Some scenes would have me punching out Mr. Parrish. Other scenes would have me being put out of school, or getting arrested. I tried to think back if I had hurt Karen. She looked okay, I thought. I wondered why she jumped up and grabbed me. Did I look like a wild man or something?

"So what's happening?"

I jumped when I heard Goldy's voice.

"You had trouble in Mr. Parrish's class?"

"Yo, man, he caught me wrong and I blew up," I said. "It's not a big deal."

"If you say so."

"I'm saying so."

"Who was right in the class just now?" he asked.

"I guess he was," I said. "He's the teacher and I'm just the student. No matter what he said, I can't do nothing about it."

"He's down in the office now trying to get you **suspended,**" Goldy said. "A couple of kids from the class came down and spoke up for you."

"Yeah?"

"They don't hate you as much as you hate yourself, it seems." Goldy looked into my soup. "What's this?"

"Barley bean soup."

"Phew! I thought it was the coffee."

ASK Yourself

- How do you feel about the way Mr. Parrish treats Slam?

Think about how you might feel if you were in Slam's place.

Words, Words, Words

situation: the condition that exists at a certain time
attitude: a feeling about someone or something
suspended: barred from school or another activity as a punishment

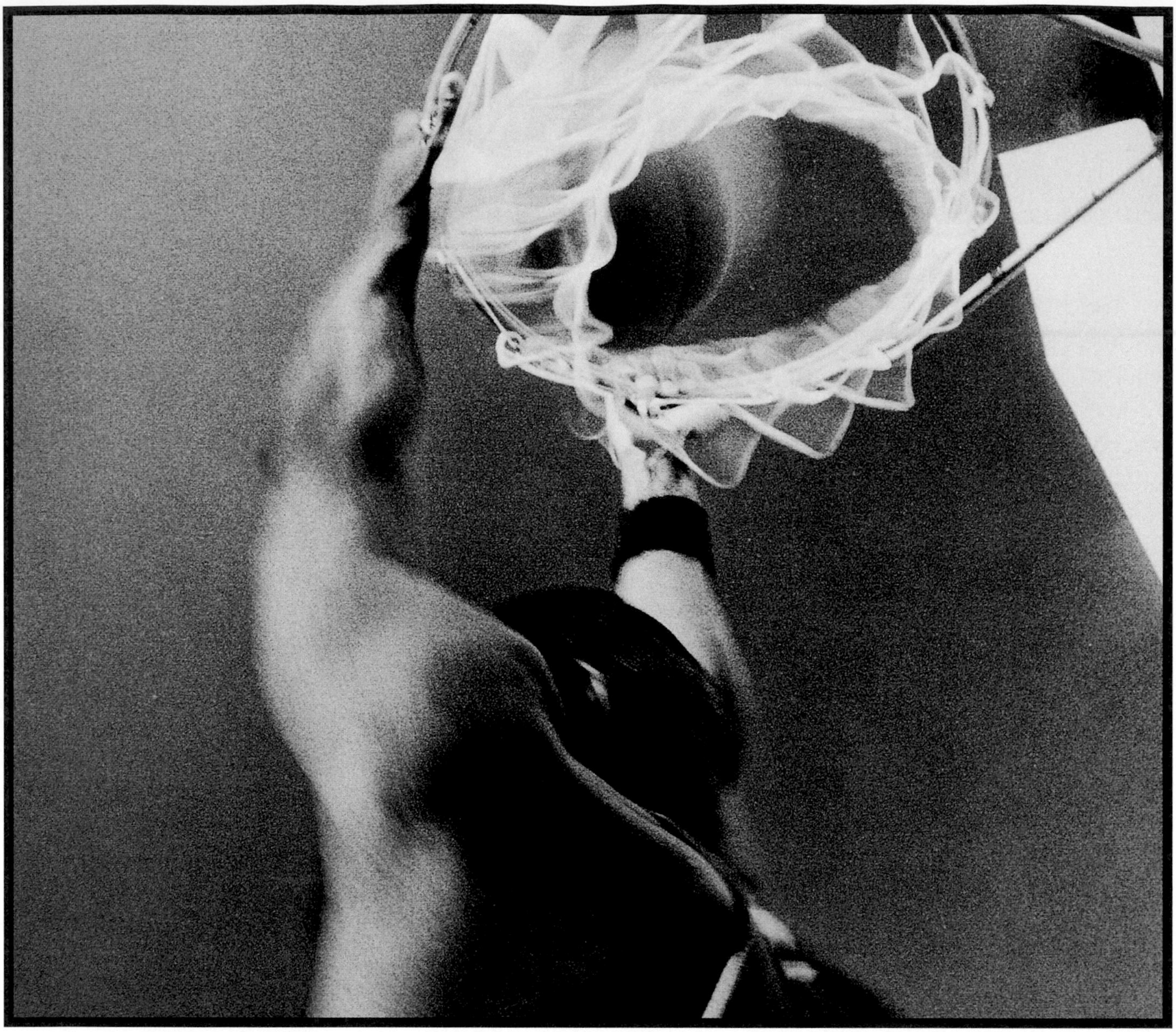

I had to smile. It was good hearing that some of the kids went and talked up for me. It was good Goldy came to the restaurant, too.

"How did you know I was here?"

"I didn't. I just looked around for you," Goldy said. "Tell me, Slam, why do you keep **self-destructing**? You find a way of making money at it or something?"

"This is going to be one of your lectures?"

"No. Why don't you make it one of *your* lectures?" Goldy said. "Why don't you tell me what's going on? You know, I'm really interested."

"Why?"

"It's just something I don't understand," he said. "It's not like you're the first kid that's been through Latimer who has trouble getting along. It happens once or twice every year. Some black kids. Some white kids."

Words, Words, Words

self-destructing: acting in a way that hurts oneself
sincere: honest and truthful
privileges: special rights or advantages given to a person or group of people
respect: a feeling of admiration or consideration for someone

"Ask the white kids."

"I got you here now," Goldy said. "And I'll make a deal with you. You tell me what's going on, and I'll work with you to get you out of this mess with Mr. Parrish."

I looked at the dude. He looked **sincere.**

"You want me to cop a plea," I said, "and I don't know what to say."

"Just tell me what you think is wrong," he said. "And if you're not going to eat the soup . . ."

"Go ahead."

He started eating the soup, and the guy behind the counter brought him over some crackers.

"Hey, how come you didn't bring me the crackers when I had the soup?" I said. "I paid for it."

"You want crackers?"

"Forget it."

"So?" Goldy had a soup mustache.

"So everybody says I'm wrong, okay? I didn't do this, and I didn't do that. I messed up a test. I forgot my homework." The guy brought the crackers and another bowl of soup.

"On the house," he said.

"You get **privileges** being with a white guy," Goldy joked.

"I'm hip."

"So go on."

"Then they start running this game about how when I get out of school, I ain't going to be into nothing. That's what Parrish ran down. I was going to be a corner guy, you know, just hanging on the block 'cause I don't have anything going for me.

"He acts like I don't see nothing. You think I don't see the dudes on my block ain't doing nothing? He sees it and I see, but when he throws it in my face, he's not showing me any **respect.** Like, if I run up to him and said he's half bald and all ugly or something like that, then I'm not showing him respect. He knows he's half bald, and he knows he ain't no movie star either. But if I throw that up in his face then everybody is going to say I'm dissing him. When he throws stuff up in my face I'm supposed to act like I'm happy with it. You know, 'Thank you Mr. Parrish for dissing me in front of the whole class because it's for my own good and I feel real glad that you did it.'"

"Is he right concerning your schoolwork?" Goldy asked.

"Yeah," I said. "He's right."

"So, say he was a ballplayer talking trash to you on the court," Goldy said. "What would you do? Punch him out?"

"If we were on the court I would have my game with me," I said. "I don't have a game off the court."

"You still don't get it, do you?" Goldy finished up his soup and took mine. "The only difference between on the court and off the court is that everybody is in the game off the court. You *will* play and you *will* win or lose. There's nobody on the bench, nobody sitting it out. You're in the game, Slam. You're in it whether you want to be or not. A lot of people fool themselves and say they're just not going to play. Believe me, it don't work that way."

"How do you know so much?"

"I'm guessing," Goldy said. "When I come back to life, I'm coming back as Michael Jordan and then I'll try a different theory. Now let's get back to the school."

"You going to talk to Mr. Tate for me?"

"About what?"

"You said you would work with me to get me out of trouble," I said.

"You're not in trouble," Goldy said.

"Once the kids took your side, Parrish backed off. He's going to be

ASK Yourself

- How would you sum up the advice that Goldy is giving Slam?

Think about what Goldy says and put it into your own words.

"I'm sorry I blew up like that," I said. "It won't happen again."

looking for you to make a mistake, though. You know that, right?"

"Yeah. I guess I dissed him, too."

"You might even be learning something," Goldy said.

"Look, thanks for coming by and talking to me."

"I just do it for the soup," Goldy said.

We got back to the school, and a few of the kids got to me and asked what was going on. I told them it was no big deal. Then I had an idea. Tony said that Mr. Parrish was in the library, and I went there and found him. He had some books in his hands, and he put them in front of his chest when I walked up to him.

"I'm sorry I blew up like that," I said. "It won't happen again."

He didn't know what to say. You could see it in his eyes. He was thinking a mile a minute and then he nodded and sort of mumbled "okay" under his breath.

I watched him walk away. Goldy had said that there were going to be winners and losers, off the court as well as on, and I knew that I didn't know what winning off the court was.

But I was going to find out. Maybe that was the way to work it. Maybe if I could get my game right, all my game, on and off the court, I would get over. ●

Walter Dean Myers

Slam is tough, cool, and an awesome ballplayer.
So is Walter Dean Myers.

Just like Slam, Walter Dean Myers grew up playing hoops on the streets of Harlem, New York. Also just like Slam, he had some trouble in school. Although Myers loved to read, he had a serious speech problem. "I was ready to conquer the world," he said, "but no one could understand a thing that I was saying."

Finally, one of his teachers suggested to Myers that he stop talking and write instead. Myers has been writing ever since. Recently, some students interviewed Myers. Here's what he had to say.

If you had a choice, what would you do besides writing books?

That's easy! I would be a star player in the NBA, of course. And I'd write in the off-season.

Why didn't you become a professional basketball player?

Well, that's an easy question, too. I wasn't good enough to land a spot in the NBA. After all, there are probably more guys in your school than there are in the whole NBA! Luckily, I had writing as a career option.

So, is the character Slam really you?

He's not exactly me, but we do have some similarities. We both grew up in Harlem and we're both ballplayers. I saw a lot of my friends who were ballplayers—good ballplayers—run into trouble just like Slam did. I also ran into some of Slam's problems. I did very well in school when I was younger, but things began to get tough for me in high school. I was still a good student, but in spite of my good grades, I knew I could never afford college. That depressed me and I began skipping school. Like Slam, I got it together eventually. I joined the army when I was 17. Later, I took some college classes.

The setting of *Slam!* is really great. How did you make it so real?

The book is set in an actual place in Harlem where I hang out. Before I started writing, I went and photographed the entire block. I referred to the photos as I was writing so I'd be sure to get the descriptions right.

When do you plan to stop writing books?

I plan to retire from writing seven minutes before I die.

Other Books by Walter Dean Myers

Harlem

Harlem

This collection of poems is illustrated by Myers's son Christopher. It celebrates the people, sights, and sounds of Harlem.

Monster

MONSTER

Illustrated by Christopher Myers. Steve Harmon, 16, is on trial for murder, and the prosecutor calls him a monster. Is Steve really guilty? Read his story and make up your mind.

Wrap-Up

Talk About It

Now that you've read *Slam!* and the author profile, what do you have to say about these questions?

- Would you want to be friends with someone like Slam? Why or why not?
- What do you like as much as Walter Dean Myers likes writing and basketball? Explain why you like these things.

Comprehension Check

Write your answers to the questions below. Use information from the novel and the profile to support your answers.

1. What happens in Mr. Parrish's class?
2. Why does Goldy go to the restaurant?
3. What lesson do you think Slam learns in this story?
4. What would Walter Dean Myers have become, if he hadn't become a writer?
5. What do Slam and Walter Dean Myers have in common?

Vocabulary Check

Complete each sentence with the correct vocabulary word below.

sincere **respect** **suspended**
privileges **attitude**

1. Coach says we can be _______ from the team if we don't make good grades.
2. Our offer to help the younger kids with their homework was _______.
3. In order to get _______, sometimes you have to give it.
4. It's hard to have a good _______ when nothing seems to be going right.
5. My parents give me special _______ if I help with the chores.

Write About It

Choose one of the writing prompts below.

- Write a letter from Slam to Goldy thanking him for his advice and concern. In the letter, explain how Slam plans to use this advice to make his experience at school better.
- Imagine that Slam becomes a big NBA star. Write a two-paragraph profile about Slam that might appear in a game program.
- Walter Dean Myers uses real-life settings for his books. Pick a location in your area that you think would make a good setting for a story. Then write a short description of the location. Also, tell what kind of story might take place there.

More to READ

If you liked this excerpt from Walter Dean Myers's book *Slam!*, you might like these other books about young athletes and the challenges they face:

Tangerine
by Edward Bloor

Paul Fisher's older brother Erik is a high school football star, but to Paul he's no hero. Paul's game is soccer, which he plays even though he has to wear thick glasses. When the Fishers move to Tangerine, Florida, Paul tries to make sense of things. Why, for example, he fits into the toughest group around, which happens to be his new soccer team. And why no one but he can see the terrifying truth about Erik.

Danger Zone
By David Klass

Jimmy Doyle is a basketball legend, the one the fans count on to make the game-winning shots that save the game. But will he be accepted by his teammates when he is picked for an American High School Dream Team?

Writing a Complaint Letter

You order a pizza. You wait and wait, but it doesn't arrive. You call the pizza place, and the employee is rude. When the pizza finally does arrive, it's cold. What can you do?

It's time to write a letter of complaint. But there's a right way and a wrong way to do that. Check out the letter below. Can you tell why it's a good letter?

My Pizza Was Late!

Call and find out who runs the business. Send your letter to him or her.

Note the date on which you received bad service. Briefly describe what happened on that date.

What can the manager do to make it up to you? You might include a suggestion or two.

270 Cedar Lane
Ridgewood, NJ 07450
June 10, 2000

Mr. Marty Pep, Manager
Pizza World
124 5th Street
Ridgewood, NJ 07450

Dear Mr. Pep:

On June 9, I ordered a pizza from your restaurant. After 45 minutes, it had not arrived. When I called to check on it, the person who answered told me that it was "on its way." After another half hour with no pizza, I called again. The person who answered was quite rude this time. He told me to stop being so impatient and that the pizza would get there "sooner or later." Finally, after two hours, we got our pizza.

I understand that your restaurant is very busy. However, waiting two hours for a pizza is unacceptable. Your employee's rudeness is also unacceptable.

Your delivery person didn't even explain why the pizza was so late. I think we should get a discount on the late pizza, or a coupon for next time.

My family has ordered from Pizza World for years. After this experience we will think twice. The pizza was for a party. The guests were hungry and unhappy when it was late. I hope in the future that other customers are treated better than my family and friends were on June 9. Thank you for your time.

Sincerely,

Billy Rollins

Billy Rollins
555-8762

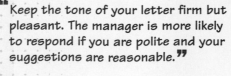

"Keep the tone of your letter firm but pleasant. The manager is more likely to respond if you are polite and your suggestions are reasonable."

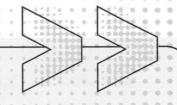

Complain in Style

You're disappointed, and you've decided to do something about it. Can you write a good complaint letter? Reread the letter and the tips that go with it. Then answer these questions. Write your answers on your own paper.

1. To whom did Billy address his letter?
  a. the pizza delivery person
  b. the Better Business Bureau
  c. the manager of the pizza place

2. Which of the following statements is true?
  a. Billy's pizza was two hours late.
  b. Pizza World sent Billy the wrong kind of pizza.
  c. The people who answered Billy's calls were helpful.

3. Which of the following suggestions did Billy make to Marty Pep?
  a. Billy wanted an apology from the person who answered the phone.
  b. Billy wanted a discount or coupon.
  c. Billy wanted the delivery person fired.

4. When did Billy write his letter? Why was it a good idea to write the letter so soon after the incident?

5. Write about it. How would you describe the tone of Billy's letter? Were his complaints reasonable?

Take Care of It

You're the manager of a pizza place. You get a letter just like Billy's. Write a paragraph telling how you'll respond to the complaint.

Send a Letter

Think about (or imagine) a time when you got bad service and didn't do anything about it. Write a letter about the incident. Remember to be firm but polite. Tell what you would like the management to do.

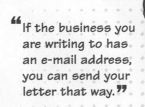

"If the business you are writing to has an e-mail address, you can send your letter that way."

Real-World Words

incident: an event; something that happens
manager: a person who runs a business
respond: to answer, reply, or react to something or someone

magazine article

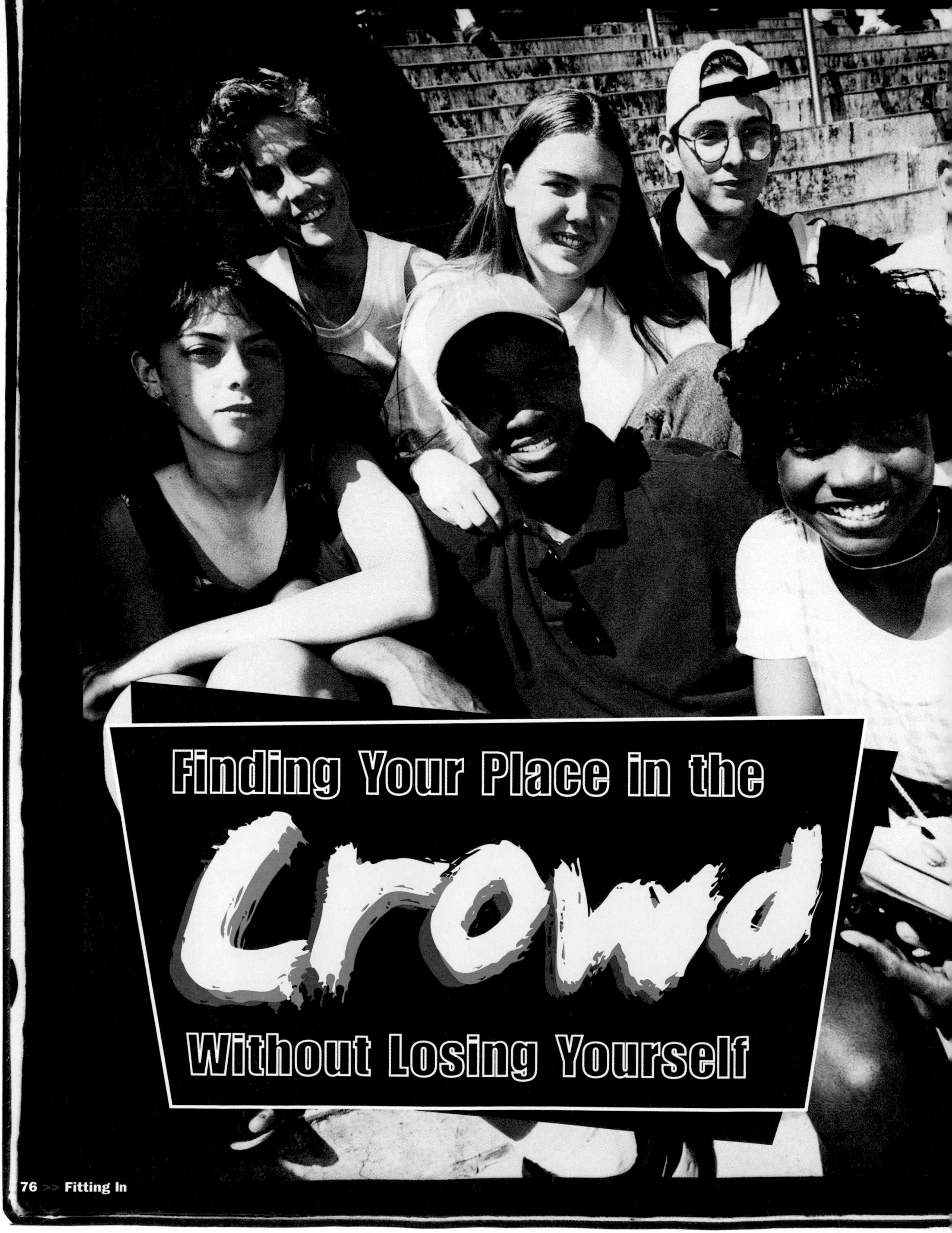

Finding Your Place in the Crowd Without Losing Yourself

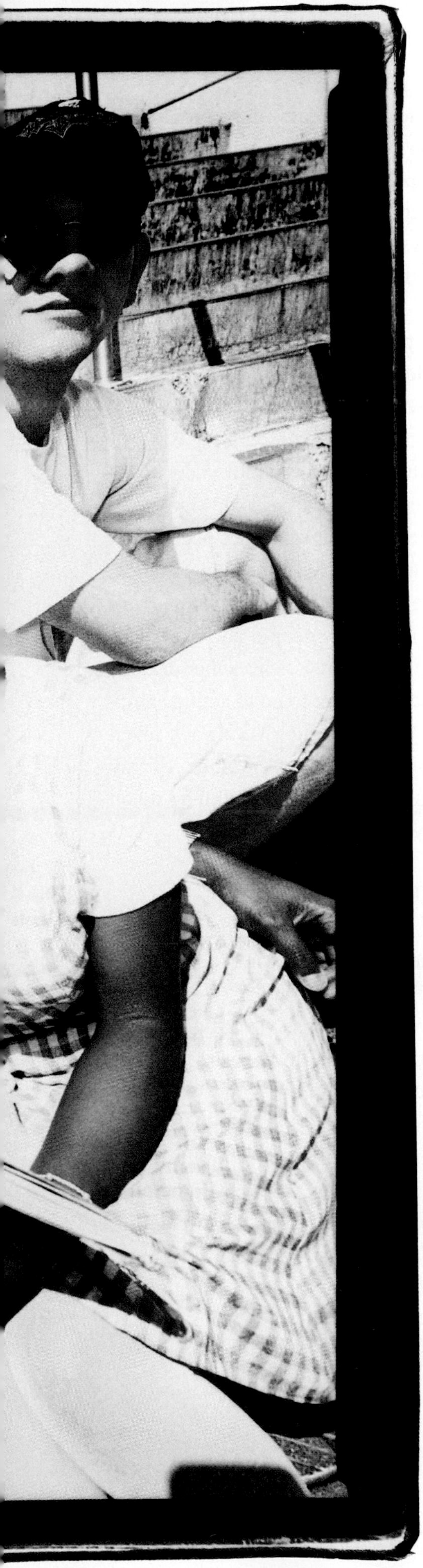

You have a group of friends you can't live without. But do they give you the space you need to be an individual?

No one could have a closer or more loyal group of friends than Mara, 16. Over the past four years, Mara and her seven girlfriends have shared experiences that bond them together like sisters. They tend each other's heartaches and cut each other's hair. They've traded faded jeans, secret confessions, and lip gloss. "They are always there for me," says Mara.

Every so often, though, maybe once a month, Mara takes a break from her girlfriends. She's met some new kids at her weekend restaurant job. They're different from her, and she enjoys spending time with them because of their varied interests. "They seem a little older," she says. "They're into different kinds of things, different music. Two of them went to Japan last year on an exchange program."

Mara would never trade her old friends for her new ones, but "different people bring out different parts of you," she says. With her new crowd, she's more intellectual and more curious. "It's good to experiment sometimes," Mara adds.

Many teenagers can relate to how Mara feels. You may have a tight group of friends that you've known for years. Or perhaps you spend your time with just one or two soul mates. They share your fries in the cafeteria and fill up your family's answering machine with their coded messages. They know how to prop you up when you're feeling low.

During adolescence, groups of friends are like second families. As teens make the transition between childhood and adulthood, friends can provide support and understanding. "Groups are tremendously important during adolescence and throughout life," says Tammy Mikinski, director of the Rockhurst College Counseling Center in Kansas City, Missouri. "Groups provide social support in difficult times. Having a support network often makes the difference between people who manage in a healthy way and those who struggle."

As much as you appreciate your group, there will be times when you want to branch out. Maybe you want to meet new kinds of people, or maybe you're fascinated by a new hobby. This is the time in your life when you're beginning to stake out your identity. You're figuring out

Students from New York City's Stuyvesant High School strike a pose.

After all, what would her friends say? "It's too bad that teens can't hopscotch between groups, experimenting with different identities," says Brown, "because that's what you should be doing at this time."

Some teens have no problem stepping away from their familiar **clique** every now and then. Some have close friends outside their regular group; others try out private hobbies or explore new activities outside of school. Mara's old friends don't mind her **occasional** "vacations" with her new friends; they even support her **endeavors** to meet new people.

Sarah, 14, leaves her friends each summer to go to acting camp. "It's something I've always loved doing," she says. "None of my friends do it. It's something I do on my own."

who you are as an individual, apart from your parents and even your close friends. This process is known as *individuation*.

Beyond the Crowd

"During adolescence, you're becoming your own person," says Bradford Brown, a **psychology** professor at the University of Wisconsin. "Having a crowd to hang out with can be an important part of finding your identity apart from your family. But that's only a step. There comes a point when you have to step beyond the crowd and just be who you are."

"A lot of kids worry if they're not exactly the same as their friends," says Annina, 15. "They don't ever look at who they are. I don't think most high school kids know who they are."

According to Brown, many teens become trapped in the image of their crowd. A kid with a nose ring may be a great basketball player, but he doesn't feel comfortable trying out for the team, even though he spends hours in his driveway shooting hoops by himself. A jock may not go out for the school play.

Grumbling Friends

Some kids try new experiences in spite of what their friends might think. Victor, 13, says his close friends used to make fun of a kid who went to church. Then the kid invited Victor to go with him. Victor knew his friends would laugh at him, too, but he went along anyway. "It was something good for me. When they made fun of me I just ignored them, and then they stopped bothering us."

Words, Words, Words

psychology: the study of the mind, emotions and human behavior
clique: a small group of people who are very friendly with each other
occasional: once in a while
endeavors: attempts or efforts
endured: put up with something painful or unpleasant

"I began to realize that if people don't like me for who I am they are not my true friends."

Rebecca, 15, also **endured** a bit of grumbling from her established group when she started hanging around with some new friends from her after-school art class. Rebecca, who is African American, thinks that her Black and Hispanic friends felt hurt because her new friends were white. "They said I was trying to be white," she says. "It hurt me at first," Rebecca adds. "But now I laugh at my friends when they hassle me. And guess what? They're still my friends."

Trying new things can build self-confidence. "I was worried about fitting in and being accepted," says Michelle, from Atlanta, Georgia. "I worried a lot about saying and doing the right things." Then she started working with Habitat for Humanity, the group that builds houses for people with low incomes. "I feel so good about helping people," she says. "It made me feel better about myself. I began to realize that if people don't like me for who I am, they're not true friends."

A Better Future

For some teens, venturing outside of the crowd is more than an interesting experiment. For Jose, 16, it was a matter of survival.

Over the past few years, Jose watched most of his friends get sucked into his neighborhood's deadly drug trade. Jose's family is poor, so he considered an offer to earn $2,000 a week as a runner, delivering drugs. Jose was very tempted, but he ultimately decided not to get involved with the whole scene. Now he knows several runners who have landed in prison. And one is even dead.

A big reason Jose turned the offer down was the help and encouragement of his new friend Nicolas. "He's a star at school," Jose says. He's into every activity. He'll go to a great college. I met him in an after-school program." Jose still loves his childhood friends. But lately he spends more time with Nicolas. Why? Nicolas opened up his mind to a better future—including college. "If he can do it, I can too," says Jose.

Stepping outside your group can do more than open your mind and broaden your perspective. Sometimes, it can change your whole attitude about yourself. The key is finding a balance between the comfort of your old group and your own individual needs.

A group of friends is important all through life, but you have to strike out on your own now and then. You have to find your own way. "My friends were troublemakers," says Chris, 15, of Monroe City, Missouri. "I'd do what they'd do because I wanted them to like me. Now I've learned what I like. I go on that instead of what everyone else likes."

ASK Yourself

- What problems did old friends present for Rebecca and Jose?

Consider how each of them wanted to change.

"I have three close friends who I talk to every day," says Raul, 16. "But sometimes I go off on my own. And if I'm interested in something new, my friends think that's great, because they want me to grow as a person."

A Healthy Balance

What do you do for yourself? What do you do just to please your friends? These tips can help you find the right balance in your life.

1. Evaluate your group.

Are your friends trustworthy and loyal? Can you count on them to come through for you? If they do, you're lucky. If your friends frequently disappoint you, rethink the friendship. If they do things that make you uneasy, limit your time with them. Build some new friendships and find a new group.

2. Pursue your interests.

If you're interested in doing something, pursue it even if you have to do it on your own. If none of your friends share your interest in computers, join an after-school club. Get a related after-school job or find someone who can teach you more about it. If your friends make fun of your interests, ignore their comments or talk to them one at a time. Tell them what you're getting out of your interest. Invite them to join you.

3. Keep an open mind.

Some people see themselves too narrowly. You may think of yourself only as a straight-A student or only as a basketball player. But what if you don't make the NBA? Do you have a backup plan? You will if you try different things. Experiment—even if it scares you. "If you are slightly interested in something, check it out," says Daphne, 18. "You can't just sit around and expect to find things you really like." Explore different options. Maybe you'd be a great chef, songwriter, or doctor.

4. Explain yourself.

Some friends may feel sad or mad at you when you spend time away from them. It's natural for that to happen, so explain to them that you're still part of the group. Make sure they know they can still count on you. You might say something like, "I'm lucky to have you as friends. You give me the courage to try new things."

5. Don't drop old friends for new groups.

What's better? Having one or two really good friends—or being part of a big group? Experts say close friendships are more important to happiness and success. So don't drop your best friend when you find a new group. There's no reason you can't have both!

Nonconformist

by Angela Shelf Medearis

Trying to fit in—or not—is something kids and teens deal with all the time. Can you relate to what this writer is saying?

I don't want to be anybody
but myself.
So, I shaved little lines
in my head and
dyed my hair purple
and green
(with just a hint of orange)
and pierced my nose and
hung a gold earring in it,
AS AN EXPRESSION OF WHO I AM
(who am I?).
Of course,
I waited until someone else did it first.
I didn't want anyone to think I'm
weird.
You know what I mean?

Wrap-Up

Talk About It

Now that you've read "Finding Your Place in the Crowd" and "Nonconformist," what do you have to say about these questions?

- Have you ever wanted to try something new but been afraid that your friends might give you a hard time? Describe the experience.
- How important is it for friends to be alike? Explain your opinion.

Comprehension Check

Write your answers to the questions below. Use information from the article and the poem to support your answers.

1. What is *individuation*?
2. Why might the kid with the nose ring feel uncomfortable about trying out for the basketball team?
3. If a close friend does not approve of a new activity you want to try, is this person really a friend?
4. In "Nonconformist," is the speaker's hair and jewelry a true expression of individuality? Explain your answer.
5. How can you be an individual and still be "one of the crowd?"

Vocabulary Check

occasional **endeavors** **clique**
endured **psychology**

Complete each sentence with the correct vocabulary word.

1. The _______ I hung out with hated sports.
2. But I liked to play ball on an _______ basis.
3. I tried out for the soccer team, but my _______ to be more athletic did not work out.
4. The aches and pains I _______ during tryouts surprised me.
5. I decided to take a class in _______ instead.

Write About It

Choose one of the writing prompts below.

- Write a letter from one best friend to another, explaining that spending time apart doesn't have to ruin the friendship.
- Write a poem that is an answer to "Nonconformist." Give an example of someone who acts like an individual and really doesn't care about what others think.
- Write a journal entry about the different groups in your school. Describe how group members define themselves—by their clothes, actions, etc.

More to READ

Fitting in is a problem that every teenager faces. If you're interested in this subject, you might enjoy these books about teens who find their own solutions.

Thief of Hearts
by Laurence Yep

Stacy thought she was like everyone else at her suburban middle school. Then a new girl at school, Hong Ch'un, comes along and things are suddenly different. Hong Ch'un says Stacy doesn't appreciate her heritage. Now Stacy must decide for herself how the Chinese and American parts of her identity fit together.

Plain City
by Virginia Hamilton

Buhlaire Sims has always felt like an outsider. Living on the "other side of the tracks" and ridiculed by her classmates, Buhlaire looks for acceptance the only place she can—within her family. But there are problems there too.

Interviewing for a Job

You answered a help-wanted ad and landed an interview. Now you need to prepare for it. How will you show the employer that you've got the qualifications for the job?

Look at the ads below. What would you say if you were interviewing for these jobs?

Help-Wanted Ads

No job experience is needed, but be prepared to talk about your great phone manners and love of reading.

Reread the ad before your interview. Know what it says about hours, pay, and experience.

Help Wanted

Local supermarket needs bagger. Must be strong, neat, and able to get along with others. Afternoons and evenings, $5 an hour. Acme Grocery, 25 Windmill Lane.

Great Summer Job

Volunteer as counselor at a sleep-away camp. Full room and board, plus a chance to live in beautiful location. No salary, but great for your resumé. Must have some experience working with children and have three references. Arts and crafts skills a plus. Write to Box 87 to apply.

Bring the phone numbers of three references to your interview.

Immediate Opening in Public Library!

Library aide wanted. No experience needed. Candidate must love books, have good telephone manners, and be able to alphabetize. Part-time, $6 an hour. Call Pat at 555-8233

Wanted: Green Thumb

Are you good at gardening and yard work? Then this is the job for you. Looking for landscaper, weekends only. Salary depends on experience. Must be energetic, able to follow directions, and have flexible hours. Call Joe at 555-2884 for information.

Now Hiring

Cleaning company needs part-time workers. Will train in household cleaning. Call Angela at 555-5456.

"Dress neatly for an interview. Smile and shake hands when you introduce yourself. Look the interviewer in the eye. Don't mumble or look at the ground."

Get to Work

The people below are looking for jobs. You're going to help them out. Reread the help-wanted ads and the tips. Then write your opinions about the questions below.

1. Sung Lee has to watch her little brother during the week, but her weekends are free. She loves to be outdoors, play soccer and basketball, and grow vegetables. Which job should she apply for?

2. Malik is a good student. He reads two books a week. He is polite, and he loves peace and quiet. Which job should he apply for? What should he talk about in his interview?

3. Victor is a popular guy. He plays football for his school, and he's president of his class. Which job should he apply for?

4. Lily has never worked before, but she cleans her family's house every weekend. She is a star athlete. She runs and lifts weights every day. Which job should she apply for? What should she discuss in her interview?

5. Jessica has been a babysitter for three years. She loves little kids. She writes music and makes pottery. She wants to go away for the summer because she can't get along with her sister. Which job should she apply for? What should Jessica discuss during her interview? What should she **not** discuss?

The Search is On

You want to hire someone to do your chores—like taking out the trash, washing the dishes, and carrying your book bag. Write a help-wanted ad for the position. Include the skills needed to do the job, and the type of person you are looking for.

Be Prepared

Choose a job from the help-wanted ads in your local paper that interests you. Then write a list of questions you might have to answer in an interview for the job.

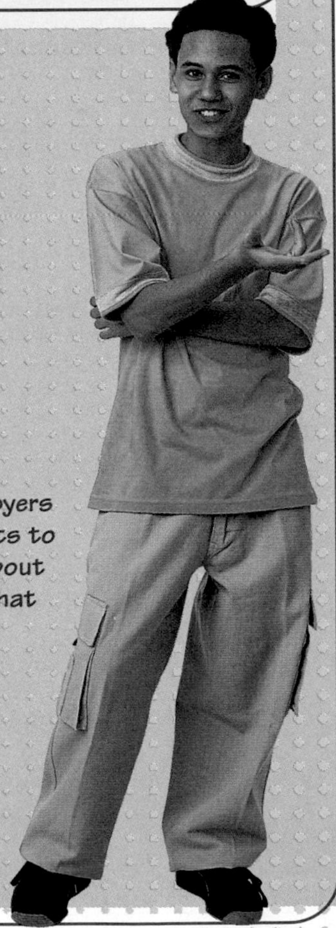

"In interviews, employers often ask applicants to tell them a little about themselves. Plan what you would say."

Real-World Words

employer: people or companies that pay you to work for them
qualifications: skills or experiences that make you fit for a job
references: people who can say that you are a good worker

profile

Sammy Sosa

Home Run Hero

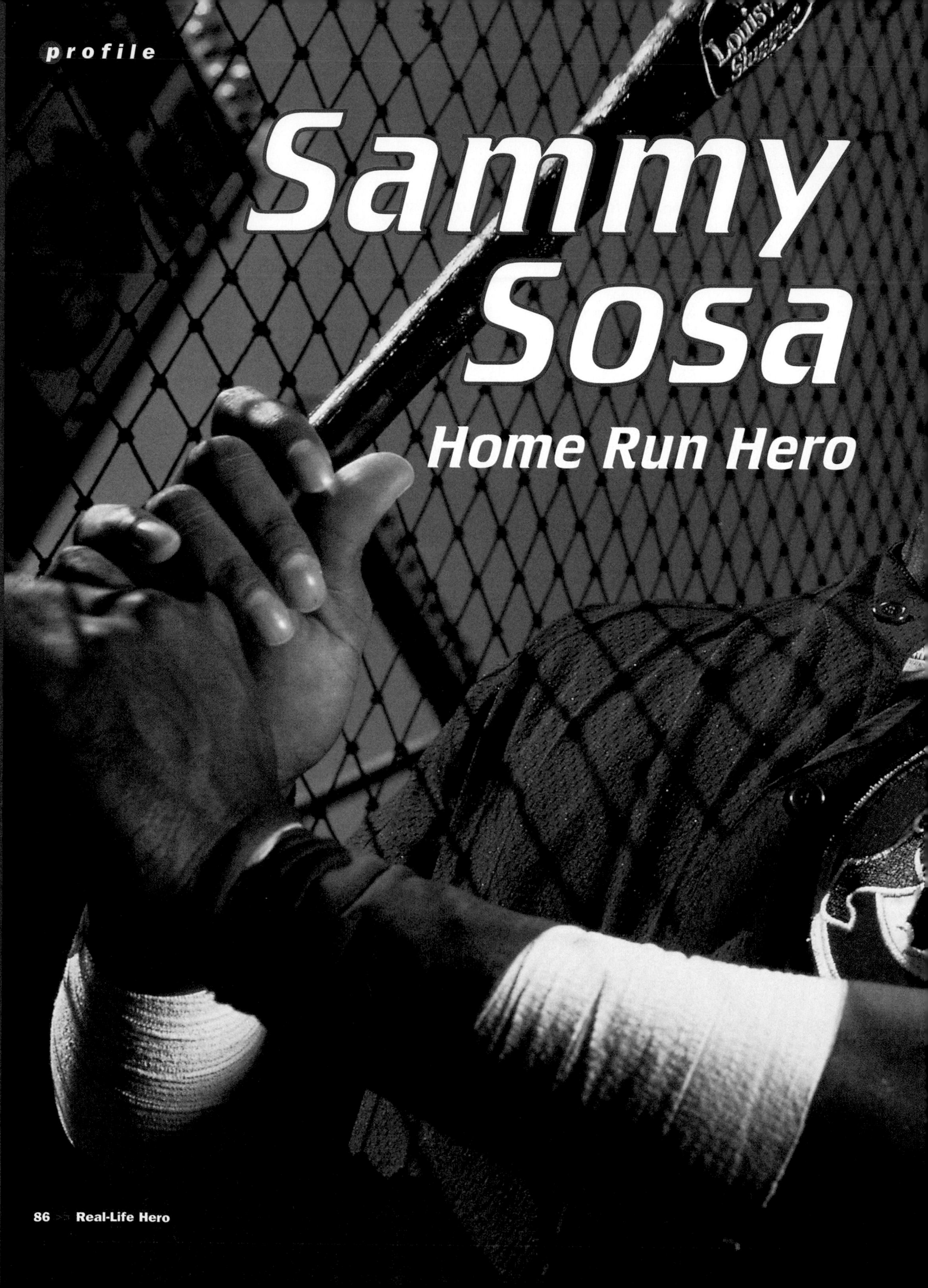

Real-Life
HERO

The world knows Sammy Sosa as a baseball slugger. But back in his homeland he's hitting another kind of "home run!"

With his home run hitting, Sammy Sosa has become one of the biggest stars in all of sports. People mob him just about everywhere he goes. Since the retirement of Michael Jordan, he has become the most popular athlete in Chicago. Fans flock to ballparks to see the man who hit a total of 129 home runs in 1998 and 1999.

But in his hometown in the Dominican Republic, Sammy is much more than just a celebrity. He is a hero. What else can you say about someone who is saving lives—and who has donated some $3 million of his money to do it?

"I remember when I was back home in the streets (as a young boy)," Sosa says. He grew up in San Pedro de Macoris, a very poor city. "People helped me and gave me money to give to my mother. Now I have the opportunity to give back."

And giving is exactly what Sammy is doing. Just ask Maria Peralta, who lives in San Pedro. When her baby daughter, Carolina, became very sick, Maria was worried. She had no money to go to a private doctor. She could not afford medicine. She did not know

Sammy and a school boy in the Dominican Republic flash Sammy's "I love you" sign that he gives after home runs.

where to turn. Then she heard a public announcement.

The announcement was telling people of a new, free health clinic. It had been started by San Pedro's favorite son: Sammy Sosa. The next morning, Maria scraped together five pesos (about 30 cents) for bus fare to get to the clinic. A doctor told Maria that the baby had a very bad cold that was close to turning into pneumonia. Maria was given medicine and told to return for follow-up care. Carolina's fever came down quickly. She began to feel better. A clinic staff member even gave Carolina a Beanie Baby.™ Maria Peralta was so grateful she had to fight back tears as she talked about it.

"I am very thankful for everything that Sammy Sosa is doing," she said. "I am very proud of him, because he is putting his country in a high place. He is doing so much for his people."

Humble Beginnings

Sammy's family was so poor when he was growing up that all six children had to work from an early age. Sammy shined shoes, collected bottles, and washed cars—anything to bring in a few pesos. His father died when Sammy was just seven, and things got even harder. Sammy and his brothers and sisters often left the table hungry. The whole family was crammed into a two-room apartment. Sammy often slept on the floor.

Sammy's baseball roots go back to the streets. There was no Little League in the Dominican Republic so Sammy and his friends played wherever they could. They used a rolled-up sock with tape on it for a ball and a stick for a bat. They didn't have money for gloves either, so they used milk cartons cut in half. Sammy got his big break in 1985, when he was 16 years old. A pro scout let him try out for the Texas Rangers. He made the team and his professional baseball career began.

By 1993, Sammy was a star for the Chicago Cubs. Baseball fans were thrilled in 1998 as they watched him hit 66 homers for the season in a home-run race against Mark McGwire. In 1999, he slugged out 63 more homers. Sammy has become a sports star and a millionaire. But he has never forgotten his humble roots.

In fact, his clinic is only a short distance from the town square where Sammy used to shine shoes. When people toss coins into the fountain in front of the building, Sammy makes sure the money is given to shoeshine boys in the park.

"If I can help people, it is something that I want to try to do," Sammy says.

ASK yourself

- How does Sammy Sosa feel about helping people?

Think of a statement that might sum up Sammy's words and actions.

Helping His Homeland

Sammy has helped people from the Dominican Republic many times in the past. After Hurricane George hit in 1998, he helped load trucks with food and

Words, Words, Words

foundation: an organization that gives money toward helping people
preventive: created to stop something from occurring
popularity: the quality of being liked or admired by many people
potential: what one is capable of in the future
generosity: unselfish acts

emergency supplies. Sammy also started a **foundation** that gave money to the island after the hurricane. He has also donated computers to Dominican schools.

Baseballs and Beanie Babies®

The clinic is another way for Sammy to help kids. With four children of his own, Sammy can relate to parents who worry about their children. "This is something that's going to be open for people who don't have money or anything to take care of their little kids," Sammy says. "It is open for all the poor people."

The clinic opened in the summer of 1999. The official name is the Sammy Sosa Children's Medical Center for **Preventive** Medicine. It is a joint project between Sammy's foundation and the Dominican government. Its goal is to provide free, quality health care to pregnant women and children. And that is no small effort in a country where chicken pox and other diseases are common.

"Every day it gets bigger and bigger," says Dr. Emmanuel Mendoza, the health director. "Our goal is not just to take care of sick people. It's to teach people about healthy habits and ways of living that prevent problems before they start." And the clinic does not forget the human touch.

The staff keeps a supply of baseballs on hand for kids too old for Beanie Babies.® Sammy also likes to stop by when he can and get a firsthand glimpse of the clinic. Because of his enormous **popularity,** he has to sneak in the back door when he visits.

Omar Minaya is someone who knows Sammy and the clinic well. He is the highest-ranking Latino official in pro baseball. Minaya was one of the first scouts to see Sammy's **potential** when he was a skinny 14-year-old. Minaya recalls giving Sammy a few dollars to help him out sometimes. And Minaya also remembers how Sammy would always turn around and give half of it away to his friends. So he is not surprised by Sammy's **generosity.**

"I'm proud of the kind of player he has become, but I'm even more proud of the things he has done outside of baseball," Minaya says. And Sammy agrees: "I'd rather people remember me for being a good person first—and a good player second." ●

Paso a Paso
Con
SAMMY
SOSA
FUENTE del LIMPIABOTAS
SAMMY SOSA 1996

In the center of the plaza by the clinic is a statue of Sammy Sosa. It is the fountain of the shoeshine boys, where Sammy once shined shoes as a little boy.

RESUMÉ

NAME: Samuel Peralta Sosa
BORN: November 12, 1968
San Pedro de Macoris, Dominican Republic

GOALS
- to give back to his homeland
- to help poor women and children receive quality medical care

WORK HISTORY
- signed first contract with Texas Rangers, July 30, 1985
- made his first major-league debut for the Texas Rangers on June 16, 1989
- traded to the Chicago Cubs, March 30, 1992

EDUCATION
- attended school until the eighth grade

MAJOR ACHIEVEMENTS
- named to National League All-Star team for first time, 1995
- hit home run No. 60 on Sep. 12, 1998 to tie Babe Ruth's 1927 record
- Chicago Cubs celebrate Sammy Sosa Day on Sep. 20, 1998 at Wrigley Field
- won National League Most Valuable Player award, 1998

Hispanic Histor

Sammy Sosa is just one of many Hispanic pioneers who've made history with their accomplishments. Just check out these various writers, politicians, artists, and others. How many do you know?

César CHÁVEZ

César Chávez (1927–1993) was a Mexican-American labor organizer. He helped form the first union for farmworkers in 1965.

César PELLI

César Pelli (1926–), an Argentine American, is an award-winning architect. His works include the World Financial Center in New York City and the United States Embassy in Tokyo, Japan.

Rebecca LOBO

Rebecca Lobo (1973–) became the first woman of Cuban descent to win an Olympic gold medal in basketball. She then went on to play with the WNBA's New York Liberty.

Octavio PAZ

Octavio Paz (1914–1998) was a distinguished Mexican poet and critic. He wrote over 40 volumes of poetry and essays in his long career. Paz received the 1990 Nobel Prize in literature.

SELENA

Selena Quintanilla (1971–1995) was a popular and talented singer who was on the forefront of bringing Tejano music to a mainstream audience. Tragically, she was killed when she was 23 and in the midst of her rising career.

Oscar HIJUELOS

Oscar Hijuelos (1951–) was the first Cuban-American writer to win the Pulitzer Prize in fiction. It was in 1990 for his novel *The Mambo Kings Play Songs of Love.*

y-Makers

Antonia C. NOVELLO

Antonia C. Novello (1944–), a Puerto Rican, was the first female Surgeon General, or chief of medicine, for the U.S. She was appointed in 1990 and served until 1993.

Ellen OCHOA

Ellen Ochoa (1958–) is the first woman of Mexican descent to become an American astronaut (in 1991). She has spent over 719 hours in space.

Frida KAHLO

Frida Kahlo (1907–1954) was an acclaimed Mexican painter. She was known for her harsh, revealing self-portraits. Many of her works were also reflective of her Mexican culture.

Fernando BUJONES

Fernando Bujones (1955–), a Cuban American, was considered one of the best ballet dancers of the 20th century. He became a soloist for the American Ballet when he was a teenager.

Nydia VELAZQUEZ

Nydia Velazquez (1953–) is the first Puerto Rican woman to serve in the House of Representatives. She was re-elected three times after her first term in 1992.

Federico PEÑA

Federico Peña (1947–) was the first Hispanic to hold the position of U.S. Secretary of Energy (served from 1997–1998). He was also the first Latino to serve as Secretary of Transportation (served from 1993–1997).

Wrap-UP

Talk About It

Now that you've read "Sammy Sosa" and "Hispanic History-Makers," what do you have to say about these questions?

- Should rich and famous people give some of their money to people who need help? Explain your answer.
- If you were to be recognized for an achievement, what would you want it to be? Why?

Comprehension Check

Write your answers to the questions below. Use information from the profile and the list to support your answers.

1. What does Sammy Sosa want to be remembered for?
2. Why did Sammy Sosa give away half of the money Omar Minaya gave him?
3. Why is it just as important to teach people healthy ways of living as it is to care for them when they are sick?
4. Who is Ellen Ochoa?
5. Why is it important to recognize the contributions that Hispanic people have made?

Vocabulary Check

Complete each sentence starter below. Before you answer, think about the meaning of the vocabulary word in bold.

1. I admire this **foundation** bccause . . .
2. To me, **generosity** means . . .
3. Everyone said that the quarterback had **potential** but . . .
4. People who are concerned with **popularity** . . .
5. It was flu season, so as a **preventive** measure . . .

Write About It

Choose one of the three writing prompts below.

- Write a thank-you letter from Maria Peralta to Sammy Sosa for the free health clinic. In the letter explain how the clinic is helping people.
- Write a speech to be read out loud on Sammy Sosa Day at Wrigley Field. How should Sosa be honored?
- Of the various Hispanic history-makers, who do you think made the most important contribution? Write a short essay stating your opinion and supporting reasons.

More to READ

Want to know more about Hispanic achievers? Check out:

At the Plate With . . . Sammy Sosa
By Matt Christopher

This book contains everything you wanted to know about the life, times, and statistics of Sammy Sosa.

Pride of Puerto Rico: The Life of Roberto Clemente
by Paul Robert Walker

This is the story of a Baseball Hall of Famer who played right field for the Pittsburgh Pirates until his life was cut short by a fatal plane crash.

Gloria Estefan (Hispanics of Achievement Series)
By Rebecca Stefoff

Gloria Estefan is a Cuban-American singer who became one of the most populuar entertainers of her time. But she had to overcome family tragedy and a life-threatening injury. Like Clemente and Sosa, she has been very generous with her success, sharing much with others.

Using a Building Directory

You've got an appointment with a new dentist. Her building has dozens of offices in it. How will you find her office?

You need to use the building directory. You can find one in the lobby of most office buildings. Check out the directory below. Could you find your way around?

The Brandford Building Directory

The suite number usually starts with the number of the floor. Suite 202 is on the second floor.

A		**N**	
B		**O**	
Gwen Brush, DDS	Suite 202	**P**	
C		The Pediatric Group	Suite 203
Kyu Hee Coleman, PhD	Suite 201	Perfect Pottery	Suite 103
D		Pro Psychiatry Practice	Suite 201
Monica Daley, MD	Suite 203	**Q**	
E		**R**	
F		Reid Publishing Company	Fourth Floor
Gary Floss, DDS	Suite 202	**S**	
G		Darryl Sanders, Att. at Law	Suite 302
The Gentle Dentists Group	Suite 202	Patricia Schmidt, Att. at Law	Suite 302
The Painting Gallery	Suite 101	Schmidt, Lee and Associates	Suite 302
H		**T**	
Hats For You	Suite 301	Twain's Paralegal Services	Suite 303
I		**U**	
J		**V**	
Mark Johnson, MD	Suite 203	**W**	
Christina Jones, PhD	Suite 201	Reba Washington, Att. at Law	Suite 302
K		**X, Y, Z**	
L			
Lovely Images Gallery	Suite 102		
M			
Elise Mayford, MD	Suite 203		
Gwen Moddel, PhD	Suite 201		

People's names are alphabetized by last name. Business names are alphabetized by the first word in the name.

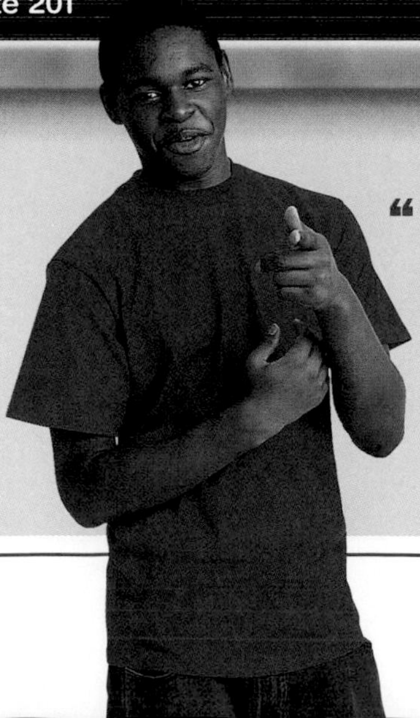

"Doctors have an M.D. after their names. Dentists have a D.D.S. after their names. Often, lawyers have 'Att. at Law' after their names. That means 'Attorney at Law.'"

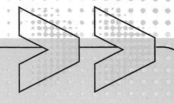

Which Floor Is It On?

You don't want to get your eyes checked when you meant to get your teeth cleaned. So you need to know how to read a building directory. Use the directory and tips to answer these questions. Write the answers on your own paper.

1. Your friend Liz has an appointment with Dr. Jones. Where does Liz need to go?
a. Suite 102
b. Suite 301
c. Suite 203
d. Suite 201

2. You have an appointment for a checkup with Dr. Daley at 9 A.M. and then an appointment with your lawyer at 11 A.M. Which floors will you go to and in what order?
a. floor one and then floor three
b. floor two and then floor three
c. floor three and then floor one
d. floor four and then floor two

3. Your friend wants to buy a hat for her mother. She also wants to buy a painting. Which suites should she go to?

4. Name two people in this building who could fill a cavity in your tooth. What suite are they in?
a. Gwen Brush, suite 202
b. Gwen Moddel, suite 201
c. Mark Johnson, suite 203
d. Gary Floss, suite 202

5. How many suites are on the first three floors of this building?
a. 5
b. 9
c. 13
d. 21

Help!

Imagine that four of the people who work in this building get stuck in the elevator. Who are they? What do they do for a living? What might they talk about? Write a dialogue of their conversation.

Make a List

Make a list of three people who might use a building directory. Tell why each person would need it.

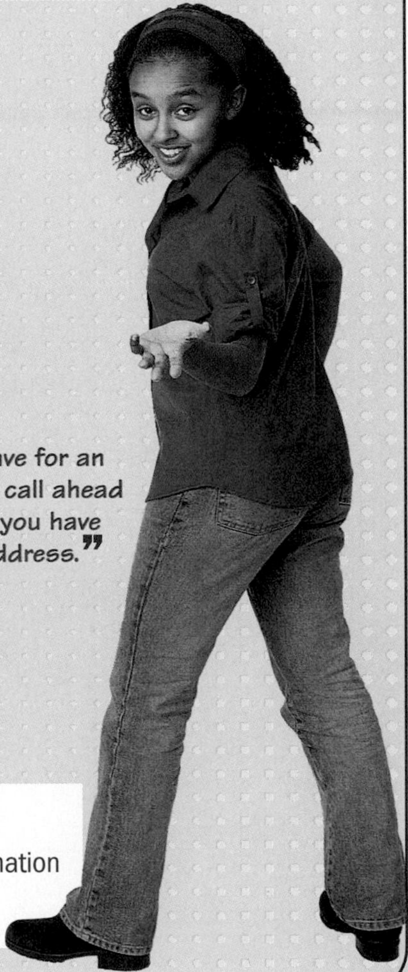

"Before you leave for an appointment, call ahead to make sure you have the correct address."

Real-World Words

appointment: a planned meeting
directory: a list of phone numbers, addresses, or other information
gallery: a business that shows and sells works of art

short story

AROUND THE RIVER BEND

**The Vietnam War killed her brother.
Can she learn to forgive and still keep his memory alive?**

by Sherry Garland

This story is set in 1969, at the height of the Vietnam War. The war took place far away in Southeast Asia. At the time, the United States was helping South Vietnam fight against North Vietnam. The North Vietnamese and Viet Cong were Communists. The United States government was against Communism. Many Americans, and many more Vietnamese, died during this war.

As this story begins, the main character is still dealing with the loss of her older brother, who had been killed a year before in Vietnam. She is camping with her parents along the banks of the Brazos River in Texas. In the night, she hears sounds of helicopters from a nearby army camp. Soldiers from the U. S. and South Vietnam are training at the camp. Those sounds make her think of Vietnam—and the war that claimed her brother.

The helicopters would not let me sleep. At first I only heard a distant hum, no louder than the buzz of a hornet. Then, one by one, the silhouettes appeared over the top of the cedar-covered mountains. They moved across the face of the moon in formation like fat dragonflies with blinking red eyes. The hum turned into loud chop-chop-chops that echoed throughout the river canyon where we camped. The choppers performed maneuvers, following the leader like squatty black geese on a southward migration.

Chill-bumps rose on my neck at the sight of the machines. I knew that American soldiers from nearby Camp Wolters rode inside them, training for combat. The terrain in this part of Texas, steep hills thick with trees and shrubs, was similar to Vietnam. Vietnam—the very word nauseated me. How many of those men in the choppers would never come back? I wondered. How many of them would end up like my brother, Larry?

I tried not to think of the last time I had seen Larry. A red-white-and-blue flag covered his closed casket. It was all the family had to look at during the chaplain's eulogy, during the hollow bugle notes playing taps, and the seven rifles firing three short bursts in salute. And not seeing Larry for a final farewell made it so much worse.

I got up from my bedroll and walked beside the river. It had been a year since Larry's funeral and I thought I had put it out of my mind in the excitement of getting ready for school to start. But now the whirl of blades reminded me of the war on the other side of the world. My heart grew sick, thinking of the waste of so many lives. And for what? For some country that I had never heard of? Who cared what happened to them?

By the time I returned to the dew-soaked bedroll, it was midnight. Hour after hour the helicopter formations crept over the mountains. It was four o'clock and even the croaking frogs and crickets and my yapping dog, Frisky, had quieted when the maneuvers stopped.

The sun was high when I awoke. By the river, my father merrily skinned and gutted freshly caught fish. From under a live oak tree, I heard the familiar sound of crunching ice and saw my mother cranking homemade ice cream. Vanilla with peaches—Larry's favorite.

This September camping trip was an end-of-summer **ritual** in our family. But it just didn't feel right doing things like this without Larry. Didn't all this dredge up painful memories for my parents? I know it did for me.

"I can't believe you're making Larry's favorite ice cream," I said. My voice was as chilly as the September night had been. "It's like you and Daddy are trying to forget Larry. You're pretending he never existed."

"Honey, I know you miss him," she said softly. "Your father and I do too. But you can't stop living."

I grabbed my fishing rod and announced: "I'm going up the river." As I stomped along the narrow trail surrounded by wild flowers, weeds, and willow trees, a rabbit jumped from a patch of purple thistles. Frisky charged after it and disappeared. A few moments later I heard her frantic yapping.

ASK yourself

- Why do the main character and her parents disagree?

Compare how these characters are reacting to Larry's death.

"Frisky!" I shouted, then whistled and slapped my thigh, hoping it wasn't a skunk or a rattlesnake. *You never know what's around the river bend,* Larry used to always say with an **optimistic** smile. He even said it the night he packed his suitcase for boot camp.

As I rounded the bend, I saw Frisky on the shore, her ears at attention. She was barking at a man standing in the river. His Army fatigues were rolled up to his knees. His boots, olive drab shirt, and cap were piled at the edge of the river. Muscles rippled as he gracefully cast out a fishing net over the water. His close-cropped raven-black hair glistened in the sunlight.

I tiptoed toward the riverbank with the intention of grabbing Frisky and running. But I slipped on a muddy spot and fell. The soldier turned around.

"You OK?" he asked. As he walked toward me, his bare feet getting coated with sand, I saw that his features were Asian. I had never met an Asian. I felt my face turn red as he helped me up.

"What you doing?" He spoke choppy English with an unfamiliar accent.

"Fishing," I muttered and brushed sand off my shorts.

"Me, too," he said, his dark eyes twinkling. "I love fishing. Back in my village, Ong-noi and me fish every day on Song Tranh River."

I glanced at the ground. "I don't see your fishing pole."

"I use net. Big, big fish in river over there." He pointed to a dark green area of the river and held his hands three feet apart. "I come every weekend to catch big fish, but he get away."

"You need a fishing pole and bait," I said, relaxing a little. "Is it a yellow catfish?"

He crinkled his eyebrows into a question.

"Cat-fish?"

With a stick I drew a fish in the sand, giving it long whiskers.

The soldier grinned. "That him. Big guy."

"My brother and father have been trying to catch Ol' Yeller for years. He must be thirty pounds. Keeps getting bigger and bigger. Show me where you saw him."

I picked up my fishing rod and followed the soldier out to a sandbar. The water gently sloshed around my ankles, then my knees, then touched the tips of my cutoffs before we crawled up onto the white island.

"There." He pointed to a greenish spot, then unfurled the net. It gracefully sailed through the air, plopped over the water and sank. He began drawing in the cord and hauling it back in. After he hoisted it on to the sandbar and emptied it, minnows, small perch, and crawdads leaped and squirmed. But no catfish. He tossed the catch back into the river, but not before I selected a lively minnow. I secured it on my hook, then cast out. The line whined as it unreeled and the sinker smacked the water with a loud plop. I gently began reeling in.

"You good fisherman. Who teach you?"

"Mostly my brother, Larry. He loved fishing more than anything in the world. He would have lived on the river, if he could."

The soldier nodded. "My village on river. Beautiful river."

"Who taught you to fish?"

"Ong-noi—my grandfather. He best fisherman in village. He skinny like a stick with white beard, but he strong. He say: 'To catch fish you must think like fish. When fish smell food, he get careless.'" The soldier heaved a sigh. "I want to be fisherman, too, like my grandfather and my father."

"The War ruined my family and ruined America. If it weren't for you and your stupid war my brother would still be alive . . ."

"I've never heard of fishing with a net," I said. "Where are you from?"

"Vietnam," he said proudly. "I am Trung Tran." He extended his hand. My heart jumped and a chill swept over my body.

"You're Vietnamese?" I said, **recoiling** from the hand. "What are you doing here? Shouldn't you be in the jungles fighting your stinking war?" My voice dripped ice, but I didn't care. I began reeling in the line as fast as I could.

I saw the look of confusion cross his face as his smile faded. I knew I was being rude, but I had to get away.

"I go back soon," he said softly. "I come to America to train in helicopter. I become pilot so I can fight Viet Cong."

His dark eyes sadly watched my jerky movements. With a set jaw I fought with the tangled fishing line. When Trung reached over to help free it, I pushed his hand away.

"I can do it myself," I hissed.

He watched in silence as I grew impatient and snapped the line in two with one **vicious** jerk. I heard him sigh.

"You no like Vietnamese," he stated calmly.

I didn't even want to look at his face again, but something inside me erupted before I could stop it.

"Vietnam ruined my family and ruined America. If it weren't for you and your stupid war my brother would still be alive. He'd be right here fishing with

WORDS, WORDS, WORDS

ritual: something that is always done in the same way as part of a ceremony or custom
optimistic: always believing that things will turn out for the best
recoiling: shrinking back in horror or disgust
vicious: fierce or dangerous

me and you'd be back in your stupid village fishing with your stupid nets. I hate Vietnam! I hate it!"

He swallowed hard and his face clouded.

"I sorry for your brother. He very brave. All American brave. They come two years ago and help my village build wall to keep out the Viet Cong. American play with kids. They laugh. I like American. My mother cook fish for soldier name Joe Bailey.

"When Viet Cong discover that our village helped Americans, they come and kill our leaders. They kill my father and my old grandfather, my big brother and two cousin. They kill my mother for feeding fish to Joe Bailey. Viet Cong burn our huts and take over our village, so I run away. I come to America to learn to fly chopper so I can help my country. I don't want America to fight our war, but I say thank you to all brave American who die."

I looked at his trembling chin and the water glistening on his dark **irises.** For a moment I didn't think he would be able to speak again, but he did.

"Sometime I say to myself, 'Why America send so many brave soldier to help little Vietnam? Must be that America love Vietnam like me.' Then I come to America and people look at me and say, 'Go home, we hate you! We hate stinky Vietnam'! What that mean—stinky?"

I saw the look of confusion, anger, and pain in his face as he waited for my answer. I drew in a deep breath.

"It's not *you* they hate. It's the war." I paused. "I'm sorry about your family. I really am."

"I hate war too. But I love Vietnam. I always love Vietnam."

As Trung rolled up the fishing net we heard a loud splash. I saw the gray shape of a fish just beneath the green surface.

"Look! It's Ol' Yeller!" I whispered.

Trung reached into a little paper bag and tossed out a live cricket. The fish circled, then snapped, causing bubbles to dance on the surface. I knelt close to the water. The **elusive** monster fish was easily three feet long. How I wished I had not jerked my fishing line in two. I saw Trung unrolling his net.

"You'll never catch him with a net," I said.

"Who say?" Trung winked. He waited, like a cat over a goldfish bowl. Soon the fish disappeared.

"He's getting away!" I screeched. "Don't just stand there."

"I study his move. Think like fish." Trung tapped his forehead and tossed out another cricket.

A minute later the fish returned, gliding under the surface, snapping at the insect. Swift as a pouncing cat, Trung flung the net out a few feet away from the fish. As the net sank, he wiggled his hand in the water. The frightened catfish darted away from the hand toward the net. Trung waited, then jerked the cord with all his might. I grabbed one end of the net and together, grunting and struggling, we hauled the twisting, flapping fish onto the sandbar.

I stood up, my mouth open as I stared at the sleek gray body. It was scarred from years of fish hooks and close calls. The glassy eyes gleamed as it rolled on its back to **reveal** a yellow underbelly.

"Ol' Yeller. I don't believe it," I said. "I just don't believe it. What are you going to do with him?"

"He make plenty fish soup," Trung said, laughing. He stroked the soft underbelly and spoke to the fish as if it were a pet, carefully avoiding the poisonous whiskers and deadly sharp fins. I looked at the angry yellow eyes and the gills fighting desperately to breathe. A sinking feeling filled my heart and suddenly I wanted to cry again.

Trung looked up into my face and his grin faded.

WORDS, WORDS, WORDS

irises: round, colored parts of the eyes around the pupils
elusive: very hard to find or catch
reveal: to show or bring into view
utensil: a tool that has a special purpose

"Ah, this fish too little for me," he said. With a grunt he shoved the fish back into the river. Ol' Yeller floated a second, then got his second wind and disappeared into the murky water.

"Why did you do that?" I asked.

Trung shrugged. "He not my fish. He your brother's fish. I have my own fish back in Song Tranh River. I go back and catch him someday." He glanced at the sun high above our heads.

"I go now. My friend need motorcycle for Big Date tonight." He sighed as he rolled up the net. "Someday when war over, maybe I have Big Date, too."

Trung slipped into his boots and shirt, then tugged his cap down low over his forehead.

"Good-bye, American girl," he said, extending his hand once again.

This time I shook it.

"Good-bye, Trung. Good luck."

I watched him climb onto an old motorcycle. He waved as it wheeled over the bank, spraying sand behind it.

I grabbed my fishing rod, woke Frisky from her snooze in the shade of a wild plum tree, and hurried back to the campsite. My parents sat on an old quilt, finishing up fried catfish and hushpuppies.

"Told you she'd be back in time for the peach ice cream," my father commented without missing a bite.

"So you did," my mother said. She rose and lifted the canister lid. Blobs of creamy white and yellow ice cream clung to the paddle.

"Want to lick the paddle?" she asked. "I remember how you and Larry used to—" She paused.

"—used to fight over the paddle?" I finished the sentence for her. I took the dripping **utensil** and tasted the sweet, creamy dessert. A million memories of Larry flooded my head and my heart.

"Yeah, I remember." I smiled and it felt good. ●

ASK yourself

- Why does Trung throw Ol' Yeller back?

Think about how the main character feels about Ol' Yeller.

DEAR A

Life wasn't easy for soldiers in Vietnam. They could seldom call home. Their main way of communicating with loved ones was to write. These real letters, from the book *Dear America: Letters Home from Vietnam,* give a glimpse of what war was like through a soldier's eyes.

Life in Vietnam

April, 1967

Dear Ma,

How are things in The World? I hope all is well. Things are pretty much the same. Vietnam has my feelings on a seesaw.

This country is so beautiful, when the sun is shining on the mountains, farmers in their rice paddies, with their water buffalo, palm trees, monkeys, birds, and even the strange insects. For a fleeting moment, I wasn't in a war zone at all, just on vacation, but still missing you and the family.

There are a few kids who hang around, some with no parents. I feel so sorry for them. I do things to make them laugh. And they call me "dinky dow" (crazy). But it makes me feel good. I hope that's one reason why we're here, to secure a future for them. It seems to be the only justification I can think of for the things that I have done!

Love to all.

Your son,
George

A U.S. soldier in Vietnam.

Private First Class George Williams served with Company B, 1st Battalion, 16th Infantry (Rangers), 1st Infantry Division, operating in III Corps, from February 1967 to February 1968. He is now a retired firefighter in Brooklyn, New York.

MERICA

An escape from the war zone: Most soldiers find that war is even worse than they had imagined.

Doing a Job

May 10, 1968

Dear Mom,

It's official! Today I received my award. But it was more than I had dreamed. Would you believe a *Silver Star*!

I was given the wrong information about a Bronze Star.

To say the least, I'm quite proud of myself! But to be broad-minded about it, as much as it means to me, it is just a rung up the ladder to success. I say this because I have so much more to accomplish—much more.

I'm sorry to rebuke all of you, but I'm no hero. Heroes are for the "Late Show." I was just trying to help a couple of guys who needed help. Keep in mind, I didn't do it alone.

That's all.

Love,
Phil

Their lifeline: A soldier in Vietnam reads the news from home.

P.S. You can tell anyone, I mean *anyone* who asks, exactly how I feel about the hero bit. They are only in comic books and television and movies. The so-called heroes over here are the guys trying to do their jobs and get home from this useless war.

Sp/4 Phillip Arterbury was assigned to Company C, 1st Battalion, 27th Infantry, 25th Infantry Division, operating in III Corps from Parrot's Beak to Saigon, between October 1967 and October 1968. He is now a silver trader in Beverly Hills, California.

GLOSSARY

The World: Soldier's slang for the United States

KIA: Killed in Action

VC: Viet Cong, the South Vietnamese Communist rebel troops Americans were fighting

WIA: Wounded in Action

Losing a Friend

November 25, 1966

Hello dear folks:

It's going to be hard for me to write this, but maybe it will make me feel better.

Yesterday after our big dinner, my company was hit out in the field while looking for VC. We got the word that one boy was killed and six wounded. So the doctor, medics, and the captain I work for went over to the hospital to see the boys when they came in and see how they were.

The first sergeant came in the tent and told me to go over to the hospital and tell the captain that six more KIAs were coming in. When I got there, they asked if anyone from A Company was there. I just happened to be there, so they told me that they needed someone to identify a boy they just brought in from my company. He was very bad, they said. So I went to the tent. There on the table was the boy. His face was all cut up and blood all over it. His mouth was open, his eyes were both open. He was a mess. I couldn't really identify him.

So I went outside while they went through his stuff. They found his ID card and dog tags. I went in, and they told me his name—Rankin. I cried, "No, it can't be." But sure enough, after looking at his bloody face again I could see it was him. It really hit me hard because he was one of the nicest guys around. He was one of my good friends. No other KIA or WIA hit me like that. I knew most of them, but this was the first body I ever saw and being my friend, it was too much.

After I left the place, I sat down and cried. I couldn't stop it. I don't think I ever cried so much in my life. I can still see his face now. I will never forget it.

Today the heavens cried for him. It started raining at noon today and has now finally just stopped after 10 hours of the hardest rain I have ever seen.

Love,

Richard

VETS

A somber tribute: The Vietnam Memorial Wall

Specialist 5th Class Richard Cantale served with the 5th Battalion, 7th Cavalry, 1st Cavalry Division, based at An Khe, from August 1966 to August 1967. He now works in New York City.

Wrap-UP

Talk About It

Now that you've read "Around the River Bend" and "Dear America," what do you have to say about these questions?

- ▶ Are the people who die the only victims of war? Explain.
- ▶ What are some of the different ways that people express their grief? Why do you think this is so?

Comprehension Check

Write your answers to the questions below. Use information from the story and the letters to support your answers.

1. What things reminded the main character of her brother Larry?
2. How are the main character and Trung Tran alike?
3. If you were in the main character's place, how would you have treated Trung Tran?
4. Who was the badly wounded boy that Richard Cantale had to identify?
5. What can you learn about war from these two selections?

Vocabulary Check

Answer each question below with a complete sentence. Before you answer, think about the meaning of the vocabulary word in bold.

1. What helps you to feel **optimistic?**
2. What is the opposite of **vicious?**
3. What color **irises** do you have?
4. Which **utensil** do you use when eating soup?
5. Why should you be careful not to **reveal** the answers when you are taking a test?

Write About It

Choose one of the writing prompts below.

- ▶ Write a journal entry about fishing with Trung Tran, as if you were the main character from "Around the River Bend." Explain how that experience changes your feelings.
- ▶ Write a letter home from Trung Tran about his experiences in America. How did Trung Tran feel about America?
- ▶ Write a short speech honoring the soldiers who fought in Vietnam. Think about the letters you read in "Dear America." What kinds of things did these soldiers have to face?

Fact FILE

The Vietnam Memorial Wall in Washington, DC, honors the brave American soldiers who died or became missing in the Vietnam War. A competition was held to establish the memorial, and a design by an architectural student from Yale, Maya Ying Lin, was the winner.

Lin's design was a black granite wall in a V-shape, with one section of the Wall pointing to the Lincoln Memorial and the other section pointing to the Washington Monument. Carved on the right side of the wall is the date of the first casualty of Vietnam. The names of those who died and those who remain missing follow in chronological order.

The wall was completed in 1982, but more names have been added to the wall since then. As of the publishing of this book, there are 58,214 names on the wall. Not even Maya Lin could have imagined the lasting impact the Vietnam Memorial Wall would have on our nation.

Reading Editorial Cartoons

You notice a cartoon in the newspaper all by itself. It's not in the comics section. What's going on? It's an editorial cartoon, and it's probably on the editorial page. That's where writers—and cartoonists—express their opinions about issues in the news.

Check out the editorial cartoon below. What's the cartoonist's point of view?

An Editorial Cartoon

First, look at the art. What's going on? A man who looks like a couch potato is watching TV. A woman is trying to show him an article.

Then read the writing in the cartoon. What's the topic of the article the woman is reading? Why do you think she wants the man to look at it?

REPORT:
TV TOO CONSUMING TO KIDS

'... Could it wait till the next commercial?..'

Source: Bennett/*Christian Science Monitor*

The caption is in quotation marks. That means it's a quote from someone in the cartoon. The man's mouth is open, so you know he's the one who's talking.

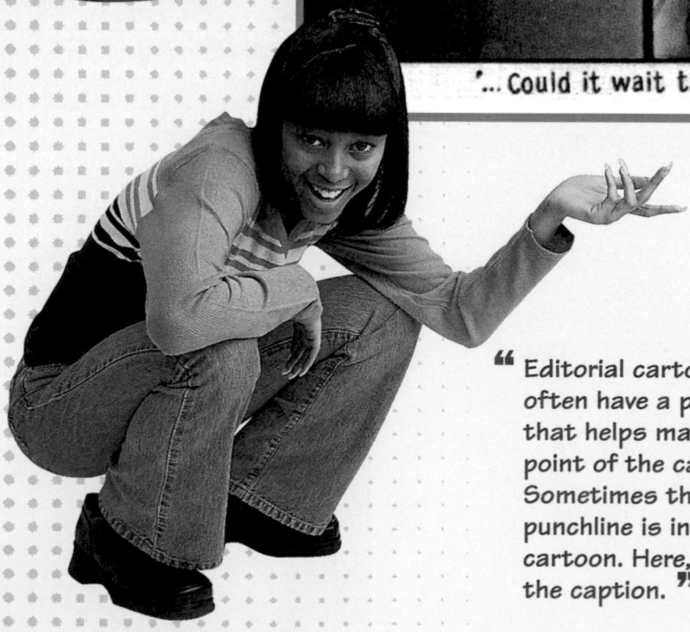

"Editorial cartoons often have a punchline that helps make the point of the cartoon. Sometimes the punchline is in the cartoon. Here, it's the caption."

That's How I See It!

When you first look at an editorial cartoon, you might not get the joke. You have to study the words and picture carefully. Reread the editorial cartoon and the tips that go with it. Then answer the questions. Write your answers on your own paper.

1. When something is "too consuming," it__________.
a. takes up too much time and attention.
b. takes no time at all to finish.
c. takes too much time to eat.
d. takes too much time to understand.

2. What can you tell about the man just by looking at the drawing of him? What about the woman?

3. Reread the caption of the cartoon. What does the man mean when he says that?
a. He'll talk with the woman during the next show.
b. He wants her to watch the next commercial with him.
c. He'll speak with her during the next commercial.
d. He's tired of waiting for the commercials.

4. What opinion is the cartoonist expressing in this editorial cartoon?
a. Kids watch TV because there's nothing else to do.
b. Many kids **and** adults watch too much TV.
c. Adults are forced to watch TV because their kids do.
d. Kids and adults spend too little time watching TV.

5. Editorial cartoons don't depict facts. They express cartoonists' opinions. Do you agree or disagree with this cartoonist's point of view? Why or why not?

See for Yourself

Look in a newspaper or magazine and find an editorial cartoon. What is the cartoon about? Do you agree or disagree with the opinion expressed in the cartoon? Why or why not?

Draw Your Own

Think of an issue in your school or town. What's your opinion about it? How could you express your point of view in a cartoon? Work with a partner to create an editorial cartoon about your opinion.

"Check the Web site of your local newspaper. There's probably a collection of editorial cartoons."

Real-World Words

caption: the words below a picture that help you understand it
depict: to show something in a picture or by using words
point of view: an opinion; what someone thinks about an issue

magazine article

Fighting for My Future

A former gang member tells how she chose a better life.

Ana* knew that getting out of a gang was not going to be easy. But she also knew that life in a gang was no life at all. It took courage for her to do what she did. Here, in her own words, is her brave story.

** This name, and all the names in this article, have been changed.*

Gang members don't snitch on each other. That is the motto I was raised on. My dad once went to jail for something he didn't do because he wouldn't turn in a "brother." So when I was called to the witness stand that fateful summer day, I was planning to lie. In fact, I didn't think I had a choice.

Paco, the main guy from our Latino gang, was on trial. I'd seen him shoot and kill a teenage boy. John, a member of a rival, African-American gang, was also on trial. John was completely innocent. I was the only eyewitness. So what I said would determine which one went to jail.

The lawyer started asking me questions. I saw Paco sitting confidently at the defendant's table. He was calm because he was sure I would lie. I looked at John, and then John's mother. She was crying because it looked like her son was going to jail for a crime he didn't commit.

I started thinking about my mom and all the times she'd cried—when I got beat up, when my brother was arrested, when my dad got stabbed and shot at. I forgot about gang rivalries and prejudice. John's mother's tears became my mother's tears. I just wanted *my* mom to stop crying.

My eyes got watery and something happened inside me.

It went against everything the gang had ever taught me. I told the truth. I said, "Paco did it!"

That day was in 1994. That's when I finally got out of the gang. I couldn't go back to the gang after **testifying** against Paco. I was 15. But my story starts way before then. . . .

I was raised in gangs. My father was in a gang; my brother was in a gang; my uncles and cousins were in gangs. I didn't know anything else. I thought drive-bys, drug deals, and beatings were normal.

When I was 5 years old, I saw one of my uncles get killed by a member of a rival gang. It took me a while to understand what had happened. I'd seen many people get shot before, but they were always taken to the hospital and then they came back. But my uncle didn't come back. At his funeral, I still didn't understand what was happening. I saw my mom crying, and she finally told me, "Your uncle's in heaven now."

After that, I got used to all the death around me. I attended many more funerals of loved ones lost to gang violence. And I watched my mom cry many more times.

An Awful Beginning

I joined the gang when I was 11 years old. That was the day I got "jumped in," which means beat up by the other gang members. First, three girls surrounded me and hit me over and over. Then, all the girls in the gang made a circle around me and hit me and kicked me more. What's really shocking to me is that I didn't fight back. I couldn't. But it didn't end there.

Then, about 20 guys lined up on one side and about 20 girls lined up on the other side, leaving a path down the middle. I had to walk through that path, as they punched and kicked me. And I had to be standing by the time I got to the end.

When I started down the path, my arm was already broken. It hurt so much. As I walked, they kept punching me in the ribs. Every time I fell down they'd kick me. I thought I was going to pass out. Toward the end of the path, I fell and they stepped on my leg and broke it. Somehow, I managed to pull myself up and limp to the end of the line.

That was my **initiation.** It was what I had to do to prove that I would do anything for them.

A lot of people say that people join gangs because they want to fit in, but to me it was more of a survival tool. In my neighborhood, you have to be from somewhere to be able to back yourself up. There were rival Asian and African-American gangs after our territory.

Before I turned 12, I'd been arrested for car-jacking, violating curfew, and drug possession. Each time I was let go on **probation.** But

"I watched my mom cry many more times."

Words, Words, Words

testifying: speaking under oath in a court of law
initiation: a task or ceremony that gives admission into a group
probation: a period of time used to test a person's behavior

"My teacher took an interest in me. . . . I began to see that I could have a future."

when I was 13, I was arrested one more time. I got sent to boot camp for eight months.

A Changing Attitude

Boot camp was the worst experience of my life. We had to get up at 5 a.m. and take cold showers, and the rooms were always cold. The guards would stand right in front of me and scream stuff like, "You may be something on the street, but you're nothing in here."

For months, I had a bad attitude. I got into fights with other girls and talked back to the guards. They wouldn't let me see my mom until I improved my behavior. In the eight months I was there, she could only visit me four times.

When I got out on probation, I knew I never wanted to go back there. But to avoid that, I had to stay in school. Otherwise I'd be violating my probation and I'd be sent back to boot camp.

The problem was, I hated school. I'd started "ditching" in the third grade. By junior high, I almost never went to school. I planned to drop out as soon as I got off probation. To me, my life was "kickin' it" with my friends.

My ninth-grade English teacher, Ms. Gruwell, changed all that. She took an interest in me, asking where I'd been if I missed class and telling me I could be the first one in my family to finish high school.

I thought she was crazy. I thought she didn't know who she was talking to. I wasn't used to people being so nice to me. When you're in a gang, you think that nobody cares about you. You think that everybody is against you.

I told Ms. Gruwell to stay out of my business. But she kept at it. In my sophomore year, her words started to sink in. I began to see that there were other things out there besides gang life—that I could have a future, that I could graduate. I started thinking about *getting out* of the gang.

ASK yourself

- What changed Ana's attitude toward school?

Think about how Ana felt before and after taking Ms. Gruwell's class.

Bird in a Cage

For Ms. Gruwell's class, I had to read *Anne Frank: The Diary of a Young Girl*, the story of a teenage girl who hid from the Nazis during the Holocaust. Anne's words had a major effect on me. I came across the line: "I feel like a bird in a cage and I wish I had the wings to fly away." I couldn't believe it. She expressed exactly how I felt—I wanted to get out of the gang, but they don't let people out. They kill people who want out.

That book really changed my **perspective**. Before I read Anne Frank, I was **prejudiced** against anybody I didn't know. I thought if you didn't look like me, you didn't understand me. But here was Anne, who was so different from me—she was Jewish and she lived 50 years before me—yet we felt the same way.

I remained a "bird in a cage" until the day of the trial in 1994.

When I was called to the stand, I said, "Paco did it." I said it for myself, to get out of my cage. I said it for my mother, and for Ms. Gruwell. I said it to end the horrible cycle of violence in my life.

Paco looked at me in shock, as they took him away to serve his 25-year sentence. He said, "Of all the people in the gang, you're the last person I thought would **betray** me."

ASK yourself

- Why was Paco surprised by what Ana did?

Explain Paco's reaction in your own words.

No More Tears

I feel guilty to this day. I feel guilty that Paco is in a jail cell because of what I said, even though I know telling the truth was the right thing to do.

After I testified, I left the gang. Although I got death threats, no one came after me. Maybe, deep down, some of them knew that I had done the right thing.

My mother doesn't cry for me anymore. She doesn't cry for my dad, either. Soon after I left the gang, my dad got out, too. My mom's very religious, and she thanks God for Ms. Gruwell every day.

Today, I am a freshman at a college in California. I plan to major in English, and then get my Ph.D. in education. I want to be the Secretary of Education and change the way kids get labeled in school as a "dropout" or a "slow learner."

If gang members could see that they have different choices and that it's never too late to change, maybe they'd get out too. I'm not a miracle. Anybody can get out.

WRITING FOR FREEDOM

For Ana and many other kids, life in Southern California was like living in a war zone. They were surrounded by gangs and violence. They were divided by race, neighborhood, and income. They felt trapped. Until they met Erin Gruwell, an English teacher. What happened in her class would change their lives forever.

One day, while Ms. Gruwell was trying to teach an English lesson, a piece of paper was passed around. It had a racist drawing on it. When Ms. Gruwell saw the picture, she became angry. She yelled at her class: "This is the type of **propaganda** the Nazis used during the Holocaust." The students' reaction to what she yelled shocked her. They had no idea what she was talking about.

"How many of you have heard of the Holocaust?" Ms. Gruwell asked. Not one person raised a hand. Then she asked, "How many of you have been shot at?" Nearly everyone raised a hand.

Why would Ms. Gruwell think that the Holocaust and being shot at were similar? During World War II, the Nazis killed people

Words, Words, Words

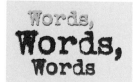

perspective: a particular way of looking at a situation
prejudiced: to have an unfair opinion of people based on race, religion, or national group
betray: to be disloyal to someone, especially a friend or family member
propaganda: information that is spread to influence the way people think

DROW-WILSON-HIGH-SCHOOL
1925
FREEDOM WRITERS
FW
CHANGING THE WORLD
The Freedom Writers with the teacher who helped change their lives. Ms. Gruwell is directly under the sign.

because of their race. In this school, gangs were made up of different races who also used hatred and guns to try to kill each other.

Ms. Gruwell's students read *The Diary of Anne Frank*. After Anne's book, the students read others, like *Zlata's Diary: A Child's Life in Sarajevo*. It tells the story of a teenager struggling to survive the war in what was once Yugoslavia.

The students were so moved by the books that they started to write their own diaries. They wrote about violence in their town and called themselves The Freedom Writers. "Writing became their ticket out," says Ms. Gruwell. "Whenever there was a problem they learned to pick up a pen and write about it as an alternative to violence."

Today, all 150 Freedom Writers have graduated from high school and are in college. "They overcame the odds," says Ms. Gruwell. "We hope the stories we wrote will also help the human race."

AUTOBIOGRAPHY IN FIVE SHORT CHAPTERS

by Portia Nelson

CHAPTER ONE

I walk down the street.
There is a deep hole in the sidewalk.
I fall in.
I am lost . . . . I am helpless.
It isn't my fault.
It takes forever to find a way out.

CHAPTER TWO

I walk down the same street.
There is a deep hole in the sidewalk.
I pretend I don't see it.
I fall in again.
I can't believe I am in this same place.
But, it isn't my fault.
It still takes a long time to get out.

CHAPTER THREE

I walk down the same street.
There is a deep hole in the sidewalk.
I *see* it is there.
I still fall in . . . it's a habit . . . but,
my eyes are open.
I know where I am.
It is *my* fault.
I get out immediately.

CHAPTER FOUR

I walk down the same street.
There is a deep hole in the sidewalk.
I walk around it.

CHAPTER FIVE

I walk down another street.

Wrap-UP

Talk About It

Now that you've read "Fighting for My Future" and "Autobiography in Five Short Chapters," what do you have to say about these questions?

- ▶ If you were Ana, what would you have said in court?
- ▶ What does it take to make a major change in your life?

Comprehension Check

Write your answers to the questions below. Use information from the article and the poem to support your answers.

1. What does Ana have to do to join her gang?
2. Why does Ana consider lying in court to protect a guilty person?
3. How is life outside the gang better than life inside one?
4. In Chapter Four of the poem, what does the author do differently?
5. If the "hole" in the poem stands for any kind of problem, what do you think that "hole" might mean to Ana? Explain.

Vocabulary Check

Complete each sentence with the correct vocabulary word below.

prejudiced **perspective** **betray**
propaganda **initiation**

1. Unfortunately, some people are influenced by hateful _______.
2. Any _______ into a group that causes you to be hurt is probably against the law.
3. People who are _______ don't give those who seem different a chance.
4. No one wants to _______ a friend, but sometimes telling the truth is more important.
5. From Ana's _______, getting an education offers a much better future than being in a gang.

Write About It

Choose one of the writing prompts below.

- ▶ Write a letter from Ana to Paco, after he was sent to prison. In this letter explain to Paco why Ana spoke the truth in court that day.
- ▶ Ana hopes to help others some day. Write a short speech that Ana might give to your class about gangs.
- ▶ Making a big life change isn't easy. Write a poem about a change you once made or one you would like to make.

More to READ

Check out the inspirational stories below. They may change the way you view the world.

Zlata's Diary: A Child's Life in Sarajevo
by Zlata Filipovic

Zlata Filipovic has been called the "Anne Frank of Sarajevo." In 1993, she was a regular, happy schoolgirl until war broke out in the capital of what was once Yugoslavia. In her moving diary, you'll read how Zlata endured bombs falling all around her and the deaths of her best friends.

The Life and Words of Martin Luther King, Jr.
by Ira Peck

Martin Luther King, Jr., was a freedom fighter if there ever was one. But his idea of fighting had nothing to do with violence. He fought unfair laws by marching, sitting-in, and speaking out. This book tells the story of this remarkable man, his philosophy, and the civil rights movement that he helped lead. With words instead of fists, King dealt a powerful blow to prejudice.

Reading a Flow Chart

Tod has become a rock star. A journalist interviews him about his rise to the top. What can he tell others to expect about the process? In response, Tod draws a flow chart.

Flow charts show each step in a process. Read Tod's chart. Can you follow his steps?

Become a Rock Star!

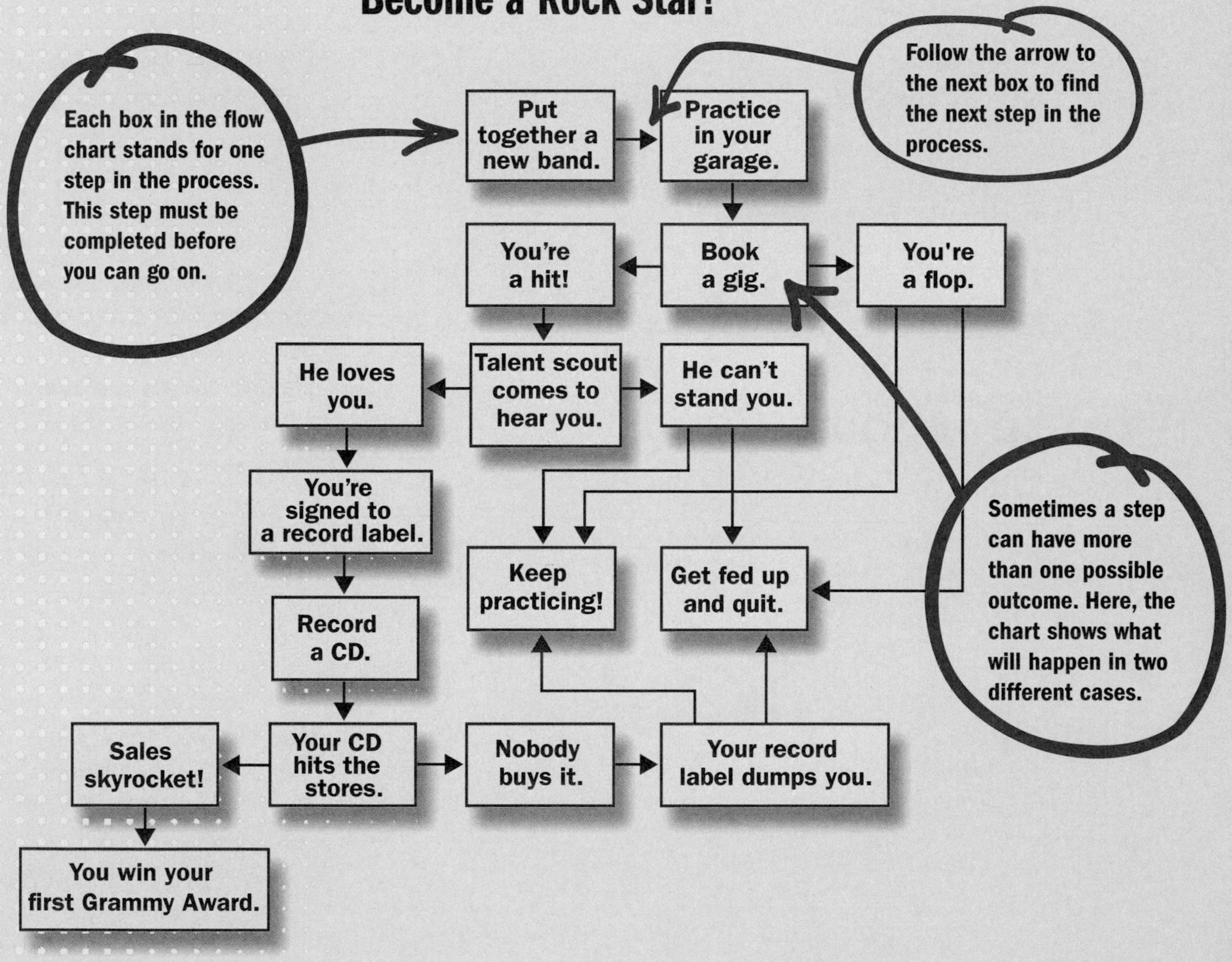
Each box in the flow chart stands for one step in the process. This step must be completed before you can go on.
Follow the arrow to the next box to find the next step in the process.
Put together a new band.
Practice in your garage.
You're a hit!
Book a gig.
You're a flop.
He loves you.
Talent scout comes to hear you.
He can't stand you.
You're signed to a record label.
Keep practicing!
Get fed up and quit.
Sometimes a step can have more than one possible outcome. Here, the chart shows what will happen in two different cases.
Record a CD.
Sales skyrocket!
Your CD hits the stores.
Nobody buys it.
Your record label dumps you.
You win your first Grammy Award.

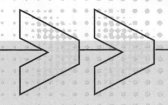

Go With the Flow

You may not be ready for the music business. But you should be getting the hang of flow charts. Use Tod's chart and the tips to answer the questions below. Write your answers on your own paper.

1. What is the **second** step in the process? If all goes well, what is the **second-to-last** step?

2. It's time to play a gig in front of an audience. According to Tod's chart, what two things could happen next?
   a. You could find a new drummer for your band.
   b. You could keep practicing.
   c. You could be a huge hit.
   d. You could do really badly.

3. Which of the following must you do **before** you are signed to a record label?
   a. rehearse with your band
   b. find one or more people who can play or sing
   c. book a gig
   d. all of the above

4. According to Tod's chart, what's the next thing you do **after** you're signed to a record label?

5. Imagine what could happen after the band wins a Grammy. List three more steps that could appear on this flow chart.

List the Steps

How do you make chocolate milk? Make a list of all the steps in the process. Then trade lists with a partner. Check each other's work. Did you leave anything out?

Chart It Out

Use your list from "List the Steps." Design a flow chart showing how to make chocolate milk.

"Many computer programs can help you to create a flow chart on the computer."

Real-World Words

gig: an engagement to perform
outcome: a result or consequence of an event or action
process: a series of actions and events progressing toward an end

play

WAR of the WORLDS

AN ADAPTATION OF A RADIO PLAY BY ORSON WELLES

THIS IS A TRUE STORY. . . . One night over 60 years ago, the radio reported that Martians were invading Earth. Millions of Americans went running in terror. Why did they fall for it? Didn't they know it was just a big joke?

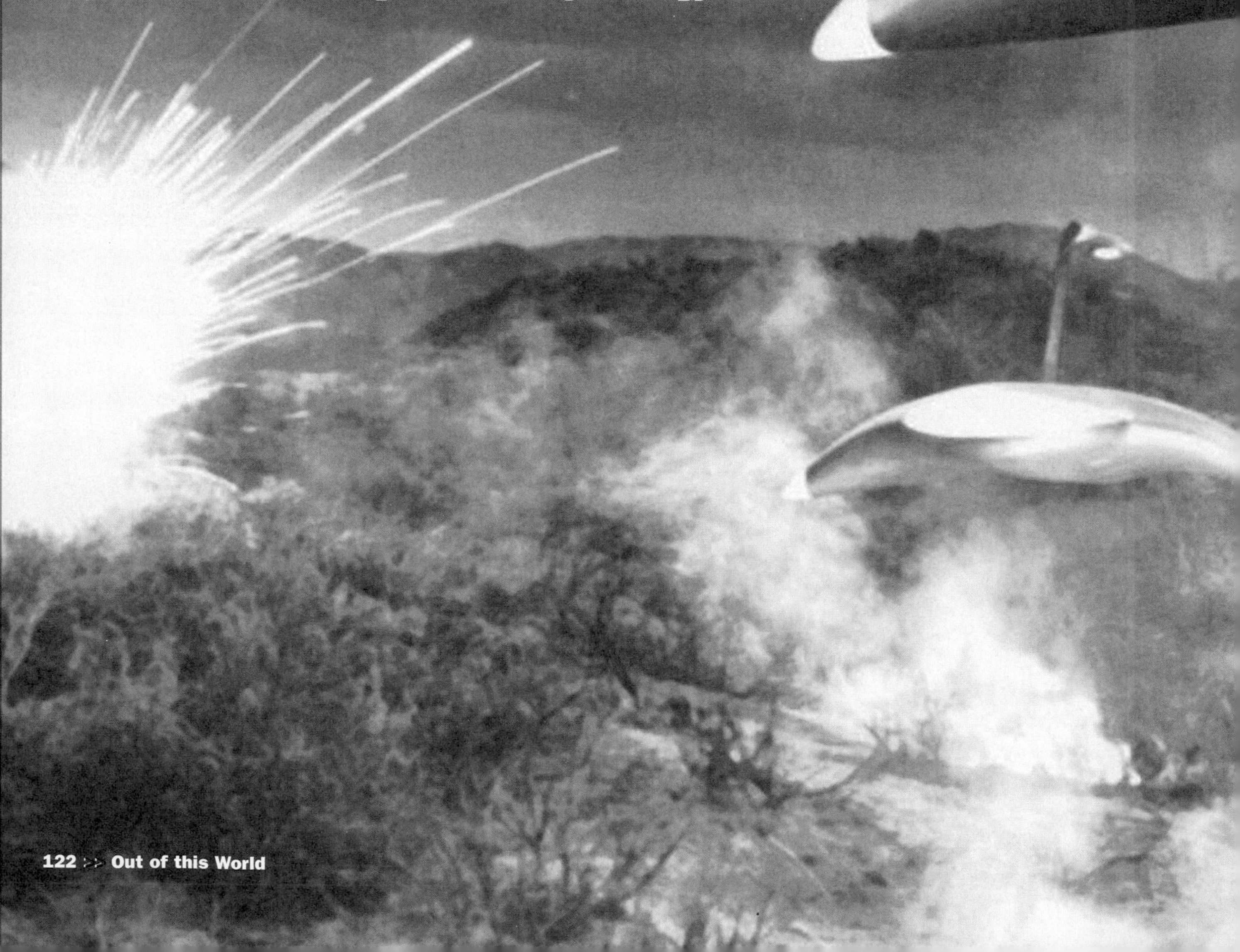

CAST OF CHARACTERS

*Starred characters are major roles

Narrator*

In New Jersey

Mrs. Springer*
Mr. Springer*
Linda Springer, 18*
Larry Springer, 16*
Grandma
Mrs. Frascetti, neighbor
Mr. Frascetti, neighbor

On the Radio

Announcer*
Carl Phillips, reporter-at-large*
Professor Richard Pierson, astronomer
Voices on the radio:
Voice 1
Voice 2
Voice 3
Brigadier General Montgomery Smith
Captain
Commander
Secretary
Radio Operator

SCENE 1

Narrator: It is October 30, 1938, in a small town in New Jersey. The Springer family is spending an evening at home. Mrs. Springer sits in a wingback chair, with Maxie the dog at her feet. Grandma, who is hard of hearing, relaxes on the couch. Larry reads a sports magazine. Linda fiddles with the radio, she has trouble finding a station.

Grandma *(loudly):* Vat's on the radio tonight?

Narrator: Grandma is a recent immigrant from Germany. She doesn't speak much English. But that doesn't keep her from talking.

Larry: It's the Jack Benny show.

Grandma: Vat?

Larry *(yelling so that Grandma can hear):* THE JACK BENNY SHOW.

Grandma: Vat are you yelling for? Ah, I hear the radio. Listen to dat Jack Benny. He's a real card, dat one.

Larry: The radio's not even tuned in yet, Grandma. Linda, what's with the static? The program's going to be over before you find it.

Linda: Wait! I think I got the show.

Narrator: The static stops and the voice of a radio announcer fills the room.

Announcer *(on the radio):* Ladies and gentlemen, from the Park Plaza in New York City, we bring you the music of Ramon Raquello and his orchestra.

Larry: Ack. That's not Jack Benny. That's mush music.

Linda: It's not mush. It's romantic.

Larry: It stinks. I'm changing the station.

Narrator: Larry reaches for the dial. Then he stops to hear an announcement.

Announcer: Ladies and gentlemen, we **interrupt** our program to bring you a special news bulletin. Minutes ago, astronomers across the country reported seeing several gas explosions on the planet Mars. We take you now to the Princeton University Observatory. There, Carl Phillips, our reporter-at-large, is interviewing the **renowned** astronomer Professor Richard Pierson.

Phillips: This is Carl Phillips on the air. Professor Pierson, tell our audience exactly what you see as you observe the planet Mars through your telescope.

Pierson: Nothing unusual. A red disk swimming in a blue sea.

Phillips: Professor, do you think that these explosions could be a sign of intelligent life on Mars?

Pierson: The chances against life on Mars are a thousand to one.

Phillips: What else could explain these gas eruptions? Why would they be occurring on the planet's surface at such regular intervals?

Narrator: Before the professor can answer, the announcer breaks in.

Announcer: Excuse this interruption. We've just received a news report from New Jersey. A huge, flaming object, believed to be a meteor, fell on a farm in Grovers Mill, near Trenton.

Larry: A real meteor, right here in Jersey? I can't believe it!

Grandma: Vat's all this commotion?

Mrs. Springer: The radio says a meteor fell on New Jersey, Mom.

Grandma: A vat?

Larry, Linda, and Mrs. Springer: A METEOR! *(The dog barks.)*

Grandma: Vy you have to yell?

Larry: Mom, do you think I could drive over there to see it?

Mrs. Springer: I don't want you going near any meteors, Lawrence. You could be hurt. I hear your dad coming in now. You can ask him about driving over there. But I don't think it's a good idea. In fact, I'm wondering if we're safe here.

> **ASK** *yourself*
>
> What causes the news report to sound realistic?
>
> Think about what is said, how it's said, and who is saying it.

SCENE 2

Narrator: Mr. Springer comes in the front door.

Mr. Springer: Hi, everybody. *(to Mrs. Springer)* What's for supper?

Larry *(interrupting):* Dad, did you hear about the meteor that hit Trenton?

Mr. Springer: A meteor hit Trenton? No way, kiddo. I was just there an hour ago. I even made a sale.

Mrs. Springer: Congratulations on the sale, sweetheart. But listen to the radio.

Mr. Springer: I didn't see a meteor. Maybe it's a joke.

Linda: It's no joke, Dad. It's all over the news. Listen.

Phillips *(on the radio):* This is Carl Phillips again, broadcasting from a farm just outside Grovers Mill. Right now, Professor Pierson and I are **investigating** the reported meteor. Hundreds of people have parked their cars in a field next to the farm. Police tried to rope off the area, but the crowd is breaking through.

Larry: Hey, Dad, could I drive over there to see it, too?

Mr. Springer: Well . . .

Mrs. Springer *(interrupting):* George, you said you were hungry. There are sandwiches in the kitchen. Go get one.

> **Words, Words, Words**
>
> **interrupt:** to stop for a short time
> **renowned:** famous or well-known
> **investigating:** searching or examining something to learn more about it
> **friction:** what occurs when two objects rub against each other

Mr. Springer: Right. Why don't I think over that question while I'm eating?

Narrator: Mr. Springer goes into the kitchen.

Larry *(frustrated):* Man. This is the most exciting thing that ever happened in Jersey. And I have to hear about it on the radio!

Linda: Shhh. Why do you have to make a joke of everything? This could be serious. *(pause)* Oh, my gosh! Listen to the radio now!

Phillips: I hardly know how to describe the strange scene before my eyes. The object, half buried in a vast pit, must have struck with terrific force. It's about 30 yards long. It doesn't look like a meteor at all. It's metal and sort of yellowish-white. Perhaps the professor can tell us more.

Pierson: I've never seen a meteor that looked anything like this. **Friction** with the earth's atmosphere usually tears holes in a meteor. This thing is smooth and cylindrical in shape. The metal is definitely extraterrestrial.

Phillips *(interrupting):* Just a minute! Something's happening! Ladies and gentlemen, this is amazing! The top of the cylinder is beginning to rotate like a screw! The thing must be hollow!

Voice 1 *(a bullhorn):* This is the New Jersey State Police. Stand back! Stand back!

Voice 2: The top looks like it's getting red-hot.

Voice 3: The top is off!

Narrator: Frightened, Mrs. Springer calls into the kitchen.

Mrs. Springer: George?

Phillips: Ladies and gentlemen, this is the most terrifying thing I have ever witnessed. Something horrible is crawling out of the hollow top!

Linda and Larry: Dad!

Grandma: Vat's happening?

Mr. Springer *(running into the room):* What's wrong?

Linda, Larry, and Mrs. Springer: Listen!

Phillips: I see something wriggling like tentacles. Now I can see the thing's body. It's large as a bear and it glistens like wet leather. But the face is indescribable. The eyes are black and gleam like a serpent's. The mouth is V-shaped. Saliva is dripping from its rimless lips. People are running, panicking.

Grandma *(leaving the room):* Nobody tells me anything. I'm going. Where's my hot-water bottle?

Mrs. Springer: I'm going to call that radio station. This can't be true.

Phillips: Ladies and gentlemen . . . Am I on? Thirty police officers are surrounding the pit. Professor Pierson is there, too. Now something else is rising out of that pit! What's that? There's a jet of flame! It leaps! It strikes! Good lord, the policemen! They're turning into flames! Now the whole field has caught fire. The woods, the barns, the gas tanks of automobiles . . . the fire is spreading everywhere. It's coming this way. . . .

Narrator: The crash of the microphone is followed by silence.

Mrs. Springer *(tearfully):* We've got to get out of here. Our home is not safe anymore.

Announcer: Ladies and gentlemen, the next voice you hear will be that of Brigadier General Montgomery Smith, Commander of the New Jersey State Militia.

Smith: The Governor of New Jersey has asked me to place the northern third of the state under martial law. No one will be permitted to enter the area, and our men will aid in the **evacuations** of homes.

Mrs. Springer *(panicking):* We'll need blankets. Linda, get all the blankets in the house. Larry, go upstairs and get suitcases. George—

Mr. Springer *(with disbelief):* Evacuate? But it's just not possible. There would be more than this radio report. We'd hear sirens, bells, something to warn us. I'm going to try calling the police station.

Mrs. Springer: George! There's no time! Leave the phone alone and start the car!

ASK yourself

Do you agree with Mr. Springer?

Consider his idea about being warned in other ways.

SCENE 3

Narrator: Just then, the next-door neighbors burst through the front door.

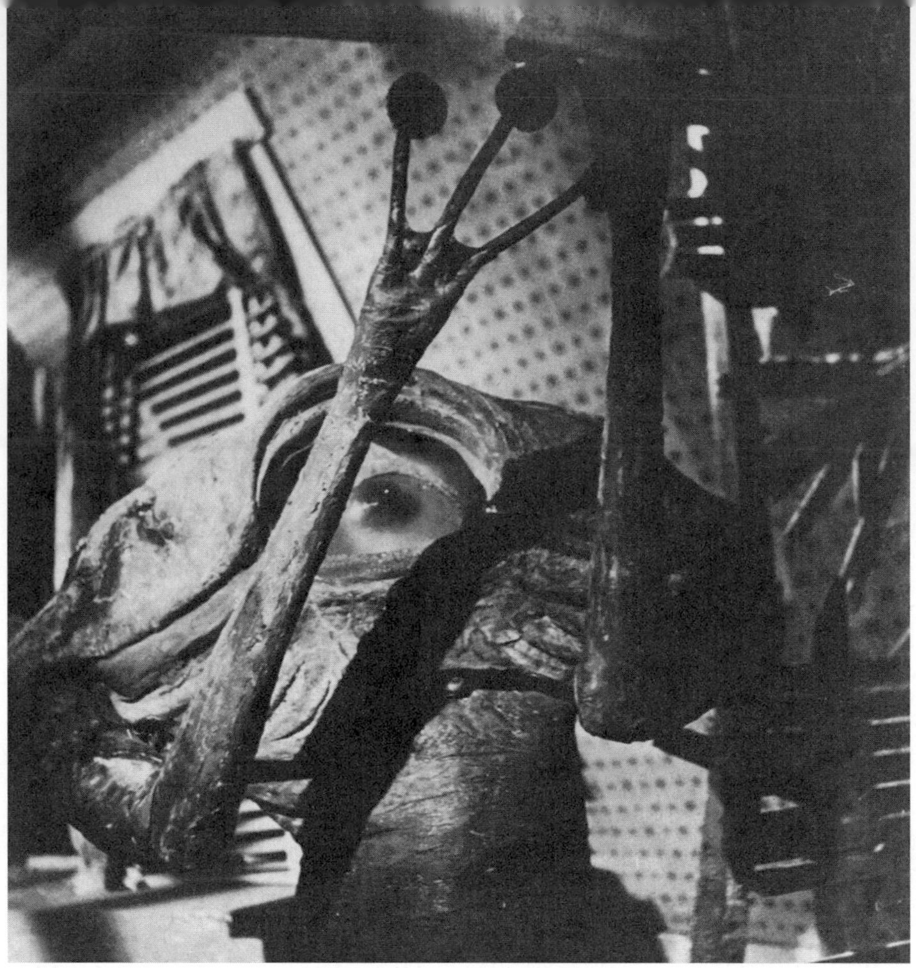

Mrs. Frascetti: The Germans have landed! They're taking over America!

Mr. Frascetti: Mama, take it easy.

Mrs. Frascetti: We don't have a cellar. So I said to him, "The Springers have a cellar. We should hide in their cellar and pray the Germans don't find us."

Mr. Frascetti: Calm down, Mama. Your heart can't take this excitement.

Linda *(breaking in):* Mom, I can't find the dog. We can't leave without Maxie!

Mrs. Springer: Don't you worry. We'll find him. Where's your grandma?

Linda: She's in the kitchen. She's reading the paper while her hot-water bottle heats up.

Announcer *(on the radio):* Ladies and gentlemen, it's confirmed that more than 40 people burned to death at Grovers Mill. We now have a live report from a captain in the New Jersey State Militia. Sir, you're on the air. Can you tell us what's happening at this site?

Captain: Eight U.S. Infantry battalions have surrounded the cylinder. No creature could withstand this kind of firepower. One quick thrust and this will all be over. *(pause)* No, wait! Something is moving. Something made of solid metal is rising out of the cylinder. It's a

Ladies and gentlemen, as incredible as it may seem, those strange beings who landed tonight are INVADERS FROM MARS!

machine standing on three giant metal legs. It's reaching above the trees, higher and higher. The searchlights are on it. Hold on! *(The sound of a loud explosion is followed by static, then . . .)*

Announcer: Ladies and gentlemen, I have a grave announcement to make. Experts now agree. There is a connection between the gas explosions on Mars and what's happening here. Incredible as it may seem, those strange beings who landed in the Jersey farmlands tonight are part of an invading army from Mars. The explosions on their planet occur as their rocket ships take off.

Mrs. Frascetti: Martians! Oh!

Narrator: Mrs. Frascetti is so frightened that she faints. Mr. Frascetti kneels beside her, fanning her.

Announcer: The battle that just took place at Grovers Mill has ended in one of the most startling **defeats** suffered by an army in modern times. Seven thousand heavily armed men were pitted against a single fighting machine from Mars. There are only 120 known survivors. The rest are strewn over the battle area. The metal monster crushed and trampled them or burned them to cinders with its heat-ray.

Linda *(crying):* What's going to happen to us? Mom, I don't want to die. I'm so scared. . . .

Mrs. Springer *(trying to be brave):* Don't worry, honey. We'll find a way out of this.

Announcer: The monsters now control the center of New Jersey. Telephone lines are down from Pennsylvania to the Atlantic Ocean.

Mr. Springer: So that's why I couldn't get through to the police station. My gosh—it *must* be true.

Announcer: Railroad tracks are in shreds. Frantic human traffic is clogging highways to the north, south, and west. Police and army reserves are unable to control the mad flight.

Mrs. Springer: We'll never get away now.

Announcer: From our Washington affiliate, here's a word from the Secretary of the Interior.

Secretary: I shall not try to conceal the **gravity** of the situation. We need calm and resourceful action. We must confront this destructive **adversary** as a nation united. We will preserve human supremacy on Earth. I thank you.

Announcer: Ladies and gentlemen, we have received bulletins from across the nation. More explosions have been observed on the surface of Mars. More metal monsters are attacking communities from St. Louis to Chicago, from Buffalo to Virginia.

Mr. Springer *(in despair):* They're trying to wipe out the whole world.

SCENE 4

Narrator: Mrs. Frascetti starts to revive from her fainting spell.

Mrs. Frascetti *(waking up)*: Where am I?

Larry: Shhh! Listen!

Commander *(on the radio):* This is Lieutenant Voght. I am currently commanding eight bombers. We have the giant tripod machines in sight. Their evident objective is to cross into New York City. The machines are staying close together. We're circling now, ready to strike. Wait! A green flash! They're spraying us with flame! Our engines are failing. . . .

Words, Words, Words

evacuations: the process of leaving a home or area for reasons of safety
defeats: the outcome of being beaten by opponents in a war
gravity: seriousness
adversary: a group of people who want to fight and destroy another group

Calling New York . . . Calling New York . . .
ISN'T THERE ANYONE ON THE AIR?

Mrs. Frascetti: It's the end of the world.

Radio Operator: Emergency! Emergency! This is an emergency broadcast. Poisonous black smoke is pouring in from the New Jersey marshes. Gas masks are useless. We urge the local population to move into open spaces. Automobiles use Routes 7, 23, 24. . . .

Mr. Springer *(leaping up):* Hurry, kids! We've got to go right now!

Larry: It's not fair! Why is this happening now? I'm too young. I've barely gotten to drive yet.

Announcer: Ladies and gentlemen, I'm speaking from the roof of our broadcasting offices in New York City. The sirens you hear behind me are warning people to evacuate. In the last two hours, three million people have jammed all roads to the north. We have no more defenses. Our army, our artillery, our air force—everything is wiped out. This may be the last broadcast from this station.

Mrs. Frascetti: It's all over.

Announcer: The enemy is now in sight across the river. The first tripod is crossing the Hudson River. Now it is reaching New York City. Its steel head is even with the skyscrapers.

Grandma *(entering)*: Vat's everybody doing? Hello, Mr. Frascetti. Mrs. Frascetti.

Mrs. Springer: Shhh, Mother.

Narrator: Grandma turns up the radio to full volume.

Announcer: The deadly Martian machines lift their metal hands. This is the end now.

Grandma *(head cocked, listening)*: Oh, this is that Martian play.

Mr. Springer *(going over to Grandma)*: What's that you said?

Grandma: Shhh. I'll tell you later. I vant to hear de end of this. It sounds very dramatic.

Announcer: Smoke drifts over the city. People in the streets see it now. They're running towards the East River. Thousands of them are dropping like rats.

Grandma: Like rats, he says. *(She laughs.)* Dat's a good one. Rats.

Announcer: Now the smoke's spreading faster. It's reached Times Square. People are trying to run away from it, but it's no use. They're falling like flies.

Grandma: Oh, like flies now. Rats or flies? These people should make up their minds.

Mr. Springer: What people?

Grandma: Orson Welles and the Mercury Theatre. I read about it in the paper just now. It's a special show, you know, a fake broadcast. Here, see for yourself.

Narrator: Grandma hands him the paper.

Announcer: Now the smoke's crossing Fifth Avenue. It's 100 yards away . . . it's 50 feet away from me. . . . *(fades off into static)*

Radio Operator: Calling New York . . . Isn't there anyone on the air?

Narrator: The radio fades into silence. At the Springers', everyone except Grandma and Mr. Springer is crying.

Grandma: Boy! I guess dat vas one pretty good play.

Mr. Springer: You have no idea, Gran.

Narrator: Mr. Springer pulls Grandma into the kitchen with him.

Mr. Springer: Come on, let's eat something. I'm starving.

Announcer: You are listening to a CBS presentation of Orson Welles and the Mercury Theatre of the Air. This is an original dramatization of *The War of the Worlds* by H.G. Wells. The performance will continue after a brief intermission.

P.E. 35

THE MARTIAN BROADCAST

How Orson Welles Tricked the Nation

On the night of October 30, 1938, thousands of American families tuned in to CBS radio and heard minute-by-minute news reports of a Martian invasion. People all over the country prayed, cried, and fled their homes, trying frantically to escape. They thought that if they'd heard it on the radio, it had to be true.

But it wasn't really a news report. It was just a radio play based on *The War of the Worlds*, the 1898 science-fiction novel by the British writer H.G. Wells. A group of actors directed by Orson Welles presented the play on a program called the "Mercury Theatre of the Air."

The play you just read features actual excerpts from the radio broadcast along with the story of a made-up family—the Springers—who heard the program. How were people like the Springers so completely taken in?

The answer is simple. Welles and his co-writer tried as hard as they could to make it seem real. The play used the names of real towns, hospitals, roads, and rivers. (They chose Grovers Mill as the touchdown point by taking a map of New Jersey and dropping a pencil on it.) The style of the radio play was also extremely realistic for the time.

The Attack Begins

The action began in a fictitious hotel in New York City, where an orchestra was playing dance music. The music went on for several minutes before an announcer's voice broke in with a report of mysterious explosions on Mars. The music resumed but was interrupted more and more often with special news reports. The reports included interviews with famous astronomers and announcements by government officials.

Welles said he knew before the broadcast that a few people would think it was real. But he said he was "flabbergasted" by the huge number of people who fell for the joke.

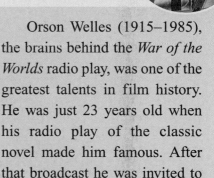

Author Bio: A Well of Talent

CBS

Orson Welles (1915–1985), the brains behind the *War of the Worlds* radio play, was one of the greatest talents in film history. He was just 23 years old when his radio play of the classic novel made him famous. After that broadcast he was invited to direct and star in his own films.

The original novel on which Orson Welles based his broadcast was written by the British author H.G. (Herbert George) Wells. Wells (1866–1946) was best known for his imaginative science-fiction stories.

Wrap-Up

Talk About It

Now that you've read *War of the Worlds* and "The Martian Broadcast," what do you have to say about these questions?

- What do you think about the possibility of life on other planets?
- What might happen today if a television station aired a phony news report about a Martian invasion?

Comprehension Check

Write your answers to the questions below. Use information from the radio play and the article to support your answers.

1. Why does Mrs. Frascetti faint?
2. Why does Mrs. Frascetti think the Germans are invading?
3. How was Orson Welles able to make his play so realistic that people actually believed it was true?
4. Did Orson Welles think people would believe his play was real?
5. What role did radio play in the lives of people in 1938?

Vocabulary Check

Complete each sentence starter below. Before you answer, think about the meaning of the vocabulary word in bold.

1. We never expected the principal to **interrupt** . . .
2. We didn't understand the **gravity** of the situation until . . .
3. The police are now **investigating** the . . .
4. After the **evacuations** of all the classrooms . . .
5. It turned out that the **friction** was caused by . . .

Write About It

Choose one of the three writing prompts below.

- Using the voice of Linda Springer, write a letter to Orson Welles explaining what happened to your family when they heard *War of the Worlds.*
- Write your own news report about a phony event. Use ideas from the play to make it sound realistic.
- If you had been fooled by the joke, how would you feel? Write a letter to Orson Welles telling him your thoughts.

More to READ

If you like stories about space invaders, you might enjoy these books.

Visitors Book 1: Strange Invaders
by Rodman Philbrick and Lynn Harnett

Twins Nick and Jessie see a strange light hover over the town. Suddenly all the adults are talking like robots and eating strange foods. Even the animals are acting weird. It looks like brain-stealing aliens have come to Harley Hills. Now it's up to the kids to save the town.

Help! I'm Trapped in an Alien's Body!
by Todd Strasser

Jake Sherman has accidentally switched bodies with a space alien. This alien, Howard, is from a planet of serious couch potatoes. So Howard has short, weak legs; long, stretchy arms; and a beak-like mouth that's perfect for ripping open bags of junk food. But why has Howard come to Earth in the first place? He's bored, bored, bored with his lazy and dull planet. Will Jake feel the same way?

Reading a Manual

You just got a new TV set. You need to hook it up to your cable box and your VCR. You've got cables everywhere, and the instruction manual looks really confusing.

Don't panic! Check out this page from a TV manual. It will help you get connected!

Hooking Up Your TV, VCR, and Cable Box

The numbers in the diagram correspond to the numbers in the step-by-step instructions.

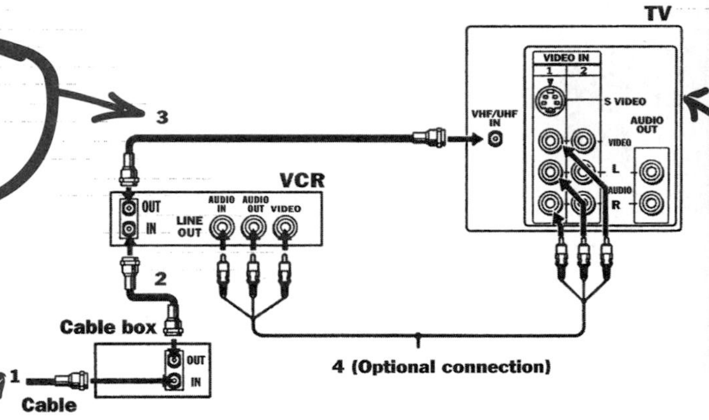
TV
VIDEO IN
1
2
S VIDEO
AUDIO OUT
VHF/UHF IN
VIDEO
L
AUDIO
R
3
VCR
OUT
IN
LINE OUT
AUDIO IN
AUDIO OUT
VIDEO
2
Cable box
OUT
IN
1
Cable
4 (Optional connection)

In this diagram, all the jacks you need to hook up your appliances are labeled. You'll find these same labels on your appliances.

Notice that the drawing of the cable is identified only once. The next time you see this drawing, you'll have to remember that it represents a cable.

1. Connect the cable wire (or the coaxial cable) that runs from your wall into the IN jack on your cable box.
2. Connect the coaxial cable from the OUT jack on your cable box to the IN jack on your VCR.
3. Connect the coaxial cable from the OUT jack on your VCR to the VHF/UHF IN jack on your TV.
4. Optional: If your VCR has video inputs, connect the A/V cables from the AUDIO and VIDEO OUT jacks on your VCR to the AUDIO/VIDEO IN jacks on your TV. Use the TV/VIDEO button to switch between the TV and VCR inputs.

"When reading an instruction manual, it helps to have the appliance in front of you. That way you can match the pictures with the parts of the appliance."

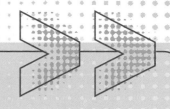

Manual Labor

Your guests are coming over to watch a movie, and you still haven't set up your new TV. Take a deep breath, and reread the manual and tips on the left. Then use them to answer the questions. Write your answers on your own paper.

1. Where does the very first cable come from?
a. the TV manufacturer
b. your wall
c. the VCR manufacturer

2. How many cables are attached to the cable box?
a. one
b. two
c. three

3. What is another name for the first cable wire?
a. the coaxial cable
b. the TV hook-up wire
c. the big wire

4. You want to hook up your TV to the VCR and cable box. Which step can you skip? How do you know?
a. step 1, because you don't want cable
b. step 2, because you don't need your VCR
c. step 4, because it is marked "optional connection"

5. What do you need to make sure you have before you hook up your TV?
a. two AA batteries
b. two cables
c. a remote

Write a Manual

Think of an activity that you do every day, such as brushing your teeth or making breakfast. List the steps you must perform to complete it. Then write instructions for completing the activity. Feel free to include a diagram.

Talk About It

Exchange manuals with a partner. Could you follow your partner's instructions? Circle anything that's incomplete or unclear. Then use your partner's comments to revise your instructions.

"Help! You read the manual carefully, and you still can't figure out what to do. Most manuals include the telephone number of a help line you can call."

Real-World Words

appliance: a household machine that runs on gas or electricity
diagram: a drawing or plan that explains something
jack: an outlet into which you plug a cable or wire

Short story

Dreaming Aloud

In Saudi Arabia during the Gulf War, two different cultures came face to face. In this story, a girl gets her first glimpse of Western culture . . . and her life will change forever.

by Rita Williams-Garcia

Staring is a bad habit, but I can't help where my eyes go and stay. With the war almost over, more American soldiers venture into the souk, or marketplace, hunting for souvenirs. I like the way they shout "Check this out!" while admiring Persian rugs and brass pots.

"What do you suppose the Americans are saying?" I whisper to my cousins.

Rabiah and Kamilah examine gold embroidery from a bolt of fabric. Kamilah replies, "What Americans always say: 'How can they wear those veils?'"

At least Rabiah is mildly curious. Together we cast quick glances at the American soldiers gathered about the jeweler, then turn inward to share a giggle.

Kamilah groans. She has no interest in Americans. Selecting the right fabric for her wedding attire is all that concerns her.

In two short months everything will come to an end. We will no longer be 16—school girls playing soccer in our school yard or making fizzes in beakers in chemistry class. We will be women like our mothers, expected to forget everything we've learned about the properties of zinc, magnesium, and iron.

Graduating is pointless, since there is no place of importance to graduate to. At least for me. When my brother Isaq graduated two years ago, there was no doubt that he would go to college. For us it's different. Kamilah will marry. Rabiah will go to London to work for our uncle and hopes to attend classes—though she has mentioned the last part only to me. My future, however, has not yet been decided by my parents.

"How must it feel to drive that jeep," I dream aloud.

A distant rumbling makes me look up. A fleet of jeeps parade slowly through the street. Rabiah and I watch them. Wanting no part of our curiosity, Kamilah practices her bargaining skills with the merchant.

One jeep is close enough to see inside. The passenger sits stiff with authority, undoubtedly an American officer of high rank. The jeep halts and out jumps the driver, the way cowboys dismount horses in American movies. The driver scurries to the passenger side, opens the door, and salutes his superior. The salute—the lifting of the arm—gives it away. The driver is a woman!

Can it be? I nudge Rabiah. We stare, utterly amazed. "How must it feel to drive that jeep," I dream aloud, my voice low—for my cousins' ears only. Women are **forbidden** to drive automobiles in Riyadh. A woman can be jailed or worse for sitting behind a steering wheel.

"Nailah!" they both scold, hitting me playfully on the shoulders. Even though they are right here **pummeling** me, I feel our impending separation more than ever. I am numb imagining Kamilah married. I can see Rabiah in London, running our uncle's household and attending classes. But somehow, when I turn my mind's mirror on myself, there is a cloud of dust where my face should be.

I leave my cousins in the souk and go home to help Momma prepare supper, though, truthfully, Momma doesn't need my help. My constant daydreaming irritates her. "How will you be a good wife?" she scolds.

She hands me a tray of fruit and coffee to serve Papa and Isaq in Papa's office. Papa owns a cable outlet and spends most of the day in his office on the phone. He and Isaq are engaged in discussion when I enter.

It's strange to watch Isaq speaking to father so seriously. Is this my Isaq? The same brother who committed prank after prank against me—even through his secondary school years? Now, after two years of college in Kuwait, he is a serious man. His beard grows thick like Papa's and he looks at us with dark, watchful eyes. Like many students forced to return home because of the war, he is uncertain about his future.

Papa listens, his face intense as he weighs Isaq's every word. My heart sinks with envy as I serve the hot coffee. Papa will never make this face for me; a girl's concerns are knitted only in her mother's brow.

Papa nods thoughtfully. He assures Isaq that he'll let him complete his education in London if he can't return to Kuwait. My brother tries to maintain the manly **composure** that two years away from home have awarded him, but Isaq is Isaq. In his eyes is the boyish triumph of the brother I grew up with. I return to the kitchen leaving them alone to discuss Isaq's future.

"Kamilah's wedding will be soon," I say to Momma.

"Soon," she says.

"And Rabiah will be in London."

"Ah! And what of Nailah?" Momma teases.

I sit down before her. "Yes, Momma. What?"

Momma sprinkles currants into the rice. "We have not yet found a suitable husband. But marriage

Words, Words, Words

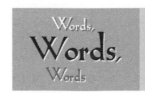

forbidden: not allowed
pummeling: punching something over and over
composure: self-control

is not on your mind." She looks at me knowingly. If I were half as beautiful as Momma, my husband would give in to all my wishes. As it is, I look too much like Papa's sisters. My nose is too round. My eyes too probing. Certainly not jewels, like Momma's.

"Nailah, I've heard your long sighs. I've seen those eyes, lost and clouded."

My words rush out all at once. "I want to study chemistry at the university. I can go back with Isaq when school reopens."

"The university? Nailah!" It is as though I'd said I want to ride through town on a two-headed goat.

"To be a scientist or a doctor, Momma. Think of what I could learn! I could research cures for diseases."

Momma laughs, convinced I am joking.

"Momma, I have the highest math and science scores in school. And my instructor has offered to inquire into a scholarship—with Papa's permission."

"And leave us, Nailah? Trees transplanted never prosper." This is a favorite saying. Parents use it to chop down their children's dreams, and girls dare not dream beyond marriage.

"But Momma, who is needed for Papa's business? Isaq, the oldest son, or I, a daughter? Papa sends Isaq to school because it gives him pleasure. But if Papa would send me also, I would return a doctor or scientist. Think of the good I could do."

"Is this what goes on in that head? Enough of this—and not a word to your father." Momma's eyes no longer sparkle. She stirs the sizzling pan of rice and currants furiously, then shoos me away with her hand.

I feel both foolish and glad to have poured myself out to Momma. But the look she gave me! I understand, though. Momma is a traditional woman. When she was my age, she'd been married two years. In her eyes her daughter *is* riding a two-headed goat. Tonight for sure, my parents will begin searching for my husband.

School is closed today. I sit in the kitchen with Momma. I know enough not to mention the conversation we had yesterday.

We hear the rumble of an auto engine just outside. Momma and I look out and see an American army jeep. It is the same jeep we'd seen in the souk yesterday, and, yes . . . the woman driver. I would give anything to be her, away from home, driving a jeep as free as I please. Papa always took us for drives. Sometimes Isaq would take the wheel, turn around to grin at me. I'd sit in the back seat, my unhappiness hidden by my veil.

ASK yourself

- What kind of unhappy thoughts might Nailah be having behind her veil?

Think about how you might feel if you were in her place.

Papa emerges from his office to greet the Americans. "Pleased to meet you, Mr. Ashkam," the officer says, extending his hand. "This lady here is my driver, Private Green."

Private Green offers her hand as the officer did, but Poppa will not take it. The officer says something to her. She straightens to attention and says, "Yes, sir!" loud and sharp like missiles going off. The officer and Papa smile and enter Papa's office.

Private Green seems relieved to be rid of the men. She pulls out a magazine and leans against the jeep. She is African-American. By the slope of her nose and her date-brown coloring, she could very well be related to the Ethiopian traders from the bay. I imagine myself sitting up front in her jeep, driving her to the bay to meet them.

Momma goes outside and calls to Private Green. "Come in! Come in!" she says in Arabic. It's funny. Private Green doesn't know what to make of Momma's ranting and repeats, "Ma'am? Ma'am?"

The American thinks Momma is a crazy woman. She hesitates, but follows Momma into the house. Momma brings her into the kitchen and seats her before me, almost as an offering.

"Hello," I say in the English I have learned in school. "I am Nailah. This is my mother, Mrs. Ashkam."

"Ah salaam alaykum," Private Green answers. Her hard accent changes the traditional Islamic greeting.

"Wa alaykum ah salaam," I return.

"My sister back in Brooklyn is a Muslim," she says, taking a photo from her wallet. It shows a young woman dressed in a white tunic and veil. Ah! A true Muslim does not submit to photographing.

"And you . . ." I do not wish to be rude, but I am curious, " . . . are Muslim?"

"Goodness, no!" she exclaims, her voice shooting off, proud like a man's. "No offense, but that's no life for *this* woman." I'm **translating** for Momma, but I leave out this part so as not to hurt her.

The American fans herself, then unfastens her top shirt button. She removes her cap and puts it in her lap. Her hair is braided like a tidy mat, close to her head. Tiny gold beads make a diagonal pattern. Momma pats them in childlike admiration.

Ordinarily, we serve coffee to guests, but Momma pours Private Green a glass of water. She drinks it like a soldier, in three large gulps. She looks about 18, Isaq's age.

"So tell me how it feels to drive this jeep," I ask.

"I hate it," Private Green says. This time her voice is flat and subdued. "Being the colonel's

Words, Words, Words

translating: turning words from one language into another language
chauffeur: a person who drives a car for someone else
illusions: things that appear to exist but really do not
indigo: a dark violet-blue color

I wonder if I should trust the dreams that cloud my vision. I wonder if I should dream at all.

driver is a lowly job," she explains. "Do you think the men in my unit want to play **chauffeur?** No way."

Momma nudges me. I translate. Momma looks at me with a face of amazement. Our **illusions** are coming unraveled.

"What I would give to drive," I say.

"You can have it," Private Green fires back. "Me? I'd rather be in a medic unit. Patching people together. I've applied to college back home. I want to be a doctor."

"A doctor!" I exclaim and grab her hand in excitement. "Me too! Or a scientist." Private Green tells me that joining the Army was the only way she could raise money for tuition.

"A small price to pay," I tell her, thoroughly envious. She drives *and* has applied to college. "I would do anything to continue school. I'd clean my brother's house just to read his books."

"A maid for your brother?" Private Green is so obviously disapproving that Momma tugs and tugs at my clothes, eager to be included.

"It's a small price to pay," I insist, though the American rolls her eyes. She opens her magazine and we gaze at the fashions. Most are quite insane looking, but fun. Then we sniff a perfume sample. Momma leaves us, then returns with a small flask of perfumed oil for Private Green.

The trooping of boots from the other room tells us the men are finalizing their business. My mother puts Private Green's army cap on her head and fastens her shirt button. Private Green is embarrassed to be fussed over, but she allows it. She thanks my mother for her kindness and gives me the magazine. As soon as the jeep is out of sight, Momma takes the magazine. She gives it back to me after she's torn out and thrown away the pictures of women wearing bikinis.

That night I watch the last missiles explode in the horizon. The sky is not its usual **indigo,** but smoky gray from the oil fire in the Gulf. I follow the bright spheres shooting up and exploding, changing the sky. I wonder if I should trust the dreams that cloud my vision. I wonder if I should dream at all. I stop thinking so loud because I hear my mother talking to my father. About me.

"Nailah is useless to me," Momma complains. "Absolutely useless."

"What would you have me do?"

"Send her off with Isaq."

A smile swells my face.

"Let her wash his clothes, cook his food, write his notes."

"A girl alone will get into mischief," Papa objects. "Trees transplanted never prosper."

"During the day she can study at the university. Isaq can keep an eye on her."

"Classes at the university?" It was as though my mother had said the unthinkable.

ASK yourself

- Why does Nailah smile even after her mother calls her "useless"?

Think about what Nailah's mother is trying to do.

"Our daughter is not so stupid she cannot learn. Rabiah will be going off to London. Jhuhadi will go to secretarial school. So will Zaidi. Are your brothers' daughters smarter than Nailah?"

"Jhuhadi! Rabiah! Zaidi! Is Kamilah the only good girl to get married?"

"Nailah is a good girl. She will make a good nurse or doctor. Her teachers pester me to send her away on scholarship."

"Enough of this!" my father roars.

I'm so happy I am almost screaming. In the morning I will wash Momma's feet, even if Papa says I cannot go. She has said my dream out loud. I'll never look at her the same way again.

The next day, Papa and Isaq leave after the first prayer to **conclude** business with the Americans. Momma invites me to her room to try on her necklaces. Wearing Momma's jewelry was my favorite treat when I was a little girl, though now I do it to please her. I'm sure she knows this.

"Nailah. Smart and beautiful. Allah willing, a doctor."

Suddenly, my mother interests me a great deal. I ask if she's ever had a dream all her own. Her eyes sparkle. She stares off the way I do. "Once, I wanted to drive my father's truck and let the wind blow my veil away." ●

A Real PLACE — A Real TIME

"Dreaming Aloud" is set in Saudi Arabia during the Gulf War. This map shows the geography of that area of the world.

Words, Words, Words

conclude: finish
coalition: two or more groups joining together for a common purpose
conservative: traditional

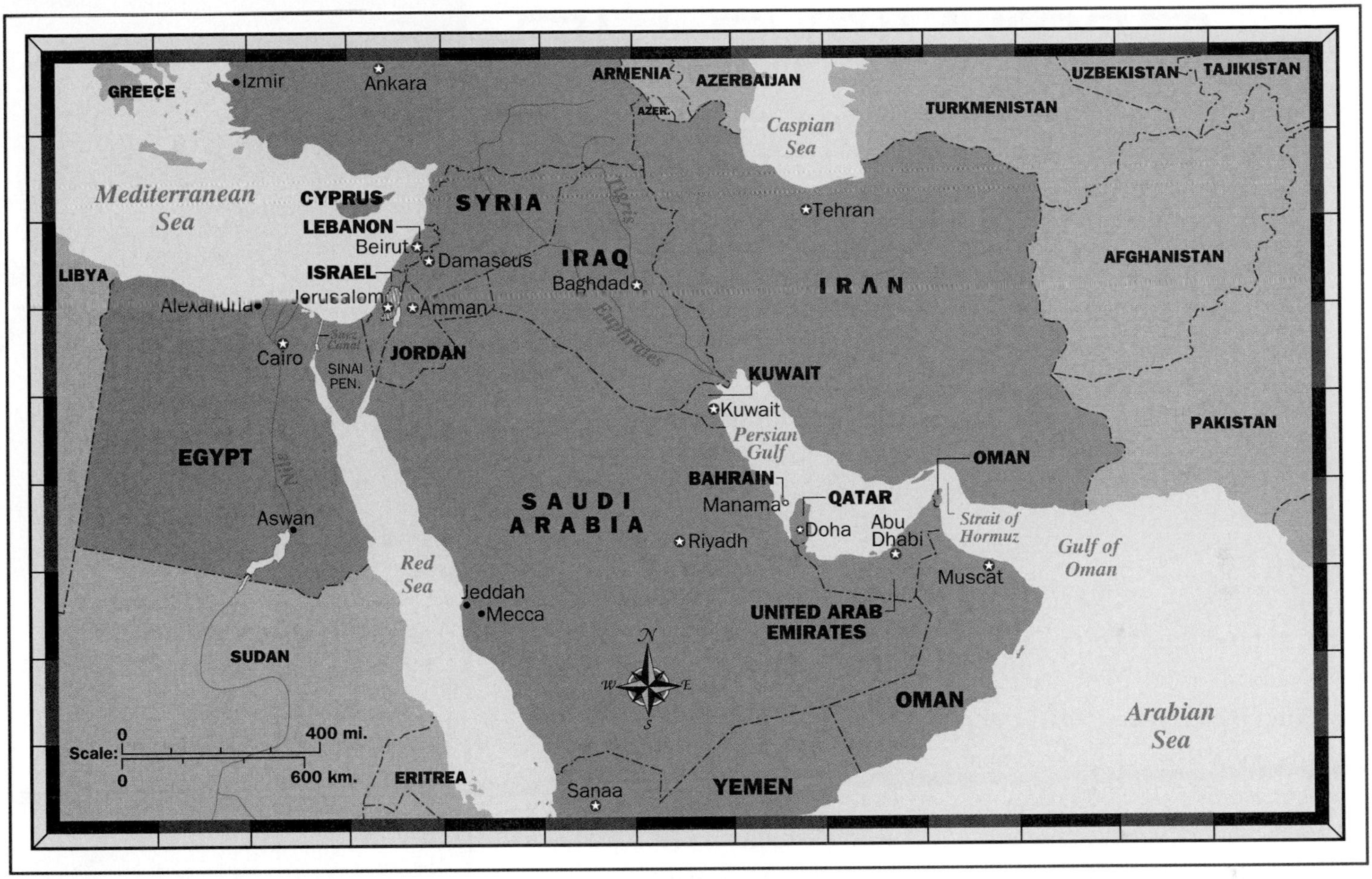
GREECE
Izmir
Ankara
ARMENIA
AZERBAIJAN
AZER.
Caspian Sea
TURKMENISTAN
UZBEKISTAN
TAJIKISTAN
Mediterranean Sea
CYPRUS
SYRIA
LEBANON
Beirut
Damascus
IRAQ
Baghdad
Euphrates
Tehran
IRAN
AFGHANISTAN
LIBYA
ISRAEL
Jerusalem
Alexandria
Amman
JORDAN
Cairo
SINAI PEN.
KUWAIT
Kuwait
Persian Gulf
PAKISTAN
EGYPT
OMAN
BAHRAIN
Manama
QATAR
Doha
Abu Dhabi
Strait of Hormuz
Gulf of Oman
SAUDI ARABIA
Riyadh
Aswan
Red Sea
Jeddah
Mecca
Muscat
UNITED ARAB EMIRATES
SUDAN
N
W
E
S
OMAN
Arabian Sea
Scale: 0 400 mi. 0 600 km.
ERITREA
Sanaa
YEMEN

This story is fiction, but it's set in a real place and a real time: Saudi Arabia in 1991, at the end of the Gulf War. The conflict began in August, 1990, when Iraqi President Saddam Hussein sent troops to invade and take over Kuwait. Hussein threatened to invade Saudi Arabia as well.

A **coalition** of 39 countries—led by the United States and the United Nations—banded together to stop him. The coalition began bombing Iraqi targets in January 1991. Ground troops took back Kuwait City a month later. Iraq agreed to a cease-fire on April 6. By that time, approximately 100,000 Iraqi troops and 480 coalition soldiers had been killed. Saudi Arabia, a **conservative** Islamic country, was home base for thousands of troops during the war. They gave many Saudis their first look at Western culture.

growing up female

Despite advances, girls and women around the world still face some special challenges.

by Amy Miller and Alexandra Hanson-Harding

When Melissa Poe was 9, she organized a group to help the environment. Today, that group, Kids For a Cleaner Environment, has more than 300,000 members. It is the largest youth environmental group in the world. "There are millions of people in the world," Melissa says, "but it just takes one to make a difference."

Not all girls feel that they can make such a difference. They may live in parts of the world where their lives are valued less than those of boys. In some countries, women get little education, cannot own property, and cannot hold a job outside the home. Life is better in most industrialized nations, such as the U.S. Since winning the right to vote in 1920, U.S. women have succeeded in breaking down barriers in education, employment, sports, and the military. The number of businesses owned by women increased from about 500,000 in 1972 to nearly 8 million in 1996.

But even in the U.S., life is not completely fair. Women make up only 12 percent of Congress. Women are paid less than men, and they shoulder more of the burden of home and child care.

And yet, all over the world, women are making progress. Even in less-developed countries such as Bangladesh, women are joining together to start businesses. More women are being educated in rural areas of the world. And they are becoming more active in politics. Women have served as heads of government in New Zealand, Pakistan, Turkey, the United Kingdom, and other countries.

Unable to sign her name, a self-employed woman in India uses a thumbprint to withdraw money from her account.

Read on to learn more about how women are doing around the world.

INDIA:
From Child Brides to Businesswomen

In the Indian state of Rajasthan (RAH-juh-stahn), the

CASH

annual Akha Teej Festival marks the day judged to be most favorable for getting married. Every city, town, and village in Rajasthan celebrates. But for many young brides, it is hardly a day for celebration.

Although India has outlawed child marriages, more than 50 percent of women in Rajasthan marry before they are 15 years old. Barely 18 percent of these young wives are able to read and write. "It is a tragedy for these little flowers . . . that they are snatched away into marriage before they even have a chance to bloom," says Mohini Giri of India's National Commission for Women.

But Indian women are working to make lives better for themselves and their daughters. More women are attending universities in India than ever before. More than 20 women's studies centers have been set up at universities throughout India.

Women who work at home now can obtain credit through organizations such as The Self-Employed Women's Association. With the association's help, women have been able to establish many successful, growing businesses. The association also provides insurance, legal aid, health care, and job training for its 250,000 members.

Massoumeh Ebtekar, Iran's Environment Minister, is the highest-ranking woman in the government.

Many woman in Kenya's rural areas get little education. Here, women farm by hand.

IRAN: Life Behind a Veil

Before the 1979 Islamic revolution, young women in Iran were encouraged to go to college and to pursue a career. Since 1979 their lives have changed dramatically, although Iranian women are still able to work outside the home with their husband's permission.

When speaking of her childhood in Iran, Batul Ebrahami, 18, recalls, "I was taught I was nothing. I could have no job. I was no use to society."

Legally, women in Iran are less valuable than men. This means that if they are the victim of a crime, they get only half the damages that men get. A female family member inherits half of what a male relative inherits.

Married women have fewer rights than their husbands. They cannot travel out of the country without permission from their husbands. When in public, women cannot talk with men who are not their husbands.

In Iran, all women above the age of nine are forced to obey a strict dress code known as hejab. They must cover their heads and part of their faces in public with a veil called a chador. They must also wrap their bodies in layers of clothing.

But Iranian women have not lost all their political rights. They can vote and hold seats in Iran's parliament. There is even a female Vice President of the Dept. of the Environment, Massoumeh Ebtekar.

KENYA: Rural Women Face Special Struggles

Both men and women suffer harsh living conditions in the East African nation of Kenya. For example, the average life expectancy is very low—49 for women, 48 for men. But women also face many other problems.

Fewer women than men are able to get an education. As a result, only 68 percent of women in Kenya can read, compared to 85 percent of men. Customs and laws make life harder for women, especially for rural women. They are expected to bear many children and to work hard at raising food to feed them.

And yet, things have improved in some ways. Although the birth rate is still high (4.9 children per

Norwegian women enjoy many opportunities and a high standard of living.

woman), it has dropped dramatically in recent years. This has given women more resources to care for the children they do have.

More women are starting their own businesses and getting involved in politics. In recent presidential elections, two major candidates were women. Some Kenyan women are even becoming world-class athletes—notably, former New York City Marathon winner Tegla Laroupe.

Educated women such as Wangari Maathai are working to help change Kenya's society. Maathai learned that poor rural women spent hours every day gathering firewood for their families. Since trees were becoming scarce, she arranged to pay these women to plant trees for more firewood. That was the start of the Green Belt movement in Kenya. Now, more than 10 million trees have been planted, helping the environment and bringing firewood closer to the women who need it.

NORWAY:
Girls' Futures Bright in Land of Midnight Sun

Women's rights are so important to Norwegians that 21 years ago they passed a law to enforce equal rights for men and women. Women hold many prominent jobs in the government. Norway elected its first woman prime minister in 1981. More than a third of the members of the Storting, Norway's parliament, are women.

In Norway, parents can take a full year off to take care of a new baby—while earning 80 percent of their pay. But in most cases, it is the mothers, not the fathers, who take time off.

In private business, women in Norway face obstacles. Only 3.5 percent of the top Norwegian executives are women, fewer than in the U.S. Women tend to choose lower-paying fields where they can work part-time and spend more time with their families. The average hourly wage of women is still lower than that for men.

Still, women have many choices in Norway. And the opportunities that exist there make it a leading nation of gender equality. ●

Wrap-UP

Talk About It

Now that you've read "Dreaming Aloud" and "Growing Up Female," what do you have to say about these questions?

- Do you think daughters and sons should always be treated the same way? Why or why not?
- Which do you think is more important: fairness or tradition? Why?

Comprehension Check

Write your answers to the questions below. Use information from the short story and article to support your answers.

1. Why is Nailah so amazed to see that the driver of the jeep is a woman?
2. Why do you think Nailah's mother changes her mind and helps Nailah after all?
3. What do you think Nailah means when she says "when I turn my mind's mirror on myself there is a cloud of dust where my face should be"?
4. How are women's rights different from men's rights around the world? Give two examples.
5. What kind of qualities would help a young woman follow her dreams if she lives in a place where women have few rights?

Vocabulary Check

Complete each sentence starter below. Before you answer, think about the meaning of the vocabulary word in bold.

1. Going into the teacher's lounge was **forbidden,** but . . .
2. People who are **conservative** usually . . .
3. My **illusions** were smashed when I learned . . .
4. I realized she had a **chauffeur** as soon as . . .
5. I need to regain my **composure** after . . .

Write About It

Choose one of the three writing prompts below.

- What would life be like if you were an exchange student living in Iran? Write a letter home explaining how the way of life there makes you feel.
- If Nailah wanted to give her father a list of ten reasons why he should let her go to college, what would be on that list?
- If you were going to start an organization, what issue would you focus on? State the problem you think needs solving and give at least two reasons why.

More to READ

If you'd like to know more about women who have dared to dream, check out:

Sally Ride: Shooting for the Stars
by Jane Hurwitz

They said it was a job for a man. But in 1983, Sally Ride proved them wrong when she became America's first female astronaut to fly in space. Ride also became the youngest American astronaut to orbit the earth. This book profiles Sally Ride, the woman, the scientist, and the astronaut as she breaks the gender barrier and shoots for the stars.

The Secret Soldier: The Story of Deborah Sampson
by Ann McGovern

This is the exciting true story of a woman who became a soldier during the American Revolutionary War. Deborah Sampson wanted to travel and have adventures. When she joined the army disguised as a man, she was caught up in the dramatic events of America's fight for independence.

Understanding Time Zones

You live in Georgia. Your best friend just moved to California. You tried to call her before school, but she was still in bed. You forgot that she had moved to a different time zone!

Look at this map that shows all the time zones in the United States. Can you figure it out?

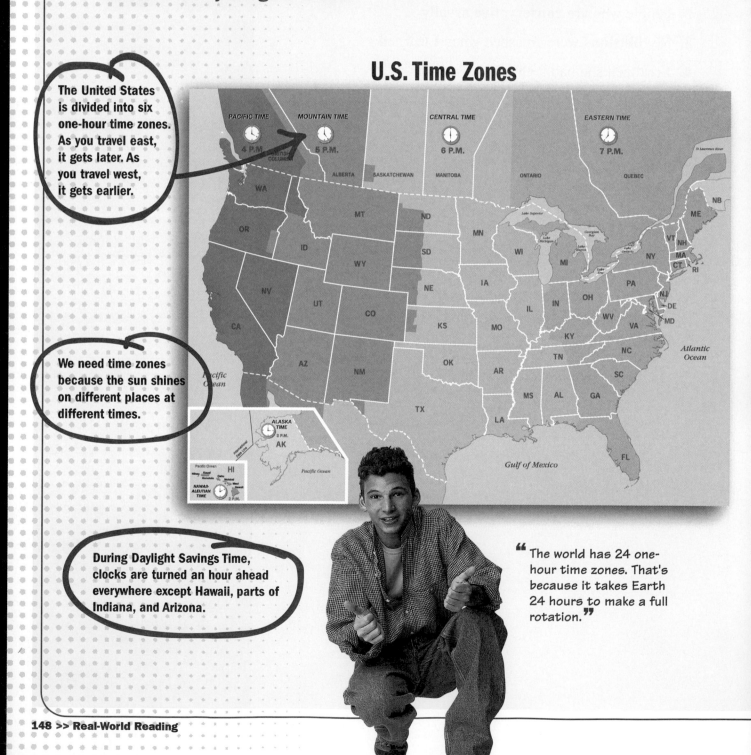

The United States is divided into six one-hour time zones. As you travel east, it gets later. As you travel west, it gets earlier.

U.S. Time Zones

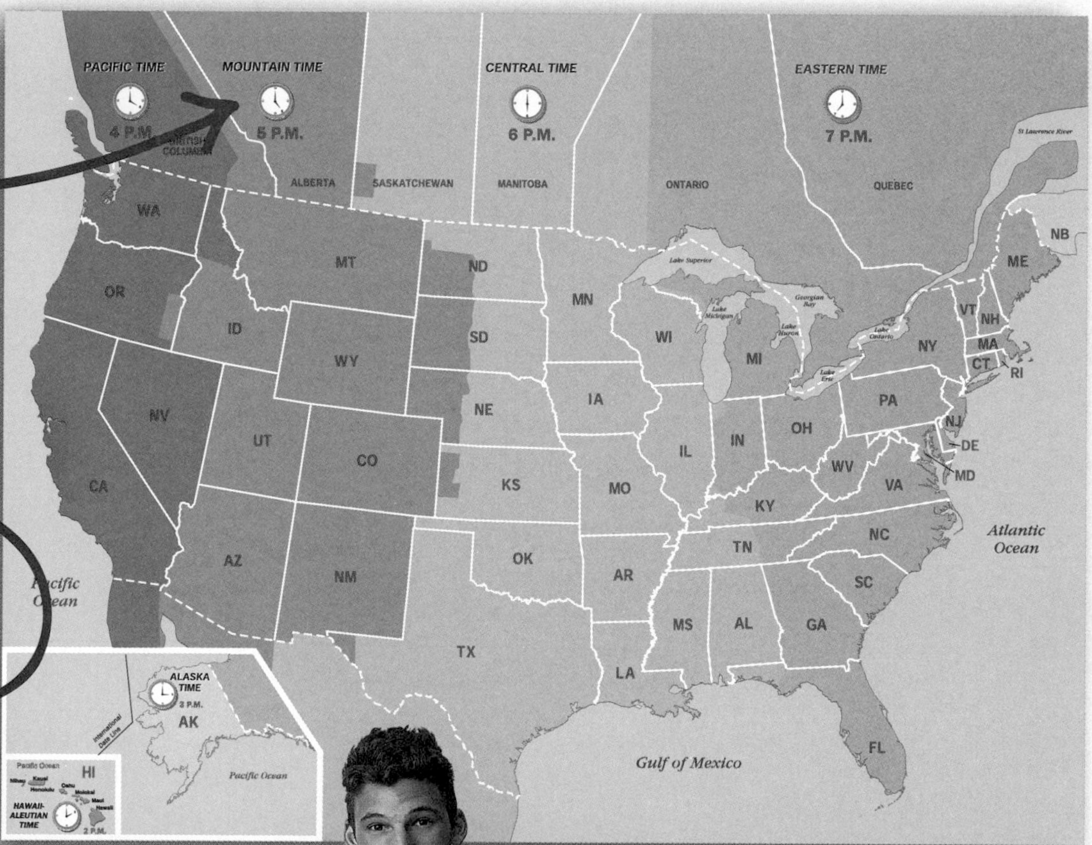
PACIFIC TIME
4 P.M.
MOUNTAIN TIME
5 P.M.
CENTRAL TIME
6 P.M.
EASTERN TIME
7 P.M.
ALBERTA
SASKATCHEWAN
MANITOBA
ONTARIO
QUEBEC
NB
WA
OR
CA
NV
ID
MT
WY
UT
CO
AZ
NM
ND
SD
NE
KS
OK
TX
MN
IA
MO
AR
LA
WI
IL
MI
IN
OH
KY
TN
MS
AL
GA
FL
SC
NC
VA
WV
PA
NY
VT
NH
ME
MA
CT
RI
NJ
DE
MD
Pacific Ocean
Atlantic Ocean
Gulf of Mexico
ALASKA TIME
3 P.M.
AK
HI
HAWAII-ALEUTIAN TIME
2 P.M.

We need time zones because the sun shines on different places at different times.

During Daylight Savings Time, clocks are turned an hour ahead everywhere except Hawaii, parts of Indiana, and Arizona.

"The world has 24 one-hour time zones. That's because it takes Earth 24 hours to make a full rotation."

In the Zone

It's vacation time! You leave Washington, D.C., at 9 A.M. on a four-hour flight to San Diego, CA. You arrive on the West Coast at 10 A.M. Are you in the twilight zone? No, you're just in another time zone. Use the map and tips to answer these questions. Write your answers on your own paper.

1. What is the name of the time zone you live in?

2. It's 3 P.M. in Atlanta, GA. What time is it in Los Angeles, CA? What time is it in Chicago, IL?

3. You live in Tulsa, OK. Your friend lives in Boulder, CO. She e-mailed you and said that she'd meet you online to chat at 8 P.M. her time. What time should you log on to your computer?

4. You just won a road race in Seattle, WA. It's 2 P.M. there. You call your parents in Miami, FL. What might they be doing?
   a. sitting down to eat breakfast
   b. getting home from their noontime walk
   c. going to bed
   d. watching an early-evening news program

5. Look at each pair of states below. Are they in the **same** time zone or **different** ones?
   a. Vermont (VT)/New York (NY)
   b. Florida (FL)/Iowa (IA)
   c. Montana (MT)/Arkansas (AR)
   d. Maine (ME)/Alaska (AK)

Real-World Words

rotation: one complete turn
zone: an area

It's About Time!

You're in Georgia (GA). You want to set up a chat with Keisha in Illinois (IL), Jamie in Idaho (ID), and Kyle in Oregon (OR). The chat must be between 3 P.M. and 10 P.M. Eastern Time. When should each person sign on?

Chat It Up

You live in Florida (FL). It's noon, and you're eating lunch. What time is it in Wisconsin (WI)? In Colorado (CO)? In Oregon (OR)? Make a chart that shows the name of each state, the time, and an activity that someone might be doing there.

"You can use an Internet search engine to find time-zone maps for the U.S. and the rest of the world."

photo essay

TWINS

A Celebration in Words and Pictures

FROM **THE BOOK OF TWINS**
BY **DEBRA** AND **LISA GANZ**
WITH **ALEX TRESNIOWSKI,**
PHOTOGRAPHS BY
BILL BALLENBERG

Everyone likes to have someone to identify with, someone to relate to and be comfortable around. Sounds like a good friend, right? Now imagine that this person also looks exactly like you do! This is the unique relationship that identical twins share, and it goes beyond just sibling closeness or friendship.

Whether it's sharing a special language or the same dream, twins have a unique relationship that most people can't understand. Read these personal reflections of three pairs of twins as they explain what it's like to experience the world with "another me."

TOP TEN
MOST ANNOYING TWIN QUESTIONS

1. Are you two twins?
2. Do you have the same parents?
3. Are your boy/girl twins identical?
4. If I hit your twin, will you feel it?
5. Do you and your twin have ESP?
6. Can your parents tell you apart?
7. Why aren't you dressed alike?
8. Are you the same age?
9. Do you ever play tricks on people?
10. Which one is older?

GEORGE AND JAMES McDONALD

"I'm the good twin and you're the bad twin."

"I'm not the bad twin; you're the bad twin."

"Most of my friends say I'm the good twin and James is the bad twin."

"No, they don't."

"You know my friend Michael in Cub Scouts? He says it."

"Me and George joined the Cub Scouts about two years ago. You start out as a bobcat, then you're a wolf, then a bear. Right now we're bears."

"The cool thing about being a twin is, when one twin is picked on, then both twins gang up on that kid. So it's always two against one."

"So if someone holds one twin, the other twin comes over and punches him."

"You always have someone on your side."

"We fight a lot too. We just fought today."

"You started it."

"No, you did."

"No, I didn't."

"I forget how it started, but he started it."

"Let's talk about something else."

"We were throwing a ball and I threw it at his head and then he kicked me."

"Sometimes we have the same dreams on the same day."

"We have the same nightmares. One time I had a dream with monsters, a skeleton, giant octopuses. Then a couple of days later George had the same dream."

"It scared the living daylights out of me."

"We have the same bedroom, and it's always messy. George cleans up things better than me."

"I make messes and I put them away; James makes messes and he makes even more messes."

"I make messes and make you clean them up."

"I wish I was the messy one, then James would have to clean up."

"You know, we just had our tenth birthday party. My dad got me a remote control car and I drove it into George's feet."

"Most times we get the same presents, sometimes different stuff."

"And if he gets something I like and I get something he likes, we swap."

"Or we both play with it. We share it."

"We like being twins. Mostly it's fun."

"Yeah, it's fun being twins. You always have someone to play with."

ASK YOURSELF

- How are George and James alike? Different?

Consider what they say about each other.

NESHMAYDA AND SUZETTE AGUAYO

Early on they knew they were different from other children, because they were the only ones who shared a face. "They loved that about themselves," says Maria Aguayo, mother of Neshmayda and Suzette. "They had a way of communicating that no one else understood. One of them would point at something or make some noise and the other would go and get what she wanted." Two kids **cavorting** through a happy world of their own, experiencing life's surprises as one—in other words, twins.

But Suzy and Neshy were different for a much greater reason—they were born profoundly deaf. "We did not know it for their first two-and-a-half years," says Maria, who contracted German measles during her first trimester. The technology in her native Puerto Rico was not as advanced as it is today, so her twins' deafness was not **diagnosed** until they were nearly three. "And when we first discovered they were deaf, I did not want to believe it. It was a mother's denial."

Maria soon accepted her daughters' condition, and as soon as she and her husband, Joaquin, heard about the Gallaudet school for the deaf in Washington, D.C., they moved their family and enrolled the twins, then five years old. "We all learned sign language so we could communicate with the girls," says Maria. "We started to talk about all the things that had happened to them in their first five years. I learned all these things that I had not known. For instance, Suzette had once been with her grandmother and wound up in the emergency room getting stitches. Her grandmother didn't know how she got hurt. Suzy later told me that she had fallen, that she was scared, that she wanted me there with her in the hospital so badly. When I discovered these things, I cried and cried."

The twins helped each other learn signs—more and more signs—**ecstatic** at the opportunity to explore each other's feelings in a new way. "Being deaf twins is a very special thing," explains Neshy. "A deaf child in a hearing world can feel very lonely and secluded, but we never experienced that. We were always together, never alone. We learned from each other every day, and we still do."

Their parents exposed them to hearing children from a very early age, determined to foster their self-sufficiency. "We would take them to soccer practice, and they would stay behind a little, not daring to go on the field," remembers Maria. "They put up this wall between them and the rest of the world. But after a while they would feel more comfortable. They might get a ball and start kicking it between them, and then before we knew it they were mixing in with the other children."

NAMES FOR TWINS AROUND THE WORLD

Afrikaans: tweeling
Czech: duojce
Dutch: tweelingen
French: jumeaux
German: zwillinge
Hungarian: ikerpar
Irish: leatchupla
Italian: gemelli
Japanese: futago
Korean: ssang dong i
Polish: bli' zniak
Portuguese: gemeos
Spanish: gemelos
Swedish: tvilling
Turkish: ikizlerden biri

ASK YOURSELF

- Why do these sisters say that having a twin made life easier?

Reread the first paragraph and consider how these twins got along.

WORDS, WORDS, WORDS

cavorting: leaping, skipping, and being playful
diagnosed: to have figured out the cause of a medical problem
ecstatic: very happy

The twins excelled at a number of sports, particularly soccer, and together they helped **establish** a women's varsity soccer team at Gallaudet. They tried water-skiing, they hit the mountain slopes, they talked about one day skydiving from a plane. "They feel that they can do anything they want to do, except hear," says their mother. "They are very secure and confident about who they are, and that has come from them being two."

It is a closeness that will be tested now that the twins are facing their first **separation.** Suzy and Neshy—both pursuing master's degrees in social work—were also both recently engaged to be married, Suzy to a hearing-impaired teacher, and Neshy to a deaf legal assistant. Suzy and her future husband will live in Wisconsin, while Neshy plans to stay behind in Washington, D.C. "Of course, we'll miss each other terribly," says Neshy. "When one of us is not present, we feel half empty, so it's going to be really difficult." For the last few months, "they have been preparing themselves for the separation," says Maria. "To even start talking about it was extremely painful, but they have been getting ready."

When Suzy spent a few weeks with her fiancé in Wisconsin, the twins got a chance to see how the separation would go. "It was really tough not being able to communicate with her regularly," says Suzy. "I would write her letters, but by the time she'd read them, it was old news. Thank goodness for the Internet. Now we talk for hours and hours on the computer. We need to be able to share our feelings all the time, and this way we can."

Busy social lives, dreams of having children, an **addiction** to the Internet—perhaps the Aguayo twins are not so different after all. "They are so incredibly independent," says their mother. "I can't remember the last time I had to do something for them."

A life without sounds has had no impact on the extraordinary love that exists between them — they simply found a way to share the quiet music of their souls. What chance do time and distance have of changing the way they feel? "It's true we are becoming more independent of each other," Neshy says. "But it really doesn't matter. The longer we are apart, the closer we become."

ASK YOURSELF

- How does their relationship now compare with the way it was when they were children?

Think about what has changed and what hasn't.

WORDS, WORDS, WORDS

establish: to set up or start something
separation: an instance of being apart from someone
addiction: the need to use something for comfort or support

NFL
21

RONDE AND TIKI BARBER

Forget helmets, running shoes, shoulder pads. The one piece of equipment the Barber brothers can't live without is a cell phone. As professional football players drafted by different teams in 1997, Ronde and Tiki led the league in long-distance bills. "Within minutes after games, they'd be on the phone to each other," says their mother, Geraldine. "Even before they got home, they'd be talking on their cell phones in their cars."

Two guys tough enough to play in the NFL gabbing away like high schoolers? Being a twin means making that connection, no matter where you are or who might think you're soft or silly. "Yeah, we SURE ran those bills up," laughs Tiki, 23, a running back for the New York Giants. "I just wasn't used to being away from my brother." Ronde, who plays cornerback for the Tampa Bay Buccaneers, says, "I think my bill cracked $300 once. And we would just talk about nothing, you know? Like, how was your day, how's the team?"

Before living six states apart in their rookie season, the Barbers had never been separated for more than four days. "That was definitely tough," says Tiki, who roomed with his twin at the University of Virginia. "In college, we had structure, we had schoolwork, and we had each other. But in the NFL, you do your job and you go home. I would get home at 4:00 PM and just sit around until I got tired. That's when the phone bills went wild."

Dependent as they are on cellular technology, the Barbers have other ways of communicating. A look, a hug, a playful tackle—as twins they share an easy **intimacy** that seems to **elude** so many brothers. Growing up in Montgomery County, Virginia, they even had a secret language. "Basically, it was English, but nobody could understand it," says Tiki. "Drove our mother crazy." Geraldine Barber remembers it well. "It wasn't really a language, it was more like whistling," she says. "One night when they were five or six, I told Tiki to go get Ronde and find out what he wants to drink with dinner. Tiki started whistling, and his brother came downstairs and said, 'I want my grape soda.' No words, no question, just whistling."

ASK YOURSELF

- What are the different ways of communicating that the brothers have used?

Recall what you've read.

WORDS, WORDS, WORDS

dependent: relying on something to make a task easier
intimacy: a close personal relationship
elude: to escape or not be present in

When it came time to decide on a college, there was little **doubt** the Barbers would be picking only one. "I remember saying, 'You know, you don't have to go to college together,'" says their mom. "And they just kind of looked at me like I had dropped in from Mars. It never came up again." **Accepted** by the University of Virginia on football **scholarships,** Ronde (whose African name means "firstborn son") and Tiki (whose African name means "fiery tempered king") were roommates all four years. Small for their sport, they had to rely on toughness, quickness, and, of course, each other. "We always trained together," says Tiki. "And because we always had someone there to push us, that's why we were so good."

And it was because they were so good that they were finally forced apart. "We kind of knew we wouldn't end up on the same pro team," says Ronde. "That's why NFL draft day was such a bittersweet day." Those first few weeks away from each other were the most difficult. "The thing is, as twins we're closer than most people are," says Tiki. "Closer even than some husbands and wives." Says Ronde, "When you really care about someone, you worry about how they're doing all the time."

COMMON MISCONCEPTION

The first-born twin is older.

Twins are exactly the same age, regardless of who was born first, because they were conceived at the same time.

Then things got a little easier. Ronde met a woman, Claudia. The two started dating and are still together. "Before Claudia, I used to call Tiki every day," says Ronde. "Then I would call him every other day, then every third day." Tiki, who is engaged to marry his longtime girlfriend, Ginny, says, "We also weren't talking for two hours anymore. It became maybe 20 minutes."

Now the Barbers are old hands at being separated, but that doesn't mean they're ready to give up their cell phones. Co-owners of a house in Tampa Bay, Ronde and Tiki will never let different uniforms drive them apart. Say it's the Super Bowl, late in the fourth quarter. Would Ronde tackle Tiki to win the game? "I'd go for it," insists Ronde, but their mom doesn't think so. "Ronde would probably just sort of push Tiki out of bounds," says Geraldine. "See, these twins are very special kids. Between them, it's just always been, 'Don't worry brother, I got your back.'"

WORDS, WORDS, WORDS

doubt: uncertainty
accepted: formally admitted into a college or club
scholarships: grants or prizes that pay for people to go to college

THE SCIENCE OF TWINS

Knowing the biology of twins helps you understand why some twins look alike—and some don't.

WHAT ARE THE DIFFERENT TYPES OF TWINS?

There are two types of twins, identical and fraternal. Identical twins look exactly alike and are always of the same sex. Fraternal twins may look no more alike than any other two siblings. With both types of twins, the babies are carried in the mother's womb at the same time.

Identical twins result from a single zygote (fertilized egg) that later divides into two eggs as it grows. Because identical twins start from the same zygote, they are also referred to as monozygotic twins. A very rare subset of identical twins is conjoined twins (also known as Siamese twins). In the case of conjoined twins, the split is incomplete. Conjoined twins are born with their bodies still connected—often they share a torso. Either way, fully split or conjoined, each twin's genetic map is the same as the other's, and that is why they are identical.

Fraternal twins (also referred to as dizygotic twins) are born when two separate eggs have been fertilized in the womb at the same time. The two fertilized eggs grow into non-identical twins. The reason they are not identical is that fraternal twins do not have the same genetic map as each other, the way identical twins do. This is so even though fraternal twins are carried in the womb at the same time. Fraternal twins' genes are no more alike than those of siblings who are born at separate times. The genes of non-identical siblings, including fraternal twins, overlap by about 50 percent. In fact, fraternal twins can be a boy and a girl, two girls, or two boys.

Most twins are fraternal. Only about 30 percent of twins are identical. What determines the inherited traits of twins, identical or not? The answer is genes.

WHAT ARE GENES?

All zygotes contain a genetic map made up of genes. At birth, a person's genes contain all the inherited traits he or she needs to physically grow into an adult. Genes decide a person's eye and hair color, height, and everything else to do with the way a person will look.

Some scientists think genes also play a role in determining personality. Generally, 50 percent of a person's genes comes from the mother and 50 percent from the father. This mixture of genes from one's parents, the genetic map, is carried in the cells of the human body. Genes are so small that people can see them only with the help of very powerful microscopes.

HOW ARE IDENTICAL TWINS NOT ALIKE?

Identical twins are not always exactly alike. First, while in the womb, one twin usually dominates and receives more of the blood supply. The dominant twin is born longer and heavier than the other twin. This size advantage is usually continued throughout puberty and adulthood. In fact, at birth there is typically more of a difference in size between identical twins than fraternal twins.

Second, there are many traits that genes do not control. Traits that are affected by a person's experiences are called learned traits. Identical twins may like different foods or music, or excel at different subjects in school. Actually, scientists do not know exactly what genes control and what they don't.

Third, rather than share identical traits, identical twins can mirror each other. For example, one will be right-handed while the other is left-handed. Sometimes mirroring goes so far that one twin's organs will be on the opposite side of the body than they should be on. Mirroring is generally a feature of identical twins who separated late in the fetus stage.

WHAT CAN WE LEARN FROM STUDYING TWINS?

Scientists have been studying twins since the late 1800s. One of the first scientists to study twins was Sir Francis Galton, Charles Darwin's cousin. Actually, the science of behavioral genetics is based on the theories and methods he developed in the 1870s. Galton suggested, based on his research, that twins who looked alike did so because they had inherited the same genetic makeup. He also believed that twins who did not look alike had not inherited the same genetic makeup.

Today, there is still information scientists want to know about genetics. Twins play an important role in the general study of genetics, not just genetics having to do with twins. By studying twins, especially those who were separated at birth, scientists hope to discover how important genes are, compared to environmental factors. Specific areas of study include the development of personality and the likelihood of being afflicted by certain diseases.

This question, or debate, is often referred to as "nature vs. nurture" or "heredity vs. the environment." Many researchers agree that nature and nurture together develop and affect our personalities and health.

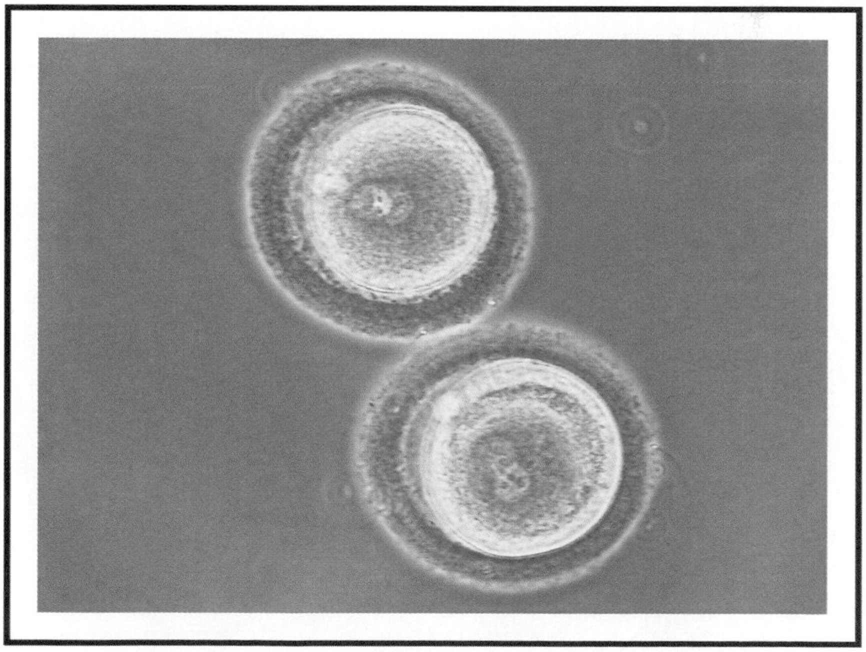

A magnified view: a single zygote (fertilized egg) that has split into two eggs.

Wrap-Up

TALK ABOUT IT

Now that you've read "Twins: A Celebration in Words and Pictures" and "The Science of Twins," what do you have to say about these questions?

- Do you wish you had a twin? Or if you have one, do you wish you didn't? Why or why not?
- Do you think we are born with our own personalities? Or are we the products of family, friends, culture, etc.? Explain.

COMPREHENSION CHECK

Write your answers to the questions below. Use information from the photo essay and the textbook selection to support your answers.

1. What do the three sets of twins all have in common?
2. Why might Neshmayda and Suzette have felt lonely and secluded without each other?
3. Why do you think it gets harder for twins to remain close as they get older?
4. What is the difference between identical twins and fraternal twins?
5. How might a scientist explain the fact that the Barber twins both excelled at football?

VOCABULARY CHECK

diagnosed **scholarships** **elude**
doubt **ecstatic**

Complete each sentence with the correct vocabulary word.

1. The doctor _______ my aches and pains as the flu.
2. My sister and I are hoping to go to college on soccer _______.
3. Luckily, the answers did not _______ me during the math test.
4. I _______ that I'll be able to get out of baby-sitting this weekend.
5. My parents were _______ with the good grades on my report card.

WRITE ABOUT IT

Choose one of the writing prompts below.

- Make a list of your physical traits. After each thing, tell who in your family shares that trait.
- If you had just been separated from your twin for the first time, how do you think it would feel? Write a letter from one twin to another, describing what it feels like to be separated.
- Finish this statement: Sharing is great, but one thing I would never want to share is. . . . Then write a paragraph explaining why you feel this way.

Fact FILE

Did you know:

- Only one out of every 36 live human births produces a twin or other multiple. These odds used to be much higher. During the 1960s about one in every 85 births produced a twin or other multiple.
- About one third of twins are identical. One third are same-sex, fraternal twins. And one third are boy-girl fraternal twins. Slightly more than one-half of all twins born are male.
- Two babies born together are twins; three are triplets; four are quadruplets; five are quintuplets; six are sextuplets; seven are septuplets; eight are octuplets; nine are nonuplets; and ten are decaplets!
- Each year, during the first full weekend in August, a festival is held in Twinsburg, Ohio. It's reported to be the largest annual gathering of twins in the world.

Analyzing a Savings Statement

You want to save some money, so you've opened a savings account. Good idea. Now you'll earn interest on your money.

Every month your bank will send a statement to tell you about your account. Will you know how to read it? Look at the statement below. Can you figure it out?

Tonya's Savings Account Statement

SAVINGS ACCOUNT #9180762370

Interest rate: 4% per year
Interest added quarterly

A "deposit" is money that you have put into your account. A "withdrawal" is money that you have taken out.

The "balance" is how much money is in your account. The balance changes whenever you make a deposit or withdrawal.

ACCOUNT ACTIVITY

	Date	Deposit/Withdrawal	Interest	Balance
Previous Balance	3/1			$217.79
	3/9	$58.23		$159.56
	3/13	$106.55		$266.11
	3/25	$33.89		$300.00
	3/31		$3.00	$303.00

Banks pay you to keep money in a savings account. That payment is called "interest."

******Savings Account Summary*******
1 Withdrawal: $58.23 2 Deposits: $140.44
Interest earned this quarter: $3.00

"Try not to take too much money out of your savings account. The more money you keep in the account, the more interest you will earn!"

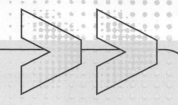

Save It!

Test your savings IQ. Reread the statement and tips. Then use the savings statement to answer the questions. Write your answers on your own paper.

1. What was Tonya's balance at the beginning of March? What was her balance at the end of March? Did the balance go up or down? By how much?

2. On what date did Tonya make a deposit of $106.55? What was the new balance in her account? What was the amount of the deposit Tonya made on March 25? What was her new balance after that transaction?

3. On April 1, Tonya will deposit $25.67 into her savings account. What will her new balance be?
a. $25.67 **c.** $328.00
b. $277.33 **d.** $328.67

4. How much interest did Tonya earn in March?

5. Tonya's bank pays interest on her savings account every quarter (three months). She got an interest payment in March. In which other months will she be paid interest?
a. December, January, and February
b. July, October, and January
c. April, May, and June
d. June, September, and December

It Pays to Save

Write down three good reasons to keep your money in a savings account.

Savings Log

You're saving for a stereo that costs $350. You start with a balance of $20. Each week you deposit a $100 paycheck and withdraw $30 to spend. Plus, the first week you have to take out $20 for an emergency. How long will it take to save $350?

"You can find the interest rates for savings accounts on many banks' Web sites. Sometimes you can even check your balance through the bank's online services."

Real-World Words

balance: the amount left after a deposit or withdrawal
quarterly: in banking, once every three months
transaction: an exchange of funds; usually, a deposit or withdrawal

profile

Eileen Collins

Space Shuttle Commander

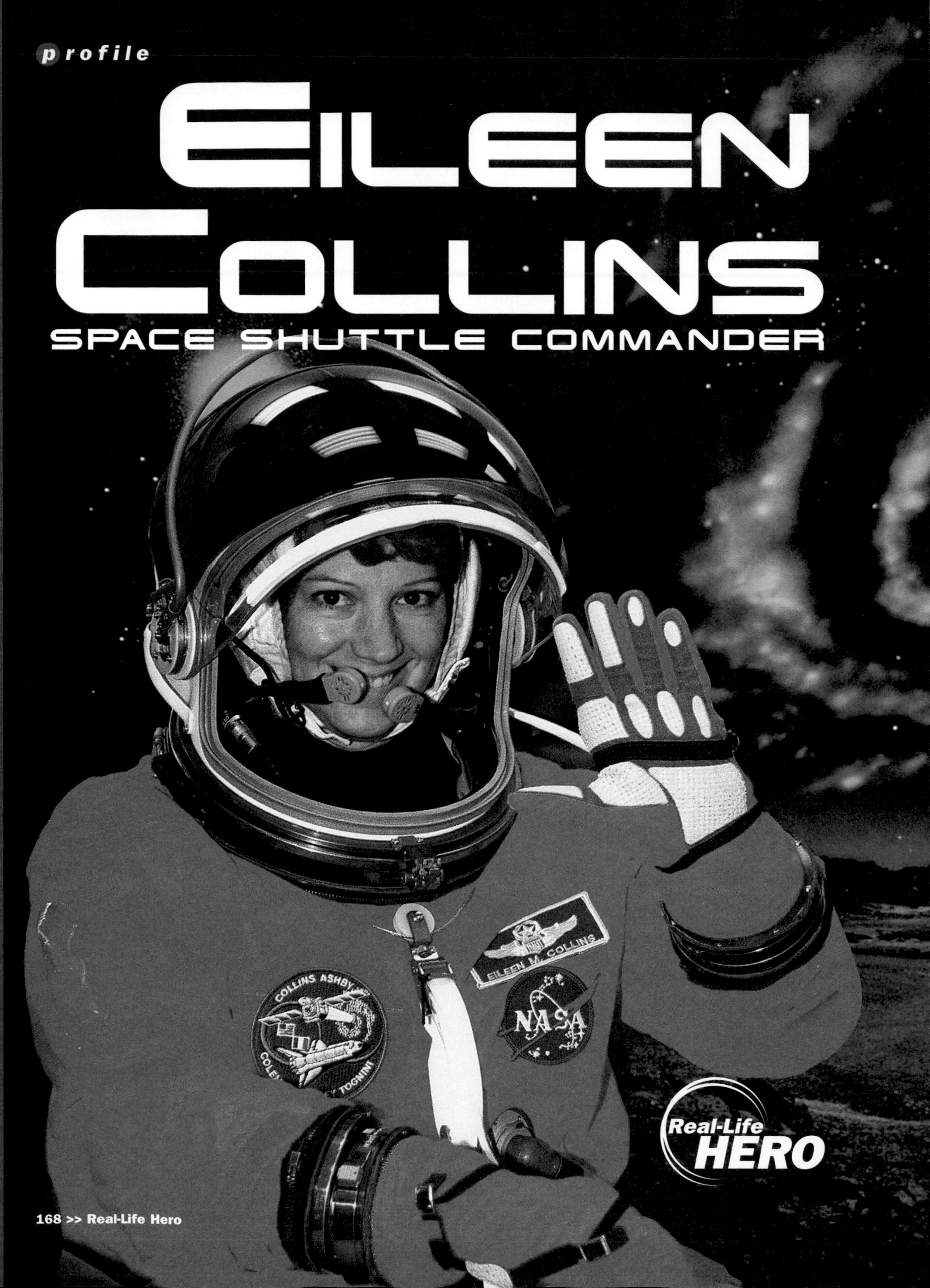
COLLINS ASHBY
EILEEN M. COLLINS
NASA
Real-Life HERO

Eileen Collins finds her wings, and a dream comes true.

How could she spend her life bent over a calculator when the sky was calling?

Finally, Eileen Collins was in the sky alone, high over upstate New York. She'd worked hard to get there, slaving nights at a pizza parlor to save $1,000 for pilot's lessons. Now, at 20, she was flying solo for the first time.

Everything went fine for several minutes. Then, all of a sudden, the cabin door popped open in a rush of air. Eileen steadied her nerves, kept her hands on the controls, and said to herself, "I'm just going to keep going."

That's exactly what she did—even after she landed. The working-class girl from Elmira, NY, kept going all the way through college and into the Air Force. She worked her way through pilot training and two master's degrees. She put in 16-hour days in the elite Air Force test pilot program. And when NASA picked her for astronaut training, she didn't stop until she'd been in orbit as the first woman ever to command a space shuttle.

On March 5, 1998, Hillary Clinton announced the news in a big ceremony at the White House. Eileen got up and told the world what the milestone meant to her. "When I was a child, I dreamed about space," she said. "I admired pilots, astronauts, and explorers of all kinds. It was only a dream that I would someday be one of them. It is my hope that all children, boys and girls, will see this mission and be inspired to reach for their dreams, because dreams do come true."

Space Dreams

To a nine-year-old girl growing up in Elmira, NASA seemed as far away as the moon. Eileen's parents had just separated and money was scarce. Her dad was changing jobs and her mom was trying to find one. Eileen and her mother lived in public housing and survived on food stamps for six months.

While her parents struggled to put food on the table, Eileen's imagination took off. She spent hours at the National Soaring Museum in town, gawking at the gliders on display. Instead of expensive trips to Cape Canaveral, the family went on outings to the local airport to watch the planes take off and land.

In high school, Eileen soon found she wasn't gifted. She made up for it by working hard and concentrating. "I was not blessed with the ability to learn things quickly," she says. "I was blessed with the ability to sit still and stay focused." Math was the subject that finally clicked for Eileen. "If you keep working at something—do the problems and assignments—eventually you will understand it, and it might even become interesting. And once you're interested, it's not work anymore, it becomes fun."

When she showed a passion for math, her father suggested she become an accountant. But Eileen still had her head in the clouds. She devoured books about famous pilots. There was Amelia Earhart, the pioneer who had disappeared mysteriously over the Atlantic in 1937. There were the WASPs (Women's Airforce Service Pilots), who flew during World War II. How could she spend her life bent over a calculator when the sky was calling?

Commander Collins at work in space.

Finding Her Path

"It wasn't until after high school that I finally decided I was going to do what I wanted—and not what everyone else was doing," Eileen says. And she recommends this to young kids today as well. "Kids need to look at themselves as individuals and do things that interest them. Explore different things they might enjoy."

After Eileen graduated, she started studying math and science at a community college. She studied by day and served pizza at night until she saved enough to learn how to fly. An Air Force scholarship put her through college. Then, in 1978, she headed for Vance Air Force Base in Oklahoma for pilot training. The class consisted of 320 men, Eileen, and three other women.

"It was like being in a fishbowl," she says of the training. "Everyone knew who we were, what we looked like, how we did on our work. People wanted to know how the 'women' were doing." It was a tough experience, but it made Eileen work even harder.

Breaking New Ground

The gender ratio improved over the next **decade** while Eileen was instructing pilots at the Air Force. But she was still a woman in a man's world. She responded by outworking everyone. In 1989 she made it into the highly **selective** test pilot program on the third try. "For one solid year, my job was to fly 26 different airplanes, study, write papers, make speeches, take check rides and get graded on every move I made," she says. "We worked 16-hour days and there was no time for anything else." In the middle of that year, the effort paid off. She was chosen for the astronaut program.

The world learned about Eileen in 1995 when she was picked to pilot the space shuttle. Suddenly reporters were knocking her door down. Strangers came up to her in diners and asked for her autograph. Everyone wanted to know about the first woman ever

WORDS, WORDS, WORDS

decade: a period of ten years
selective: having the power to choose carefully
motivated: encouraged someone to do something
reflects: thinks back on something
conflict: a clash or disagreement

to steer a space shuttle into orbit.

Eileen just shrugs her shoulders and tries to focus on the thing that's always **motivated** her: the work. "I don't think about being the first," she tells reporters. "I just worry about getting the job done."

As usual, she did just that. On February 2, 1995, she took the shuttle into orbit at 40 miles per *second*. She and her crew linked up with the Russian space station, launched and retrieved a satellite, conducted a space walk, and more. They circled the earth 129 times and returned for a smooth landing, all in 10 days. "Being up in space can be difficult," Eileen **reflects.** "But when you take a break from the work, and can look out the window at the earth—that is the best reward."

By the time Eileen went up as commander, in July 1999, she had a three-year-old daughter to watch the liftoff. "She's the only shuttle commander with baby bottles on her office desk, between the stacks of checklists," says her pilot, Jeffrey Ashby.

That is a situation some people still aren't ready for. NASA had to make sure they picked a crew of open-minded men to go up with Commander Collins. "There are probably still a lot of men around who don't like taking orders from women," says David Leestma, director of NASA flight crew operations.

If she's had any **conflict** on her way up, Eileen prefers to shrug it off. "Eventually, having a woman in these roles won't be news anymore," she says. "It will be both accepted and expected."

If that's the case, Commander Collins's hard work will pay off for generations of girls—not to mention her own daughter. As Eileen was preparing for her mission as commander, Bridget started declaring that she wanted to be an astronaut. "Have you ever been to the moon?" she would ask her mom.

"No," Eileen would reply, "but someday *you* can go there." ●

ASK YOURSELF

- How did Eileen's life change after 1995?

List the most important events and put them in order.

EILEEN COLLINS RESUMÉ

NAME:
- Eileen Marie Collins

BORN:
- November 19, 1956
  Elmira, New York

GOALS:
- to explore the world and space
- to inspire kids around the world to pursue their dreams

WORK HISTORY:
- ten years as an instructor pilot in the Air Force
- three years as a math professor at the Air Force Academy
- nine years as a NASA astronaut, shuttle pilot, and commander

EDUCATION:
- bachelor's degree in math and economics, Syracuse University, 1978
- master's degree in operations research, Stanford University, 1986
- master's degree in space systems management, Webster University, 1989

MAJOR ACHIEVEMENTS:
- became first woman to pilot space shuttle, on mission to link up with Russian space station, 1995
- placed 50,000-pound X-ray telescope in space as first woman shuttle commander, 1999

Space Exploration

The development of rockets has allowed us to visit the Moon and to study space—from space. Humans can now live and work in space using space shuttles and stations.

Going Into Space

Three hundred years ago, there was a scientist named Isaac Newton. He had an idea that a cannon placed on the top of a high mountain might be able to fire an object so fast that it would fly around Earth in a circle. He thought this would happen without it ever crashing back to the ground. His idea became reality in 1957. That's when the first artificial satellite (spacecraft) was launched.

To go into space and stay above Earth, a satellite has to reach a speed of about 17,500 miles per hour. At that speed, the satellite's power is shut off. It then coasts on an orbit around Earth. The satellite is still in Earth's gravity. However, the pull of gravity back toward Earth is canceled out by the speed at which the satellite is traveling.

Sergei Korolev

Wernher von Braun

Rocket Pioneers

Two of the first people to build rockets were Sergei Korolev (1906–1966) and Wernher von Braun (1912–1977). Korolev worked in Russia and developed the first artificial satellite, *Sputnik-1*.

Von Braun built long-range rockets for the German Army. Then in the 1950s, he went to America and switched to space research. Von Braun was responsible for the first American satellites as well as directing the Apollo Moon missions.

The photograph (left) shows the *Saturn V* rocket launching the *Apollo 11* spacecraft on July 16, 1969. This was for the first moon landing.

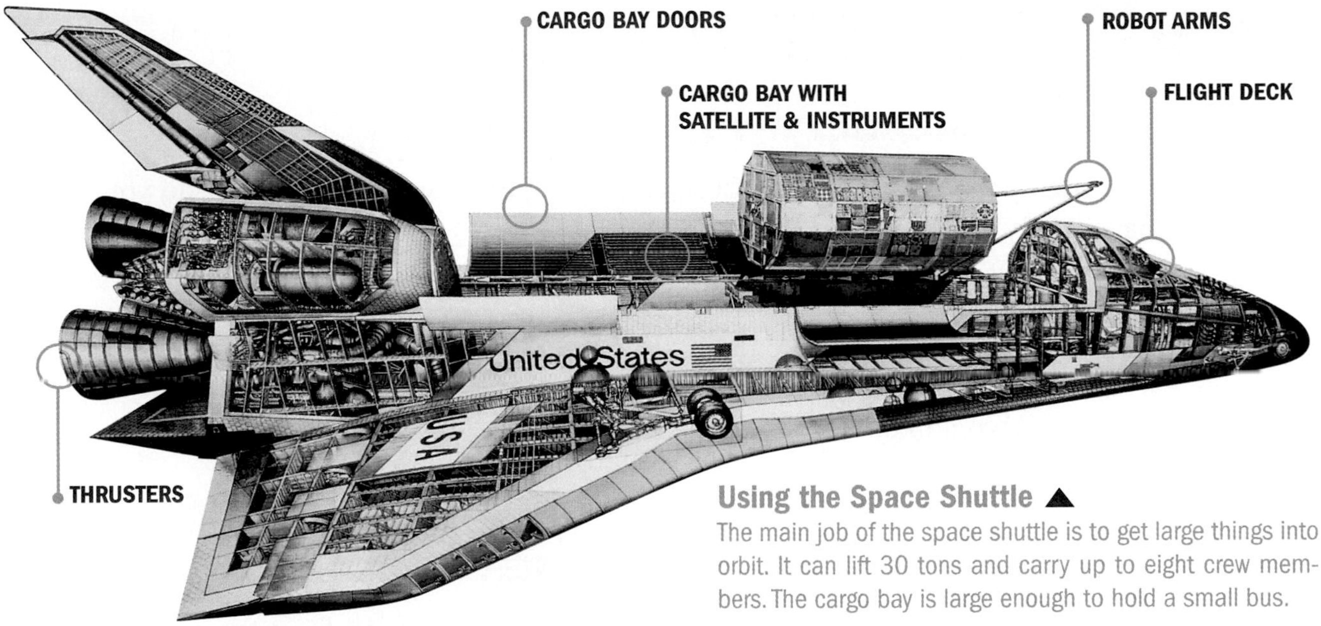
CARGO BAY DOORS
CARGO BAY WITH SATELLITE & INSTRUMENTS
ROBOT ARMS
FLIGHT DECK
THRUSTERS
United States
USA

Using the Space Shuttle ▲
The main job of the space shuttle is to get large things into orbit. It can lift 30 tons and carry up to eight crew members. The cargo bay is large enough to hold a small bus.

Types of Satellite

There are three main types of satellite: scientific, commercial, and military. Scientific satellites include telescopes, weather satellites, and space stations. Commercial satellites include communications satellites that are used for telephones and television transmissions. Military satellites may be used for spying.

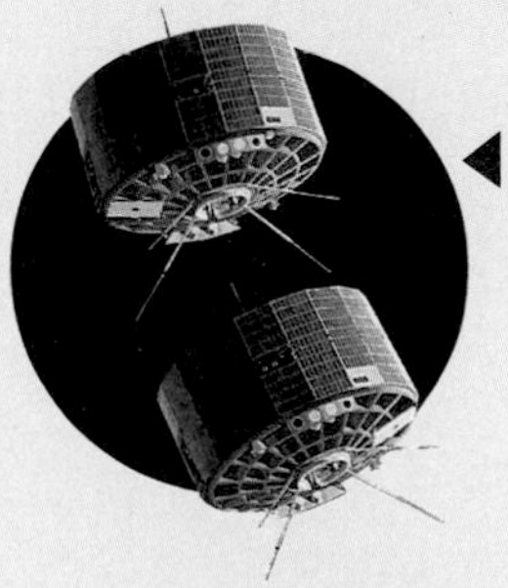

◀ Weather Satellite

Communications Satellite ▶

◀ Astronomy Satellite (Telescope)

The Space Shuttle

Most rockets can be sent into space only once. The space shuttle is the only reusable space vehicle.

At launch, its three rocket thrusters and two fuel boosters provide almost the same lift as a *Saturn V* rocket. They get the shuttle into space in less than five minutes. The shuttle takes off vertically like a rocket, and it glides back to Earth to land like a normal airplane. The shuttle will carry crews and supplies to the *International Space Station*. ●

Space Stations

A space station is a place for living and working. There, astronauts can spend many months at a time in space. Inside the stations, astronauts are weightless.

They must use exercise machines to keep their bones and muscles strong. The bathrooms are designed to work in the weightless environment, and the astronauts can wear everyday clothes. The U.S.A.'s first space station, *Skylab*, was placed in orbit in 1973.

The *International Space Station* is a joint project between the U.S. and 15 other nations. Several sections of the *International Space Station* will be put together over several years into the 21st century.

Wrap-Up

TALK ABOUT IT

Now that you've read "Eileen Collins" and "Space Exploration," what do you have to say about these questions?

- Eileen was the first female commander of a space shuttle. Would you like to be the first person to do something? If so, what? If you said no, why not?
- Would you be interested in taking a trip up to a space station? What do you think it would be like? Explain.

COMPREHENSION CHECK

Write your answers to the questions below. Use information from the profile and the encyclopedia entry to support your answers.

1. When Eileen Collins was growing up, how did she satisfy her interest in flying?
2. Why did Eileen's father suggest she become an accountant even though she wanted to be an astronaut?
3. Why do you think Eileen recommends that all young people should follow their own interests?
4. What are the three main types of satellites?
5. What is the importance of the *International Space Station*?

VOCABULARY CHECK

Complete each sentence starter below. Before you answer, think about the meaning of the vocabulary word in bold.

1. In a **decade,** I see myself . . .
2. A person who **reflects** before acting . . .
3. Sometimes it's hard to get **motivated** to . . .
4. People who are **selective** about their friends might . . .
5. A good way to settle a **conflict** is . . .

WRITE ABOUT IT

Choose one of the writing prompts below.

- As the commander of a space shuttle, write three journal entries about what it is like to be in space circling the earth.
- You have just been chosen to be the first kid in space. Write a speech to give to the world.
- Write a poem titled "Reach For Your Dream."

Fact FILE

Women in Space

Eileen Collins was the first female commander of a space shuttle. But long before Collins, there were many women who dreamed of flying to the stars.

- **The late 1950s.** Women were first considered as potential astronauts, and thirteen women completed the initial screening used for Mercury astronauts.
- **1959.** Jerrie Cobb becomes the first woman to report for astronaut testing.
- **June 18, 1983.** Sally Ride becomes the first American woman in space.
- **September 12, 1992.** Mae Jemison becomes the first African-American woman in space.
- **September 26, 1996.** Shannon Lucid breaks the record for longest period in space of any American—188 days, 4 hours, 14 seconds.

Writing a Resumé

You've spotted an ad for the perfect part-time job—manager of a snack bar. What can you do to show the employer that you're perfect for the job? Write a resumé! A resumé is a short history of your education, skills, and job experiences.

Check out the resumé below. What would yours say?

Sample Resumé

A resumé must include your name, address, and phone number so the employer can contact you.

What were your duties at other jobs? Be sure to describe them to show what kinds of skills you've learned.

After-school activities show employers that you are hardworking and responsible. That's especially important if you have no job experience.

Julie Garrison
123 Morning Court
Silver Spring, MD 20903
(410) 555-3580

Work Experience

Dog- and House-sitting, 2000–2002
Responsibilities: watch homes and pets while owners are on vacation; feed and walk dogs; water plants; make sure windows and doors are locked/undisturbed; 5 clients

Lawn and Yard Maintenance, 1999-2002
Responsibilities: keep to schedules and cut neighbors' lawns on a weekly basis; 10 clients

Paper Route, 1998-1999
Responsibilities: organize newspapers; know neighborhood streets and addresses; collect subscription money; deliver newspapers in a timely manner

Other Interests

Student Council, homeroom representative
Theater Club, stage crew
School Newspaper, sports reporter

Education

Martin Luther King Jr. Middle School, 1999-2002
Hillandale Elementary School, 1993-1999

References

Marilyn and James Finkel (house-sitting clients)
(410) 555-8976
Jennifer Gleason (school-paper advisor)
(410) 555-1463

"A reference is someone employers can call to find out whether you're a good worker. It's a good idea to use adults, especially people you've worked for. Make sure it's okay with your references before you use their names."

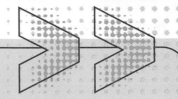

Help Wanted!

Julie Garrison is applying for the job at the snack bar. Does her resumé show she's the right person for the job? Review her resumé and the tips. Then use them to answer the questions below. Write your answers on your own paper.

1. The snack-bar owner wants someone who has handled money. In what way does Julie meet this qualification?
   a. She used to collect newspaper-subscription money.
   b. She was in the stage crew of a school play.
   c. She was a clerk at a bank.

2. The owner also wants someone who will be good with customers. Which item on Julie's resumé shows that she gets along well with people?
   a. She watches houses and dogs.
   b. She participates in many school activities.
   c. She always delivered the newspaper on time.

3. The owner of the snack bar needs to hire someone who can work alone, without much supervision. Do you think Julie could do it? Why or why not?

4. Who are Julie's references? Why do you think she chose these people to include on her resumé?

5. Do you think Julie is a good candidate for the job of snack-bar manager? Why or why not?

Plan It

On a sheet of paper, list the work experiences, activities, interests, and skills that you could put on a resumé. Then list the names, addresses, and phone numbers of two people you could use as references.

Write It

Use your list from "Plan It." Arrange the information into a resumé format. Use Julie's resumé as a model. Have a partner review it.

"A resumé doesn't have to be fancy. But it should be neat and legible. Type yours on a computer. Be sure to check it carefully for spelling mistakes."

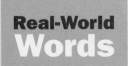

Real-World Words

candidate: a person who seeks a job or political office
qualification: a skill or experience that makes someone fit for a job
supervision: direction; guidance

short story

Broken Chain

By Gary Soto

Alfonso thinks he can have it all—except straight teeth. With no money for braces, can he ever look good enough to get a girl?

Alfonso sat on the porch trying to push his crooked teeth to where he thought they belonged. He hated the way he looked. Last week he did fifty sit-ups a day, thinking that he would burn those already apparent ripples on his stomach to even deeper ripples, dark ones, so when he went swimming at the canal next summer, girls in cut-offs would notice. And the guys would think he was tough, someone who could take a punch and give it back. He wanted "cuts" like those he had seen on a calendar of an Aztec warrior standing on a pyramid with a woman in his arms. The calendar hung above the cash register at La Plaza. Orsua, the owner, said Alfonso could have the calendar at the end of the year if the waitress, Yolanda, didn't take it first.

Alfonso studied the magazine pictures of rock stars for a hairstyle. He liked the way Prince looked—and the bass player from Los Lobos. Alfonso thought he would look cool with his hair razored into a V in the back and streaked purple. But he knew his mother wouldn't go for it. And his father, who was *puro Mexicano,* would sit in his chair after work, sullen as a toad, and call him "sissy."

Alfonso didn't dare color his hair. But one day he had had it butched on the top, like in the magazines. His father had come home that evening from a softball game, happy that his team had drilled four homers in a thirteen-to-five bashing of Color Tile. He'd swaggered into the living room, but had stopped cold when he saw Alfonso and asked, not joking but with real concern, "Did you hurt your head at school? *Qué pasó*?"

Alfonso had pretended not to hear his father and had gone to his room, where he studied his hair from all angles in the mirror. He liked what he saw until he smiled and realized for the first time that his teeth were crooked, like a pile of wrecked cars. He grew depressed and turned away from the mirror. He sat on his bed and leafed through the rock magazine until he came to the rock star with the butched top. His mouth was closed, but Alfonso was sure his teeth weren't crooked.

Alfonso didn't want to be the handsomest kid at school, but he was determined to be better-looking than average. The next day he spent his lawn-mowing money on a new shirt, and, with a pocketknife, scooped the moons of dirt from under his fingernails.

He spent hours in front of the mirror trying to herd his teeth into place with his thumb. He asked his mother if he could have braces, like Frankie Molina, her godson, but he asked at the wrong time. She was at the kitchen table licking the envelope to the house payment. She glared up at him. "Do you think money grows on trees?"

His mother clipped coupons from magazines and newspapers, and kept a vegetable garden in the summer. Their family ate a lot of *frijoles,* which was OK because nothing else tasted so good, though one time Alfonso had had Chinese pot stickers and thought they were the next best food in the world.

GLOSSARY

puro Mexicano: truly Mexican
qué pasó?: What happened?
frijoles: beans
abuelitas: grandmothers
pendejos: fools
chale: no way
menso: dummy

He didn't ask his mother for braces again, even when she was in a better mood. He decided to fix his teeth by pushing on them with his thumbs. After breakfast that Saturday he went to his room, closed the door quietly, turned the radio on, and pushed for three hours straight.

He pushed for ten minutes, rested for five, and every half hour, during a radio commercial, checked to see if his smile had improved. It hadn't.

ASK Yourself

- How do you think Alfonso feels about himself?

Think about what you've learned about his character so far.

Eventually he grew bored and went outside with an old gym sock to wipe down his bike, a ten-speed. His thumbs were tired and wrinkled and pink, the way they got when he stayed in the bathtub too long.

Alfonso's older brother, Ernie, rode up on *his* bicycle looking depressed. He parked his bike against the peach tree and sat on the back steps, keeping his head down and stepping on ants that came too close.

Alfonso knew better than to say anything when Ernie looked mad. He turned his bike over, balancing it on the handlebars and seat, and flossed the spokes with the sock. When he was finished, he pressed a knuckle to his teeth until they tingled.

Ernie groaned and said, "Ah, man."

Alfonso waited a few minutes before asking, "What's the matter?" He pretended not to be too interested. He picked up a wad of steel wool and continued cleaning the spokes.

Ernie hesitated, not sure if Alfonso would laugh. But it came out. "Those girls didn't show up. And you better not laugh."

"What girls?"

Then Alfonso remembered his brother bragging about how he and Frostie met two girls from Kings Canyon Junior High last week at a costume party. They were dressed as gypsies, the costume for all poor Chicanas—they just had to borrow scarves and gaudy red lipstick from their *abuelitas*.

Alfonso walked over to his brother. He compared their two bikes: his **gleamed** like a handful of dimes, while Ernie's looked dirty.

"They said we were supposed to wait at the corner. But they didn't show up. Me and Frostie waited and waited like *pendejos*. They were playing games with us."

Alfonso thought that was a pretty dirty trick but sort of funny too. He would have to try that some day.

"Were they cute?" Alfonso asked.

"I guess so."

"Do you think you could recognize them?"

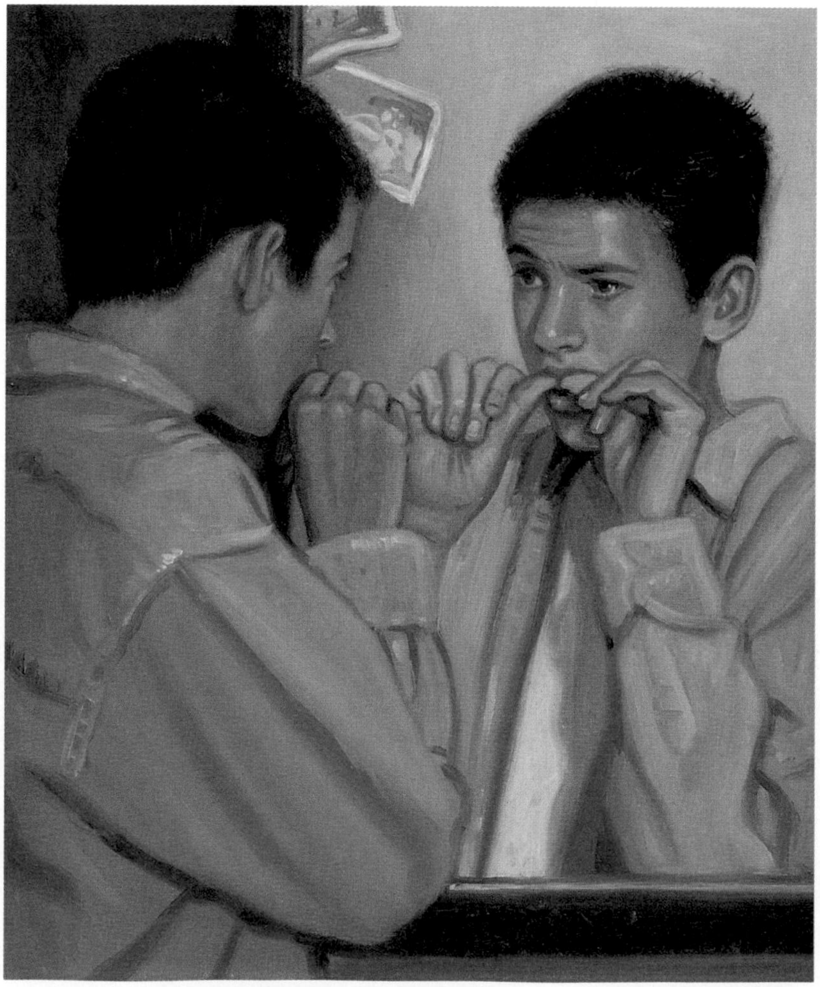

"If they were wearing red lipstick, maybe."

Alfonso sat with his brother in silence, both of them smearing ants with their floppy high tops.

Later that day, Alfonso sat on the porch pressing on his teeth. Press, relax; press, relax. His portable radio was on, but not loud enough to make Mr. Rojas come down the steps and wave his cane at him.

Alfonso's father drove up. Alfonso could tell by the way he sat in his truck that his team had lost their softball game. Alfonso got off the porch in a hurry because he knew his father would be in a bad mood. He went to the backyard, where he unlocked his bike, sat on it with the kickstand down, and pressed on his teeth. He punched himself in the stomach, and growled, "Cuts." Then he patted his butch and whispered, "Fresh."

After a while Alfonso pedaled up the street, hands in his pockets, toward Foster's Freeze, where he was chased by a rat-like Chihuahua. At his old school, John Burroughs Elementary, he found a kid hanging upside down on the top of a barbed-wire fence with a girl looking up at him. Alfonso skidded to a stop and helped the kid untangle his pants from the barbed wire. The kid was grateful. He had been afraid he would have to stay up there all night. His sister, who was Alfonso's age, was also grateful. If she had to go home and tell her mother that Frankie was stuck on a fence and couldn't get down, she would get scolded.

"Thanks," she said. "What's your name?"

Alfonso remembered her from his school and noticed that she was kind of cute, with ponytails and straight teeth. "Alfonso. You go to my school, huh?"

"Yeah. I've seen you around. You live nearby?"

"Over on Madison."

"My uncle used to live on that street, but he moved to Stockton."

"Stockton's near Sacramento, isn't it?"

"You been there?"

"No." Alfonso looked down at his shoes. He wanted to say something clever the way people do on TV. But the only thing he could think to say was that the governor lived in Sacramento. As soon as he shared this **observation,** he **winced** inside.

Alfonso walked with the girl and the boy as they started for home. They didn't talk much. Every few steps, the girl, whose name was Sandra, would look at him out of the corner of her eye, and Alfonso would look away. He learned that she was in the same grade as him, and that she had a pet terrier named Queenie. Her father was a mechanic at Rudy's Speedy Repair, and her mother was a teacher's aide at Jefferson Elementary.

When they came to the street, Alfonso and Sandra stopped at her corner, but her brother ran home. Alfonso watched him stop in the front yard to talk to a lady he guessed was their mother. She was raking leaves into a pile.

"I live over there," she said, pointing.

Alfonso looked over her shoulder for a long time, trying to **muster** enough nerve to ask her if she'd like to go bike riding tomorrow.

Shyly, he asked, "You wanna go bike riding?"

"Maybe." She played with a ponytail and crossed one leg in front of the other. "But my bike has a flat."

"I can get my brother's bike. He won't mind."

She thought for a moment before she said, "OK. But not tomorrow. I have to go to my aunt's."

"How about after school on Monday?"

"I have to take care of my brother until my mom comes home from work. How 'bout four-thirty?"

"OK," he said. "Four-thirty." Instead of parting immediately, they talked for a while, asking questions

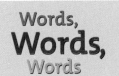

Words, Words, Words

gleamed: shined brightly
observation: a comment about something
winced: made a quick movement because of pain or embarrassment
muster: to gather something together

like, "Who's your favorite group?" "Have you ever been on the Big Dipper at Santa Cruz?" and "Have you ever tasted pot stickers?" But the question-and-answer period ended when Sandra's mother called her home.

Alfonso took off as fast as he could on his bike, jumped the curb, and, cool as he could be, raced away with his hands stuffed in his pockets. But when he looked back over his shoulder, the wind raking through his butch, Sandra wasn't even looking. She was already on her lawn, heading for the porch.

That night he took a bath, **pampered** his hair, and did more than his usual set of exercises. In bed, in between the push-and-rest on his teeth, he pestered his brother to let him borrow his bike.

"Come on, Ernie," he whined. "Just for an hour."

"*Chale,* I might want to use it."

"Come on, man, I'll let you have my trick-or-treat candy."

"What you got?"

"Three chocolates and some hard candies."

"Who's going to use it?"

Alfonso **hesitated,** then risked the truth. "I met this girl. She doesn't live too far."

Ernie rolled over on his stomach and stared at the outline of his brother, whose head was resting on his elbow. "*You* got a girlfriend?"

"She ain't my girlfriend, just a girl."

"What does she look like?"

"Like a girl."

"Come on, what does she look like?"

"She's got ponytails and a little brother."

"Ponytails! Those girls who messed with Frostie and me had ponytails. Is she cool?"

"I think so."

Ernie sat up in bed. "I bet you that's her."

Alfonso felt his stomach knot up. "She's going to be my girlfriend, not yours!"

"I'm going to get even with her!"

"You better not touch her," Alfonso snarled, throwing a wadded tissue at him. "I'll run you over with my bike."

For the next hour, until their mother threatened them from the living room to be quiet or else, they argued whether it was the same girl who had stood Ernie up. Alfonso said over and over that she was too nice to pull a stunt like that. But Ernie argued that she lived only two blocks from where those girls had told them to wait, that she was in the same grade, and, the clincher, that she had ponytails. Secretly, however, Ernie was jealous that his brother, two years younger than himself, might have found a girlfriend.

Sunday morning, Ernie and Alfonso stayed away from each other, though over breakfast they fought over the last tortilla. Their mother, sewing at the kitchen table, warned them to knock it off. At church they made faces at one another when the priest, Father Jerry, wasn't looking. Ernie punched Alfonso in the arm, and Alfonso, his eyes wide with anger, punched back.

Monday morning they hurried to school on their bikes, neither saying a word, though they rode side by side. In first period, Alfonso worried himself sick. How would he borrow a bike for her? He considered asking his best friend, Raul, for his bike. But Alfonso knew Raul, a paper boy with dollar signs in his eyes, would charge him, and he had less than sixty cents, counting the soda bottles he could cash.

Between history and math, Alfonso saw Sandra and her girlfriend huddling at their lockers. He hurried by without being seen.

During lunch Alfonso hid in metal shop so he wouldn't run into Sandra. What would he say to her?

Words, Words, Words

pampered: treated with special care
hesitated: stopped for a short time before doing something
impulse: a sudden desire or action
desperation: the state of having an urgent need or desire

If he weren't mad at his brother, he could ask Ernie what girls and guys talk about. But he *was* mad, and anyway, Ernie was off with his friends.

Alfonso hurried home after school. He did the morning dishes as his mother had asked and raked the leaves. After finishing his chores, he did a hundred sit-ups, pushed on his teeth until they hurt, showered, and combed his hair into a perfect butch. He then stepped out to the patio to clean his bike. On an **impulse,** he removed the chain to wipe off the gritty oil. But while he was unhooking it from the back sprocket, it snapped. The chain lay in his hand like a dead snake.

Alfonso couldn't believe his luck. Now, not only did he not have an extra bike for Sandra, he had no bike for himself. Frustrated, and on the verge of tears, he flung the chain as far as he could. It landed with a hard slap against the back fence and spooked his sleeping cat, Benny. Benny looked around, blinking his soft gray eyes, and went back to sleep.

Alfonso retrieved the chain, which was hopelessly broken. He cursed himself for being stupid, yelled at his bike for being cheap, and slammed the chain onto the cement. The chain snapped in another place and hit him when it popped up, slicing his hand like a snake's fang.

"Ow!" he cried, his mouth immediately going to his hand to suck on the wound.

After a dab of iodine, which only made his cut hurt more, and a lot of thought, he went to the bedroom to plead with Ernie, who was changing to his after-school clothes.

"Come on, man, let me use it," Alfonso pleaded. "Please, Ernie, I'll do anything."

Ernie could see Alfonso's **desperation,** but he had plans with his friend Raymundo. They were going to catch frogs at the Mayfair canal. He felt sorry for his brother, and gave him a stick of gum to make him feel better, but there was nothing he could do. The canal was three miles away, and the frogs were waiting.

Alfonso took the stick of gum, placed it in his shirt pocket, and left the bedroom with his head down.

He went outside, slamming the screen door behind him, and sat in the alley behind his house. A sparrow landed in the weeds, and when it tried to come close, Alfonso screamed for it to scram. The sparrow responded with a squeaky chirp and flew away.

At four he decided to get it over with and started walking to Sandra's house, trudging slowly, as if he were waist-deep in water. Shame colored his face. How could he disappoint his first date? She would probably laugh. She might even call him *menso.*

He stopped at the corner where they were supposed to meet and watched her house. But there was no one outside, only a rake leaning against the steps.

ASK Yourself

- How do you feel when plans you've made don't work out?

Think about how you would handle this in your own life.

Why did he have to take the chain off? he scolded himself. He always messed things up when he tried to take them apart, like the time he tried to repad his baseball mitt. He had unlaced the mitt and filled the pocket with cotton balls. But when he tried to put it back together, he had forgotten how it laced up. Everything became tangled like kite string. When he showed the mess to his mother, who was at the stove cooking dinner, she scolded him but put it back together and didn't tell his father what a dumb thing he had done.

Now he had to face Sandra and say, "I broke my bike, and my stingy brother took off on his."

He waited at the corner for a few minutes, hiding behind a hedge for what seemed like forever. Just as he was starting to think about going home, he heard footsteps and knew it was too late. His hands, moist from worry, hung at his sides, and a thread of sweat raced down his armpit.

He peeked though the hedge. She was wearing a sweater with a checkerboard pattern. A red purse was slung over her shoulder. He could see her looking for him, standing on tiptoe to see if he was coming around the corner.

What have I done? Alfonso thought. He bit his lip, called himself *menso,* and pounded his palm against his forehead. Someone slapped the back of his head. He turned around and saw Ernie.

"We got the frogs, Alfonso," he said, holding up a wiggling plastic bag. "I'll show you later."

Ernie looked through the hedge, with one eye closed, at the girl. "She's not the one who messed with Frostie and me," he said finally. "You still wanna borrow my bike?"

Alfonso couldn't believe his luck. What a brother! What a pal! He promised to take Ernie's turn next time it was his turn to do the dishes. Ernie hopped on Raymundo's handlebars and said he would remember that promise. Then he was gone as they took off without looking back.

Free of worry now that his brother had come through, Alfonso emerged from behind the hedge with Ernie's bike, which was mud-splashed but better than nothing. Sandra waved.

"Hi," she said.

"Hi," he said back.

She looked cheerful. Alfonso told her his bike was broken and asked if she wanted to ride with him.

"Sounds good," she said, and jumped on the crossbar.

It took all of Alfonso's strength to steady the bike. He started off slowly, gritting his teeth, because she was heavier than he thought. But once he got going, it got easier. He pedaled smoothly, sometimes with only one hand on the handlebars, as they sped up one street and down another. Whenever he ran over a pothole, which was often, she screamed with delight, and once, when it looked like they were going to crash, she placed her hand over his, and it felt like love.

Tin Grin

Cassandra Walker is a former "brace face." Here's how she survived four years of teasing with a smile on her face.

by Cassandra Walker

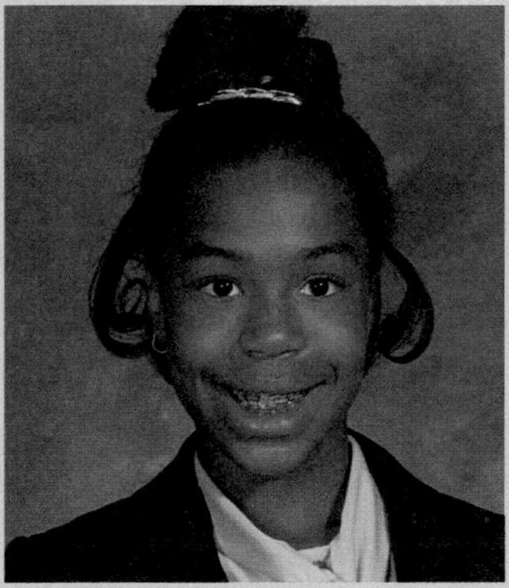

"I never liked my braces . . . "

" . . . now I can't stop smiling."

WHAT?! I DON'T WANT TO HAVE BRACES!

That is what I told the orthodontist and my mother. They both insisted that I would be so happy . . . when I had my braces removed. That may be true, I thought, but what about in the meantime? After all, we're talking four years of my life! Think about it. A person gets to be President of the United States for four years. You can graduate from college in four years, and for a 12-year-old, four years is the time it takes to go from riding a bike to driving a car. Four years is a big chunk of anyone's life, and this life was mine.

I must admit that my orthodontist, Dr. Greenfield, was very nice and comforting each time I had to visit him. He also had some excellent stories of people who had braces and how it helped improve their lives. But I couldn't take Dr. Greenfield with me to school. So there I was, all alone, with echoes in my head of "Hey, brace face!" "How's it going, Tin Grin?" and the worst, "Can I put a magnet on your teeth and see if it will stick?"

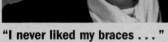

I'm not going to tell you that I learned to "grin and bear it." I never liked my braces, not for one minute. But when I ran out of tears and had heard all the stupid braces jokes that had ever been thought of, I decided to do something.

I took the attention away from my teeth and put it on me, a person—not a walking braces factory. I styled my hair in new and different ways that drew attention. I took extra care in matching my clothes and wearing accessories like bows and pins. Most of all, instead of being upset and cruel to the people who ridiculed me, I was nice to them and even laughed at some of their braces jokes.

Soon the jokes stopped and I blended in with everyone else. It's no fun for the people who tease you if it doesn't affect you. Also, by taking time to draw attention to other things about myself, I started taking more pride in how I looked, and I have been doing that ever since.

When the braces finally did come off and I looked in the mirror, Dr. Greenfield and my mother were right. I did like my new teeth.

Now I can't stop smiling.

Wrap-Up

Talk About It

Now that you've read "Broken Chain" and "Tin Grin," what do you have to say about these questions?

- How important is it to you how a person looks?
- What would you do if you overheard someone being teased about wearing braces or glasses?

Comprehension Check

Write your answers to the questions below. Use information from the story and the essay to support your answers.

1. How do Alfonso and Sandra meet?
2. How does Alfonso feel about his looks?
3. Why do you think most people are nervous around someone they like?
4. How did Cassandra respond when people teased her about her braces?
5. What do you think Alfonso might have said to Cassandra about getting braces?

Vocabulary Check

Complete each sentence starter below. Before you answer, think about the meaning of the vocabulary word in bold.

1. The bicycle **gleamed** after I . . .
2. I **winced** because . . .
3. I feel really **pampered** when . . .
4. The student **hesitated** before . . .
5. I once had a crazy **impulse** to . . .

Write About It

Choose one of the writing prompts below.

- Write a short contract between Alfonso and his brother for the use of his brother's bike. In it, make a list of the terms; for example, how long the bike will be used, what Alfonso will offer in exchange, and anything else you can think of.
- Have you ever suffered from shyness? Write a few short paragraphs telling about a time when you felt shy. What caused it? What did you do about it?
- Write a list of five to seven beauty tips for someone who wears braces. Think about what Cassandra did, and then add your own advice.

About the AUTHOR

Gary Soto is a Mexican American from California, just like many of his characters. Also like his characters, he had to work hard for what he had. To earn money as a young man, Soto worked in fields picking crops. When he first began to write, he wrote only poetry. Later, he got the idea that he might be able to earn money writing stories. Today, he has sold over a million copies of his books.

Want to know more? Check out Gary Soto's official Web site at www.garysoto.com.

More Books by Gary Soto

Baseball in April
Local News
Neighborhood Odes
Taking Sides

Analyzing Ads

Ads are designed to get you to buy something. When you read one, it's important to read carefully. A great deal isn't always so great when you check out all the details.

Take a look at the ads below. Do you understand what each one offers?

Four Ads

Did you notice that you get a free CD only if you buy a CD player? That's not exactly free!

Putting just a few items on sale is a way to attract customers who may wind up buying full-priced merchandise.

Eddie's Electronics
Free CD!!
With purchase of our slammin' CD player for only $140.
Lifetime warranty for an additional $29.99
Sale this weekend on select CD players by Tuned In and Jamasonic!
Small Pizza FREE
with purchase of large pizza when you bring this coupon to
JOE'S PIZZA
Victory Video
Rental Fee Only 99¢
• For members only
• $2.99 for non-members
• Membership: $30 per year
• Tapes must be returned within 3 days
• Late fee is $6 per day
SALE!!
1/24 through 1/31
ALL sneakers 40% off
• Sizes 6-10 only • Laces not included
SPORTS WORLD

Six dollars is a big late fee. Of course, such fine print is easy to miss—and that's just what the advertiser hopes you'll do.

"Be a smart consumer. Don't buy something you're not really crazy about, just because it's on sale. If you don't use it, it's not a good deal."

Are These Deals or Steals?

You need to read ads carefully to make sure that what you're buying is really a good value. Review the ads and the tips that go with them. Then use them to answer the questions below. Write your answers on your own paper.

1. You and your sister are ordering a pizza. Should you use the coupon from Joe's to get a free small pizza? What if you were ordering a pizza with five friends? Explain.

2. You wear a size 5 shoe. Could you buy sneakers on sale at Sports World? What if you wore size ten? What would you need to buy before you could wear sneakers you bought on sale at Sports World?

3. Which of the following statements are true of the Victory Video store? (Pick two.)
- **a.** The video rental fee is $.99 cents for members only.
- **b.** There is a one-time membership fee of $30.
- **c.** To avoid paying a late fee, you must return videos within 48 hours.
- **d.** There is a yearly membership fee of $30.

4. What is the total cost of the CD player and lifetime warranty from Eddie's Electronics?
- **a.** $140.00
- **b.** $29.99
- **c.** $169.99
- **d.** $99.00

Selling Points

Check out some ads in newspapers or magazines. How do the advertisers catch consumers' interest? List some words and phrases advertisers use to make shoppers think they're getting a good deal.

Market It

Pick a product. Create your own ad for it. Use some words and phrases from "Selling Points." Trade ads with a partner. Would you buy your partner's product? Why or why not?

"When you're surfing the Web, ads may pop up on your screen. They can be as tricky as any other ad, so read them carefully."

Real-World Words

consumer: a person who buys a product or uses a service
merchandise: items for sale in a store
warranty: a contract stating broken goods will be fixed or replaced

autobiography

LITTLE ROCK CENTRAL HIGH SCHO

WARRIORS DON'T CRY

Melba Pattillo wanted to go to a school that didn't want her. Her brave fight for her rights helped change our world.

by Melba Pattillo Beals

INTRODUCTION

In 1957, Melba Pattillo turned 16. That was also the year she became a warrior on the front lines of a civil rights battle—the fight to integrate Central High School in Little Rock, Arkansas.

Melba stood up for her right to go to school—a school that in the past only white students had attended. In doing this, she had acid thrown in her face, was spit at, kicked, threatened, and called every horrible name you can imagine.

How could this be?

Until the Supreme Court made its famous *Brown* vs. *Board of Education* ruling in 1954, schools throughout the South were segregated by race. White students went to one set of schools and African-American students went to another. In the *Brown* decision, the Supreme Court ruled that segregation was discriminatory and that all schools must be integrated.

Brave Warrior: Melba in 1957

Despite that, officials in many states—including Arkansas—did not want their schools integrated and did everything they could to stop it. Finally, in 1957, a federal court ordered all schools to begin integration at once.

Local civil rights groups in Little Rock chose Melba and eight other African-American high school students—from among many volunteers—as the ones who would integrate Central High School.

When the first day of school arrived, Arkansas Governor Orval Faubus vowed that integration would not take place and ordered a unit of the National Guard to go to Central High School and stop the African-American students from entering the school.

Later that week, President Dwight D. Eisenhower stepped in. He seized control of the National Guard and sent the Army's 101st Airborne Division to Little Rock. On the morning of September 25, Army soldiers with guns surrounded the school and escorted Melba and the others into Central High.

For the first months of the school year, Melba was escorted

◀ **White students look on as the heavily guarded African-American students climb the steps to Central High School.**

Soldiers form a protective ring around Melba and the other African-American students as they enter the school.

from class to class by an Army guard named Danny. After one unusually tough day, Danny told Melba: "It takes a warrior to fight a battle and survive." As the year went on, Melba took on the attitude of a warrior, telling herself "Warriors don't cry." That's what she titled her book about that year.

From *Warriors Don't Cry:*
The First Day

Once the paratroopers had delivered us safely inside the front door of Central High School, all of us—the soldiers, we nine students, white school officials—were standing absolutely still, as though under a spell. No one seemed to know what to do next. The commander of the troops who'd brought us in spoke a few words. Soon our military protectors fell into formation and marched away. I felt naked without that blanket of safety. A warning alarm surged through my body.

Principal Jess Matthews greeted us with a forced smile on his face. He directed us to our classrooms. It was then that I saw the other group of soldiers. They were wearing a different uniform from the combat soldiers outside, but they carried the same hardware and had the same **placid** expressions. As the nine of us turned to go our separate ways, one by one a soldier followed each of us.

Along the winding hallway, near the door we had entered, I passed several clusters of students who stared at me, whispered obscenities, and pointed. They hurled insults at the soldier as well, but he seemed not to pay attention. My class was more than a block away from the front door. I saw other 101st soldiers standing at intervals along the hall. I turned back to make sure there really was a soldier following me. He was there. As I approached the classroom he speeded up, coming closer to me.

"Melba, my name is Danny." He looked me directly in the eye. He was slim, about five feet ten inches tall, with dark hair and deep-set brown eyes. "I'll be waiting for you here. We're not allowed to go inside the classrooms. If you need me, holler."

Despite Danny and the other guards who were around, groups of white students tried to drive Melba and the others out of school. Every day was a struggle and brought new attacks and ***confrontations.*** *Still, the nine students were determined to stay strong and keep integration alive.*

Four Months Later

It was just before the start of the Christmas holidays, and we were very aware of a last-minute drive to get us out of school before the new year. Fliers and cards appeared say-

WORDS, WORDS, WORDS

placid: calm
confrontations: threatening meetings
harassment: the state of pestering or annoying someone
intervening: getting involved in a situation to change what is happening

ing "Two, four, six, eight, we ain't gonna integrate—no, not in '58." There was lots of talk about how we wouldn't come back when the new semester started.

When we had one more day to go before the break, five of us entered the cafeteria. Lunchtime was always a hazard, and recently even more so. I had been avoiding the cafeteria, eating my sandwich alone in any safe place I could find. The cafeteria was such a huge place, with so many of our attackers gathered at one time. There were no official-looking adults or uniformed Arkansas National Guardsmen inside. We knew we could expect some form of **harassment.**

As always on Tuesday the hot lunch was chili, which Minnijean Brown—one of the other African-American students—loved. So while I took my seat with the others, she got in line to buy her chili. As Minnijean made her way back toward us, her tray loaded down with a big bowl of chili, we saw her hesitate. She had to inch her way through a tight spot where mostly boys sat at tables on either side of her path. She had stood dead in her tracks. We all froze, realizing she must be in real trouble. We could see two boys near her—one directly in her path. Something awful was happening, but there was no way any of us could do anything to rescue her. We had been instructed that in such instances we were never to move toward the person in danger for fear of starting a riot.

I felt panic-stricken. Minnijean was being hassled by those boys. Snickering among themselves and taunting her, they had pushed a chair directly in front of her. For a long moment, she stood there patiently, holding her tray high above their heads.

The nine students being escorted to school by the military. Melba is behind the soldier's arm.

It was all I could do to hold on to my chair and not go to help her. Like a broken record, the words played over and over in my head—**intervening** on her behalf would blur the lines between who was the victim and who was the person at fault. If other white students joined the fight to rescue the other side, we'd have a brawl. They outnumbered us at least two hundred to one. Still, I wanted to go to her, move the chair, take her tray, tell her to back up and go another way, do something, anything.

> **ASK YOURSELF**
>
> - Why might helping Minnijean make the situation worse?
>
> Think about what Melba was told and what you know about people.

All Was Quiet

As more and more people realized something was brewing, the chatter in the cafeteria quieted down. I could tell Minnijean was trapped and desperate, and very fast running out of patience.

Frantically, I looked around to see if there were any adults nearby who could be trusted to help. The vice-principal for girls, Mrs. Huckaby, had made some efforts to be fair during these situations, but she was nowhere in sight. I beckoned to Minnijean to go around her hasslers, but she was standing perfectly

"DIGNITY IS A STATE OF MIND."

still. It was as though she were in a trance, fighting within herself.

Later, she would explain that the boys had been taunting her, sticking their feet in the aisle to trip her, kicking her, and calling her names. But we weren't close enough to see them. All we saw was her wavering as though she were trying to balance herself—and then her tray went flying, spilling chili all over two of the boys.

Everyone was stunned, silent for a long time. Her attackers sat with astonished looks on their faces as greasy chili dropped down over their heads. All at once, the lunchroom workers, most of whom were African American, began to applaud. This was greeted by an **ominous** silence, and then loud voices, all chattering at once, as the chili-covered boys stood up. I wondered whether we'd ever get out of there alive. Suddenly a school official showed up, and Minnijean was whisked away, while we were hustled out of the cafeteria.

ASK YOURSELF

- Why do you think all the African-American students were taken out of the cafeteria?

Think about what Melba was afraid might happen.

They Wanted Us Out

Word got around school immediately. Clusters of people gathered along the hallway, chanting, "Two, four, six, eight, we ain't gonna integrate." Some were applauding and laughing. I wondered why some students were jubilant, almost celebrating.

"Looking for your little friend?" one of the students said as I walked down the stairs to study hall. "She's done got herself suspended. She can only get back in if the superintendent lets her, and you know what that means."

"One down and eight to go" was the cry we heard as we left Central High for Christmas vacation. I could hear those declarations shouted even above the festive Christmas carols being played.

Minnijean Brown became the only one of the nine students who didn't finish the school year at Central. After a series of incidents that arose from this one, she was expelled. Melba was terribly disappointed to lose one of her ***allies,*** *but she stuck it out. The next part shows how a raw egg and some advice from her grandmother helped her survive.*

Change the Rules

"Ooooooo, no, no," I heard myself shout as I was walking up the Fourteenth Street stairwell one morning. It wasn't yet 8:40, and I'd just become the victim of a dousing with raw eggs from someone standing on the stairs above my head. The odor bothered me, but even more, it was the feel of that slimy substance oozing very slowly through my hair and onto my face, while at the same time raw egg slithered over the sweater Auntie Mae Dell had given me for Christmas.

"She's come to have breakfast. I can tell, she's wearing eggs," one boy called. I never said a word back to them. I knew they were just hoping I'd do or say something that would result in my expulsion. I backed down the stairs and out the door to go home.

At home, Grandma tried to wipe as much of the egg out of my hair as she could; then I would have to bathe and wash my hair. "Hold still," she said. "After a nice long bath, you can hurry back to school, and this will have been just a refreshing break in your morning."

"I've never been so embarrassed."

"Oh, I'll bet there've been other times and there'll be more. Embarrassment is not a life-threatening problem. It can be washed away with a prayer and a smile, just like this egg is washed away with a little water."

"I know, but it's the same way I feel when they spit on me. I feel like they've taken away my **dignity.**"

"Dignity is a state of mind, just like freedom. These are both precious gifts from God that no one can take away unless you allow them to," Grandma continued. "You could take charge of these mind games, you know."

"How do you mean?"

"Take, for example, this egg in your hair. Suppose you'd have told the boys who did this, 'Thank you,' with a smile. Then you've changed the rules of the game. What they want is for you to be unhappy. That's how they get pleasure."

"But that would be letting them win."

"Not exactly. Maybe it would defeat their purpose. They win when you respond the way they expect you to. Change the rules of the game, girl, and they might not like it so much."

"They'd think I was crazy."

"They'd think you were no longer their victim."

For the rest of the morning as I walked the halls, amid my hecklers, I kept thinking about what it would be like to feel as though I were in charge of myself. I always believed Grandma India had the right answer, so I took her advice.

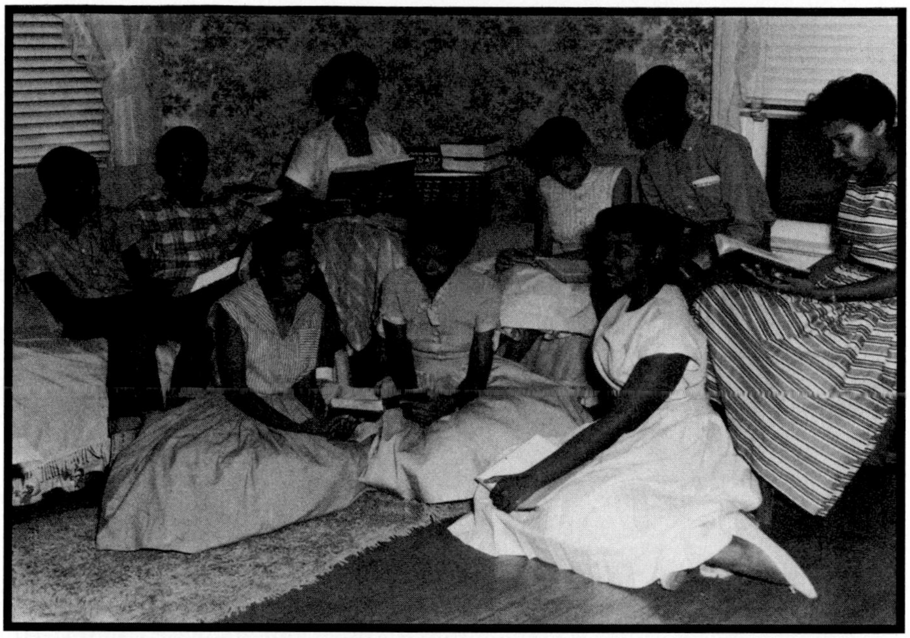

Melba (front row, far right) and the other students needed each other for support. In this photo they are studying together.

As I tried to open a classroom door, two boys pushed it closed. At first I tried to pull it open, but then I remembered changing the rules of the game. I stood up straight, smiled politely, and said in a friendly voice, "Thank you. I've been needing exercise. You've done wonders for my arm muscles." I chatted on and on as if they were my friends. They looked at me as though I were totally nuts, then they let go of the door. I felt great power surging up my spine, like electricity. I left them standing there looking at each other.

Melba and her friends made it through the year. Unfortunately, the next fall, Governor Faubus shut down all the schools and got a court order delaying integration. Melba went to California to finish high school. It wasn't until September of 1960 that Central High opened to integration again.

Melba didn't return to Central High until 1987. On that day, she was greeted by the school's student-body president—Derrick Noble. Derrick is African American.

The brave warriors—known as the Little Rock Nine—made their mark on America. And most Americans, as they learn about this story ask themselves, "Would I have been as brave?" Would you? ●

WORDS, WORDS, WORDS

ominous: threatening
allies: people who give support to someone
dignity: a quality that makes a person worthy of respect

The following is an editorial that appeared in The Washington Post *on September 25, 1997. The author was the Secretary of Transportation at that time. An editorial expresses one person's views or opinions on a subject.*

When the Doors Opened at Central High

Forty years after the Little Rock Nine entered Central High School, a nation looks back.

by RODNEY E. SLATER

Forty years ago today, nine African-American students took a long walk down a short block and integrated Central High School in Little Rock, Ark. Today President Clinton will be at Central High to open the door for the nine men and women whose courageous walk opened doors for so many others. He will be introduced by student-body president Fatima McKendra, honor student, aspiring surgeon, African American. This young woman could not have been student-body president in 1957.

My Own Experience

How far have we really come in 40 years? How far have we left to go? I was two years old when those brave students walked through angry, jeering crowds, past armed soldiers to the front door of Central High. It was not until years later that, as an African-American teenager, I had the occasion to go to school with white children in Marianna, Ark.

How far have we come in 40 years? How far have we left to go?

And still it was not easy. After my school canceled a program celebrating the Rev. Martin Luther King Jr.'s birthday, students staged a sit-in. They were chased from the school grounds by firemen spraying them with high-powered blasts of water. The student officers, including myself, who had been meeting in the principal's office were taken to the police station. We did not go back to school that year. And when I did go back, I was not allowed to play sports, a severe penalty for someone who later went to college on a football and academic scholarship.

It was a [turning-point] experience for me. I learned that you have to take a stand in what you believe is right. There is always a cost. But often there is a higher cost for not taking a stand.

Tolerance actually got an early start in Arkansas. The city of Little Rock already had desegregated its public buses, its zoos, its library, and its park system. Its citizens were poised to deal with integration in a positive way. They were guided by what President Abraham

The Little Rock Nine met discrimination every day. Here, Elizabeth Eckford, one of the nine students, faces a harsh crowd.

Lincoln called the better angels of our time. But the actions of a few [made it very hard for the Little Rock Nine. Still], justice prevailed, the school was integrated, and Ernest Green, the lone senior of the Little Rock Nine, graduated in May 1958.

A Brighter Future

We have come a long way since then. Our economy is healthy, unemployment is low, and the African-American middle class has grown substantially.

But we have to learn to live together, because the face of America is changing. Today in Hawaii, everyone is a minority.

Soon this will be true of California. And 40 years from now, there will be no majority race in America.

We can look at statistics and know what America will look like in the 21st century. But we have to look inside ourselves to determine what America will *be* like in the 21st century.

A Call for Dialogue

The president is asking all Americans to join him in a national conversation about race to face one another honestly across lines that still divide us. Clearly, now is the time for honest dialogue, the time to build a society that recognizes the worth of all people and honors the dignity of every person.

Laws can change institutions, but they cannot change what is in people's hearts. ●

Wrap-Up

Talk About It

Now that you've read *Warriors Don't Cry* and "When the Doors Opened at Central High," what do you have to say about these questions?

- Have you ever known a person to be treated unfairly just because of what they look like? Describe the experience.
- What issue do you feel strongly enough about to take action?

Comprehension Check

Write your answers to the questions below. Use information from the autobiography and the editorial to support your answers.

1. How did the boys react when Melba thanked them for closing the door to the classroom?
2. Why did the lunchroom workers applaud when Minnijean's chili spilled all over the heads of the white boys?
3. Why do you think so many African-American teenagers volunteered to be among the Little Rock Nine?
4. What happened to Rodney E. Slater after he took part in a sit-in?
5. Why do you think people choose to take a stand, even if they suffer for it?

Vocabulary Check

harassment **placid** **confrontations**
ominous **dignity**

Complete each sentence with the correct vocabulary word.

1. The day of the test, I woke up with an _______ feeling in the pit of my stomach.
2. As I sat down to take the test, I was surprised at how _______ I felt.
3. During the test, the boy sitting behind me kept tapping his pencil and it began to seem like _______.
4. I just ignored the noise because it wasn't the time or the place for any _______.
5. Getting an A on the test gave me a great sense of _______.

Write About It

Choose one of the writing prompts below.

- Write a speech that Melba Pattillo Beals might give if she returned to her old high school today. Think about how she might feel about the way things have changed.
- How did you feel about the situation when Minnijean spilled the chili and got suspended from school for it? Write an editorial for the school paper that gives your opinion about what happened.
- What issue might be worth standing up for today? State your five best reasons why this issue is so important.

Fact FILE

A FAMOUS SPEECH

In 1954, the Supreme Court heard the case of *Brown vs. Board of Education of Topeka.* Thurgood Marshall, who eventually became the first African-American Supreme Court Justice, argued the case. In a famous speech, he said:

"I got the feeling (from what has been said here) that when you put a white child in a school with a whole lot of colored children, the children would all fall apart or something. Everybody knows this is not true. Those same kids . . . they play in the streets together, they play on their farms together, they go down the road together, they separate and go to school, they come out of school and play ball together."

Marshall said, "Equal means getting the same thing, at the same time and in the same place." Marshall won this case and made it illegal to segregate schools. This paved the way for the Little Rock Nine and the Civil Rights movement.

Reading a Line Graph

You're doing some research on movie attendance over the years. You've found a line graph that shows how ticket sales went up and down between 1946 and 1998.

Check out the graph below. Can you figure it out?

Movie Tickets Sold in the U.S.

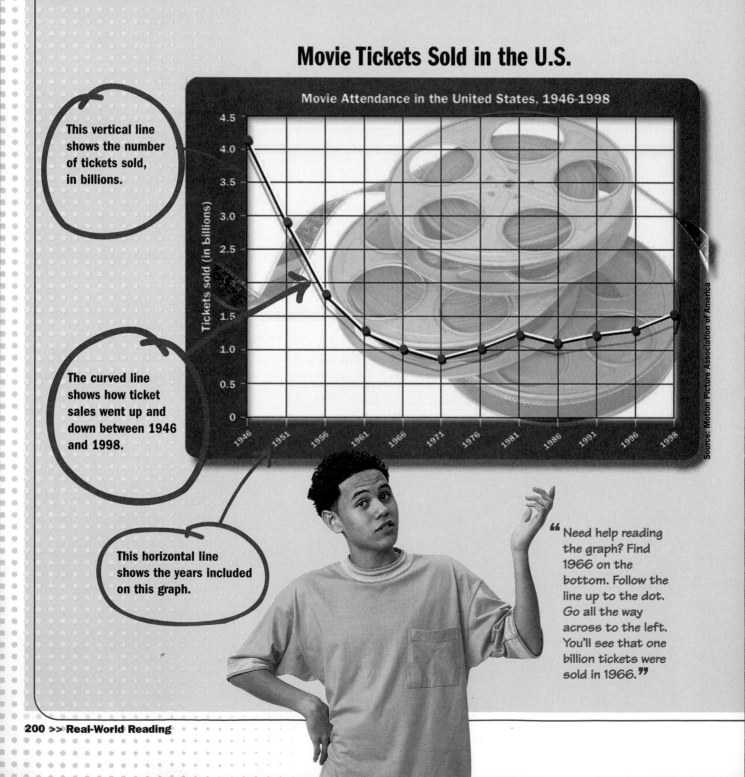

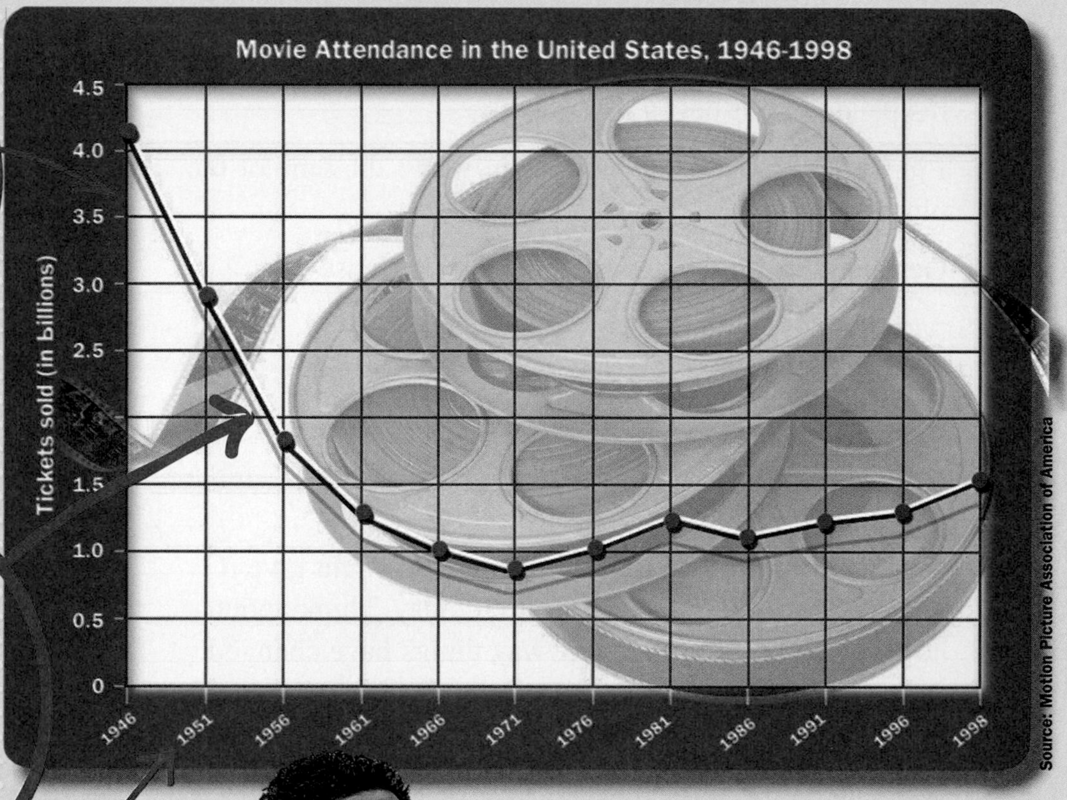
Movie Attendance in the United States, 1946-1998
Tickets sold (in billions)
4.5
4.0
3.5
3.0
2.5
1.5
1.0
0.5
0
1946
1951
1956
1961
1966
1971
1976
1981
1986
1991
1996
1998
Source: Motion Picture Association of America

This vertical line shows the number of tickets sold, in billions.

The curved line shows how ticket sales went up and down between 1946 and 1998.

This horizontal line shows the years included on this graph.

"Need help reading the graph? Find 1966 on the bottom. Follow the line up to the dot. Go all the way across to the left. You'll see that one billion tickets were sold in 1966."

Let's Graph It!

Line graphs present facts and figures in a way that makes it easy to see a trend. This one tells you about American movie attendance. Use the line graph and tips to answer these questions. Write your answers on your own paper.

1. What was the total number of tickets sold in the United States in 1976?
a. approximately 10 billion
b. approximately 1 billion
c. approximately 4.2 billion
d. approximately 1.2 billion

2. In what year were the fewest tickets sold? In what year were the most tickets sold?

3. Between the years 1971 and 1996, did ticket sales go up or down? Did ticket sales go up or down between 1951 and 1971?

4. Within which five-year span was there the largest change in movie attendance?
a. 1951–1956
b. 1961–1966
c. 1971–1976
d. 1986–1991

5. What is the main trend shown on this graph?
a. Movie attendance in the United States will never reach 4 billion again.
b. Movies are a popular form of entertainment.
c. More and more people are going to the movies.
d. Movie attendance has gone down since 1946.

Think About It

Why do you think that movie ticket sales have gone down since 1946? List a few reasons. (Hint: Think about what you do now for entertainment.)

Graph It

Graph a soccer star's goals. Here's the number of goals she scored each school year. Grade 6: 8 goals. Grade 7: 9 goals. Grade 8: 11 goals. Grade 9: 6 goals. Grade 10: 8 goals. Grade 11: 12 goals. Grade12: 13 goals.

"A graph like this gets dated quickly. Check the source if you need up-to-date information. Call the organization, or check their Web site."

Real-World Words

approximately: about
attendance: the number of people at an event
trend: the general direction in which things are changing

short story

Opening Act

For Amanda, writing poetry is a way to express her deepest feelings. Will her famous mother ever understand how important it is to her?

By Jane Yolen and Heidi Elisabet Yolen Stemple

Well, she's not exactly famous.

Not like Janet Jackson or Mariah Carey, or even Barbra Streisand. More like well known. At least if you live in our county you'd know her name. Probably you'd have heard her sing at church or at somebody's wedding.

She won the grand prize on a show like *Star Search* about ten years ago before there even *was* a *Star Search,* when I was small enough to think that was a big deal. I must have watched the tape Daddy made of the show a hundred times. But to tell the truth, it's real embarrassing now—the songs about love gone wrong and how another guy dumped her. Once I asked how she would even know what being dumped felt like when she's been married to Daddy for about a million years. I mean sometimes they still act like teenagers. She just laughed and said it was a feeling no one ever forgets, even if it was a million years ago.

Ever since I can remember, everyone has always asked me if I wanted to be a singer like my mom when I grow up. Mom used to take me onstage with her. When I was three and four and five, I guess it was cute. But when it got painful—for both the audience and me—she stopped. One day I was the star of the family, the next day I was nothing. And I didn't understand, really, till I turned twelve and was kicked out of the school choir. Seems I can't carry a tune. Not even in a bucket loader.

I guess I have my dad's genes when it comes to music. He left Woodstock and became an accountant. Anyway, these days I can't even imagine how terrifying it must be to get up and sing in front of people. I think I'd rather be an accountant, not that anyone ever asks about that.

On the other hand, my older brother Aaron is a bigger ham than Mom. He has his own band in Minneapolis and he sings, plays guitar, even writes his own music. He's the real star. Mom walks around the house humming his tunes. My dad, Mr. "I only listen to country music," even abandoned his Willy Nelson CDs for Aaron's newest tape. And sometimes I catch myself singing his songs as well, with *my* voice!

Maybe I can't sing, but I *do* know about the kind of heartbreak in my mom's songs—which brings me to my reason for telling this story. Right after school started this fall, I heard from some "friend" that my boyfriend, Jeff, had been eyeing Marie McCall. Now, I had never liked the way he looked at her in the school hallways between classes. But a lot of the boys looked at Marie that way, especially now because she grew quite a bit over summer vacation—and I didn't. Since Jeff hadn't called me since school started, I suspected that meant we were breaking up after a whole summer together, though I hoped I was wrong.

now performing...
So
sad and Lo-oo-onely
mom
me & dad
neat
neat-o
me & mom
Thank you and good night!
my brother

However, the last thing that I would have done was to get up onstage and sing about it. "As summer slipped into the fall, you dumped me for Marie McCall." What a catchy tune.

I've always thought the best way to deal with heartbreak was to write poetry in secret. Better than singing about fake heartbreak on a stage anyway. Like the 27 poems I wrote about Brian, my last boyfriend, who moved to Texas when his mom was offered a great job there. I keep those poems safely tucked away in a box in the back of my closet. After all, they're no one's business but my own.

> **ASK Yourself**
>
> - What causes Amanda to write poetry?
>
> Think about the feelings she describes.

When the phone rang last week at 10:30, I jumped to answer it. I was up studying for my math test and my parents were watching TV. I knew, in that way that you just *know,* that the phone was for me. Sure enough, it was my best friend, Kaytlin. She had been shopping at the mall.

"Manda," she said, out of breath. "This couldn't wait till morning. It's too important." There was an edge to her voice I couldn't quite grasp. "Are you sitting down?"

"Yes," I said, although I wasn't.

"Manda, it's Jeff. I saw him with Marie." That's when I sat down. "They were coming out of the movies and I followed them."

Although there was nothing funny about this, I almost smiled. Kaytlin wants to be a police officer like her father and three older brothers and she tends to act as if she were already undercover.

"Were you lurking?" I asked.

I could just see her pulling her jacket up around her face and sneaking about. Sometimes I am jealous that she knows exactly what she wants to be.

"After about half an hour of **surveillance** . . . are you sure you're sitting?"

I made an affirmative sound.

"He kissed her."

Suddenly I hadn't wanted any more details. "Kate, I've got to go. My mom is calling me," I lied. I'm sure she knew I wasn't telling the truth.

I abandoned my books and ran upstairs. I hate crying, really. But it seemed the appropriate thing to do. So I did, into my pillow, where no one could hear me.

After I'd cried as much as I could, I started writing in my poetry journal. I was inspired. Heartbreak does that to me. And the rhymes had nothing to do with Marie or McCall. Jeff either. It had to do with me. And with poetry.

I'm picking up the pieces of my heart
First you mended it, then tore it all apart
You've made ***despair*** *an art form*
And cheating an art.

I was feeling better in a strange sort of way. I'd read somewhere that many poets find poetry a **catharsis.** I could understand that. So, I continued:

You tore down my palace and my throne,
The ones I'd built of mortar and of bone.
You ***razed*** *it piece by piece,*
Each precious little stone.

I loved that word "razed," the way it made me feel. As if razor blades had been drawn across my fingertips.

I wrote for another hour or so. Crossing lines out, rewriting the rhymes. It always happens that

> **Words, WORDS, Words**
>
> **surveillance:** watching someone or something
> **despair:** a loss of hope
> **catharsis:** a process for getting rid of emotional stress
> **razed:** tore down

way. The first stanza or two come quickly, but the following ones need to be worked and reworked. As I wrote, the writing itself became my entire universe, rhyme and meter replacing tears and pain.

When I was done, I reread the whole poem aloud. I was happy with it—and exhausted.

I must have fallen asleep, because the next moment it was morning and I was still in my clothes. But, curiously, someone had tucked me neatly under the covers. And the lights were off.

My journal, however, was nowhere to be found. Worrying about my math test and wondering what could have happened to my journal, I went downstairs to breakfast.

When I got there, my dad was reading the financial section of the paper, per usual. Mom was sipping her tea. It seemed normal enough until I spotted my poetry notebook right by her bread plate, covered with crumbs.

I snatched up the notebook and screamed. For all I knew, they'd been having a good laugh at my expense over cereal and toast.

"Manda, honey," Mom began, "these are . . ."

I cut her off, too mad to hear her excuses. Or worse—her criticisms of my work. "You had no right to violate my privacy!"

I squeaked. I always squeak when I am really angry, which sort of undercuts the effect. Turning, I stomped out, slamming the door behind me. That made a great punctuation, like one enormous exclamation point. I was halfway to school before I realized I had come out without my books or jacket. And to make things worse, I was early for school.

My anger brewed through first-period civics. My stomach growled through the second-period math test. By the time I reached lunch, I had decided that *not* speaking to my mother was the only way to deal with her. She might READ my words, but I sure wasn't going to let her HEAR them. I was so mad, I forgot to be heartbroken, till I saw Jeff walking hand in hand with Marie McCall. Then it all flooded back.

"I don't know who I hate worse," I told Kaytlin.

"What do you mean?" she asked.

"My mom or Jeff. They both broke faith with me," I said.

"I thought Jeff broke your heart," she said.

Are you sitting down?
yes
I saw Jeff with Marie

morning
morning
morning

"Whichever."

I didn't want to talk anymore to Kaytlin. She just didn't get it. What I really wanted to do was call my brother, Aaron, but he was on tour with his band. However, since they were headed our way for a Friday night gig at the Iron Horse Cafe, three days away, I supposed I could hold out until after the show. I might not want to talk to Mom, and I couldn't talk to Kaytlin, but—boy—was Aaron going to get an earful!

ASK Yourself

- What do you think Amanda will say to Aaron?

Think about what's bothering Amanda.

The three long days until Friday seemed closer to a year and a half, but somehow I made it through.

Mom tried several times to talk to me. Once in the kitchen, she stopped me in the middle of making a peanut butter sandwich and said: "Manda, your poem is . . ." And once at the dinner table she began: "Honey, you've got to let me . . ." But I walked out each time, letting the door slams be double exclamation points. She got the message and left me alone. Just maybe, I thought, she knew she was wrong. Just maybe, I thought, I'd stop being mad a year from now.

Even Dad tried to get into the act, saying: "Your mom thought the notebook was homework, Manda. It's a terrific poem and . . ."

And I cut him off too, saying: "She sings about broken hearts. I live them. I don't want to talk about it." So we didn't.

To make things easier, Mom had nightly rehearsals with her group, as they were the opening act for Aaron's band. So every night when she got home, I was already in bed. Pretending to sleep.

And then—suddenly—it was Friday. I was so excited to see my brother, I didn't mind having to listen to Mom's group first. She had already left for her sound check, so Daddy and I drove over together talking about everything: the new pizza parlor in town, my math test, my brother's band. Everything, in fact, except my fight with Mom. Daddy was too **diplomatic** to bring that up again. Came from dealing with crazed clients at tax season, I guess.

At the Iron Horse, we were given the best table in the house and treated like the family of royalty, which, on this night, I guess we were. The owner of

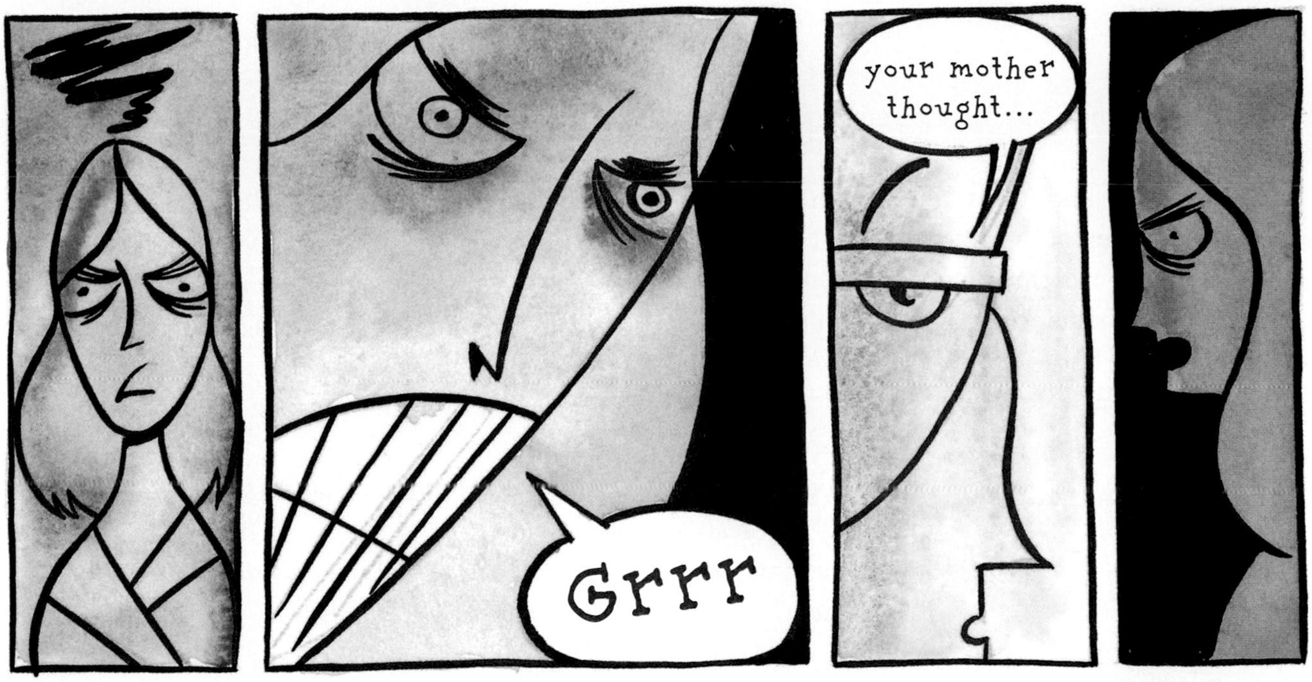
Grrr
your mother thought...

the café, Mom's self-professed "biggest fan," came to our table twice to make sure we were comfortable.

Finally, the lights dimmed and it was time for Mom to take the stage. At other times, I had found this a magic moment, the lights going down, her name called over the speakers, the applause, and then her entrance. But I was still too mad at her to let the magic work. And for the first time it all seemed a little—I don't know—**tawdry,** maybe?

She started her set with a **raucous** jazzy number that got the entire audience clapping in time with the beat. I didn't clap on principle. After all, she was still the woman who had stolen my journal and read my most secret poetry. But I had to admit, she looked wonderful in her white gauzy dress and she sounded great, too. So maybe a little bit of the magic still worked. I couldn't help but tap my foot under the table. When I realized what I was doing, I made myself stop.

Then, she pulled up a stool and sat for a soulful ballad that cried out for a lost lover, long gone, but not forgotten. As usual, it made me blush. But something more, too. It made me think about Jeff and how he had left me for Marie McCall. I let the lyrics wash over me, tell me my own story. And—you know—I felt better. Other people had suffered before and it wasn't the end of the world. Maybe that's what music does best—reminds us that we are like other people.

Mom sang three more songs and then finished with an old lullaby—one she used to sing to me whenever I was sick or scared of the dark. This time she sang it with a slight blues beat and it seemed—somehow—like a kind of apology. Then she blew kisses to the audience, acknowledged her band, bowed, and turned to go.

This was a ploy I had seen many times before. She wasn't ready to leave yet; she knew the audience would yell for just one more song. Even though I knew it was a practiced routine, she seemed believable when she turned and slowly walked back to the microphone.

"As many of you know," she started, her voice low and husky, "tonight is a special night for me. My son's band is patiently awaiting our departure from the stage so they can come out and show you their stuff."

I could feel the excitement building and had to

Words, WORDS, Words

diplomatic: tactful and good at dealing with people
tawdry: showy and cheap
raucous: wild and noisy

admire the way she controlled the audience. Even I was energized.

"But, what I know that you all don't know—and I wasn't even fully aware of until this very week—is that he isn't my only talented child."

I heard my mother's words, but didn't quite get it. Call me slow, but I guess I was just waiting for Aaron to come on.

"Amanda, honey, could you join me onstage?" I heard my name, and suddenly there was a spotlight on me and my dad was pulling me to my feet. As if in a haze I stood. I looked at my mother, who was motioning to me. My anger at her for embarrassing me in front of all these people was small compared to my overwhelming fear. I hadn't been up onstage in ten years. She couldn't possibly mean for me to go up there. And do what? *Sing?* With my voice?

ASK Yourself

- How does her mother's concert affect Amanda?

Consider how Amanda's feelings change.

Then Daddy gave me a push from behind and my feet seemed to move on their own. I walked, shaking all the way, onto the stage.

Mom hugged me, though I was rigid with anger and fear. I smiled a weak smile and attempted a feeble escape, but she led me to the empty stool, where she sat me down. Then she began talking again. I only made out parts of what she was saying.

". . . which she wrote . . . doesn't know . . . music . . . apology . . . hope you like it as much as . . ."

And as I sat, red-faced and shaking, her backup group started to play.

When she sang the opening lines, I could hardly believe it.

I'm picking up the pieces of my heart; first you mended it, and then tore it apart. You've made despair an art form, and cheating an art. I'm picking up the pieces of my heart.

After the first stanza, she looked at me and smiled. My face must have registered shock and horror, because she moved closer while the band played an instrumental section. Then she picked up my limp right hand and her eyes told me to look out into the crowd. I looked. It was better than staring at her. I could only see a couple of rows into the darkened café.

You tore down my palace and my throne . . .

As she started singing again, my dad's face was the first I focused on. He had an awfully odd expression. I couldn't tell if there was a kind of feedback from the spotlight, but he almost seemed to have tears in his eyes. I may have started to smile.

You excited?
No
Could you join me...

The ones I'd built of mortar and of bone.

I looked past him to strangers in the audience. They were swaying to the music. Now I *know* I was smiling.

You took it down slow piece by piece. Each precious little stone.

I looked just offstage to my right. Aaron and the guys in his band were all watching and listening. And grinning. I grinned back. I just couldn't help it.

You tore down my palace and my throne.

Mom squeezed my hand. I closed my eyes while she finished the song.

Our song.

When the music ended, I opened my eyes again. Everyone was clapping and cheering. One by one they began to stand. Mom released my hand and took a bow. Then she turned to me and pulled me up by the shoulders to stand beside her.

"Razed," I whispered. *"Razed* it piece by piece. You changed my words. How *could* you?"

"Words on a page," she whispered back, "are different than words in the mouth. Trust me on this one, sweetie. Now bow. The applause—it's for you."

I looked for my brother, but he had disappeared. Only his band remained, applauding right along with the crowd. Suddenly I realized what Mom had said. I was supposed to bow. So I tried. But have you ever bowed when your knees are shaking with anger? And with joy? All I managed was some sort of bob. The audience loved it, roaring even louder this time. So I bowed again, this time a deep one. When I came up from my bow, Aaron was there with a bouquet of red roses. He handed them to me and kissed my cheek.

"So," he said, "you've been holding out on me, Sis. And me struggling along with my own lousy lyrics. You going to write me something, too?"

"You don't sing about heartbreak," I said. "No one ever dumped you."

"I sing about lots of things that never happened to me," he said.

"What about *razing?"* I asked.

He laughed. He didn't know what I was talking about, but it didn't matter. "Up or down?" he asked. Then he laughed again. "Now get offstage. It's my turn."

As I sat next to Daddy, I thought: *"You raised me up, I razed you down . . ."* It was the start of a song and Aaron could sing it. Or Mom. Whichever.

you going to write me something too?

A Song and Poem by Jewel

Jewel turns words into poetry and song.

Jewel became a popular singer in the '90s, but not just because of her beautiful voice. Jewel writes songs that touch people's hearts. Her sad songs about life and love have helped to make her a star.

Long before Jewel started to write songs, however, she wrote poems. Her poetry—and lyrics—became enormously popular with people of all ages. Why? Some people think that Jewel has the ability to take her own experiences and make everyone feel like they are experiencing them, too.

Like Amanda in "Opening Act," Jewel writes very personal poems and song lyrics. In the song "I'm Sensitive" we get a glimpse into Jewel's inner thoughts and how she feels about herself.

When she was only eight years old, Jewel's parents were divorced. Jewel remembers what her life was like then in the poem "After the Divorce." Watch for the lines "scatter us like seeds." What do you think Jewel means?

Read the following song and poem by Jewel. Can you relate to the words and feelings she expresses?

I'm Sensitive

I was thinking that I might fly today
Just to disprove all the things that you say
It doesn't take a talent to be mean
Your words can crush things that are unseen.

Chorus:
So please be careful with me, I'm sensitive
And I'd like to stay that way.

You always tell me that it's impossible
To be respected and be a girl
Why's it gotta be so complicated?
Why you gotta tell me if I'm hated?

So please be careful with me, I'm sensitive
And I'd like to stay that way.

I was thinking that it might do some good
If we robbed the cynics and took all their food
That way what they believe will have taken place
And we can give it to people who have some faith.

So please be careful with me, I'm sensitive
And I'd like to stay that way.

I have this theory that if we're told we're bad
Then that's the only idea we'll ever have
But maybe if we are surrounded in beauty
Someday we will become what we see
'Cause anyone can start a conflict
It's harder yet to disregard it
I'd rather see the world from another angle
We are everyday angels
Be careful with me 'cause I'd like to stay that way.

After the Divorce

After the divorce
we moved to Homer
to live in a one bedroom apartment
behind Uncle Otto's machine shop.

My brothers slept in the water closet
after my dad painted it any color
they wanted. The pipes looked like
silver trees sprouting up through the
frames of their bunk beds.

For me, we took the door
off the coat closet
and built a narrow bed
four feet off the ground
with a ladder of rough wood
to climb up that hurt my bare feet.
My dad tried hard
to keep us all together
and work at the same time,
but things just weren't the same.
He pulled my hair when he brushed it
and didn't sing to us at night
before we went to sleep.

I was eight and started cooking.
Shane grocery shopped
and Atz, well, he was a kid.
By 7 A.M. every morning
we walked ourselves out to the road
and waited for the school bus
with all the other kids.
Looking for signs
of when life might strike random again
and scatter us like seeds
on the unknowable winds
of chance.

Wrap-Up

Talk About It

Now that you've read "Opening Act" and "A Song and Poem by Jewel," what do you have to say about these questions?

- Has a friend or family member ever admired a talent of yours? Describe the experience.
- Why might writing help a person to feel better?

Comprehension Check

Write your answers to the questions below. Use information from the story and lyrics and poem to support your answers.

1. Why did Amanda stop appearing onstage with her mother?
2. How do you think Amanda feels when her mother calls her up onstage at the end of the story?
3. What do you think Amanda's mother means when she says "Words on a page are different than words in the mouth?"
4. In "I'm Sensitive," how does Jewel want to be treated?
5. Which of the poems or songs in these selections could you relate to the most? Why?

Vocabulary Check

Complete each sentence with the correct vocabulary word below.

despair **surveillance** **catharsis**
diplomatic **raucous**

1. The police officer was on a routine _______ of the area when he heard some music blasting.
2. There was a loud and _______ party going on inside the house at the end of the block.
3. He tried to be as _______ as possible when he asked them to turn down the music.
4. Jane likes to take long walks as a _______.
5. Suddenly, she was filled with a feeling of _______.

Write About It

Choose one of the writing prompts below.

- If Amanda wrote a journal entry about the night of the concert, what do you think she would say? Write a journal entry in her voice, telling about the experience.
- Amanda's brother wanted some new lyrics, too. Write original lyrics to any tune you know.
- If Amanda wanted some advice about songwriting, she could always ask Jewel. Write a list of five tips you think Jewel might offer a young songwriter.

About the AUTHORS

Jane Yolen and Heidi Stemple are the mother-daughter team who wrote "Opening Act." Like Amanda, Stemple has grown up with a semi-famous mother, who has published more than 200 books for children, teens, and adults. Not surprisingly, Stemple remembers being asked over and over if she wanted to be a famous writer just like her mom. Her answer? "No way." Time has changed that, however. "Opening Act" is the second story by Yolen and Stemple.

Although Yolen is famous for fantasy stories about mermaids and unicorns, this story owes a lot to real life. Like the mother in the story, Yolen says that she also used to be a singer (a job she took for extra money during college). Aaron, the brother in the story, is based on Stemple's two younger brothers. And Stemple, like Amanda, still hides a journal under her bed, filled with poems.

Understanding Credit Cards

Your new credit card really came in handy during your last shopping spree. It made shopping fun and easy. But now you're staring at the monthly statement. And the fun is definitely over.

Don't worry. It's not really that hard to read a statement. Check out this one and read all about it.

Jack's Credit Card Statement

VITA CREDIT CARD MONTHLY STATEMENT

CLOSING DATE	CARD NUMBER	CREDIT LIMIT		PAYMENT DATE
11/04	123456789	1000.00		11/28

TRANSACTION DATE	DESCRIPTION	AMOUNT
	TRANSACTIONS FOR CARD NUMBER 123456789	
10/05	NO WAY CAFE SANTE FE, NM	$ 28.50
10/11	SPORTS WORLD ALBUQUERQUE, NM	125.00
10/23	JJ RECORDS SANTE FE, NM	19.04
10/24	RETURN SANTE FE, NM	31.47CR
	PAYMENTS, ADJUSTMENT, AND OTHERS	
	10/29 PAYMENT RECEIVED, THANK YOU	55.00CR

Account Activity Summary	Previous Balance +	Purchases +	ITEMIZED FINANCE CHARGES: Charge This Month	Monthly Periodic Rate	Annual Percentage Rate	− Payments	− Credits	= NEW BALANCE
	255.00	172.54	3.38	1.5%	18%	55.00	31.47	$344.45
							Minimum Payment due	$ 50.00

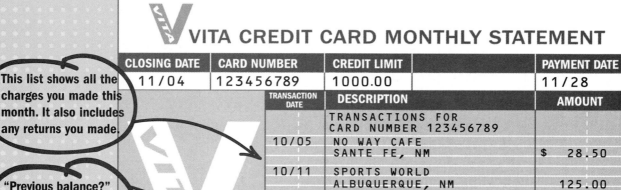

This list shows all the charges you made this month. It also includes any returns you made.

"Previous balance?" That's what's owed from last month! "Purchases" is the total spent this month.

If you don't pay your whole bill at once, you must pay a finance charge. This company charges 18% of your unpaid balance every year. That's 1.5% a month.

"In a few months, that finance charge really adds up. By the time you pay for a purchase, it may have cost you a lot more than its original price!"

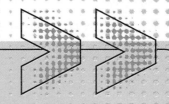

Paying With Plastic

Always read your credit card statement carefully. It will tell you how much you owe, and when your payment is due. Reread the credit card statement and tips. Then use them to answer the questions. Write your answers on your own paper.

1. Did Jack make a purchase or a return on October 5? Did this transaction make Jack's bill larger or smaller? By what amount? Now look at the transaction on October 24. Did Jack make a purchase or a return?

2. When is payment for this bill due? What is the smallest amount that the credit card user can pay?

3. How much money does Jack still owe from purchases made before October? (In other words, what is Jack's previous balance?)

a. $31.47 **c.** $255.00
b. $55.00 **d.** $172.54

4. What was the total amount of Jack's purchases this month?

5. What is the yearly finance charge on this credit card? What is the monthly finance charge?

Great Rates

Look through newspapers, magazines, or the Internet for five different credit card rates. What is the lowest annual interest rate you can find? What's the highest?

Write About It

What are the benefits of shopping with a credit card instead of cash? Make a list of reasons to use a credit card. Then make a list of reasons it may be better not to use a credit card.

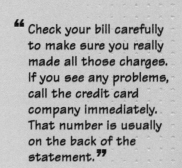

"Check your bill carefully to make sure you really made all those charges. If you see any problems, call the credit card company immediately. That number is usually on the back of the statement."

Real-World Words

annual: yearly
balance: a remainder; amount of money that is left
transaction: an exchange of goods, services, or money

poetry/nonfiction article

Out of the Dust

A Story in Poems

by Karen Hesse

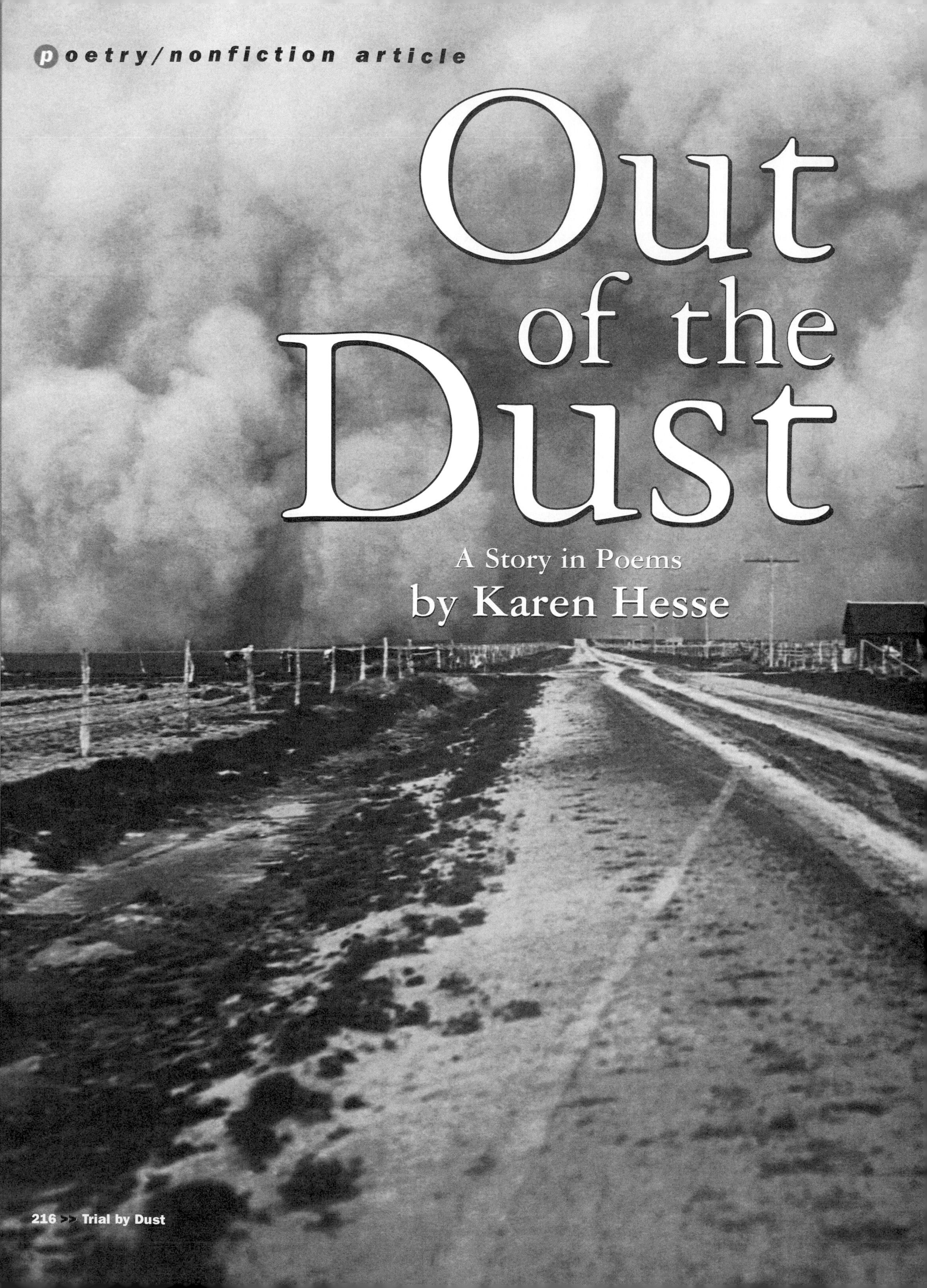

Out of the Dust is an unusual book. It's a novel—a book that tells a made-up story—but it's not written the way most novels are. The story is told purely through poetry. In a series of poems, the main character, 14-year-old Billie Jo, describes her life.

The poems are set in the Oklahoma Dust Bowl during the Depression. They explore what it was like to live with the ever-present dust sweeping through the land. Before reading Hesse's poems, it's helpful to know more about the Oklahoma Dust Bowl. The following information will give you an idea of what life was like during that time.

Black Blizzard

Imagine this: You're eating breakfast one Tuesday morning, minding your own business. You chance to look out the window.

"Ma! Dad!" you yell. "It's back. Take cover!"

Even though it's nine A.M., the sky in the distance is pitch black. A dry tidal wave of dust and dirt—7,000 feet high—is rolling, howling towards you. Your parents race to cram wet towels in the spaces under doors and windows, as the huge black cloud rumbles closer.

It's an eerie sight. In front of the cloud, birds fly and rabbits run, terrified. Soon the cloud is here. The sky is pure black. The wind is screaming, pelting your tiny house with dirt. Your mom hands you a wet towel, which you put over your face, but you can still taste the dust, feel it with every breath, gritty between your teeth. You huddle in the middle of the room with your family in the total darkness, and wait for the dust storm to end.

A Natural Disaster

In the mid 1930s, large areas of Oklahoma, Texas, Kansas, New Mexico, and Colorado were hit by hundreds of these storms. Together, the storms made up one of the worst natural disasters in America's history.

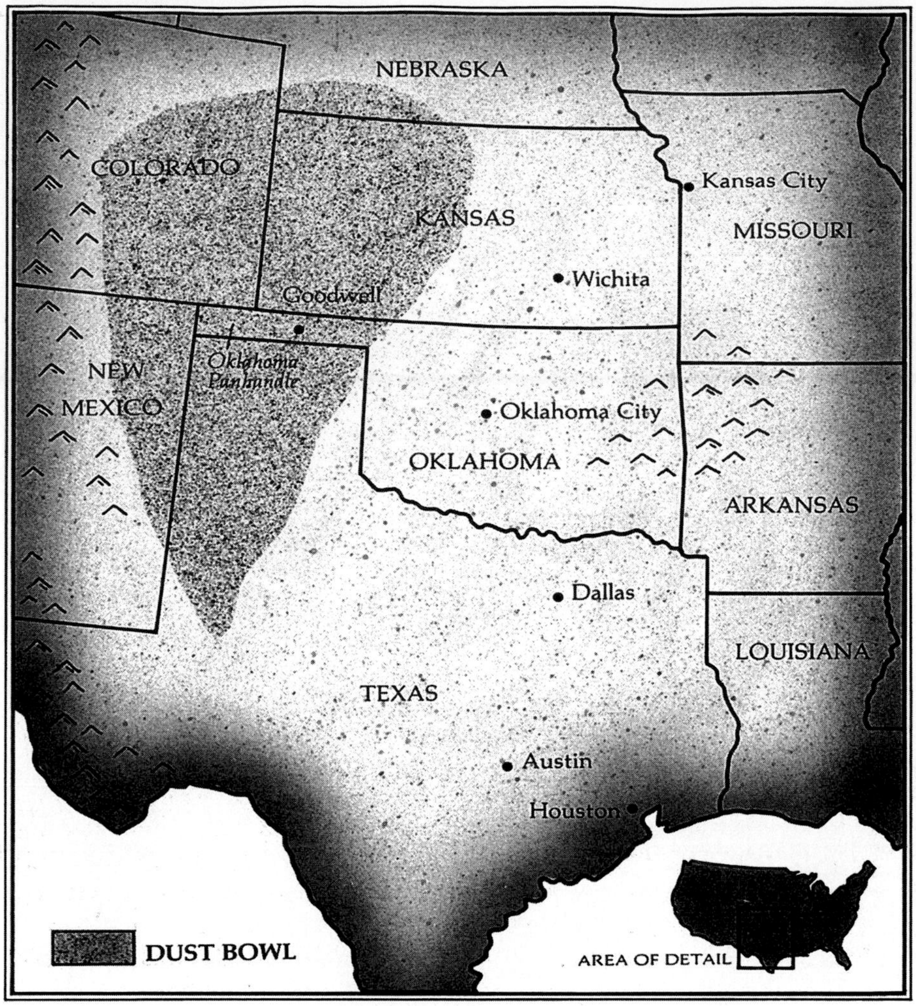
NEBRASKA
COLORADO
KANSAS
Kansas City
MISSOURI
Wichita
Goodwell
Oklahoma Panhandle
NEW MEXICO
Oklahoma City
OKLAHOMA
ARKANSAS
Dallas
LOUISIANA
TEXAS
Austin
Houston
DUST BOWL
AREA OF DETAIL

A map of the Dust Bowl, 1939. The dust storms affected the lives of people in six states.

The dust storms destroyed the land, ruined the economy of the whole area, and **threatened** the lives of most of the population. Everyone who could, picked up and moved west. It became the greatest peacetime migration ever in America. How did it happen?

From 1900 to 1930, many families bought or leased small parcels of land in the Plains states, and built farms. The area was mostly dry grasslands, where crops are difficult to grow. With hard work, the farmers were able to grow wheat and corn, and to raise cattle.

But in 1931, a terrible drought fell across the middle of the nation. America was already suffering from the stock market crash of 1929 and the Great Depression. Now, from 1931 to 1935, the farmers got almost no rain at all. For five years in a row, their corn and wheat crops failed. Farmers had no income, and couldn't pay their

Words, Words, Words

threatened: put in danger
suffocated: died from a lack of oxygen
impoverished: very poor
relentless: harsh and endless

mortgages. And soon their financial troubles were matched by the horror of their surroundings.

The Soil Blew Away

With no rainfall, the soil in the area became loose, dry, and dusty. The region's native wild grasses, which had served to hold the soil together, had been replaced long ago by crops, which now dried up and blew away. Soon, heavy winds began to howl, picking up the dust and soil. When the winds reached 50 or 60 miles an hour, they picked up the topsoil right off the ground. The flying dust buried roads and flew through the walls and windows of flimsy farmhouses. It killed cattle, and ruined the engines of vehicles. Old people and children caught outside were **suffocated.** Thousands of others died slowly of "dust pneumonia."

The dust storms were the last straw for many area farmers. They had already suffered through five years with little or no income because of the drought. Now, banks and mortgage companies took their farms—sending tractors to knock their houses down and run them off the land. The farmers, with no other choice, packed up their families and meager belongings and headed west.

More than one million people migrated west from the Plains states during that time. Poor, dirty, and hungry, they rumbled down Route 66, searching for work picking crops, digging roads—anything that would keep their families from starving.

Tough Times

But things were tough in the West, too. There were not enough jobs for all the new arrivals. Few could afford housing. Most of the migrant families camped or "squatted" wherever they could.

Many native Californians resented the migrants, calling them "Okies" and spreading rumors that they were not trustworthy. They felt the migrants were ruining local schools with overcrowding. Mobs of local men, armed with clubs and ax handles, raided the squatters' camps and tried to beat the migrants into leaving.

The migrating "Okies" became a media event after articles about them appeared in national magazines. In 1939, John Steinbeck, a California journalist and now a classic author, wrote *The Grapes of Wrath,* a fictional account of a family of **impoverished** Oklahoma farmers, and their journey to California. The book was an instant best-seller. A year later, a movie version came out. Now all of America knew the plight of the "Okies." Eventually, as America came out of the Great Depression, things began to improve for the migrants in California. Within a few years, the rains returned to the Dust Bowl, and people began farming again. Over the decades since, there have been several other serious droughts in the Plains states. But the Dust Bowl of the 1930s will always be remembered as the worst of all.

ASK yourself

- What caused the Great Dust Bowl of the 1930s?

Think about what the weather conditions did to the land.

Out of the Dust Came Poetry

So, why did author Karen Hesse decide to use poems to tell the dust story? "Billie Jo and her family had reached a point where they said only what needed to be said to get through each day," said Hesse. "I felt the use of poetry would be a good way to describe the rhythm of their daily lives."

The poems that follow are excerpts from *Out of the Dust.* The first poem gives an impression of the hardships of the Dust Bowl, and the battle farmers fought against their **relentless** enemy—dust. Some of the poems describe everyday life for Billie Jo in the midst of the dust—from going to school to playing the piano. In another poem, Billie Jo struggles to move on after a terrible accident that took her mother's life, and left her badly burned.

Here, Billie Jo describes the intensity of the dust and how it engulfs her family's house.

Fields of Flashing Light

I heard the wind rise,
and stumbled from my bed,
down the stairs,
out the front door,
into the yard.
The night sky kept flashing,
lightning danced down on its **spindly** legs.

I sensed it before I knew it was coming.
I heard it,
smelled it,
tasted it.
Dust.

While Ma and Daddy slept,
the dust came,
tearing up fields where the winter wheat,
set for harvest in June,
stood helpless.
I watched the plants,
surviving after so much
drought and so much wind,
I watched them fry,
or
flatten,
or blow away,
like bits of cast-off rags.

It wasn't until the dust turned toward the house,
like a fired **locomotive,**
and I fled,
barefoot and breathless, back inside,
it wasn't until the dust
hissed against the windows,
until it **ratcheted** the roof,
that Daddy woke.
He ran into the storm,
his overalls half-hooked over his union suit.
"Daddy!" I called. "You can't stop dust."
Ma told me
to cover the beds,
push the scatter rugs against the doors,
dampen the rags around the windows.
Wiping dust out of everything,
she made coffee and biscuits,
waiting for Daddy to come in.

Sometime after four,
rubbing low on her back,
Ma sank down into a chair at the kitchen table
and covered her face.
Daddy didn't come back for hours,
not
until the temperature dropped so low,
it brought snow.

Ma and I sighed, grateful,
staring out at the dirty flakes,
but our relief didn't last.
The wind snatched that snow right off the fields,
leaving behind a sea of dust,
waves and
waves and
waves of
dust,
rippling across our yard.

Daddy came in,
he sat across from Ma and blew his nose.
Mud streamed out.
He coughed and spit out
mud.
If he had cried,
his tears would have been mud too,
but he didn't cry.
And neither did Ma.

March 1934

ASK yourself

- What problems is the dust storm creating for Billie Jo's family?

Think about what is happening to the crops they were growing.

Once the dust hits, nothing is the same for Billie Jo . . . not even school.

Tested by Dust

While we sat
taking our six-weeks test,
the wind rose
and the sand blew
right through the cracks in the schoolhouse wall,
right through the gaps around the window glass,
and by the time the tests were done,
each and every one of us
was coughing pretty good and we all
needed a bath.

I hope we get bonus points
for testing in a dust storm.

April 1934

Heading for shelter during a dust storm.

Words, Words, Words

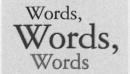

spindly: long, thin, and weak
locomotive: an engine
ratcheted: moved

In this poem, Billie Jo describes a horrible accident.

The Accident

I got
burned
bad.

Daddy
put a pail of **kerosene**
next to the stove
and Ma,
fixing breakfast,
thinking the pail was
filled with water,
lifted it,
to make Daddy's coffee,
poured it,
but instead of making coffee,
Ma made a rope of fire.
It rose up from the stove
to the pail
and the kerosene burst
into flames.

Ma ran across the kitchen,
out the porch door,
screaming for Daddy.
I tore after her,
then,
thinking of the burning pail
left behind in the bone-dry kitchen,
I flew back and grabbed it,
throwing it out the door.

ASK yourself

- Why was the kitchen "bone dry"?

Think about the effects of the dust storms.

A dust storm hits a small town.

I didn't know.
I didn't know Ma was coming back.

The flaming oil
splashed onto her apron,
and Ma,
suddenly Ma,
was a column of fire.
I pushed her to the ground,
desperate to save her,
desperate to save the baby, I
tried,
beating out the flames with my hands.
I did the best I could.
But it was no good.
Ma
got
burned
bad.

July 1934

Billie Jo's hands have been badly burned, and her mother dies after the fire. But she doesn't give up playing the piano, or ***pursuing*** *her dreams.*

Dreams

Each day after class lets out,
each morning before it begins,
I sit at the school piano
and make my hands work.
In spite of the pain,
in spite of the stiffness
and scars.
I make my hands play piano.
I have practiced my best piece over and over
till my arms throb,
because Thursday night
the Palace Theatre is having a contest.
Any man, woman, or child
who sings,
dances,
reads,
or plays worth a lick
can climb onto that stage.
Just register by four P.M.
and give them a taste of what you can do
and you're in,
performing for the crowd,
warming up the **audience** for the
Hazel Hurd Players.
I figure if I practice enough
I won't shame myself.
And we sure could use the extra cash
if I won.
Three-dollar first prize,
two-dollar second,
one-dollar third.
But I don't know if I could win anything,
not anymore.
It's the playing I want most,
the proving I can still do it.
without Arley making excuses.

I have a hunger,
for more than food.
I have a hunger
bigger than Joyce City.
I want tongues to tie, and
eyes to shine at me
like they do at Mad Dog Craddock.
Course they never will,
not with my hands all scarred up,
looking like the earth itself,
all **parched** and rough and cracking,
but if I played right enough,
maybe they would see past my hands.
Maybe they could feel at ease with me again,
and maybe then,
I could feel at ease with myself.

February 1935

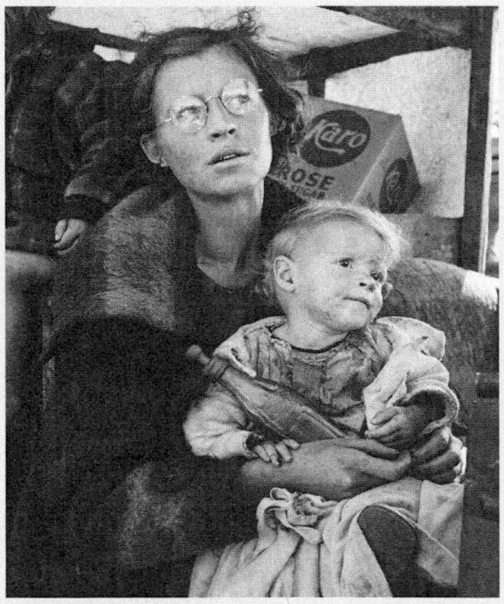
Karo
ROSE
A family heads west to escape the dust bowl, 1939.

Words, Words, Words

kerosene: fuel
pursuing: working towards a goal
audience: a group of people who listen to a performance
parched: very dry

Will things ever get better for Billie Jo? She doesn't think so, until it starts to snow.

Hope

It started out as snow,
oh,
big flakes
floating
softly,
catching on my sweater,
lacy on the edges of my sleeves.

Snow covered the dust,
softened the
fences,
soothed the parched lips
of the land.

And then it changed,
halfway between snow and rain,
sleet,
glazing the earth.

Until at last
it slipped into rain,
light as mist.

It was the kindest
kind of rain
that fell.

Soft and then a little heavier,
helping along
what had already fallen
into the
hard-pan
earth
until it
rained,
steady as a good friend
who walks besides you,
not getting in your way,
staying with you through a hard time.

And because the rain came
so patient and slow at first,
and built up strength as the earth
remembered how to yield,
instead of washing off,
the water slid in,
into the dying ground
and softened its stubborn pride,
and eased it back toward life.

And then,
just when we thought it would end,
after three such gentle days,
the rain
came
slamming down,
tons of it,
soaking into the ready earth
to the primed and greedy earth,
and soaking deep.

It kept coming,
thunder booming,
lightning
kicking,
dancing from the heavens
down to the prairie,
and my father
dancing with it,
dancing outside in the drenching night
with the gutters racing,
with the earth puddled and pleased,
with my father's near-finished pond filling.

When the rain stopped,
my father splashed out to the barn,
and spent
two days and two nights
cleaning dust out of his tractor
until he got it running again.
In the dark, headlights shining,
he idled toward the freshened fields,
certain the grass would grow again,
certain the weeds would grow again,
certain the wheat would grow again too.

May 1935

Karen Hesse

Author Karen Hesse took a trip into the Dust Bowl. She came back with a vivid tale of a young survivor.

You never know what might happen in a Karen Hesse story. One of her characters is raised by dolphins. Another lives through a nuclear accident. And in *Out of the Dust,* Billie Jo Kelby is trapped in the middle of a natural disaster.

Does that mean Hesse herself has lived through all those things? Well, no. In fact, she wasn't even alive during the Dust Bowl. But Hesse knows how to bring characters and stories to life in ways that make you feel like you are there. Here, she talks about *Out of the Dust.*

The Dust Bowl sounds like a major nightmare. How did you decide to write about it?

I was working on a picture book called *Come On Rain*, about a very hot day. That made me think about times in history when people really needed rain. So, I began to research the Dust Bowl. What happened to the Plains states was incredible. Dust from the Plains blew away and actually landed on ships 200 miles out on the ocean. That's a long way for a dust cloud to travel!

Some terrible things happen in *Out of the Dust.* Are they based on real life?

Oh, yes. I often base my stories on real-life events. To research *Out of the Dust*, I read a lot of old newspapers. Many things that happen in the book come from real newspaper stories.

Billie Jo had so many problems to deal with. How did she manage to go to school and play piano, too?

Even in a disaster like the Dust Bowl, normal life goes on. That's what I learned from my research. Those newspapers had stories about concerts and plays and things, too. I wanted readers to know that, so I made Billie Jo a poet and a piano player.

Is there anything you would change about *Out of the Dust*?

I wouldn't make it so sad. A while ago, I went on the *Today Show* to talk about the book. I had to reread it first so I could answer questions. And as I read, I thought, Wow, it's so sad! The book ends on a note of hope. But if I rewrote it, I'd make the beginning more hopeful, too. ●

Other Books by Karen Hesse

Letters from Rifka

It is 1919. The leaders of Russia are making trouble for Jewish people. Through a series of letters, 12-year-old Rifka tells the story of her family's escape to America.

The Music of Dolphins

Mila has lived on a tiny island and been raised by dolphins since the age of 4. Now she's a teenager and has been rescued from the island. Can she adjust to life among humans?

Wrap-Up

Talk About It

Now that you've read *Out of the Dust* and the author profile, what do you have to say about these questions?

- What recent disasters might compare to the dust storms of the mid-1930s?
- How do you think people cope with such great tragedies?

Comprehension Check

Write your answers to the questions below. Use information from the poems, the article, and the profile to support your answers.

1. What were two effects of the dust storms?
2. How do you think Billie Jo feels in the poem "Tested by Dust"?
3. Why did it take courage for Billie Jo to enter that contest?
4. How far did dust clouds from the Dust Bowl travel?
5. How does Karen Hesse feel about what happens to her characters in *Out of the Dust?*

Vocabulary Check

Answer each question below with a complete sentence. Think about the meaning of the vocabulary word in bold, and use that word in your sentence.

1. How could a young child's questions seem **relentless**?
2. What would you do if you felt **threatened** by a stray dog?
3. What would you do if you were feeling **parched**?
4. When is the last time you were part of an **audience**?
5. What career can you imagine yourself **pursuing**?

Write About It

Choose one of the writing prompts below.

- Billie Jo's father doesn't say much in these poems. Rewrite one of the poems from his point of view.
- Write a newspaper headline and short article about the Dust Bowl. Describe what happens, as if you were an eyewitness.
- Is there a historical time that you think is interesting? Write a letter to Karen Hesse telling her about it. Give three reasons why you think it would make a good setting for a story.

More to READ

For other glimpses of history through the eyes of young people, check out:

I Thought My Soul Would Rise and Fly: The Diary of Patsy, a Freed Girl
by Joyce Hansen

When the story begins, Patsy is a freed slave. As a joke, some children teach her to read so she can be the dunce in their game of "school." But Patsy is a good student, and later, she proves to be a good teacher, too.

Under the Blood-Red Sun
by Graham Salisbury

When the Japanese attack Pearl Harbor on December 7, 1941, Tomi's father and grandfather are arrested simply for being Japanese. Now, Tomi must become the man of the family. Luckily, he can still count on his baseball buddies, the Rats.

Responding to an Emergency

A basketball player gets knocked down—hard! The coach runs onto the court and yells, "Someone call for help!"

You know that you can call 911 in an emergency. But what do you say when the operator answers? Look over this dialogue. Then be prepared.

It's an Emergency!

Tell the 911 operator who and where you are right away. If you're cut off, the operator can call you back.

Tell the operator everything you know about the emergency. If you can't answer a question, tell the operator you don't know the answer.

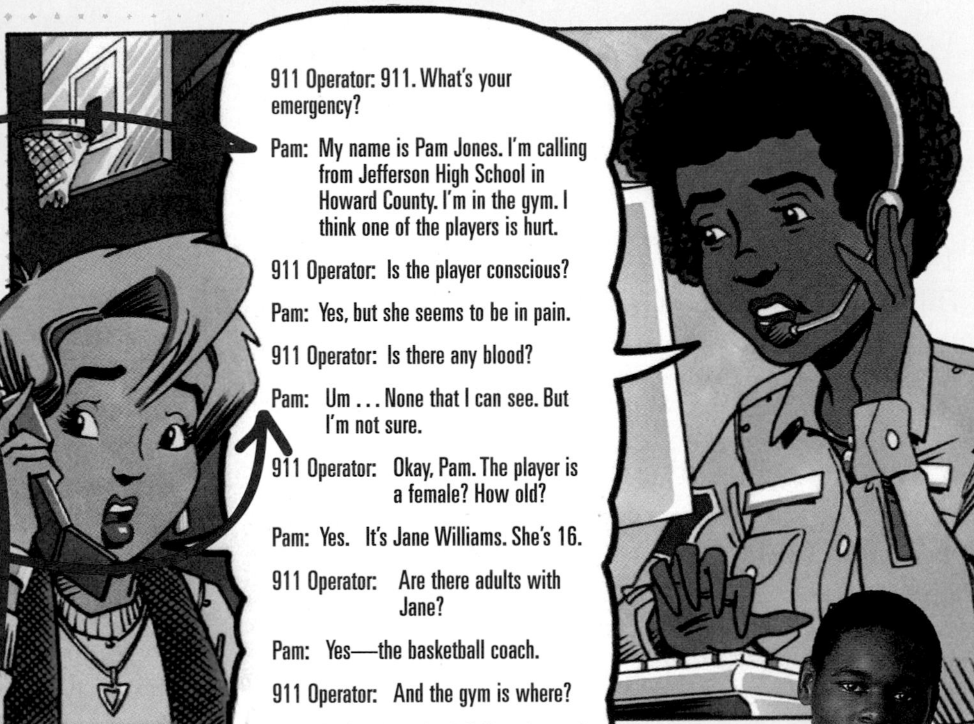
911 Operator: 911. What's your emergency?
Pam: My name is Pam Jones. I'm calling from Jefferson High School in Howard County. I'm in the gym. I think one of the players is hurt.
911 Operator: Is the player conscious?
Pam: Yes, but she seems to be in pain.
911 Operator: Is there any blood?
Pam: Um . . . None that I can see. But I'm not sure.
911 Operator: Okay, Pam. The player is a female? How old?
Pam: Yes. It's Jane Williams. She's 16.
911 Operator: Are there adults with Jane?
Pam: Yes—the basketball coach.
911 Operator: And the gym is where?
Pam: Behind the school. Follow the road to the left of the school.
911 Operator: Okay, Pam. An ambulance is on its way.

When telling the operator where you are, give as much detail as you can. If the ambulance driver has good directions, he or she will get to the emergency more quickly.

"911 calls are for emergencies only. Don't tie up emergency phone lines with calls about small problems."

Time to React

Are you prepared to respond to an emergency? Reread the dialogue and tips. Then use them to answer these questions. Write your answers on your own paper.

1. If you call 911, it's most important that your answers
a. are funny and helpful.
b. are clear and correct.
c. are short and fast.
d. show how upset you are about the emergency.

2. You're at school. Someone gets hurt. Which piece of information do you **not** need to tell the 911 operator?
a. your name
b. your e-mail address
c. the name and address of your school
d. what you know about the student's injury

3. An emergency happens at your school. You don't know the street address or the phone number. What could you tell the 911 operator so he or she can help the ambulance driver find it?

4. Why would an operator need to know if the injured player is conscious or bleeding?

5. When should you call 911? (Pick two.)
a. You have a test tomorrow, and you need help studying.
b. There's a big car wreck in front of your house.
c. A lifeguard at the pool yells for someone to get help.
d. Your little brother trips and scrapes his knee.

Just the Facts

There's been a serious accident at your home. Your sister has just cut herself badly. Create a fact sheet. Make a list of all the information you would need to give to the 911 operator.

Write a Dialogue

Use your fact sheet from "Just the Facts" to write a dialogue between you and a 911 operator. Use the dialogue from this lesson as a model.

"What happens if you need to call 911 but you don't have change for the pay phone? Don't worry. Calls to 911 are always free."

Real-World Words

conscious: awake; not asleep or passed out
injured: hurt
operator: a person who handles calls

short story

AMIGO BROTHERS

By Piri Thomas

Antonio and Felix are best friends who share a dream. They both dream of becoming a champion. But will their friendship survive when they come face to face in the ring?

Antonio Cruz and Felix Vargas were both seventeen years old. They were so together in friendship that they felt themselves to be brothers. They had known each other since childhood, growing up on the Lower East Side of Manhattan in the same tenement building on Fifth Street between Avenue A and Avenue B.

Antonio was fair, lean, and lanky, while Felix was dark, short, and husky. Antonio's hair was always falling over his eyes, while Felix wore his black hair in a natural Afro.

Each youngster had a dream of someday becoming lightweight champion of the world. Every chance they had the boys worked out, sometimes at the Boys Club on 10th Street and Avenue A and sometimes at the pro's gym on 14th Street. Early morning sunrises would find them running along the East River Drive, wrapped in sweatshirts, short towels around their necks, and handkerchiefs around their foreheads.

While some youngsters were into street negatives, Antonio and Felix slept, ate, rapped, and dreamt positive. Between them, they had a collection of *Fight* magazines second to none, plus a scrapbook filled with torn tickets to every boxing match they had ever attended, and some clippings of their own. If asked a question about any given fighter, they would immediately zip out from their memory banks divisions, weights, records of fights, knock-outs, technical knock-outs, and draws or losses.

"We both know that in the ring the better man wins. Friend or no friend, brother or no brother."

Each had fought many bouts representing their community and had won two gold-plated medals plus a silver and bronze medallion. The difference was in their style. Antonio's lean form and long reach made him the better boxer, while Felix's short and muscular frame made him the better slugger. Whenever they had met in the ring for sparring sessions, it had always been hot and heavy.

Now, after a series of **elimination** bouts, they had been informed that they were to meet each other in the division finals that were scheduled for the seventh of August, two weeks away. The winner would represent the Boys Club in the Golden Gloves Championship Tournament.

The two boys continued to run together along the East River Drive. But even when joking with each other, they both sensed a wall rising between them.

One morning less than a week before their bout, they met as usual for their daily workout. They fooled around with a few jabs at the air, slapped skin, and then took off, running lightly along the dirty East River's edge.

Antonio glanced at Felix who kept his eyes purposely straight ahead. He kept pausing from time to time to do some fancy leg work and throw some punches to an imaginary jaw. Antonio then beat the air with a **barrage** of body blows and short **devastating** lefts with an overhand jawbreaking right.

After a mile or so, Felix puffed and said. "Let's stop a while, bro. I think we both got something to say to each other."

Antonio nodded. It was not natural to be acting as though nothing unusual was happening when two good buddies were going to be blasting each other within a few short days.

They rested their elbows on the railing separating them from the river. Antonio wiped his face with his short towel. The sunrise was now creating day.

Felix leaned heavily on the river's railing and stared across to the shores of Brooklyn. Finally, he broke the silence.

"Man, I don't know how to come out with it."

Antonio helped. "It's about our fight, right?"

"Yeah, right." Felix's eyes squinted at the rising orange sun.

"I've been thinking about it too, *panín.* In fact, since we found out it was going to be me and you, I've been awake at night, pulling punches on you, trying not to hurt you."

"Same here. It ain't natural not to think about the fight. I mean, we both are *cheverote* fighters and we both want to win. But only one of us can win. There ain't no draws in the eliminations."

Felix tapped Antonio gently on the shoulder. "I don't mean to sound like I'm bragging, bro. But I wanna win, fair and square."

Antonio nodded quietly. "Yeah. We both know that in the ring the better man wins. Friend or no friend, brother or no . . ."

Felix finished it for him. "Brother. Tony, let's promise something right here. Okay?"

GLOSSARY

panín: pal
cheverote: great
hermano: brother
sí: yes
Suavecito: take it easy
sabe: understand
salsa (music): Latin American dance music
señores y señoras: gentlemen and ladies
mucho corazón: much courage

"If it's fair, *hermano,* I'm for it." Antonio admired the courage of a tugboat pulling a barge five times its welterweight size.

"It's fair, Tony. When we get into the ring, it's gotta be like we never met. We gotta be like two heavy strangers that want the same thing and only one can have it. You understand, don'tcha?"

"*Sí,* I know." Tony smiled. "No pulling punches. We go all the way."

"Yeah, that's right. Listen, Tony. Don't you think it's a good idea if we don't see each other until the day of the fight? I'm going to stay with my Aunt Lucy in the Bronx. I can use Gleason's Gym for working out. My manager says he got some sparring partners with more or less your style."

Tony scratched his nose **pensively.** "Yeah, it would be better for our heads." He held out his hand, palm upward. "Deal?"

"Deal." Felix lightly slapped open skin.

"Ready for some more running?" Tony asked lamely.

"Naw, bro. Let's cut it here. You go on. I kinda like to get things together in my head."

"You ain't worried, are you?" Tony asked.

"No way, man." Felix laughed out loud. "I got too much smarts for that. I just think it's cooler if we split right here. After the fight, we can get it together again like nothing ever happened."

The *amigo* brothers were not ashamed to hug each other tightly.

"Guess you're right. Watch yourself, Felix. I hear there's some pretty heavy dudes up in the Bronx. *Suavecito,* okay?"

"Okay. You watch yourself too, *sabe?*"

Tony jogged away. Felix watched his friend disappear from view, throwing rights and lefts. Both fighters had a lot of psyching up to do before the big fight.

The days in training passed much too slowly. Although they kept out of each other's way, they were aware of each other's progress via the ghetto grapevine.

The evening before the big fight, Tony made his way to the roof of his tenement. In the quiet early dark, he peered over the ledge. Six stories below the lights of the city blinked and the sounds of cars mingled with the curses and the laughter of children in the street. He tried not to think of Felix, feeling he had succeeded in psyching his mind. But only in the ring would he really know. To spare Felix hurt, he would have to knock him out, early and quick.

Up in the South Bronx, Felix decided to take in a movie in an effort to keep Antonio's face away from his fists. The flick was *The Champion* with Kirk Douglas, the third time Felix was seeing it.

The champion was getting hit hard. He was saved only by the sound of the bell.

Felix became the champ and Tony the challenger.

The movie audience was going out of its head. The challenger, confident that he now had the championship in the bag, threw a left. The champ countered with a dynamite right.

Felix's right arm felt the shock. Antonio's face, superimposed on the screen, was hit by the awesome blow. Felix saw himself in the ring, blasting Antonio against the ropes. The challenger fell to the canvas.

ASK YOURSELF

- Why do you think the two friends have decided to train separately?

Explain the problem these friends have in your own words.

WORDS, WORDS, WORDS

elimination: removal by being defeated
barrage: a large amount of something that all comes at the same time
devastating: shocking and distressing
pensively: thoughtfully

When Felix finally left the theater, he had figured out how to psyche himself for tomorrow's fight. It was Felix the Champion vs. Antonio the Challenger.

He walked up some dark streets, deserted except for small pockets of wary-looking kids wearing gang colors. Despite the fact that he was Puerto Rican like them, they eyed him as a stranger to their turf. Felix did a fast shuffle, bobbing and weaving, while letting loose a **torrent** of blows that would demolish whatever got in its way. It seemed to impress the brothers, who went about their own business.

Finding no takers, Felix decided to split to his aunt's. Walking the streets had not relaxed him, neither had the fight flick. All it had done was to stir him up. He let himself quietly into his Aunt Lucy's apartment and went straight to bed, falling into a fitful sleep with sounds of the gong for Round One.

Antonio was passing some heavy time on his rooftop. How would the fight tomorrow affect his relationship with Felix? After all, fighting was like any other profession. Friendship had nothing to do with it. A gnawing doubt crept in. He cut negative thinking real quick by doing some speedy fancy dance steps, bobbing and weaving like mercury. The night air was blurred with perpetual motions of left hooks and right crosses. Felix, his *amigo* brother, was not going to be Felix at all in the ring. Just an **opponent** with another face. Antonio went to sleep, hearing the opening bell for the first round. Like his friend in the South Bronx, he prayed for victory, via a quick clean knock-out in the first round.

Large posters plastered all over the walls of local shops announced the fight between Antonio Cruz and Felix Vargas as the main bout.

WORDS, WORDS, WORDS

torrent: a flow of violent and swift actions
opponent: someone who is against you in a fight or contest
improvised: did the best you could on the spur of the moment
acknowledgment: recognition that something exists

The fight had created great interest in the neighborhood. Antonio and Felix were well liked and respected. Each had his own loyal following. Antonio's fans counted on his boxing skills. On the other side, Felix's admirers trusted in his dynamite-packed fists.

Felix had returned to his apartment early in the morning of August 7th and stayed there, hoping to avoid seeing Antonio. He turned the radio on to *salsa* music sounds and then tried to read while waiting for word from his manager.

The fight was scheduled to take place in Tompkins Square Park. It had been decided that the gymnasium of the Boys Club was not large enough to hold all the people who were sure to attend. In Tompkins Square Park, everyone who wanted could view the fight, whether from ringside or window fire escapes or tenement rooftops.

The morning of the fight Tompkins Square was a beehive of activity with numerous workers setting up the ring, the seats, and the guest speakers' stand. The scheduled bouts began shortly after noon and the park had begun filling up even earlier.

The local junior high school across from Tompkins Square Park served as the dressing room for all the fighters. Each was given a separate classroom with desk tops, covered with mats, serving as resting tables. Antonio thought he caught a glimpse of Felix waving to him from a room at the far end of the corridor. He waved back just in case it had been him.

The fighters changed from their street clothes into fighting gear. Antonio wore white trunks, black socks, and black shoes. Felix wore sky blue trunks, red socks, and white boxing shoes. Each had dressing gowns to match their fighting trunks with their names neatly stitched on the back.

The loudspeakers blared into the open windows of the school. There were speeches by dignitaries, community leaders, and great boxers of yesteryear. Some were very well prepared, some **improvised** on the spot. They all carried the same message of great pleasure and honor at being part of such a historic event. This great day was in the tradition of champions emerging from the streets of the Lower East Side.

Interwoven with the speeches were the sounds of the other boxing events. After the sixth bout, Felix was much relieved when his trainer Charlie said, "Time change. Quick knock-out. This is it. We're on."

Waiting time was over. Felix was escorted from the classroom by a dozen fans in white T-shirts with the word FELIX across their fronts.

Antonio was escorted down a different stairwell and guided through a roped-off path.

As the two climbed into the ring, the crowd exploded with a roar. Antonio and Felix both bowed gracefully and then raised their arms in **acknowledgment.**

Antonio tried to be cool, but as the roar was starting to build, he turned slowly to meet Felix's eyes looking directly into his. Felix nodded his head and Antonio responded. And both as one, just as quickly, turned away to face his own corner.

Bong—bong—bong. The roar turned to stillness.

"Ladies and Gentlemen, *Señores y Señoras.*"

The announcer spoke slowly, pleased at his bilingual efforts.

"Now the moment we have all been waiting for — the main event between two fine young Puerto Rican fighters, products of our Lower East Side. In this corner, weighing 134 pounds, Felix Vargas. And in this corner, weighing 133 pounds,

ASK YOURSELF

- Who do you think will win the fight—Antonio or Felix?

Think about what you've read so far, and make your best prediction.

Antonio Cruz. The winner will represent the Boys Club in the tournament of champions, the Golden Gloves. There will be no draw. May the best man win."

The cheering of the crowd shook the window panes of the old buildings surrounding Tompkins Square Park. At the center of the ring, the referee was giving instructions to the youngsters.

"Keep your punches up. No low blows. No punching on the back of the head. Keep your heads up. Understand. Let's have a clean fight. Now shake hands and come out fighting."

Both youngsters touched gloves and nodded. They turned and danced quickly to their corners. Their head towels and dressing gowns were lifted neatly from their shoulders by their trainers' nimble fingers. Antonio crossed himself. Felix did the same.

BONG! BONG! ROUND ONE. Felix and Antonio turned and faced each other squarely in a fighting pose. Felix wasted no time. He came in fast, head low, half hunched toward his right shoulder, and lashed out with a straight left. He missed a right cross as Antonio slipped the punch and countered with one-two-three lefts that snapped Felix's head back, sending a mild shock coursing through him. If Felix had any small doubt about their friendship affecting their fight, it was being neatly dispelled.

Antonio danced, a joy to behold. His left hand was like a **piston** pumping jabs one right after another with seeming ease. Felix bobbed and weaved and never stopped boring in. He knew that at long range he was at a disadvantage. Antonio had too much reach on him. Only by coming in close could Felix hope to achieve the dreamed-of knockout.

Antonio knew the dynamite that was stored in his *amigo* brother's fist. He ducked a short right and missed a left hook. Felix trapped him against the ropes just long enough to pour some punishing rights and lefts to Antonio's hard midsection. Antonio slipped away from Felix, crashing two lefts to his head, which set Felix's right ear to ringing.

Bong! Both *amigos* froze a punch well on its way, sending up a roar of approval for good sportsmanship.

Felix walked briskly back to his corner. His right ear had not stopped ringing. Antonio gracefully danced his way toward his stool none the worse, except for glowing glove burns, showing angry red against the whiteness of his midribs.

"Watch that right, Tony." His trainer talked into his ear. "Remember Felix always goes to the body. He'll want you to drop your hands for his overhand left or right. Got it?"

Antonio nodded, spraying water out between his teeth. He felt better as his sore midsection was being firmly rubbed.

Felix's corner was also busy.

"You gotta get in there, fella." Felix's trainer poured water over his curly Afro locks. "Get in there or he's gonna chop you up from way back."

Bong! Bong! Round two. Felix was off his stool and rushed Antonio like a bull, sending a hard right to his head. Beads of water exploded from Antonio's long hair.

Antonio, hurt, sent back a blurring barrage of lefts and rights that only meant pain to Felix, who returned with a short left to the head followed by a looping right to the body. Antonio countered with his own flurry, forcing Felix to give ground. But not for long.

WORDS, WORDS, WORDS

piston: something that moves back and forth quickly to create energy
feinted: moved to fool an opponent
flailed: swung one's arms wildly
commenced: started something

“Neither **fighter** was giving an **inch.**”

Felix bobbed and weaved, bobbed and weaved, occasionally punching his two gloves together.

Antonio waited for the rush that was sure to come. Felix closed in and **feinted** with his left shoulder and threw his right instead. Lights suddenly exploded inside Felix’s head as Antonio slipped the blow and hit him with a piston-like left catching him flush on the point of his chin.

Bedlam broke loose as Felix’s legs momentarily buckled. He fought off a series of rights and lefts and came back with a strong right that taught Antonio respect.

Antonio danced in carefully. He knew Felix had the habit of playing possum when hurt, to sucker an opponent within reach of the powerful bombs he carried in each fist.

A right to the head slowed Antonio’s pretty dancing. He answered with his own left at Felix’s right eye that began puffing up within three seconds.

Antonio, a bit too eager, moved in too close and Felix had him entangled into a rip-roaring, punching toe-to-toe slugfest. It brought the whole Tompkins Square Park screaming to its feet.

Rights to the body. Lefts to the head. Neither fighter was giving an inch. Suddenly a short right caught Antonio squarely on the chin. His long legs turned to jelly and his arms **flailed** out desperately. Felix, grunting like a bull, threw wild punches from every direction. Antonio, groggy, bobbed and weaved, evading most of the blows. Suddenly his head cleared. His left flashed out hard and straight catching Felix on the bridge of his nose.

Felix lashed back with a harsh punch, right off the ghetto streets. At the same instant, his eye caught another left hook from Antonio. Felix swung out trying to clear the pain. Only the frenzied screaming of those along ringside let him know that he had dropped Antonio. Fighting off the growing haze, Antonio struggled to his feet, got up, and ducked. Then he threw a smashing right that dropped Felix flat on his back.

Felix got up as fast as he could in his own corner, groggy but still game. He didn’t even hear the count. In a fog, he heard the roaring of the crowd, who seemed to have gone insane. His head cleared to hear the bell sound at the end of the round. He was very glad. His trainer sat him down on the stool.

ASK YOURSELF

- How does each fighter plan to beat his opponent?

Think about what each fighter knows about the other’s strengths and weaknesses.

In his corner, Antonio was doing what all fighters do when they are hurt. They sit and smile at everyone.

The referee signaled the ring doctor to check the fighters out. He did so and then gave his okay. The cold water sponges brought clarity to both *amigo* brothers. They were rubbed until their circulation ran free.

Bong! Round three—the final round. Up to now it had been tic-tac-toe, pretty much even. But everyone knew there could be no draw and that this round would decide the winner.

This time, to Felix’s surprise, it was Antonio who came out fast, charging across the ring. Felix braced himself but couldn’t ward off the barrage of punches. Antonio drove Felix hard against the ropes.

The crowd ate it up. Thus far the two had fought with *mucho corazón.* Felix tapped his gloves and **commenced** his attack anew. Antonio, throwing boxer’s caution to the winds, jumped in to meet him.

Both pounded away. Neither gave an inch and neither fell to the canvas. Felix's left eye was tightly closed. Bright red blood poured from Antonio's nose. They fought toe-to-toe.

The sounds of their blows were loud in contrast to the silence of a crowd gone completely mute. The referee was stunned by their savagery.

Bong! Bong! Bong! The bell sounded over and over again. Felix and Antonio were past hearing. Their blows continued to pound on each other like hailstones.

"No matter what the decision, they knew they would always be champions to each other."

Finally the referee and the two trainers pried Felix and Antonio apart. Cold water was poured over them to bring them back to their senses.

They looked around and then rushed toward each other. A cry of alarm surged through Tompkins Square Park. Was this a fight to the death instead of a boxing match?

The fear soon gave way to wave upon wave of cheering as the two *amigos* embraced.

No matter what the decision, they knew they would always be champions to each other.

BONG! BONG! BONG! "Ladies and Gentlemen. *Señores* and *Señoras*. The winner and representative to the Golden Gloves Tournament of Champions is . . ."

The announcer turned to point to the winner and found himself alone. Arm in arm the two champions had already left the ring. ●

SHOULD BOXING BE BANNED?

Antonio and Felix loved boxing. It kept them in top shape and helped them focus on the positive. But not everyone thinks that boxing is good. In fact, the American Medical Association (AMA)—a national group of doctors—has called for a ban on the sport. They say that boxing often causes brain damage. But many people in the boxing world say that their sport is no more dangerous than skiing or racing cars. They believe it should be left up to fighters to decide whether boxing is worth the risk.

WHAT DO YOU THINK? READ THIS DEBATE AND DECIDE FOR YOURSELF.

yes

Athletes get hurt all the time. But boxing is the only sport in which the main goal is to beat up your opponent. Every year, at least three or four fighters are killed in the ring. Sudden death isn't the only risk boxers face. Unlike other sports, boxing has long-term effects on the brain. As many as 70% of pro boxers wind up with permanent brain damage. And even in amateur boxing, where the fighters wear headgear, many boxers have suffered brain injuries. An outright ban on boxing is the only way to prevent this problem.

If you said yes:

- Should other dangerous sports, like skiing and car racing, also be banned?

no

Boxing teaches kids discipline, gives them goals to work for, and keeps them off the street. Plus, it's a great workout and a good sport for athletes who don't enjoy team sports. Of course, boxing has its risks. But don't we live in a free country? Like other athletes, boxers should be free to decide for themselves whether their sport is worth the risks involved. Besides, more people are killed or disabled every year in sports such as football and car racing than in the boxing ring.

If you said no:

- Should teens who want to box be warned that the sport may cause brain damage?

What's your point of view?

Wrap-UP

TALK ABOUT IT

Now that you've read "Amigo Brothers" and "Should Boxing Be Banned?" what do you have to say about these questions?

- If you were the judge, who would you say won the fight between Antonio and Felix? Why?
- Why do you think people enjoy dangerous sports like boxing, football, and race-car driving?

COMPREHENSION CHECK

Write your answers to the questions below. Use information from the story and the debate to support your answers.

1. What are both boxers afraid of?
2. Do you think Felix and Antonio are evenly matched? Why or why not?
3. Do you think it's a problem for friends to compete?
4. What are two possible dangers of boxing?
5. What do you think might have happened if one of the amigo brothers had seriously hurt the other during the match?

VOCABULARY CHECK

Answer each question below with a complete sentence. Before you answer, think about the meaning of the vocabulary word in bold.

1. What is the opposite of something that's **improvised**?
2. What might cause someone to be **pensively** silent?
3. How does it feel to get **acknowledgment** for a difficult job?
4. If a friend heard some **devastating** news, what would you do?
5. If a person **flailed** about in the water, what could you do to help?

WRITE ABOUT IT

Choose one of the writing prompts below.

- Create a flyer announcing the boxing match between Felix and Antonio. Include a short paragraph about the match that will make people want to go.
- What do you think Felix and Antonio might say to a reporter after the match? Write a short interview that might appear in the sports section of a newspaper. The interview should include at least three questions for the fighters and their answers.
- Does boxing have enough rules? Come up with a list of five rules that you think might make this sport safer.

More to READ

If you like books about friendship, check out:

Taking Sides
by Gary Soto

Eighth-grade basketball player Lincoln Mendoza moves to a new neighborhood and changes schools. Now he has to play against his former teammates. To make matters worse, his new coach holds a grudge against Lincoln's old school—and Lincoln, too. Pressure builds as the day of the big game approaches. Lincoln can't decide who he really wants to win.

Walk Two Moons
by Sharon Creech

Thirteen-year-old Salamanca Tree Hiddle travels with her grandparents from Ohio to Idaho, on a trip to find her mother. Along the way, she tells her grandparents the strange story of her friend Phoebe whose mother disappears and then returns. Despite her father's warning that she is "fishing in the air," Salamanca hopes that she too will get her mother back. The truth waits at the end of the journey.

Understanding Labels

You want to plant a garden, so you head to the plant nursery to buy fertilizer. There are several kinds on the shelves. How can you tell which kind to buy? You need to read the labels.

Check out the sample labels below. Can you tell how the products are different?

Finding the Right Fertilizer

This fertilizer is not for all seasons or plants. Read labels closely to make sure you buy the product you need.
$15.95
Maxi Flor
FERTILIZER
For Evergreens, Bushes, Fruit Trees
Directions: Sprinkle on wet ground. Do not dilute with water. Apply once.
LATE SUMMER EARLY FALL
20 lbs.
Caution: Poison! Keep away from children and pets. Keep tightly closed.
GREEN THUMB
FERTILIZER FOR LAWNS
Directions: Mix 1/4 cup to a gallon of water per 50 sq. ft. Apply twice a year.
10 lbs. $7.95
EARLY TO LATE FALL
EARLY SPRING
ALL-GROW
FERTILIZER
MULTI-PURPOSE
(bushes, trees, vegetable gardens, bulbs, flowers)
Early Spring
10 lbs.
$7.95
Directions: Use with special hose adapter. Fill hose adapter to line with fertilizer and fill with water. Attach hose. Water area with fine spray. Use entire mixture for maximum of 20 sq. ft.
Check out the weight or amount of the product. Which is the best value? Pick a size that's right for your needs.
Make sure you have everything you need to use the product. Don't buy a product that will be too hard for you to use.

"Pay attention to brand names. When you find a brand name that works well for you, you'll know which one you might want to buy next time."

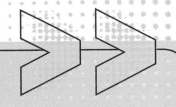

Looking at Labels

At first glance, all three fertilizers look the same. Did you see the difference when you read the labels? Reread the fertilizer labels and the tips that go with them. Then answer the following questions. Write your answers on your own paper.

1. It's August. Helen Gatsby needs to fertilize the bushes in front of her house. Which fertilizer should she buy?
a. Maxi Flor
b. Green Thumb
c. All-Grow

2. The grass really **is** greener on the other side of Mr. Sanchez's fence. He needs to fertilize his lawn. Which fertilizer should he buy?
a. Green Thumb
b. All-Grow
c. Green Thumb or All-Grow

3. The Jacksons have three young children and two dogs. Which fertilizer should they buy for their apple trees? Explain why.

4. Jim Hank has some bushes to fertilize. He doesn't own a garden hose and doesn't want to buy one. Which fertilizer should he buy? Why?

5. Mrs. Dunhart needs to fertilize a rosebush, some tulip bulbs, a vegetable patch, and her lawn. She doesn't want to spend more money than necessary. Which two products should she buy?

Chart It

Make a chart that compares the information from the three fertilizer labels. Label the columns as follows: Brand, Price, Number of Pounds, Season to Use, Type of Plant, Method of Use.

Compare It

You have to paint your baby brother's room. The paint must be water-based and easy to clean. Look at paint labels in a hardware store or on the Web. Find paint you could use for the job. Write down the brand name you choose.

"If you want to do some additional research on a product before or after purchase, try the company Web site."

Real-World Words

dilute: to make weaker by adding water
fertilizer: a substance added to soil to help plants grow
multi-purpose: having more than one use

Not Your Average Jobs

Want to spend the rest of your life sitting behind a desk? No? Then read about these jobs where a desk and office aren't required.

Animal Keeper & Friend

Whether she's grooming rhinos or feeding warthogs, Michele Gaffney has a bear of a job.

It's just another day at the office for Michele Gaffney. Same old drill: Get a cup of coffee. Relax. Clip a rhino's toenails. Break up a deer fight. Feed a warthog.

It's a jungle out there. The work world can be a zoo, and that's just fine with Michele. That's because she works at the San Diego Wild Animal Park in Escondido, CA. It's a place where you can see wild animals like giraffes, rhinos, and tigers in their own habitats. Michele is an animal keeper. It's her job to make sure that the animals are healthy and happy in their homes.

"I loved animals when I was a kid, and I always wanted to work with them," says Michele, 38. Then she got her master's degree in zoology. "Of course, I loved cats—not warthogs. I never really had experience with animals like these, but the more you work with them, the more you learn to respect them."

From Zebras to Foxes

The Wild Animal Park is home to animals from all over the world. Michele has worked there for 16 years. First, she worked with large animals from Africa and East Asia, like giraffes, zebras, and gazelles. Now, she tends to animals from Central Africa. Many of these animals are exotic creatures that usually live in rainforests, like the colobus monkey or the bat-eared fox. But Michele says that working with any animal—from an elephant to a mouse—is all a matter of learning their personalities and gaining their trust.

"To a certain extent you have to treat animals like humans," she says. "You have to learn who they are and what they like. Then you look for any sign of change that might show they aren't feeling well." For example, if the usually-ravenous warthog is shying away from his food, he might have a stomachache or a bad tooth. If the always-calm giraffe is suddenly kicking up her heels, she might be sick—or even pregnant.

"There's a whole world going on in here," Michele says. "You have to keep your eye on everyone."

Michele begins her day by making sure that all the animals are fed—and that can be quite a project in itself. She loads her truck with 50 pound feed bags and bails of hay. Then she visits all the animals in her section. "There's a lot of physical labor in this job," she says. "And you

"If you have a sincere love of and interest in animals, I can't think of anywhere better to be."

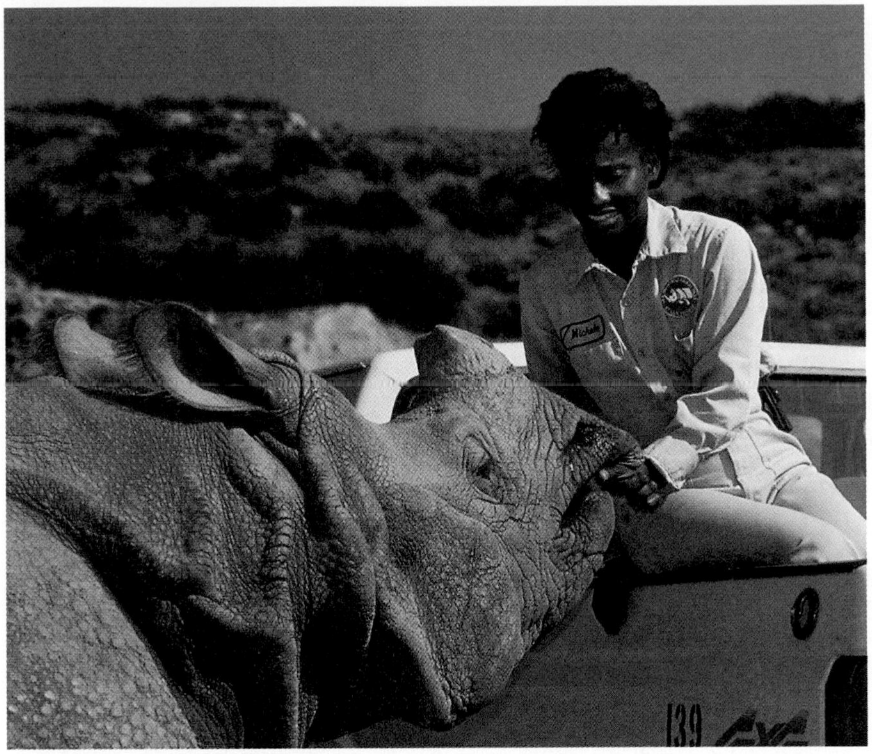

Michele Gaffney loves working with animals.

get a little tired of cleaning up after some of these guys too."

Then it's time for the animal roll call. Michele counts all the animals, just to make sure that no one is missing or hiding because of an injury. Sometimes Michele finds an unexpected treat in her head count: an animal who has given birth in the middle of the night.

The babies can be hard to find, though. Many animals hide their young because they are worried that predators will attack them. So, sometimes Michele has to climb high into the hills or check behind rocks and fallen trees to find a baby.

Animal Personalities

Then it's on to the daily chores, which are different for every animal. Sometimes there is a warthog to be cleaned. "I love them, they have such great little personalities," she says. "And they are so ugly, they're actually cute." Sometimes the rhino needs a little personal grooming. That's when Michele has to clip the animal's toenails. She doesn't sedate him before pulling out the giant clippers. She merely relaxes him with a bucket of sweet grass and then rubs his tummy until he rolls over. "He's like a big puppy dog," she says. "Except he weighs 5,000 pounds."

Not all of her jobs are fun, though. Sometimes she has to assist the park's veterinarians in caring for sick animals. And, unfortunately, seeing an animal die is just a daily part of her job. "It's hard to lose an animal, but you have to accept what happens in nature," she says. It was especially hard for Michele when she cared for a Przewalski's Horse from Russia that was born sickly. She treated the foal for two weeks and thought the animal was gaining strength. But the baby horse died days later. "You just have to realize that there are some animals you are not going to be able to save, no matter how hard you try," she says.

Luckily, she gets to experience the other side of nature too. She recently helped in the difficult delivery of a deer calf. It was touch and go for a while, but now both mother and baby are back on their feet—umm—hoofs.

"You see it all on this job," Michele says. "You work very hard. But if you have a sincere love of and interest in animals, I can't think of anywhere better to be."

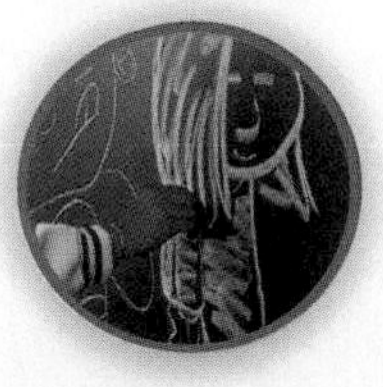

Sketch Work

Cartoonist Robb Armstrong turns his life into art.

Robb Armstrong has some advice for kids who want to travel in his career footsteps. First, follow your passion. Second, stay true to your vision.

And third, keep your pencils sharpened and your drawing table clean.

"If I told you the time I spend clearing all the mail and scrap papers off my desk," Robb laughs. "It takes me a half hour to find space to draw."

OK, maybe a clean table isn't all it takes to be a cartoonist. It takes dedication, creativity, and talent. All of which helps Robb produce "Jump Start," a comic strip that appears seven days a week in 350 newspapers from Los Angeles to Chicago to Robb's hometown of Philadelphia. "Jump Start" is a strip about a young hardworking African-American couple, Joe and Marcy. It's a cheerful cartoon that follows the couple's **hectic** lives as they raise their little girl, Sunny, and their baby boy, Joe Jr.

"I'm really very fortunate to be able to do what I'm doing," says Robb, 37, who works from his home and helps his wife, Sherry, care for their two kids.

Robb is one of only a handful of **syndicated** African-American cartoonists in the country. That puts pressure on him to make "Jump Start" a positive picture of a black family. But it's a task he's also embracing. "It's not like I'm **conscious** of being a black cartoonist when I'm writing," he says. Instead, he tries to make "Jump Start" reflect the people he's known. "I don't know anybody who's car-jacking or playing basketball or rapping," he says. "If my characters are human and ring true, maybe I can change just one person who has a negative **perception** of an African American."

From Doodles to Art

Do you spend lazy lunch periods doodling pictures of the X-Men in the margins of your math book? Maybe you can put your talents to work. Robb began his cartoon career by drawing sketches of Charlie Brown when he was five. The youngest of five kids, Robb was supported and encouraged to draw by his mother. She was a seamstress who raised the family by herself. Robb's mother saw more talent in him than he did.

"She absolutely went nuts over my artwork," Robb says. "I mean, she never treated it as trivial. She never said 'Stop doodling in your science book.' By the time I was ten, she was submitting my work to magazines."

Another influence helped him perfect his craft. One of Robb's teachers worked hard at making sure he took his drawings to the

Words, Words, Words

hectic: very busy
syndicated: having work published in many newspapers at the same time
conscious: aware of something
perception: a way of seeing something that may be unfamiliar

next level. "I was just an imitator, like most kids," he says. "One of my art teachers in high school was really tough on me. She would rip up my work in front of me and make me do it again. But that's what I needed to get better. She's still a friend of mine. And I'm thankful for both her and my mother."

Robb's mom helped him get to Syracuse University, where he majored in art design and drew a regular strip for the college newspaper. After school, and a few false starts, Robb hit on a strip that touched a chord in readers.

Making people laugh is all in a day's work for Robb Armstrong.

Writing About Real Life

The reason, he thinks, is that "Jump Start" is based on his family's real life. And readers—black and white—can see themselves in the stories of a family balancing mortgage payments, wacky in-laws, and busy jobs, all while raising children. "It sounds weird, but characters have to take on a very real life that people can relate to," he says. "I know they are just drawings on a piece of paper, not flesh and blood. But in the mind of the cartoonist and the reader, they sort of become real."

And writing about real life means there's never a shortage of ideas. "All the simple, everyday acts of waking up, brushing your teeth, having a conversation. I factor in all of these and say to myself, 'Is there an idea there?'" he explains. "Something my kids did. Something my wife said. There are ideas in everything."

Still, being a successful cartoonist requires hard work and more than a little bit of luck. Even kids with talent can be sidetracked by a lack of confidence. Robb, who spends a lot of time visiting schools, says there are many kids who have good stories to tell. They just need to believe that someone wants to hear them.

"I see a lot of kids who are really talented, but they are writing strips about spaceships and super heroes and stuff they really don't know about," Robb says. "Good writers always tell you to write about what you know. And that's really true. Even if what you know is how to be a 15-year-old. That will speak to another 15-year-old—and anyone who's been 15."

ASK YOURSELF

- Why did Robb Armstrong become a cartoonist?

Think about what you read and choose the most important idea.

On a Mercy Mission

When disasters strike, Cesar Rivera lends a helping hand.

Cesar Rivera thought he had seen it all. He worked as a firefighter in New York City for 18 years. He pulled people from burning buildings. He saw some families lose everything they owned—and others lose their lives.

But Cesar had never seen anything like this.

In 1989, Cesar and 16 other New York-area firefighters **volunteered** to travel to Puerto Rico and help victims of Hurricane Hugo. The devastating storm had crashed through the island's cities and countryside. As Cesar drove a Red Cross van through the mountains, searching for survivors, he found row after row of **demolished** houses, overturned trees, and piles of debris.

"It was like someone took an eraser and just wiped Puerto Rico off the map," says Cesar, 43.

But Cesar uncovered some triumphs amid the tragedy. While looking for families who needed his help, he found a home that had been ripped apart by the hurricane's winds. The only thing left was a cement foundation with a slab of concrete overhang. A family of four was cramped under the slab. They were warming what little food they had on a butane heater and drying their rain-soaked clothes over exposed pipes.

When the family saw Cesar, they welcomed him into what was left of their home. And they didn't ask for his aid. They asked if he wanted a cup of coffee.

"People are just so amazing," he says. "Something so terrible and so huge can happen, and they can still be so generous. When you see something like that, you know that humans can survive anything."

DART to the Rescue

But when a disaster hits—a hurricane, a tornado, a flood—people still need help. And that's where Cesar comes in. The mission to Puerto Rico inspired Cesar to create a new agency, a partnership between the Red Cross and the New York City Fire Department. Cesar called it DART—the Disaster Assistance Response Team. DART is a group of 350 New York firefighters and emergency medical technicians. When a disaster strikes, DART volunteers hurry to sites throughout the U.S. and in American territories like Puerto Rico and Guam.

In the nearly ten years since he helped form DART, Cesar has dispatched rescuers to aid people in New York during crises like the 1993 World

Words, Words, Words

volunteered: offered to do a job, usually without pay
demolished: destroyed
ravaged: severely damaged
chaos: total confusion

American
Red Cross
DISASTER
SERVICES

Who needs help? Cesar checks the situation on the map.

Trade Center bombing. And he's sent them around the country to help families after disasters. His team pitched in after Hurricane Andrew's assault on Florida in 1992 and the Midwest Floods that badly **ravaged** Missouri, Illinois, and Iowa in 1993.

"We can ship people out to a disaster within a few hours," he says. It's really important that rescuers arrive on a scene as quickly as possible. DART never sends volunteers into an area until a disaster is over. But once a tornado has passed or an earthquake has subsided, the DART members are on the way. That's a blessing to victims.

"After a disaster, it's usually **chaos,**" he says. "People have lost everything and they need the basics—food, water, shelter, medical help. And they need it quick. If people go a day or two without seeing help, they lose all hope."

From Tragedy to Hope

Cesar and his DART co-workers are in the business of giving people hope. Usually, that means helping people rebuild their lives after tragedy hits. Sometimes Cesar finds them a place to sleep if their homes

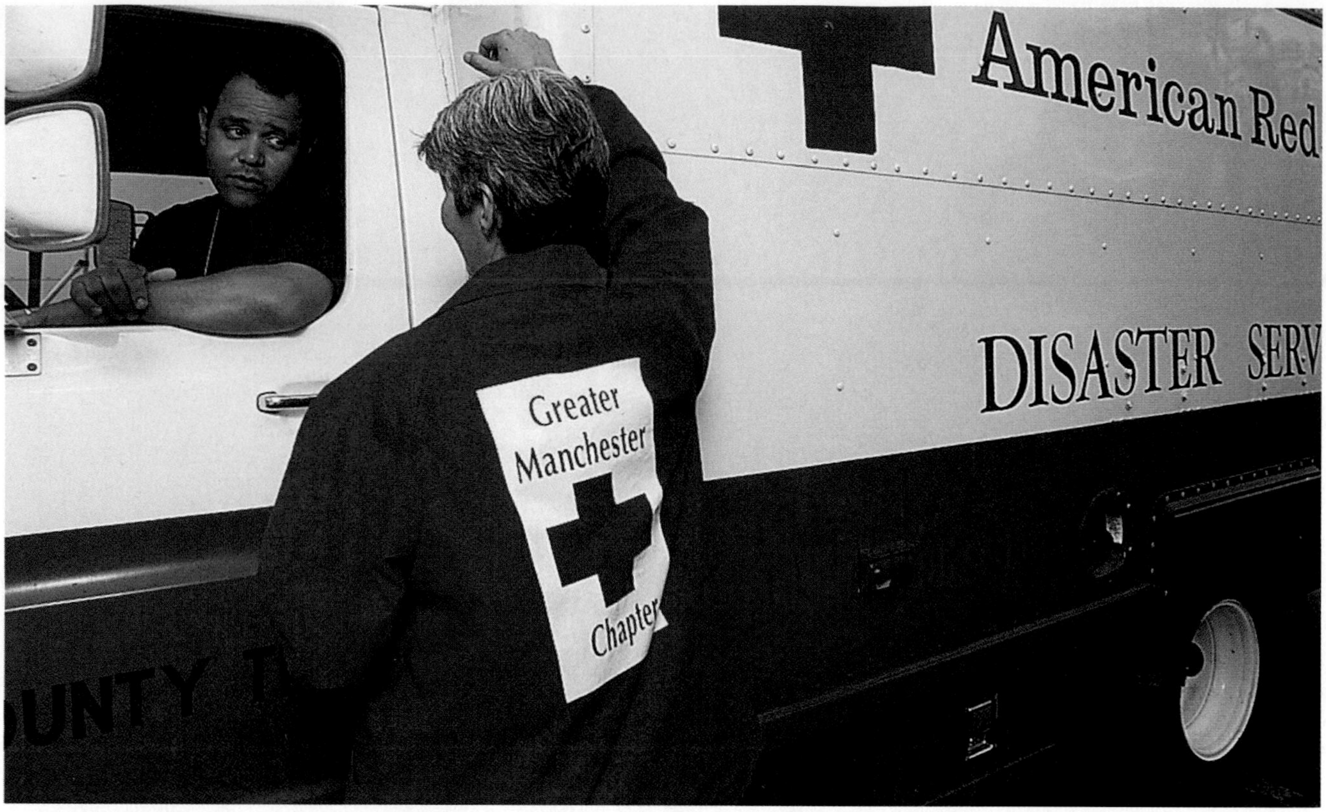
American Red
DISASTER SERV
Greater Manchester Chapter
UNTY

Cesar, on the go and ready to help out after a disaster.

have been destroyed. Sometimes he helps them rebuild a collapsed roof, find a hot meal, or even search for a lost pet. "We just want to make sure that, when something terrible happens, nobody falls through the cracks," he says. "Everybody gets a helping hand."

Helping people isn't always easy. The disasters that Cesar has seen have been heart-wrenching. Hurricane Andrew leveled whole cities in Florida. "One day you'd see people who had a nice way of living. And the next day, they were sleeping in their station wagon," he says.

Still, Cesar's job isn't depressing. In fact, he says it's **rewarding** to watch people fight back in difficult times. He's seen people at their best—husbands putting off their medical aid until their wives have been treated, mothers giving their last scraps of food to children. "The **sacrifices** people make are remarkable," he says. "People who do this job aren't doom-and-gloomers. Even when the worst tragedies happen, you see some human kindness that just inspires you."

While cleaning up after the Midwest floods, a woman whose house was washed away gave Cesar a long hug. "She was just grateful that someone came all the way from New York to help her," he says. "That's the message we try to give: that everybody is important. We're here to help everyone, every way we can." ●

Words, Words, Words

rewarding: satisfying
sacrifices: the giving up of valuable things to benefit someone else

Worst U.S. Natural Disasters

WINTER STORM 1888

March 11-14, East Coast: the Blizzard of 1888. As much as 5 feet of snow fell and 400 people died. Damage was estimated at $20 million.

FLOOD 1889

May 31, Johnstown, PA: more than 2,200 died in the flood that caused fires, explosions, and drownings.

HURRICANE 1900

August 27-September 15, Galveston, TX: more than 6,000 died from the devastating combination of high winds and a tidal wave.

EARTHQUAKE 1906

April 18, San Francisco: earthquake accompanied by fire razed more than 4 sq. mi.; more than 500 dead or missing.

TORNADO 1925

March 18, Great Tri-State Tornado: Missouri, Illinois, and Indiana; 695 deaths. Eight additional tornadoes in Kentucky, Tennessee, and Alabama raised the toll to 792 dead.

Source: National Weather Service; U.S. Department of Commerce

DROUGHT 1930s

Many states: longest drought of the twentieth century. Peak periods were 1930, 1934, 1936, 1939, and 1940. During 1934, dry regions stretched from New York and Pennsylvania across the Great Plains to the California coast. A great "dust bowl" covered some 50 million acres in the south central plains during the winter of 1935-1936.

ASK YOURSELF

- What natural disaster hit during the 1920s?

Go back and check the chart for the information.

How a Hurricane Grows

1. Heat from the sun causes the oceans to warm. Warm, moist air rises from the water to form thunderclouds and rain.
2. Strong winds and the Earth's rotation cause thunderclouds to spin in a counterclockwise motion.
3. Some air sinks to the center, forming a calm tunnel called the eye.
4. Hurricanes quickly lose strength once they hit land.

▶ Tropical storms in the Atlantic Ocean begin as clusters of thunderstorms off the western coast of Africa. The storms take in humid air and gain strength as they travel westward toward the U.S.

▶ Scientists identify tropical storms by the bodies of water over which they travel. Storms reaching hurricane strength are called cyclones in the Indian Ocean and typhoons in the Pacific Ocean.

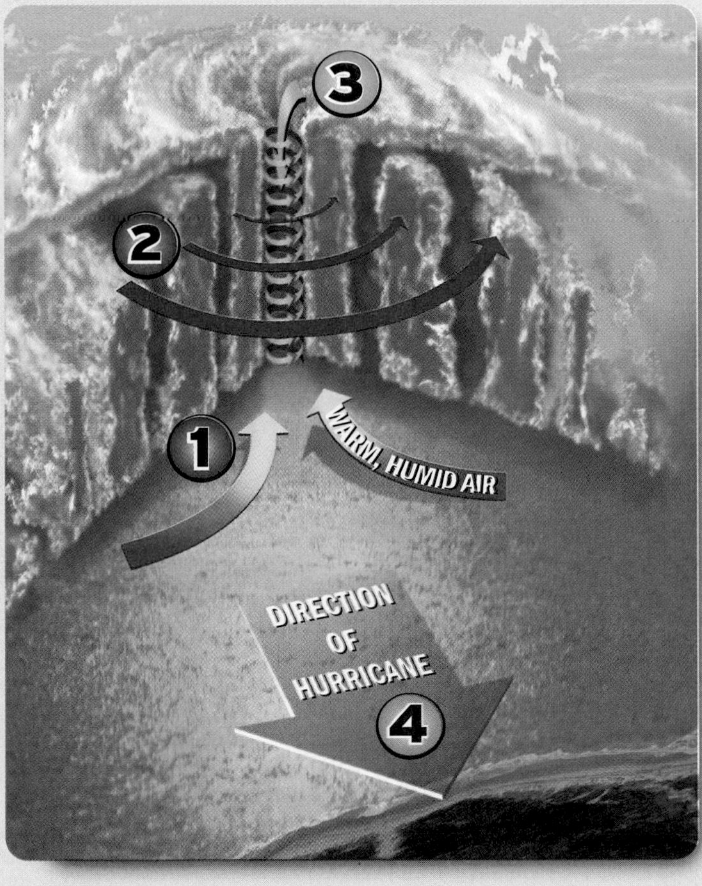
3
2
1
WARM, HUMID AIR
DIRECTION OF HURRICANE
4

Wrap-Up

Talk About It

Now that you've read "Animal Keeper & Friend," "Sketch Work," and "On a Mercy Mission," what do you have to say about these questions?

- What is most important to you—doing what you love, doing what you're good at, or doing something that helps others? Explain.
- When thinking about a career, do you see yourself working in an office—or in a different type of environment? Why?

Comprehension Check

Write your answers to the questions below. Use information from the career profiles to support your answers.

1. What three things does Michele Gaffney do everyday at her job?
2. What is the most difficult thing about working with wild animals?
3. Why does Robb Armstrong think it is a good idea for people to write about what they know?
4. Would you want to be a DART volunteer? Why or why not?
5. Of the three jobs mentioned, which do you think is the best one? Why?

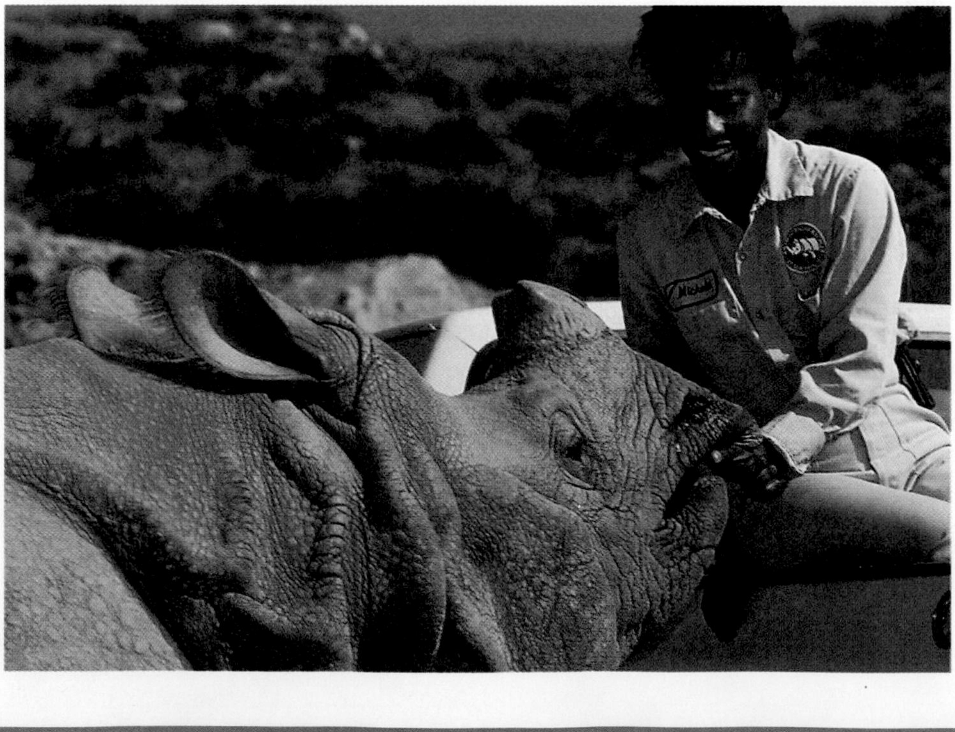

Vocabulary Check

Complete each sentence starter below. Before you answer, think about the meaning of the vocabulary word in bold.

1. In the middle of a very **hectic** day . . .
2. I was **conscious** of a low rumbling noise that was coming from . . .
3. The earthquake **demolished** the . . .
4. His **perception** of the situation was wrong because . . .
5. Everyone would have to make **sacrifices** in order to . . .

Write About It

Choose one of the three writing prompts below.

- ▶ Describe a job that you would like to have. Mention the skills you would need for this job and how you might plan to get them.
- ▶ Write a letter to Cesar Rivera from someone he has helped. What would this letter say?
- ▶ Turn something funny that happened at school into a comic strip.

Take ACTION

Have you ever wondered what career is in your future? There are lots of ways to find out what interests you, and what doesn't.

You could become a volunteer and work in one of the following places: a hospital, animal shelter, nursing home, homeless shelter, library, and more.

You could get an internship; some are paying, some are not. Even if you don't make any money, it's a great way to get behind the scenes and see if a certain field is for you.

Or become an entrepreneur and start your own business. You can make money while you learn a lot about your talent for business. Here are some ideas to get you started:

- ▶ **Baby-sitting**
- ▶ **Cutting lawns, raking leaves, shoveling snow, etc.**
- ▶ **Teaching someone to use a computer**
- ▶ **Washing cars**
- ▶ **Walking dogs or pet-sitting**
- ▶ **Running errands for busy people**

Reading Stock Prices

When you buy a "share" of a company's stock, you actually buy a tiny piece of the company. If the company increases in value, your stock will, too. Then you'll be able to sell your shares at a profit.

Stock quotes tell you the dollar value of one share of stock. Here are some quotes. Read all about them.

This column gives the name of the company. Often the name is abbreviated.

Stock prices go up and down all day. These columns show the highest and lowest prices of the day. The column labeled "Last" shows the prices at the end of the day.

Here are the highest and lowest prices for this stock during one year.

Selected Stock Prices: 1 Day

52-Week High	52-Week Low	Stock	High	Low	Last
72.625	52	LeCola	67.4375	66.75	67.0625
108.75	70.375	Biznix	108.5	107.3125	108.3125
41.25	19.875	TheGrape	41.1875	40.0625	40.9375
66.1875	43.75	ChocInc	64.375	63.50	63.6875
54.875	42.125	BurgrCo	48.6875	48	48.5625
156.125	87.50	Softwar	158	155.0625	156.8125
52.875	25.50	Nikybok	29	28.1875	29

"When a company does well—or even when people just think it's doing well—the price of the stock goes up. When things go wrong for the company, it goes down."

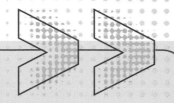

Take Stock of Stock!

Knowing how to read stock quotes is the first step toward making smart investments. Review the stock market quotes and tips. Then use the information to answer the questions. Write your answers on your own paper.

1. What was the highest price for one share of Nikybok stock over the past 52 weeks? What was the lowest price?

2. Which stock hit a new 52-week high today?

a. Biznix **c.** Softwar
b. BurgrCo **d.** LeCola

3. Which company had the biggest difference between its high price for the day and its low price for the day?

a. Softwar **c.** ChocInc
b. TheGrape **d.** BurgrCo

4. Richy Rich bought 500 shares of BurgrCo stock at the day's highest price. What was his total cost?

a. \$27,437.50 **c.** \$24,000.00
b. \$24,343.75 **d.** \$21,375.00

5. You bought 10 shares of TheGrape stock at its 52-week high price. You need some fast cash, so you had to sell it at today's last price. How much money did you lose?

a. about \$3.13 **c.** about \$412.50
b. about \$5.00 **d.** you broke even

Think it Over

If you were given \$1,000 to invest in any two companies from this lesson, which two would you choose? Why?

Follow a Stock

Choose a real company. Find out its abbreviation. Each day for one week, look up its price in the newspaper or on the Internet. Record how the price changes. Would your company be a good one to invest in?

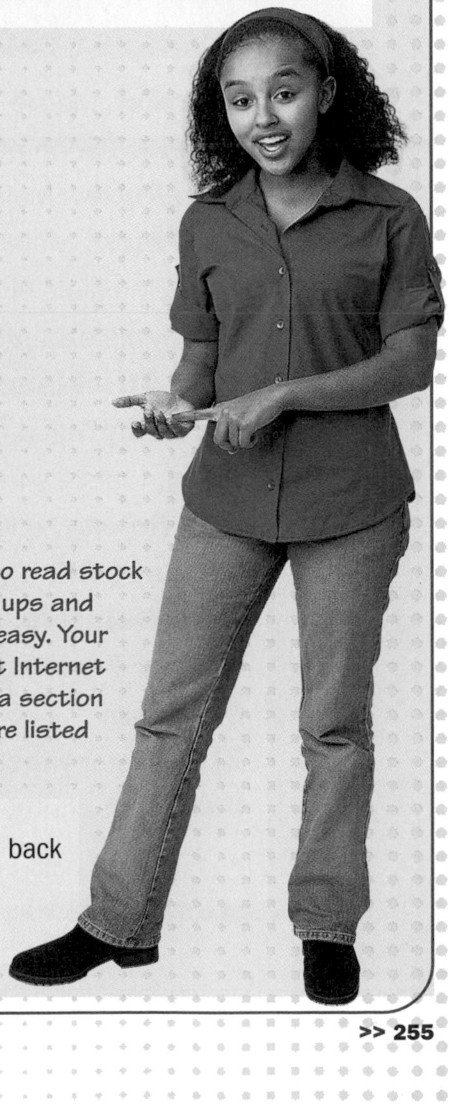

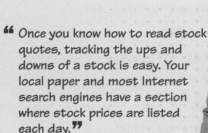

"Once you know how to read stock quotes, tracking the ups and downs of a stock is easy. Your local paper and most Internet search engines have a section where stock prices are listed each day."

Real-World Words

invest: to spend or loan money in the hope of getting more back
profit: the money you earned minus the money you spent
stock quote: the price of one share of stock

play

THERE'S A *Girl* IN MY HAMMERLOCK

Adapted from the novel by **Jerry Spinelli**

Joining the boys' wrestling team was not the easiest move Maisie ever made.

CAST OF CHARACTERS

Narrator, Maisie recalling the events*
Maisie, 13, an athlete*
Mrs. Potter, Maisie's mom*
Mr. Potter, Maisie's dad
John, Maisie's older brother
P.K., Maisie's little sister
Miss Strickland, cheerleading coach
Liz Lampley, a cheerleader
Holly, Maisie's friend
Eric Delong, a wrestler
Mr. Cappelli, a wrestling coach*
Tina McIntyre, a basketball player
George Bamberger, a wrestler
Principal
Kruko, star wrestler
Coach, of another team

* starred characters are major roles

STATE CHAMPIONS WOMEN'S GOLF 1992
STATE CHAMPIONS WRESTLING 1999
ATHLETIC DEPT.

SCENE one

Narrator: It was the end of the first week of school. Miss Strickland was finally posting the list of girls who'd made cheerleader. I'd been the best in tryouts. But when I ran to look at the bulletin board, my name wasn't on the list.

Maisie: *(to herself)*: I can't believe it!

Narrator: Then, I spotted Miss Strickland leaving school and ran after her.

Maisie *(upset)*: Miss Strickland! My name's not on the list! There must have been a mistake!

Miss Strickland: There was no mistake, Maisie. Forty-six girls tried out, and we had spots for only five.

Maisie *(suspicious)*: Who voted against me?

Narrator: I knew that cheerleaders already on the **squad** voted for new members.

Miss Strickland: Maisie, you know I can't answer that.

Narrator: She got in her car and drove off.

Maisie *(shouting at the car)*: It was Liz Lampley, wasn't it? I know it was her!

SCENE two

Narrator: I deserved to be on the squad! The year before, I'd won a medal for being the best female athlete in school. At dinner that night, I was still angry.

Maisie: Why didn't I make it? I was the best!

John: That's easy—you're ugly.

Narrator: Later that night, I sat in my room with Mom and my little sister, P.K.

Maisie *(upset)*: John's right, isn't he? I'm ugly.

Mrs. Potter: Where have I been? I didn't even know I had an ugly child!

Maisie: Maybe it's because I don't wear makeup. I'm not the Lizard Lampley type.

Mrs. Potter: Why don't you just go out for hockey again? You enjoyed it last year.

Maisie: I did like it, but it's time to move on. Every great woman was a cheerleader once.

Mrs. Potter: I wasn't.

Maisie: You don't count. Mom, you have to help me. You can teach me to use makeup. Then I'll go see Miss Strickland. She'll say, "Whoa! I think we can find space for another cheerleader!"

Mrs. Potter: I wouldn't want you to lower yourself like that.

Maisie: Then I'm doomed. Maisie Potter: Cut from cheerleading. Cut from life.

Mrs. Potter *(gently)*: Maisie, there's something you aren't telling me, isn't there?

Maisie: Huh? Uh, no.

Narrator: But there *was* something else. His name was Eric Delong.

SCENE three

Narrator: Eric had changed my life the summer before. One day at the swimming pool, he accidentally bumped into me underwater. He came up, dripping wet, and spoke the words I'll never forget.

Eric: Oh, sorry.

Narrator: I was taken completely by surprise. I'd never felt like this before. I was amazed. I was in love.

Maisie ***(awestruck)***: Oh, that's OK.

Narrator: Then he swam away. Eric was a year ahead of me in school and a big athlete. I didn't

Words, Words, Words

squad: a group of people involved in the same activity
awestruck: feeling wonder and admiration for someone
trance: being awake but not aware of what is happening around you

"The problems don't end in the gym. Other students can be harsh."

even tell my friend Holly I was in love. Then, the second day of school, I saw Eric at the water fountain.

Maisie: Hi, Eric!

Eric: Hi.

Narrator: A moment later, he was gone. But then Lizard Lampley oozed by, smiling her rattlesnake smile.

Liz: I didn't know you liked him, too.

Maisie *(playing dumb)*: Like? Who?

Liz: Eric. Who else? Remember? Three seconds ago? The water fountain?

Maisie: I'm not allowed to say hello?

Liz: Not that way.

Narrator: Then she slithered away. When she got to the door, she turned to me.

Liz: Are you going out for hockey again, Maisie?

Maisie: What's it to you?

Liz: I was just thinking. It's too bad we don't cheer for hockey like we do for football. I'll be cheering right behind Eric all season. They made him quarterback, you know—because he makes such good passes.

Narrator: That was when I decided to try out for cheerleader.

ASK yourself

- Why does Maisie want to be a cheerleader?

Think about what Liz has just told her.

SCENE four

Narrator: In the end, I never was a cheerleader. I did play field hockey, and I had a great season. But a few days after it ended, I ran into Eric and Liz.

Liz: Going out for basketball, Maisie?

Maisie: Maybe.

Liz: Eric's going out for wrestling. I *love* those sexy wrestling suits.

Narrator: I told myself I didn't care about Eric anymore. And if I did care, there was nothing I could do about it. But the next day after school, I found myself in room 116. I kept asking myself, "Why am I here?" Other kids stared at me. Then the coach came in.

Cappelli: Gentlemen, welcome to wrestling.

Narrator: After dinner that night, my brother came storming into my room.

John: Kruko just called me. I know what you did. You're not funny.

Narrator: Kruko was our star wrestler.

Maisie: Who says I was trying to be funny?

John *(angry)*: Get yourself over to girls' basketball, where you belong.

Narrator: But I didn't. The next day, I went to the wrestling room again. It was almost like being in a **trance.** This time the coach handed me a note.

Cappelli: Potter, give this note to your parents. I want to meet with the three of you.

Narrator: We met that night. The principal was there, too.

Principal: You played girls' basketball last year, didn't you, Maisie?

Maisie: Yeah. But I wanted to try something new this year. So I went out for wrestling.

Mr. Potter *(to the principal)*: Is she allowed?

Principal: The law says that since there's no girls' wrestling team, she may try out for the boys' team. The real question is—do you say she's allowed?

Mrs. Potter *(to Maisie)*: Do you really want to wrestle?

Maisie: I do.

Mr. Potter *(sighing)*: She's allowed.

Cappelli: I've never had a girl try out before. And I don't want one now. But I won't try to stop her. Some coaches would make her so miserable, she'd quit.

Mr. Potter: But you wouldn't do that, would you?

Cappelli: No, I wouldn't. But I have the toughest workouts around.

Mrs. Potter: Maisie wouldn't have it any other way.

Principal: The problems don't end in the gym. Other students can be harsh.

Mrs. Potter: OK. Let's get this settled. Maisie, do you realize the situations you could get into? On the mat? Wrestling with boys?

Maisie: Yeah.

Mrs. Potter: And the kinds of things they might say? Or other people might think?

Maisie: Yes.

Mrs. Potter: Do you care?

Maisie: No.

Mrs. Potter *(to the coach)*: Maisie doesn't quit. Nobody is as strong in the heart as this little girl right here.

SCENE five

Narrator: I was back at practice the next day. I was in the 105-pound class. When we did sit-ups, I kept up fine. After that, Mr. Cappelli showed us how to do the referee's position. I practiced with George Bamberger, another 105-pounder. When he wrapped his arm around my waist, I started giggling.

ATHLETIC
DEPT.

Cappelli: Potter! What's so funny?

Maisie: Um. It . . . uh . . . tickled?

Cappelli: Potter, stand up. Give me five laps around the school. And if you want to run on home, nobody's going to stop you!

Narrator: When I got back to the gym, Mr. Cappelli looked surprised to see me. He made me do lots more sit-ups and push-ups. Later, in the locker room I stood on the scale. I was down to 103. Then I lost more weight: I threw up. The next morning, I was so sore and tired that my mother had to drag me out of bed. When I got to school, things got even worse. Holly nabbed me.

Holly *(hurt)*: You went out for wrestling? Are you crazy? Why didn't you tell me? I'm supposed to be your best friend! And I have to hear about this from 50 other people! I feel like such a jerk!

Maisie *(sarcastic)*: I'm sorry. From now on, every time I do something, I'll get your permission. Then you won't feel like a jerk.

Holly *(angry)*: Don't you care what other people think?

Maisie: No. Why do *you?* Huh?

Holly *(yelling)*: I don't! But I learned your dirty little secret.

Maisie: Want to tell me about it? I didn't know I had one.

Holly: Eric Delong! Your good buddy Liz Lampley told me. Are you that desperate? Chasing him onto the wrestling team?

Narrator: I had nothing to say. So I just stomped off.

ASK yourself

- How do you feel about what Maisie is doing?

Consider your own ideas about girls playing on boys' teams.

SCENE SIX

Narrator: At practice that day, Mr. Cappelli told us to work on the referee's position. So I paired up with Bamberger again. We wound up joking around. The coach didn't like it.

Cappelli: Bamberger and Potter! Five laps, 20 push-ups, and into my office!

Narrator: We did as he said. Then we went in to see the coach.

Cappelli *(to Bamberger)*: Get out of here.

Narrator: George left.

Cappelli: What game are you playing? It's clear to me that you're a fake, a troublemaker. You don't want to wrestle. You want attention: The girl who wrestles boys.

Maisie: But . . .

Cappelli: Listen. Your days are numbered. Law or no law, I pick my team. Go home to your family and friends. On Monday, be at girls' basketball. Not here.

Narrator: I went home. Holly was supposed to sleep over that night, but she didn't show up. Later, Dad got a call from the father of another wrestler. He said he'd pull his kid off the team if I didn't quit.

Maisie *(depressed)*: It's OK. I'm quitting anyway.

Narrator: If I quit, maybe things would go back to normal. Maybe I could get my best friend back.

Mrs. Potter: Honey, it's your decision.

Narrator: On Monday, I went to school planning to quit. Then I saw Bamberger **moping** by the bulletin boards.

Maisie: Hey, George. You're going to be late for practice.

George: I'm not going. I'm quitting.

Maisie: Is it because he yelled at you? *(pause)* It's not because of me, is it?

George *(smiling)*: Nah. You're no problem.

Narrator: I don't know what came over me. I guess I just wanted to **encourage** him.

Maisie: You are not quitting.

George: It's not up to you. It's up to me.

Maisie: You're not quitting because I'm not quitting. I was. But now I'm not. I just found one person who says I'm not a problem. And I'm going to keep him. Come on. We're going to practice.

George: No. I don't want to.

Maisie: George, we need each other. You can't quit wrestling. What's next? School? Life?

Narrator: Neither of us quit. And at the end of the week, the coach announced final cuts. I made the team! After I saw the list, I ran up to Mr. Cappelli.

Maisie: I really made the team? It's not a mistake?

Cappelli: I'll tell you a secret. You made the team when you came in after I told you to forget it.

Narrator: I told my family. Mom gave me a kiss. Dad shook my hand. My brother was a jerk. My little sister was proud. That was Friday. On Saturday, I went to the gym to shoot baskets. Eric and Liz were there. So was Holly, who hadn't spoken to me since our

Words, Words, Words

sarcastic: speaking in an unkind way that is meant to hurt someone
moping: acting sad and depressed
encourage: to give someone confidence with praise or support

fight. I got into a game of HORSE with Eric and won. When I got home, Holly called me.

Holly: You're so stupid. You don't know anything about guys. You don't go beating them in sports if you want them to like you. Besides Eric loves Liz.

Narrator: I could tell someone else was on the other extension with Holly. I suspected it was Lizard.

Maisie: Hey, Lizard. Is that you?

Narrator: The phone went click. Twice. I had definitely lost my best friend.

ASK yourself

- Why do you think that Maisie went out for wrestling?

Think about Maisie's character—there might be more than one reason.

SCENE seven

Narrator: We started learning to really wrestle. I hardly ever lost. I figured I had a knack for it. George didn't want to wrestle me, though. I guessed he was mad that Mr. Cappelli picked me to be on varsity and him to be backup. But I was still miserable.

Mrs. Potter: What's the matter, honey? Is it Holly? I haven't seen her around lately.

Maisie: She dumped me.

Narrator: I wound up telling her everything—even about Eric Delong.

Mrs. Potter: Is he why you went out for wrestling?

Maisie: That's what everyone at school thinks, but I just don't know. Was I stupid to beat him at HORSE?

Mrs. Potter: If a boy can't handle getting beaten by a girl, that's his problem. Just be yourself, honey.

Narrator: Of course, I **ignored** her advice. I went back to the gym the next Saturday and let Eric beat me. It didn't make him fall in love with me, though. I talked to Mom about that too.

Maisie: I blew it, Mom. I lost to Eric on purpose. I feel gross.

Mrs. Potter: Honey, let's go to the pet shop. You can pick out something cute. You deserve it. You've had a very hard month.

Narrator: I looked at kittens and puppies. None of them seemed quite right. Then I saw a guy buying a cute-looking rat to feed to his snake. I had to save it.

Maisie: Um, excuse me. I'll take that rat.

Narrator: Mom was shocked when she saw the rat, but she got over it.

Maisie: I'm naming her Bernadette.

Mrs. Potter: That's a nice name.

SCENE eight

Narrator: At practice on Monday I was still in a bad mood. I wasn't really trying. But I still pinned Beans Agway, a guy two weight classes above me. Everybody was cheering. Then I flashed back to the last game of HORSE I'd played with Eric. I realized what had been going on for a long time. The boys were all letting me win.

Maisie: Hey! You're cheering for Agway—not me! Mr. Cappelli, I want the nutcracker!

Cappelli: Forget it.

Narrator: In the nutcracker, one person wrestles ten people in a row for 30 seconds—or until somebody gets pinned.

Maisie: No, *you* forget it. I need to make them accept me. Your way doesn't work. I'm just a joke to them.

Words, Words, Words

ignored: did not pay attention to something on purpose
revive: to wake someone up after they collapsed or fainted
drastic: extremely sudden and severe

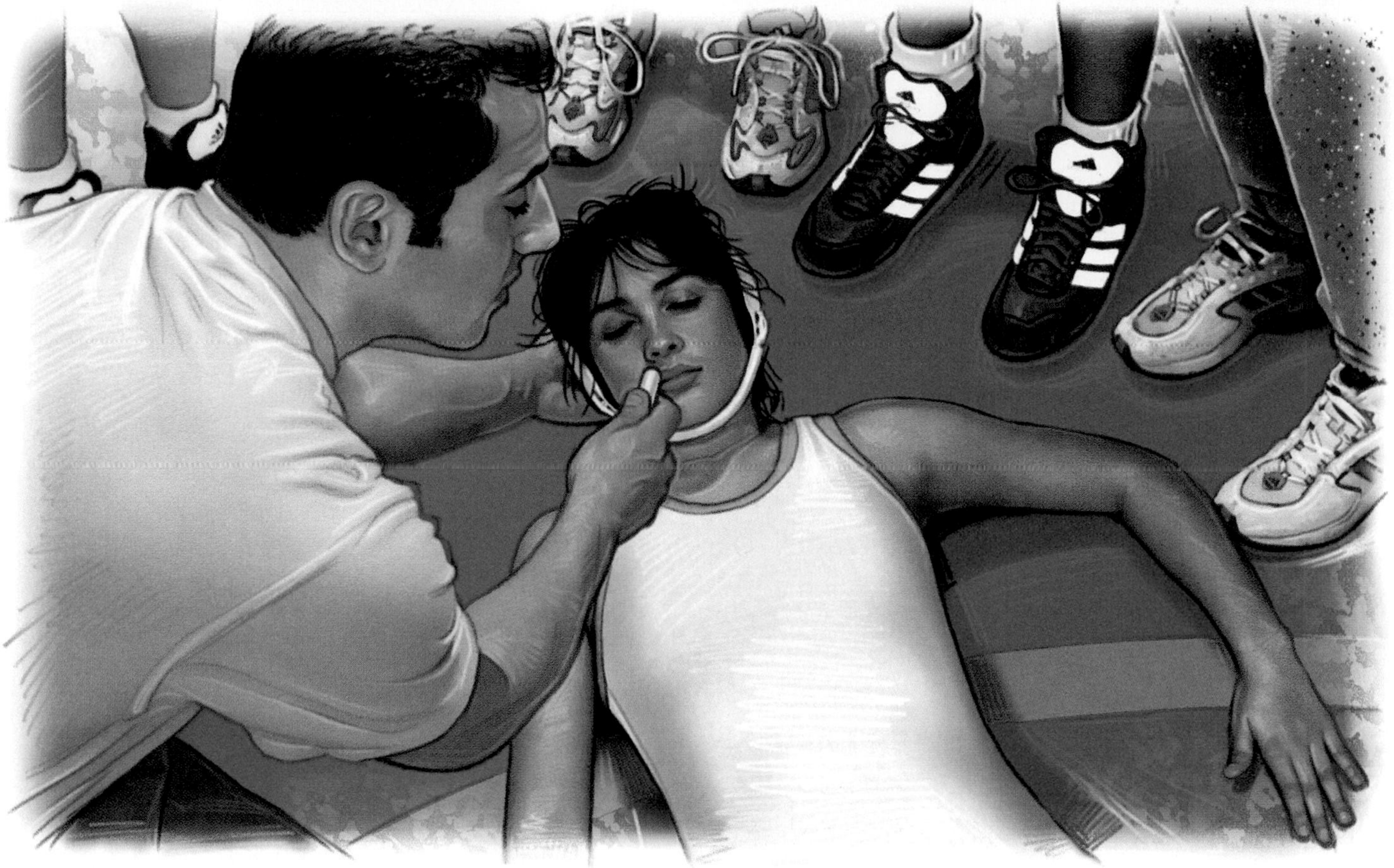

Narrator: Agway was laughing, so I shoved him. Mr. Cappelli grabbed my arm.

Maisie: Nutcracker or I quit!

Cappelli *(quietly)*: OK.

Narrator: This time the guys practically fought to wrestle me. Agway was first. He pinned me in a couple of seconds.

Kruko: You're stupid, Agway. You should have kept it going.

Narrator: Kruko, all 145 pounds of him, was next. He didn't beat me right away. He took the full 30 seconds.

Cappelli: That's 30 seconds. Next!

Narrator: After that, it's blurry. I wrestled ten guys. In the end, Mr. Cappelli had to **revive** me with smelling salts.

Cappelli: Are you OK, tiger?

Maisie: Yeah.

Narrator: I heard clapping and wondered why. Then I realized people were cheering for me. Even Agway and Kruko. Mr. Cappelli asked me some questions to make sure I was OK. Then he got real serious.

Cappelli: I don't know whether to be mad at you—or at myself—for letting you get away with that. I'll be satisfied as long as you can walk out of here tonight. This is as new to me as it is to you. I let you do that because I thought something **drastic** was called for. I didn't have any better ideas.

Narrator: Then he sighed and sent me to the locker room. I must not have looked too good.

Tina: What happened to you?!

Narrator: Tall Tina McIntyre was our girls' basketball star. We'd been friendly when we played together the year before. But we weren't really friends off the court.

Tina: There's blood on your sweatshirt, and your lip's as big as . . .

Narrator: I was trying to take my shoes off. But I couldn't manage it. Tina helped me.

Tina: I hope you're not doing this for *him.*

Narrator: She helped me get the rest of my clothes off. Then she shoved me in the shower.

Tina: That's as far as I go.

Narrator: Mr. Cappelli had George wait for me outside the locker room. He and Tina walked me home.

Maisie *(to George)*: Now I know why you wouldn't wrestle me. You didn't want to join in the little joke.

Tina: You could have told her what they were doing. (*after a pause*) So, George. You think she's going to catch loverboy Delong? Think he's worth it?

Narrator: I kicked Tina in the shins. George didn't say anything.

Tina: I hope she's doing it just to be **outrageous!**

Narrator: We'd reached my house. I went inside, fed Bernadette, and fell asleep. I woke up when I felt a hand on my fat lip. I opened my eves. It was P.K. and a kid I'd never seen before.

P.K.: Hi, Maisie! This is my friend Tank. He wants to touch your lip.

Maisie: Yo, Tank.

P.K.: Tank wants to see you wrestle. Can we?

Narrator: So P.K. and Tank started coming to practice every day. That meant I had three friends: a rat and two 5-year-olds.

ASK yourself

- Would you want to be friends with someone like Maisie?

Think about the qualities you look for in a friend.

SCENE nine

Narrator: Our first match was after semester break. When my turn came, I headed for the mat.

Cappelli: You can do it, Maisie.

Narrator: My opponent didn't come to the mat. His coach **motioned** for Mr. Cappelli to meet him at the timer's table.

Cappelli: I was afraid of this.

Narrator: Then the announcer said, "In the 105-pound class we have a **forfeit.** The winner is Maisie Potter."

Narrator: The next morning, P.K. ran into my bedroom with the newspaper.

P.K.: You're famous, Maisie!

Maisie *(reading a headline)*: "There's a Girl in My Hammerlock." That's so stupid.

Narrator: The letters to the editor later that week were worse than the silly little story. Tina came over after school the day they were printed.

Tina: People are fools. Listen to this: "When I opened your paper and saw a picture of a male and female wrestling, I was shocked. How could the school allow this?"

Maisie: I got a note on my locker like that.

Tina: Listen. There's a dance at school tonight. Let's go. It'll be good for you.

Narrator: But it turned out to be a huge disaster. Someone put a sign up that said "Hunkiest Boy at the Dance: Eric Delong. Runner-Up: Maisie Potter." The next day was our second wrestling match. The other team forfeited again. The same thing happened the next week. At the fourth match, the other team's coach weighed me in.

Maisie: So, are you guys going to forfeit?

Coach: Hey! We're no chickens.

Maisie *(smiling)*: All right!

Narrator: The noise was amazing when I trotted out to the mat. Some people were cheering. A lot more were booing.

Cappelli: Here you go. It's what you've been waiting for. You can do it, Maisie.

Narrator: I hit the floor running—and got pinned in 22 seconds. But I was so happy to wrestle that I didn't care that I lost.

Kruko and Bamberger: Nice try.

Narrator: After my match, the cheering went on and on. But the match was at home. My own school was happy that I lost. I didn't feel so good anymore. Once we got home, my parents tried to cheer me up.

Mrs. Potter: Not everybody was cheering—just a couple of nitwits.

Maisie *(upset)*: Until I heard them, I didn't mind getting pinned.

Mr. Potter: Back in the principal's office, you said you wouldn't care. Your coach tried to tell you . . .

Maisie *(almost crying)*: Yeah, but I didn't count on being voted the hunkiest boy at the dance! I didn't count on having my own friends cheer against me. Dad, you're always so big on being fair. Well, this isn't fair! And it isn't easy.

Narrator: I ran up the stairs to my room. My mother called after me.

Mrs. Potter: We know.

Narrator: People kept writing to the paper about how I was unnatural. But Tina became my friend. That was the one good thing.

Maisie: I'm at the point where the only time I'm happy is during the actual bouts.

Tina: That's about two minutes a week.

Maisie: Yeah. It would be nice if I could last beyond the first period for once.

Narrator: Against Upper Jonesford, I finally did. I still lost, but not until 20 seconds into the second period. I saw Tina afterwards.

Tina: I loved that chant they did in the stands: "Potter, Potter, she's our man . . ."

Maisie: Yeah, I heard it.

Tina: And did you hear this? Eric and Lizard broke up.

Narrator: And I was still shocked when I answered the phone Thursday.

Eric: Want to go out tomorrow?

Maisie: OK.

Eric: OK. Bye.

Narrator: I wondered where we'd go and what we'd do. Then I worried that he wouldn't call back. But he did.

Eric: Meet me at Shirts Plus at 7 o'clock.

Maisie: OK.

Narrator: Dad drove me to the mall. It was snowing, and I worried that the whole thing would fall through. I didn't know if Eric would be there when I got to Shirts Plus. He was.

Eric: Hi. Let's go to the arcade.

Narrator: He demolished me at video games. Then we went to the pizzeria. Eric and I sat down and had a slice.

Eric: My brother is at the mall, too. We drove here in his Mustang convertible.

Maisie *(smiling)*: Not with the top down, I hope.

Eric: Nah, but I wanted to. Want to go sit in it? I have a key. We can listen to music.

Maisie: OK.

Narrator: He put his arm around me, and we trudged through the snowy parking lot. In the car, Eric played a new CD.

Eric: Do you hear that? Quadraphonic sound!

Narrator: Then he was on me. His lips mashed against my teeth. My head hit the door. My shoe got stuck in the steering wheel. And I punched him. It's hard to explain why. Maybe I was just shocked. I wanted to take it back to last summer, to the swimming pool. I wanted to start over. I could almost hear myself shouting *Not this way! Not yet!* And I punched him again.

Eric: Hey! What are you doing?

Maisie *(yelling)*: What are you doing?

Eric: I thought you liked me!

Words, Words, Words

outrageous: shocking and surprising
motioned: told someone something through a movement or gesture
forfeit: an act of giving up the right to something

Maisie: I did.

Narrator: But I didn't anymore. I got out of the car. I ran to the phone in the mall.

Maisie *(to her dad)*: Pick me up! Now!

Narrator: When I got home, Mom, P.K., and Tank were in the living room. They looked at me really strangely. It was as if they had been waiting for me. But they couldn't know what had happened to me. Or could they? I didn't want to talk about it. So I went up to my room. I'd play with Bernadette, my rat. She'd make me feel better.

Maisie: Where is Bernadette? Bernadette!!

Narrator: She wasn't there. She was missing. Moments later, my mother and sister and Tank were in my room.

Mrs. Potter: I'm sorry, Maisie. I let P.K. and Tank play with Bernadette downstairs. Tank accidentally let her out the door. She's gone.

P.K.: It wasn't Tank's fault. Don't be mad.

Maisie *(yelling)*: Oh, I'm not mad. I just had the worst night of my life. Then I come home and find out my rat's gone. *(moving toward Tank)* And it's your fault!

Narrator: I was sorry as soon as I said it. Tank ran out the door and into the street. I followed him. Just then, a snowplow turned the corner. It was bearing down on Tank. I made a flying leap and scooped Tank out of its way. I threw him toward the house.

Maisie *(to herself)*: Please, please land in the snow.

Narrator: Then the plow's blade picked me up.

SCENE ten

Narrator: I woke up in the hospital.

Mrs. Potter: You're going to be OK.

Maisie: The snowplow hit me. Is Tank . . .

Mrs. Potter: Tank's fine. Perfect.

Narrator: I had bruises and a concussion. But basically I was OK. I went home the next day. And guess what? Bernadette was there, too.

Mrs. Potter: The mailman found her in the mailbox. I don't know how she got there.

Narrator: Mr. Cappelli came to visit.

Cappelli: Everyone on the team stopped by to ask me how you were doing.

Maisie: Not Kruko?

Cappelli: Even Kruko.

Narrator: Then Mr. Cappelli gave me a get-well banner that the whole team had signed. I was also in the paper that day. The article told about my "daring rescue" of Tank. The next time I was in the paper was our last bout of the season. There was a photo of the crowd cheering as the team carried me off the mat. I had gone three full periods against my opponent. I never won. But by the end, I had people's approval. The funny thing is that by then I didn't need it. I had the approval of the person who counted most: Me. ●

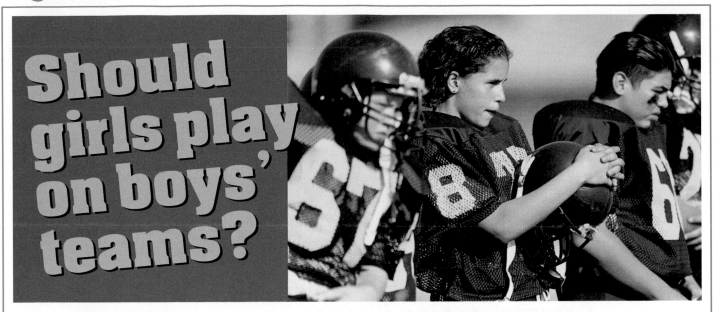

Should girls play on boys' teams?

Maisie Potter's wrestling coach didn't really want her on the team at first. He had to let her try out, though. It's the law. If a public school has a boys' sports team, it must offer the same sport for girls. Many schools don't have enough female players to form girls' teams in sports like wrestling. That means the schools must let girls join boys' teams. So, many girls have been doing just that. In 1997–1998, almost 800 girls played high-school football.

Some people think that's fine. Why shouldn't girls join boys' teams if they want to and they're good enough? Other people say it's dangerous. Girls simply aren't big enough or strong enough to play contact sports with boys.

What do you think? Read this debate and decide.

yes Of course girls should be allowed to play on boys' teams. Girls who want to play contact sports should be given the chance. Sometimes, that can't happen unless they join boys' teams.

Some girls may be too small or weak to compete against boys. But they'd probably quit or get cut from the team anyway. Its up to girls and their parents to decide whether they're tough enough to play with the boys.

If you said yes:

- Who should be held responsible if a girl gets hurt while playing for a boys' team?

no Girls who want to play contact sports should form their own teams. By middle school or high school, most boys are lot bigger, heavier, and stronger than their female classmates. Girls could get hurt badly playing sports in which boys have to hit them or pin them.

Plus, lots of boys feel that they can't play their hardest if they're playing against a girl. Schools and parents should do what they can to avoid having girls on boys' teams.

If you said no:

- What should happen when a girl wants to play football, but her school doesn't have a girls' team?

What's your point of view?

Wrap-Up

Talk About It

Now that you've read *There's a Girl in My Hammerlock,* and "Should Girls Play on Boys' Teams?" what do you have to say about these questions?

- Do you think Maisie was a hero or a fool? Why?
- In what circumstances might you let another person win a game? Any? Explain.

Comprehension Check

Write your answers to the questions below. Use information from the play and the debate to support your answers.

1. What does Maisie do to prove she's serious about being on the wrestling team?
2. Why does Holly stop being Maisie's best friend?
3. Why do you think the crowd finally begins to cheer for Maisie?
4. Why might girls join boys' sports teams in some schools?
5. Who should have the final decision about whether a girl should be allowed to join a boys' sports team?

ATHLETIC DEPT.

Vocabulary Check

Answer each question below with a complete sentence. Before you answer, think about the meaning of the vocabulary word in bold.

1. What would you do if someone made a **sarcastic** remark to you?
2. If your friend wants to try a new sport, should you **encourage** her?
3. What would you say to a friend who was just **moping** around the house?
4. After you **revive** someone who has almost drowned, what should you do?
5. Why might a sports team have to **forfeit** a game?

Write About It

Choose one of the three writing prompts below.

- ▶ Write an article about Maisie for the school paper.
- ▶ Write a letter from Holly to Maisie about why she doesn't want to be her friend anymore.
- ▶ Write a short essay about sports teams in your school. Are the teams for girls and boys given equal support and attention?

About the AUTHOR

Jerry Spinelli likes to write about kids. Whenever students ask Jerry Spinelli where he gets his ideas, he replies "From you. You're the funny ones."

Humor is a large part of Spinelli's novels. He believes that a person's life is a mixture of happy, sad, and funny events. So he tries to write books that combine all three of these elements.

Of all the books he has written, *Space Station Seventh Grade* is Spinelli's favorite because it was the first he ever published. But Spinelli says that if he could only recommend one of his novels to students, it would be *Maniac Magee.* He likes the message, the story, and the language of that book.

Managing a Checkbook

Can't keep track of your checking account? Check it out: There's a log in your checkbook that can help. You just list all the checks you write, as well as all your deposits and withdrawals.

Look over the log below. Does everything balance out?

Julio's Checkbook

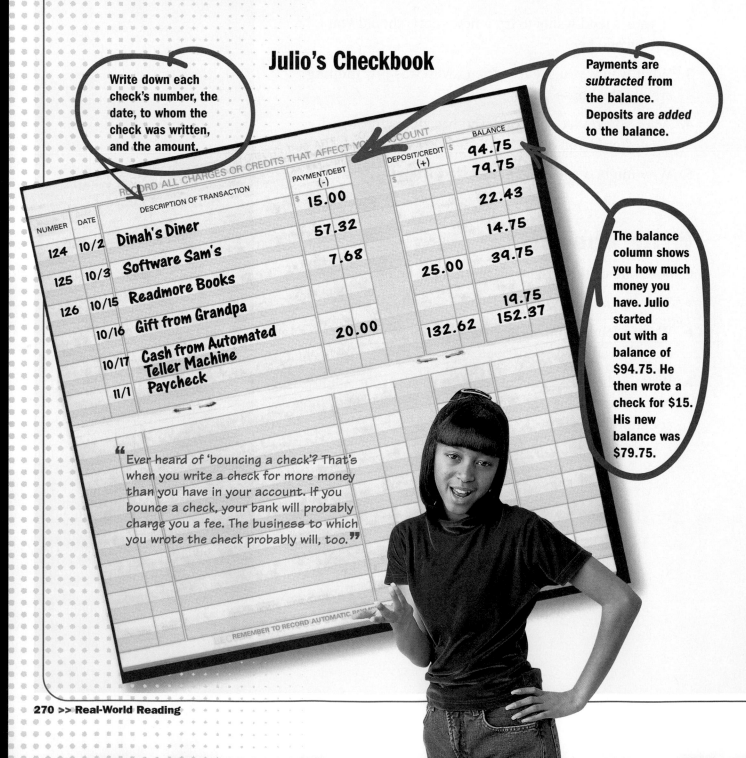

Write down each check's number, the date, to whom the check was written, and the amount.

Payments are *subtracted* from the balance. Deposits are *added* to the balance.

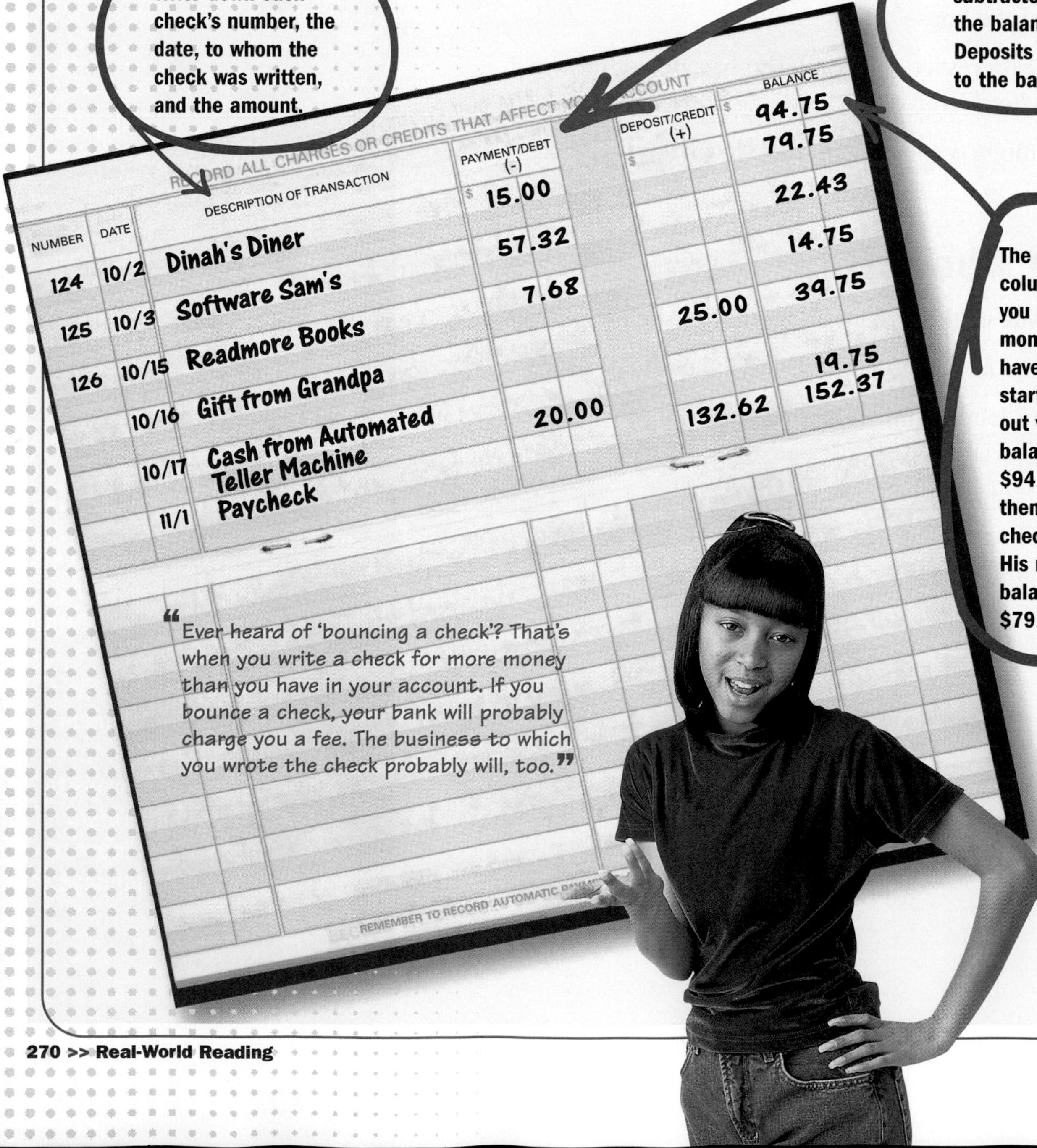

RECORD ALL CHARGES OR CREDITS THAT AFFECT YOUR ACCOUNT

NUMBER	DATE	DESCRIPTION OF TRANSACTION	PAYMENT/DEBT (-)	DEPOSIT/CREDIT (+)	BALANCE
					94.75
124	10/2	Dinah's Diner	15.00		79.75
125	10/3	Software Sam's	57.32		22.43
126	10/15	Readmore Books	7.68		14.75
	10/16	Gift from Grandpa		25.00	39.75
	10/17	Cash from Automated Teller Machine	20.00		19.75
	11/1	Paycheck		132.62	152.37

The balance column shows you how much money you have. Julio started out with a balance of $94.75. He then wrote a check for $15. His new balance was $79.75.

"Ever heard of 'bouncing a check'? That's when you write a check for more money than you have in your account. If you bounce a check, your bank will probably charge you a fee. The business to which you wrote the check probably will, too."

Check, Please!

Review the sample checkbook again. Then use it to answer the questions below. Write your answers on your own paper.

1. To whom did Julio write check #124? What was the amount of the check? What was the balance after he wrote this check?

2. What kind of transaction did Julio make on October 17? What amount was it for? What was the balance after this transaction?

3. On October 3, Julio wrote a check to Software Sam's. What was the amount of the check? What was his new balance?
a. $15.00. The new balance was 79.75.
b. $57.32. The new balance was 22.43.
c. $57.32. The new balance was 137.05.

4. On November 1, Julio deposited a paycheck. What was the amount of this check? In which column in the checkbook was this amount written?
a. $25. It was recorded under "Payment."
b. $25. It was recorded under "Deposit."
c. $132.62. It was recorded under "Deposit."

5. Starting November 2, Julio will withdraw $20 from the ATM every day. About how many days will his money last if he makes no deposits?
a. 4 days
b. 5 days
c. 7 days
d. 9 days

Track Your Cash

For one week, keep a log of all the money you spend and receive. Be sure to include dates, as well as descriptions of where the money was spent or came from. How did your balance change?

Write About It

You work at a bank. A customer brings in a checkbook filled with math mistakes. Give this customer three reasons to keep a correct checkbook log. Write down the reasons.

"An ATM can show your account balance. However, that balance won't include checks and deposits that have not yet cleared your account."

Real-World Words

deposit: money put into a bank account
withdrawal: money taken out of a bank account
transaction: an addition to or subtraction from your account

nonfiction selection

ALCATRAZ

The Prison for America's Most Wanted

by C.J. Henderson

Alcatraz was built to hold the toughest criminals in the country. It was built with the strongest materials. It was armed with the latest weapons. It was staffed with the most experienced guards. And it was surrounded on all sides by cold, deep water.

Prisoners who survived Alcatraz were never the same. Those who tried to escape were never heard from again.

Step inside this super-prison for super-prisoners.

You'll be very happy to leave . . .

Fighting Back

It was the 1920s in America. Police were fighting crime everywhere. Gangsters were shooting it out on the streets. Robbers were stealing from each other. Many ordinary Americans were breaking the law every day. Much of this crime and **mayhem** began when a new law was passed. This law made it illegal to make, sell, or drink alcohol. It was called the National Prohibition Act.

How did this law lead to a crime wave? Even though it was against the law, many people still wanted to buy alcohol.

So criminals took over. They saw a new way to make money—and they decided to take advantage of it. Some criminals started sneaking alcohol in from other countries; others made their own.

Illegal bars opened around the country. You could find them everywhere. Before Prohibition, New York City had 15,000 bars. After the new law, 32,000 illegal ones took their place.

The criminals made huge profits. Some of them lived like kings. They paid local police and politicians to leave them alone. They murdered the ones they could not bribe.

Even when these men were caught, nothing changed. They ruled from jail. They paid guards to pass messages for them, and if the guards said no, the gangsters threatened to hurt their families.

The gangsters laughed at justice. They knew that even in jail they couldn't be stopped. Alcohol was on every corner. Crime was **rampant** in the streets.

Then a man named Homer C. Cummings came up with an idea.

His idea involved an island.

The island's name was Alcatraz.

A Super-Prison

Homer C. Cummings had an extremely tough job. He had to stop the gangsters. He had to get them into jail. But that was only the first step. He also had to cut them off from the outside world.

Cummings decided he needed a "super-prison for super-prisoners." Once inside, the gangsters wouldn't be able to talk to their men on the outside. They wouldn't be able to threaten the guards' families. They would be put away once and for all. And Cummings knew it would take extreme security **precautions** to make it work.

Cummings decided Alcatraz was the answer. It was a big, rocky island that was located far out in California's San Francisco Bay. The nearest land was over a mile away. The water around it was cold all year. The currents were too powerful for swimmers. And there was an old prison on the island already.

Cummings was given five years to make his idea work. He hired a man named James Johnston as the first warden. Johnston started work right away.

First, he **reinforced** the existing prison. He made the old buildings stronger by replacing old iron bars with steel ones. Then he added new buildings. Telephones and radios came next. That way

The prisoners' first glimpse of "The Rock" as they arrived on the island.

the guards could communicate with each other from any point on the island. Tall guard towers were built around the prison—and each one had huge searchlights. Tear gas came next. If prisoners rioted, the guards could drop gas from slots in the ceiling.

Then the gun boxes were built. They were steel boxes set high on the walls. Guards would sit inside. They pointed machine guns through small holes. And they kept watch 24 hours a day. Next, electric gates and doors were added. Guards could lock any part of the jail just by pushing a button. Metal detectors were placed everywhere. Prisoners would pass through them at least eight times a day. Barbed wire went on all the fences.

Johnston then built one main control center. It was open only to the outside. All the weapons were kept there. A single man stayed in the control center. Dozens of microphones were placed around the prison. This man could hear every sound in Alcatraz. He also knew if any phone was off the hook for 15 seconds. He could send a guard to find out if anything was wrong. Guards counted the prisoners 12 times a day and reported to the man in the control center. If anyone was missing, he called for help.

Finally, guards were hired. Johnston picked them carefully from other prisons. They were expert shots. They knew judo and other forms of self-defense. They were tough and experienced men. There were a lot of them, too. There was one guard for every three prisoners. Most prisons had just one for every ten prisoners.

Guards stood in the towers and at every door. They watched the roads and the stairs.

ASK YOURSELF

- What steps did James Johnston take to secure the prison?

Think about the things he added.

The guards and their families had to live on the island, too. Their kids even went to school there. There was no way any gangster could threaten a guard's family.

By August of 1934, "The Rock" was open for business.

It was time for the prisoners.

The Prisoners Arrive

Reporters were full of questions about the first prisoners—but no one was talking. The operation was top-secret.

Where were the prisoners coming from? No answer.

When would they arrive? No answer.

Was Al Capone, the most famous gangster of all, coming to Alcatraz? Johnston said he was not. (He was.)

Johnston had one big fear. The prisoners would arrive by train from all around the country. Each train would be packed with the most terrible criminals alive. Gangsters might attack the trains. The gang leaders could be set free . . . if their friends knew where they were.

At midnight on August 18, the prison in Atlanta, Georgia, was quiet. A special train moved through the darkness into the yard. Guards made 53 prisoners leave the jail. Each had his legs and wrists chained. They moved into the train. When they were chained to their seats, the train pulled off.

The train reached San Francisco several days later. Even

WORDS, WORDS, WORDS

mayhem: random or deliberate violence
rampant: wild and without restraint
precautions: things you do to prevent something dangerous from happening
reinforced: strengthened something

This view of one cell block area is what the prisoners saw, day after day.

Prisoners spent most of their time in the 9-by-5 foot cells.

102

Every day on the Rock was the SAME ROUTINE.

The mess hall is where the prisoners ate every meal.

then, the prisoners did not get off. A special boat had been built so that the train could be driven right onto the boat. Then the train was transported to the island. Warden Johnston was taking no chances.

More trains soon arrived. The prisoners quickly learned about Alcatraz.

For the first few years, prison ers couldn't even speak to each other. They could ask for salt at a meal, or they could ask for a tool at work—but that was it. Sometimes guards caught prisoners talking. Those prisoners ended up in the cellar.

Prisoners called the cellar the "Hole." It was a group of small cells under the prison. Prisoners were chained to a brick wall. They stayed there 24 hours a day in the dark and in **isolation.** There was no one else in sight. They were fed bread and water. Every 19 days they could have a shower. They could be in the Hole for ten days, a month, or even a year.

Prison Life

Every day on the Rock was the same routine. Prisoners got up at 6 A.M. They washed with cold water. They put on gray shirts and pants. They marched to breakfast. There was plenty of food, and it was good. But prisoners who left food on their plates had to skip the next meal. The next time it happened they were sent to the Hole for ten days.

The rest of the day was spent working and eating. On Sunday, prisoners got a two-hour break in the yard. They could go to church in the morning, but if they did, they got less time in the yard.

Day after day passed. Each one was the same. No one spoke. No radios played. Visitors were allowed only once a month. And a guard was always there, listening.

This **monotonous** and **sparse** life drove some prisoners crazy. A prisoner named Al Loomis spent 16 months on Alcatraz. "It's driving the men nuts," Loomis said. "The walls were the barest things I ever saw. If a man tried to put up a photo of his mother he was headed for the Hole. They never give a guy a break."

Warden Johnston thought his rules were working. "We have some tough customers," he said. "But we have torn them down to size. We have [made them realize] that they are not as big as they thought they were."

ASK YOURSELF

- What was life like for the prisoners?

Describe their daily routine in your own words.

The Most-Wanted

Who were the criminals inside this "super-prison"?

THE BIRDMAN

Robert Stroud killed a man when he was 19. He was sent to prison for 12 years. Then, just before Stroud's sentence was over, he stabbed a guard. No one knows why. He was sent to a prison in Kansas for life.

One day Stroud found a nest of sparrows in the exercise yard. He took the baby birds to his cell. He gave them bits of bread and he nursed them back to health.

Stroud became very interested in birds. He read all the books on birds in the prison library.

He brought more birds into his cell. He fed them flies and bits of his own meals. Stroud studied birds for years. He even wrote two books on bird illnesses. Few people in the world knew more about the diseases of birds.

Stroud was moved to Alcatraz a few years after it opened. He wasn't allowed to have birds there, but he became known as the "Birdman of Alcatraz" anyway. Many people **rallied** to get Stroud

WORDS, WORDS, WORDS

isolation: the state of being alone or separate from others
monotonous: boring and lacking in variety
sparse: lacking in quantity and quality
rallied: joined together to help support a person or cause

released because of his work with birds. They wrote letters, and they formed protests. No one listened. Once Alcatraz got its hold on a prisoner, it never let go.

Robert Stroud died while still in prison. He was 73 years old. He spent 56 of those years behind bars, and more than 15 of them were on the Rock.

AL CAPONE

The Rock's most famous prisoner was Al Capone. By the age of 26, Capone was the king of Chicago's gang world. In fact, he was the most powerful criminal in the world. Capone sold alcohol to millions of drinkers, and his business made him very rich. He was making about five million dollars a year.

Capone was a very violent man. He was responsible for more than 1,000 murders. Capone ordered the deaths of policemen, politicians, and gangsters. He killed anyone who got in his way. He committed many of the murders himself and would even kill his own men if they didn't obey him.

Capone ran Chicago. He paid the police and politicians to do what he said. Most of them obeyed him without questions.

Finally, the U.S. government came after Capone. They could not prove that he had murdered anyone. There was no one brave enough to tell on Capone.

So the government brought Capone to trial for not paying his taxes. He was sentenced to ten years in prison for tax **evasion.**

Capone started his term in a prison in Georgia. There, he bribed guards. They did him special favors and gave him perks. They brought him good meals and fine cigars. He spent his days eating, smoking, relaxing, and listening to the radio.

Then one night he was ordered out of his cell. Guards searched him. They chained him and pushed him onto a train. Several days later, Capone had a new home: Alcatraz.

Life was never the same for Capone. The silence drove him crazy. His first week there he tried to talk during a meal. He got ten days in the Hole.

When he got out of the Hole, he wanted to talk about it. He got another ten days. A week after that, he tried to bribe a guard for news. That got him 19 days. Capone had no power in Alcatraz. He couldn't get special favors. He ate prison food. He had no cigars. There was no radio. He had to clean toilets.

In the end, Capone became insane. He would not leave his cell. He spent hours making and remaking his bed. In 1939, Capone was freed. He died a few years later. He was powerless and forgotten. Alcatraz had destroyed him.

Escape!

Warden Johnston wanted to make it impossible to escape from Alcatraz. And he may have succeeded. Most people think that no one ever escaped the Rock.

Not alive anyway.

Teddy Cole was a murderer and a kidnapper. He was sent to Alcatraz for 50 years. When he arrived, he said, "I don't think I'll like it here. I doubt I'll stay long." He didn't. In December 1937, he teamed up with a bank robber named Ralph Roe.

They sawed the bars off a window. They kicked out two panes of glass. They dropped to the ground in **dense** fog. Then they smashed a lock on the fence gate. They jumped 20 feet off a cliff. Then they jumped another 30 feet into San Francisco Bay.

They were never seen again. But this did not mean they escaped. The water was freezing that day, and the current was running fast. Most people assume the two men were washed out to sea.

John and Clarence Anglin were brothers. They were both

WORDS, WORDS, WORDS

evasion: the act of avoiding something you should do
dense: thick

Al Capone was one of the most powerful criminals in America.

A scene from the movie, Birdman of Alcatraz

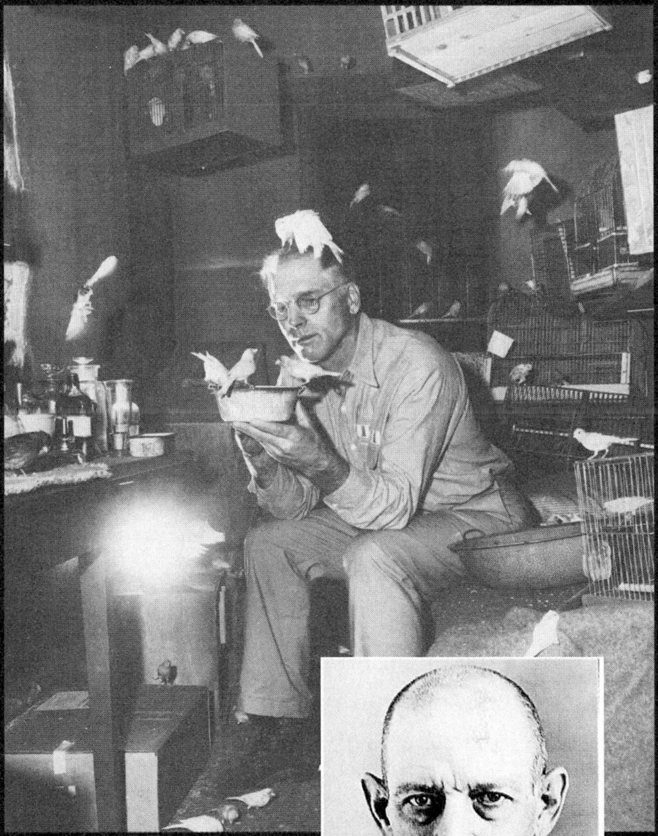

Robert Stroud—the real Birdman—was sent to prison for life.

The Rock held the most DANGEROUS prisoners alive.

U. S. PENITENTIARY
ALCATRAZ
1441
1 20 60

Three who tried to escape: John and Clarence Anglin and Frank Morris (left to right).

sent to Alcatraz. In 1962, John, Clarence, and their friend Frank Morris decided to escape.

They spent months digging holes through the back walls of their cells. When the prison first opened, its walls were in perfect condition. But after 25 years, the salt air had **eroded** and worn them down. Now they could be chipped away with a spoon!

The three men had planned their escape perfectly. They worked at night and they were very careful. Guards counted the prisoners' heads during the night. So the prisoners saved newspaper, wire, paint, and their own hair. They made models of their own heads. Then they put the fake heads in their beds at night to fool the guards.

Next, they replaced the metal air grates in their cells with fake grates. They made these out of cardboard. They hid their tools in an empty hall behind the walls. They hid their escape equipment there as well.

By the summer, they had dug their way through the walls. Then they made their move. On the night of June 11, 1962, the three climbed into the hidden hallway. They climbed from floor to floor behind the cells.

They made their way to the roof. On the roof, they headed to the north of the island where they slipped into the water. They paddled away on a raft made out of raincoats. And like Ralph Roe and Teddy Cole, they disappeared.

Did they make it? No one knows. No bodies were ever found. The current was slow that day, but the water was cold and land was a mile and a half away. Besides, these men had never been able to stay out of trouble. They were never arrested again, so it seems unlikely that they made it.

But no one will ever know for sure.

ASK YOURSELF

- How did the Anglin Brothers and Frank Morris escape?

Retell the details of their plan.

Riot!

Most of the escape attempts at Alcatraz were very quiet. They ended without much violence. Then Bernie Coy tried to escape.

Coy was a bank robber from Kentucky. The guards didn't think he was dangerous, so they made him a janitor. That meant he was allowed to go into areas of the prison that were off limits to other inmates.

It was Thursday, May 2, 1946. Coy was pushing a broom quietly around a cell block. A cell block is a group of cells. Coy's partner was also cleaning nearby.

Bert Burch, a guard, sat in the gun box above. Officer W.H. Miller was on duty in the cell block.

At exactly 1:40 P.M., Burch walked into a walled-off section of the gun box. Coy had a plan. At the right moment, he knocked on the cell-block door. Miller came to the door. Coy hit him from behind. The partner knocked him **unconscious.** They locked him in a cell and took his keys.

A couple of prisoners lifted Coy to the gun gallery. He climbed onto its roof and worked his way into that secure area. When Burch came back, Coy hit him with a club. Coy took a pistol and a rifle. Then he released the rest of the prisoners.

Coy and several others headed for the door to the prison yard. Coy planned to break into the yard. Then he and his friends would take the prison boat. They would disappear into San Francisco.

But there was one problem. The key to the door of the yard was gone. Miller had taken it off his key ring. Coy and his friends were unable to get outside.

After his **futile** escape attempt, Coy returned to the cell block. Then a riot began.

WORDS, WORDS, WORDS

eroded: worn away over time
unconscious: not awake
futile: useless

For 48 hours, the prisoners ruled The Rock. They terrified the guards they had captured. Finally, U.S. Marines were sent in. They stormed the island and took control of the prison.

Many prisoners died in the riot. Coy and two of his friends died. One of his friends was given 99 more years in prison. The other two were killed in the gas chamber. Two guards died.

It was the only riot in the history of Alcatraz.

The Rock Falls Apart

Alcatraz was the most successful prison ever built in America. The Rock held the most dangerous prisoners alive. And it kept them safely locked away.

But in 1963, the Rock opened its doors. The prisoners were shipped to jails around the country. The problem: Alcatraz was too expensive to run. It cost twice as much as any other federal prison. Since Alcatraz was an island, all the supplies had to be brought over on boats. Even fresh drinking water arrived by boat.

Frank Morris and the Anglin brothers had something to do with the closing, too. Their escape shook prison officials and the public. They had dug through the walls with a spoon.

The Rock was literally falling apart. And it was too expensive to fix.

Many people also felt that there was no longer the need for a super-prison. Prohibition had ended in 1933, and the gangsters seemed under control.

On March 21, 1963, the government shut down the Rock. Nine years later, Alcatraz became a national park. Today, visitors from all over the world come to see it.

You can walk in and hear the doors close behind you.

Then, when you get tired of the Rock, you can make your escape.

"MAXIMUM SECURITY, MINIMUM PRIVILEGE"
—the motto of Alcatraz when it was chosen as a federal prison in 1934.

One of the eight guard towers that existed on the island.

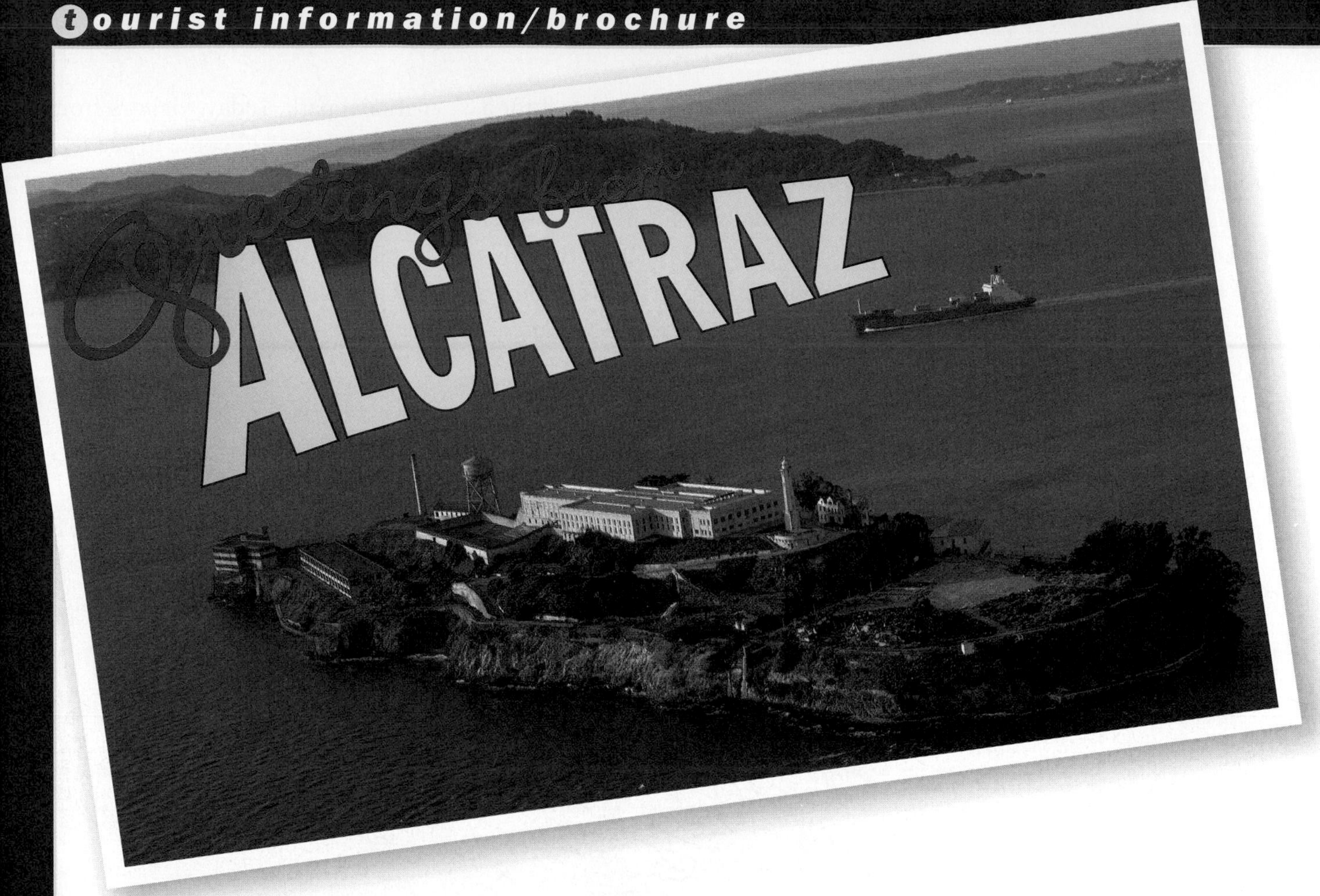
Greetings from
ALCATRAZ

A GREAT PLACE TO VISIT.....
But You Wouldn't Want to Live There!

Millions of tourists pour into San Francisco each year. In fact, it is one of America's most visited cities. What's the big attraction? Why do crowds continue to flock here? It might be because of San Francisco's rich history with its gold rush and earthquakes. Maybe it is because of its unique tourist attractions—the trolley cars, Fisherman's Wharf, and the Golden Gate Bridge. Maybe it's the food. But maybe—just maybe—tourists come here to see the world's most notorious prison—Alcatraz! You, too, can visit Alcatraz. Just turn the page and let the tour begin.

SO CLOSE AND YET SO FAR ▶

One of the best overall views of San Francisco is from the former prison on Alcatraz Island. This incredible view, however, was pure torture for the inmates of Alcatraz. How come? They could see—and even hear—the life of the city while knowing they would never experience it. Never.

POWELL
25

Take a Tour of the Rock!

Now remember, Alcatraz isn't your typical tourist attraction. No sunny beaches. No thrilling rides. What it does have is the Rock. That's the nickname of the famous former prison where inmates such as Al Capone spent their last days. And if you get a chance to visit the rock—here's what to expect.

▲ **DON'T GET LEFT BEHIND! Through the heavy wire fencing, you can see the rows and rows of prison cells. Once they were all full. Now they are empty . . . and waiting for you—as a tourist, of course! When you visit Alcatraz you can enter an empty cell. Close the cell door and imagine what life must have been like for the prisoners.**

GETTING THERE There's only one way to reach Alcatraz. (And only one way to leave, too!) You'll take a ferry ride from Fisherman's Wharf. The journey is one-and-a-half miles long. You'll land on the island's only dock—the same one where prisoners took their first steps into the dreary world of the Rock.

THE GUARD HOUSE Check out the guard house that overlooks the prisoner's landing. From this tower, guards watched to make sure that newly arriving prisoners didn't decide to take a little swim . . . back to the mainland.

THE GARDENS Flowers and plants on Alcatraz? You bet! Even though the twelve-acre island really is just a big rock—it's waterless and has almost no soil, you'll see lots of plants and flowers. They grow in soil that was brought to the island so prison guards could grow gardens.

THE TOURS There are a few different tours that might appeal to you. One is the Time on the Rock Tour. Another is the Escapes Tour—where you get to see how and when the few escapes were attempted. Were these attempts successful? Find out here!

PRISONERS TALK! Using the audiocassette player and headphones, you'll walk through the prison with company—the tour is narrated by former guards and prisoners.

THE CELLBLOCK Chances are that you'll want to spend some time in the main prison cellblock. Here's where you'll get a look at the tiny cells, the mess hall, the library, and the horrible dark holes where prisoners were placed in solitary confinement.

BROADWAY The prisoners of Alcatraz spent almost the entire day alone inside their tiny cells. Only nine feet long by five feet

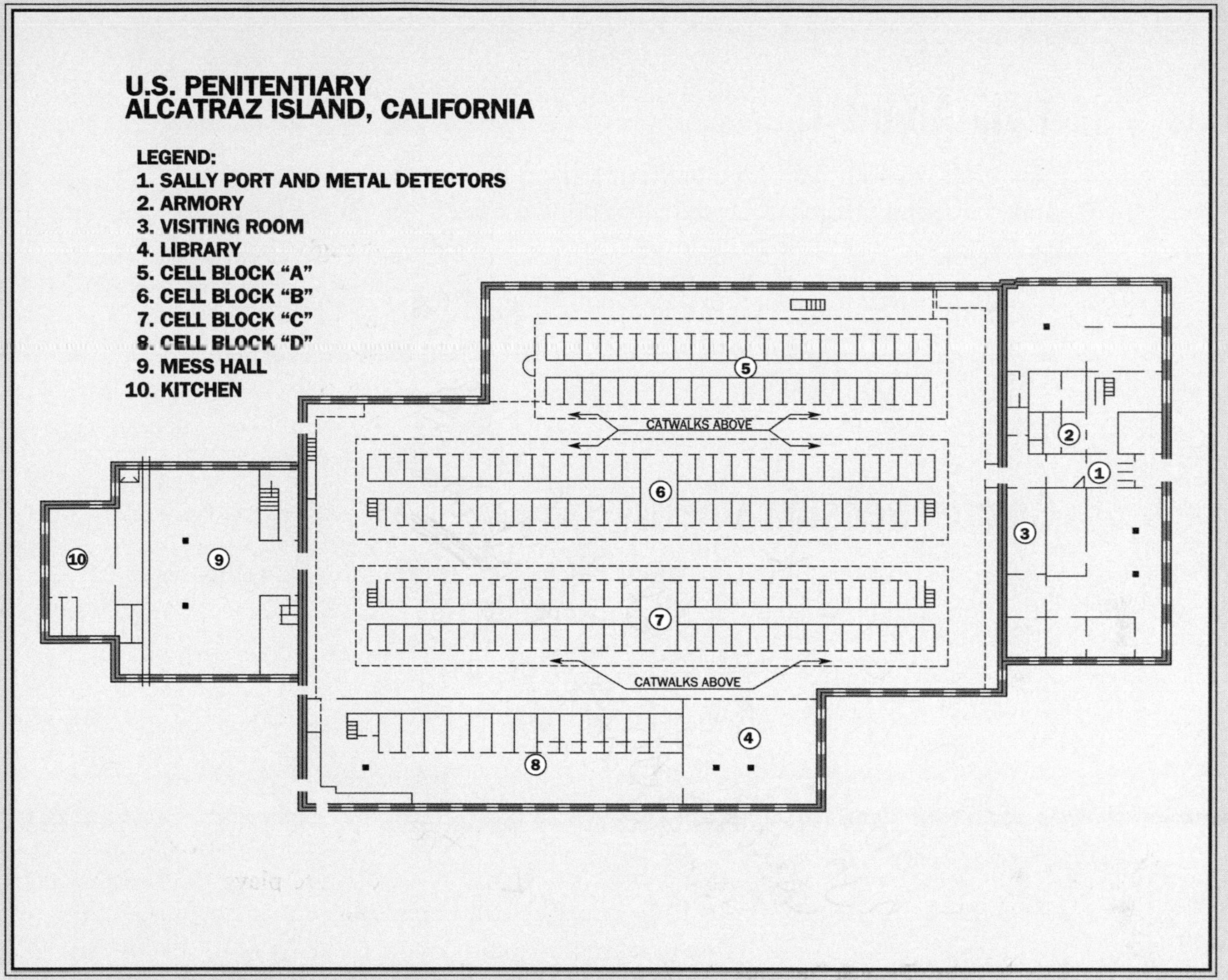
U.S. PENITENTIARY
ALCATRAZ ISLAND, CALIFORNIA
LEGEND:
1. SALLY PORT AND METAL DETECTORS
2. ARMORY
3. VISITING ROOM
4. LIBRARY
5. CELL BLOCK "A"
6. CELL BLOCK "B"
7. CELL BLOCK "C"
8. CELL BLOCK "D"
9. MESS HALL
10. KITCHEN
CATWALKS ABOVE
CATWALKS ABOVE

ALCATRAZ FLOOR PLAN

This is a floor plan of the cell house on Alcatraz. The legend lists all the main areas of the building.

wide, each cell contained nothing but a hard bunk and a toilet. You'll see rows and rows of these miserable cells along "Broadway." That's the inmates' nickname for the hallway connecting Cell Blocks B and C.

Are you the kind of tourist who likes to wander around on your own? WARNING: Don't miss the boat that takes you back. The night could get really long—

TOURS OF ALCATRAZ

Tours of Alcatraz begin with a ferry ride from Pier 41 (at Fisherman's Wharf). The fare includes the crossing, entry to the island's public areas, and loan of an audiocassette guided tour and a cassette player. Departures are at 30-minute intervals throughout the day. Tickets go on sale at 8 AM. During the summer, reserving tickets two days in advance is recommended. For more information: (415) 546-2700.

Wrap-Up

Talk About It

Now that you've read "Alcatraz: The Prison for America's Most Wanted" and "Greetings from Alcatraz," what do you have to say about these questions?

- ▶ Was Alcatraz too tough or just tough enough? Explain your opinion.
- ▶ Why do you think so many people are fascinated with this former prison? Would you want to see Alcatraz, why or why not?

Comprehension Check

Write your answers to the questions below. Use information from the selection and the brochure to support your answers.

1. Why was it so difficult to escape from Alcatraz?
2. What effect did the Prohibition Act have on crime?
3. Why do you think life at Alcatraz drove some prisoners crazy?
4. What different types of tours could you take at Alcatraz today? Name two.
5. What do you think some of the criminals who lived at Alcatraz would say, if they were giving a tour of the prison today?

Vocabulary Check

Answer each question below with a complete sentence. Before you answer, think about the meaning of the vocabulary word in bold.

1. How would you describe a **monotonous** weekend?
2. What are some **precautions** that you could take before going on a vacation?
3. How can you tell when your confidence in something has **eroded**?
4. How does being in a very **dense** crowd make you feel?
5. What is something that you and your classmates might have **rallied** together to change?

Write About It

Choose one of the three writing prompts below.

- It's 1950 and Alcatraz is still open for business. Imagine that you are a reporter who goes there undercover in order to write a story. Write a short article about the one day and night you spent there.
- Oops! Something went wrong on your tour of Alcatraz. Write about it in a letter to a friend.
- Many movies have been made about Alcatraz. Write an outline for a movie plot about this famous prison.

Fact FILE

Native Americans and Alcatraz

What caused Alcatraz to finally shut down? The costs and difficulties of running an island prison were some of the reasons. So on March 21, 1963 the last 27 prisoners of Alcatraz were transferred to other prisons. But these criminals were not the last citizens of Alcatraz.

A group of Native Americans made their way to Alcatraz Island and claimed it for the Sioux Indian nation. They said it was their birthright to inhabit the island. They used a treaty that was written in 1868 as their defense. The treaty said that the Sioux nation had rights to "any unused government land." Alcatraz Island, they said, was now indeed unused government land.

Over 400 Native Americans lived on the island. Their occupation—or takeover—of Alcatraz lasted until 1971. Then, in 1972, President Nixon turned Alcatraz into a national park. So Alcatraz was once again being used by the federal government. That meant the claim by the Sioux nation was no longer valid.

Reading a Floor Plan

You and your family are looking for a new place to live. You see an ad for an apartment that says it's "sunny with cozy rooms." What does that really mean? If you want the facts, you need to check the floor plan.

Look at this floor plan. Can you tell what this space is like?

Floor Plan for an Apartment

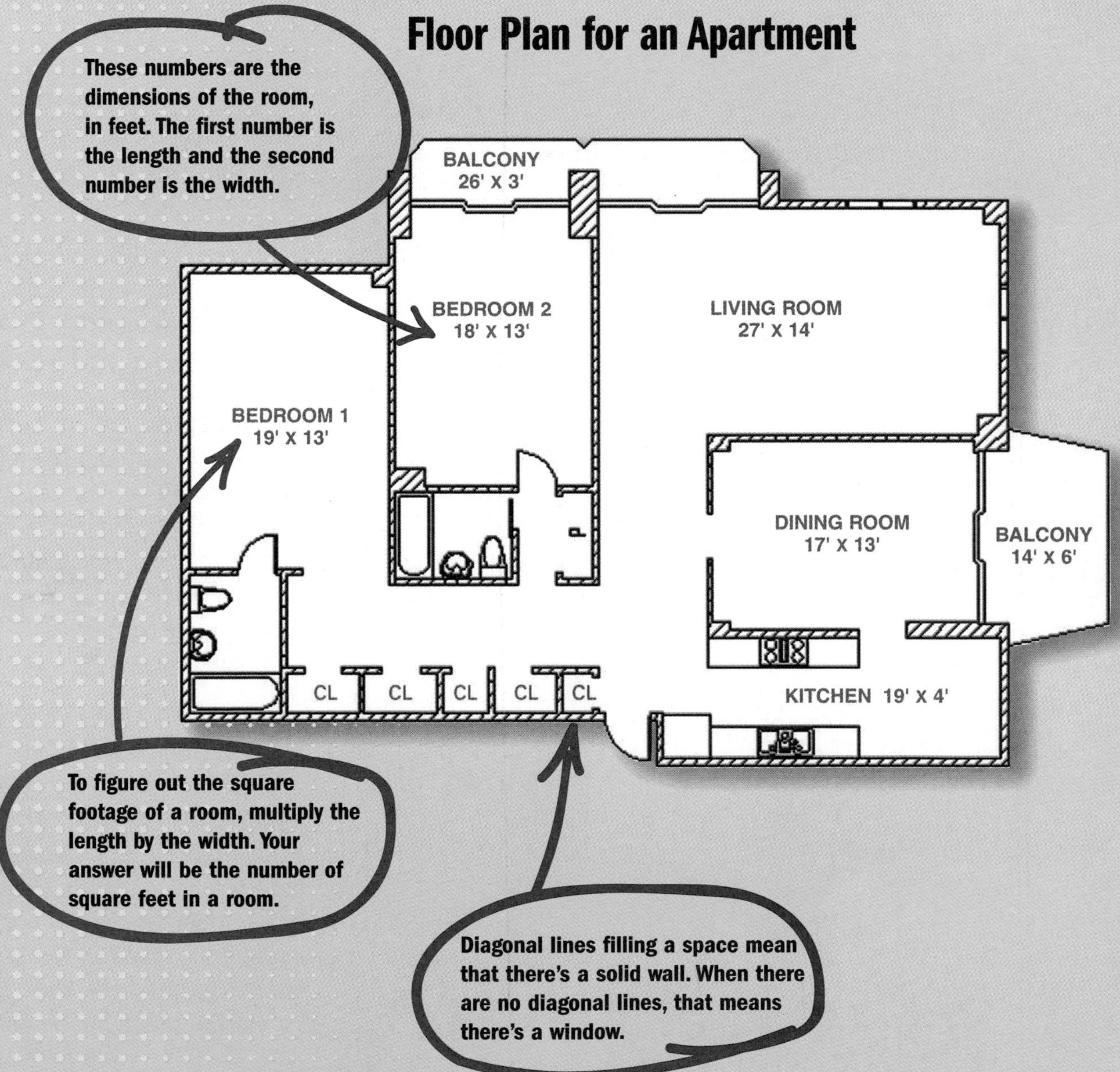
These numbers are the dimensions of the room, in feet. The first number is the length and the second number is the width.
BALCONY 26' X 3'
BEDROOM 2 18' X 13'
LIVING ROOM 27' X 14'
BEDROOM 1 19' X 13'
DINING ROOM 17' X 13'
BALCONY 14' X 6'
CL
CL
CL
CL
CL
KITCHEN 19' X 4'
To figure out the square footage of a room, multiply the length by the width. Your answer will be the number of square feet in a room.
Diagonal lines filling a space mean that there's a solid wall. When there are no diagonal lines, that means there's a window.

Explore the Floor!

After you've "toured" the apartment on the left, use the floor plan and the tips to answer the following questions. Write your answers on your own paper.

1. Without doing any math: Which room on the floor plan seems to be the biggest? (Don't count the kitchen, bathrooms, closets, or balconies.)

2. What is the length of the dining room? What is the width? Now look at the measurements for the other rooms. Which room is the longest? Which is the widest?

3. You own many plants that need sunlight. Which room would you **not** put them in?
   a. bedroom 1
   b. bedroom 2
   c. the living room
   d. the dining room

4. What is the square footage of the balcony off the living room and bedroom 2?

5. Your bed is 6 feet long. Your dresser is 3 feet long. Your desk is 5 feet long. In which bedroom (or bedrooms) could you place this furniture side by side along the length of the room?
   a. both bedroom 1 and bedroom 2
   b. bedroom 1 only
   c. bedroom 2 only
   d. neither bedroom

Measure It

Use a tape measure to find the length and width of two rooms in your home. Then figure out the square footage. Which room is bigger? Which is smaller?

Draw a Plan

Design the floor plan for your dream apartment. Label each room. Don't forget to include bathrooms, closets, and windows.

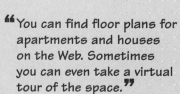

"You can find floor plans for apartments and houses on the Web. Sometimes you can even take a virtual tour of the space."

Real-World Words

length: the longer measurement in a room
square footage: the length of a room times its width
width: the shorter measurement in a room

TREASURE ISLAND

A GRAPHIC CLASSIC BY
ADAM GRANT

BASED ON THE NOVEL BY
ROBERT LOUIS STEVENSON

Robert Louis Stevenson wanted to become a writer. He also wanted adventure. In 1872, when he was 22, he started traveling the world.

First, he explored Europe. Then he went to San Francisco. There, he met and married Fanny Osbourne, who had a son named Lloyd.

Stevenson wrote his first novel, *Treasure Island,* to entertain his new stepson. It was an exciting tale about pirates, a mysterious map, and buried treasure.

In 1888, Stevenson became very sick. He moved with his family to the island of Samoa, which had a warm and beautiful climate.

Stevenson lived only six more years. Before his death, he traveled around the world—and wrote many unforgettable tales. But the most memorable tale is the one you are about to read.

IT ALL STARTED WHEN I WAS JUST A KID. MY MOTHER AND I RAN A SMALL INN CALLED THE ADMIRAL BENBOW. ONE DAY, AN OLD SEA CAPTAIN CAME TO STAY WITH US. HIS NAME WAS BILLY BONES.
ADMIRAL BENBOW
This here's a handy inn. Have you got a room?
Uh, yes.
I think I'll stay awhile. The name is Billy Bones.

BONES CAUSED LOTS OF TROUBLE FOR MY MOTHER AND ME. HE SPENT MANY NIGHTS GETTING INTO MISCHIEF AND SINGING HIS STRANGE SEA SONGS.
Fifteen men on a dead man's chest! Yo ho ho . . .

ASK YOURSELF

- Does this story take place in the past, present, or future?

Look for clues in the words and pictures of this story.

BILLY BONES ALSO TOLD STRANGE STORIES FROM HIS DAYS SAILING WITH A FAMOUS PIRATE CALLED CAPTAIN FLINT.
... We had already fed most of his crew to the sharks. And I said to him, "You're next, Admiral. If you can't walk the plank yourself, I'll be glad to help you!"

ONE DAY, BONES OFFERED ME A FEW PENNIES IF I WOULD DO A LITTLE JOB FOR HIM.
Keep your eyes open for a seafaring man with one leg, Jim. My life depends on it.

I DID AS HE ASKED. SO I HARDLY NOTICED AN OLD BLIND MAN WHO WALKED UP TO ME ONE DAY.
Would some kind soul help me to find the Admiral Benbow Inn?
Sure. I can help you. I live there.
SUDDENLY, HE GRIPPED MY ARM AND PULLED ME CLOSE.
Where is Billy Bones? Take me to him, or I'll break your arm!
I TOOK THE MAN INTO THE BENBOW.
No! It can't be! Blind Pew!
Don't try to run, Billy. I cannot see, but I can hear your little finger move. Get ready to give up Captain Flint's secret, or get what's coming to you! Now, give me your hand.
AS HE LEFT, PEW DROPPED SOMETHING INTO BONES'S HAND. IT WAS THE BLACK SPOT. THAT'S A NOTE THAT PIRATES GIVE TO ANOTHER PIRATE WHEN THEY ARE GOING TO KILL HIM.
The black spot! I can't b-breathe! I c-c-can't—
I'LL BE BACK TO KILL YOU AT 10 O'CLOCK

AN HOUR LATER, WE FOUND BILLY BONES IN HIS ROOM.
He must have died of fright!
BONES OWED MY MOTHER MONEY, SO WE DECIDED TO LOOK IN HIS SEA CHEST.
Just take what he owes us.
I will. Wait, this looks like a map. But what is it a map of? I have an idea who might know....
WE WENT TO OUR FRIEND SQUIRE TRELAWNEY'S HOUSE. HE WAS HAVING DINNER WITH ANOTHER FRIEND OF OURS, DR. LIVESEY.
You say this Billy Bones sailed with old Captain Flint? Flint was the most bloodthirsty old pirate who ever sailed. And maybe the richest!
They say Flint buried most of his treasure somewhere. Then he died before he could ever dig it up. Let's take a look at that map.

North Inlet
Spy-glass Hill
Bulk of treasure here
Fort
Cape of the Woods
Jim, it looks as if you have found the map to Captain Flint's treasure!
We've got to go after that treasure! Tomorrow, I will hire the finest ship money can buy. And I'll get the best captain and crew in England.
I'll be the ship's doctor. Jim, you'll work as the cabin boy. The squire here will be the admiral. If all goes well, we'll be rich!
But won't it be dangerous to steal a pirate treasure?
Not really. Captain Flint's dead. He can't hurt us.
But we must keep this trip a secret. If any of Flint's old friends find out, we will pay with our lives.
TEN DAYS LATER, I RECEIVED A LETTER FROM THE SQUIRE, TELLING ME TO REPORT TO THE SHIP.
I'm worried. And I'll miss you terribly.
I'll miss you too. But don't worry, Mother. I'll be fine.

A FEW DAYS LATER, WE SET SAIL.
I QUICKLY MADE FRIENDS WITH A SAILOR NAMED LONG JOHN SILVER. HE WAS THE COOK, SO THE MEN CALLED HIM 'BARBECUE.'
Jim Hawkins, I'm pleased to meet you. Come by any time, and I'll tell you tales of the high seas.
I SPENT MANY HOURS WITH SILVER ...
This here's my parrot. I call him Flint, after the old pirate.
Pieces of eight! Pieces of eight!
Pieces of eight? What's that?
He's talking about gold coins. He learned that talk from his old owners — some pirates.
You'll walk the plank for that, mate!

ASK YOURSELF

- Who is Captain Flint?

Stop and make sure you know who all the characters are.

THE OTHER SAILORS LOOKED UP TO SILVER. THEY TOLD AMAZING STORIES ABOUT HIM.
He's no common man. He's been to school and can talk like a professor. And he's brave. Like a lion. I once saw Barbecue take on five strong men and knock their heads together. And he was unarmed!
Don't lie to that boy, you mutt! It was only four!
AT NIGHT, I'D SIT OUT ON THE DECK WHILE SILVER CLEANED UP THE POTS AND PANS. I'D EAT AN APPLE AND LISTEN TO HIM TALK.
This is where we belong, Hawkins. The sea is our home.
ONE NIGHT, I FELL ASLEEP ON DECK. I WAS BEHIND AN APPLE BARREL. WHEN I AWOKE, TWO MEN WERE TALKING NEARBY. THEY THOUGHT THEY WERE ALONE.
I sailed with that pirate Flint for years. I've seen that treasure, and I plan to have it. And I won't share it with that prissy squire or the doctor!
IT WAS LONG JOHN SILVER TALKING! HE WAS A PIRATE!
We'll let **them** find the treasure and load it on board.
Then, we'll cut their throats!
You're a mean one, Silver. Just like Flint.

AS SOON AS THEY LEFT, I RUSHED BELOW TO TELL THE SQUIRE AND THE DOCTOR ABOUT SILVER'S PLAN TO KILL US. THEY WERE WITH THE SHIP'S CAPTAIN, CAPTAIN SMOLLETT.
We must figure out who else is on Silver's side.
I'm afraid we must consider the other 20 sailors our enemies.
Our best weapon against those cutthroats is surprise. They don't know that we know what they're up to.
You're right. For now, we do nothing.
WE SPOTTED OUR ISLAND THE VERY NEXT DAY.
I saw that Captain Flint's fort was marked on the map. Once we're on the island, we'll meet there.
Let's all head off in different directions to confuse the pirates. Meet at the fort by sundown.
THE CAPTAIN AND DR. LIVESEY HEADED FOR THE FORT. I RAN INTO THE HILLS.

SUDDENLY, I SAW SOMETHING LEAP BEHIND A TREE. I COULD NOT TELL IF IT WAS A BEAR, A MAN, OR A MONKEY.
I REMEMBERED WHAT I HAD HEARD ABOUT MAN-EATING CANNIBALS ON THESE ISLANDS. I WAS SCARED AND STARTED TO RUN AWAY. BUT THE CREATURE STOPPED ME.
Wait!
I'm Ben Gunn. I was left on this island three years ago. I've had nothing to eat but wild goats and berries. Tell me the truth, lad. That's not old Captain Flint's men I saw, are they?

I TOLD HIM THAT CAPTAIN FLINT WAS DEAD. BUT SOME OF HIS CREW WERE ON THE ISLAND.
Is there a man with one leg among them?
That's Long John Silver, their leader. Do you know him?
He's the worst of them. I know him from when we both sailed with Captain Flint.
But I'm not a pirate anymore. I'll help you if you promise to take me back to England with you.
I'll tell my friends what you said. I'm headed back to the fort now.
THE SQUIRE AND DR. LIVESEY WERE WAIT- ING FOR ME AT THE FORT. I TOLD THEM ABOUT BEN GUNN.
This Gunn might be able to help us later. But we're safe for now.
Silver and his men can't do anything without our map. Silver will probably try to bargain with us for it.
We have the fort and a few days' worth of food.

THE NEXT MORNING, LONG JOHN SILVER STOOD OUTSIDE THE FORT, ASKING FOR A MEETING.
CAPTAIN SMOLLETT WENT OUT TO TALK WITH SILVER.
I'll tell you plain, Captain. We have taken over the ship. You can't go anywhere. We want the map. If you give it to us, we'll spare your lives. Otherwise, the talking is over, and the shooting starts.
Look here, Silver. It's *you* who are out of choices. You'll never find the treasure without our map. And none of you can sail the ship. I'll give you one chance to surrender.
SILVER WAS FURIOUS. HE LOOKED TERRIFYING, BUT THE CAPTAIN JUST CHUCKLED.
Go ahead and laugh, Captain. But when we return, you'll be begging for your lives.
WHEN SILVER LEFT, WE PREPARED FOR BATTLE.

THAT AFTERNOON, THE BATTLE BEGAN. THE PIRATES QUICKLY HAMMERED THEIR WAY INTO THE FORT.
SOMEHOW, WE KEPT OUR HEADS. SOON, A FEW OF THE PIRATES HAD FALLEN. WITHIN MINUTES, THE REST OF THEM WERE HEADED BACK TO THE TREES. I WAS SURE THE FORT AND THE MAP WERE STILL OURS!

THEN I THOUGHT OF SOMETHING. THE PIRATES WERE ALL FIGHTING US. SO WHO WAS GUARDING THE SHIP? MAYBE I COULD STEAL IT BACK FOR US. I KNEW MY FRIENDS WOULDN'T LIKE THIS PLAN. SO AS SOON AS IT WAS DARK, I SNEAKED AWAY.
I WENT TO THE SPOT WHERE BEN GUNN HAD TOLD ME HE HAD A BOAT. SURE ENOUGH, IT WAS THERE.
I FOUND THE HISPANIOLA ANCHORED IN THE BAY. IT LOOKED LIKE THERE WASN'T A SOUL ON BOARD. I CLIMBED UP THE ANCHOR ROPE.
THE DECK WAS COVERED WITH BODIES. THE PIRATES SILVER HAD LEFT TO GUARD THE SHIP HAD KILLED EACH OTHER! BUT THEN I SAW ONE OF THE BODIES MOVE....

I GRABBED TWO PISTOLS FROM A DEAD PIRATE.
I've come aboard to take over this ship. Consider me your captain!

ASK YOURSELF

- Why does Jim take such a big risk to get control of the ship?

Think about the setting and why a ship is so important.

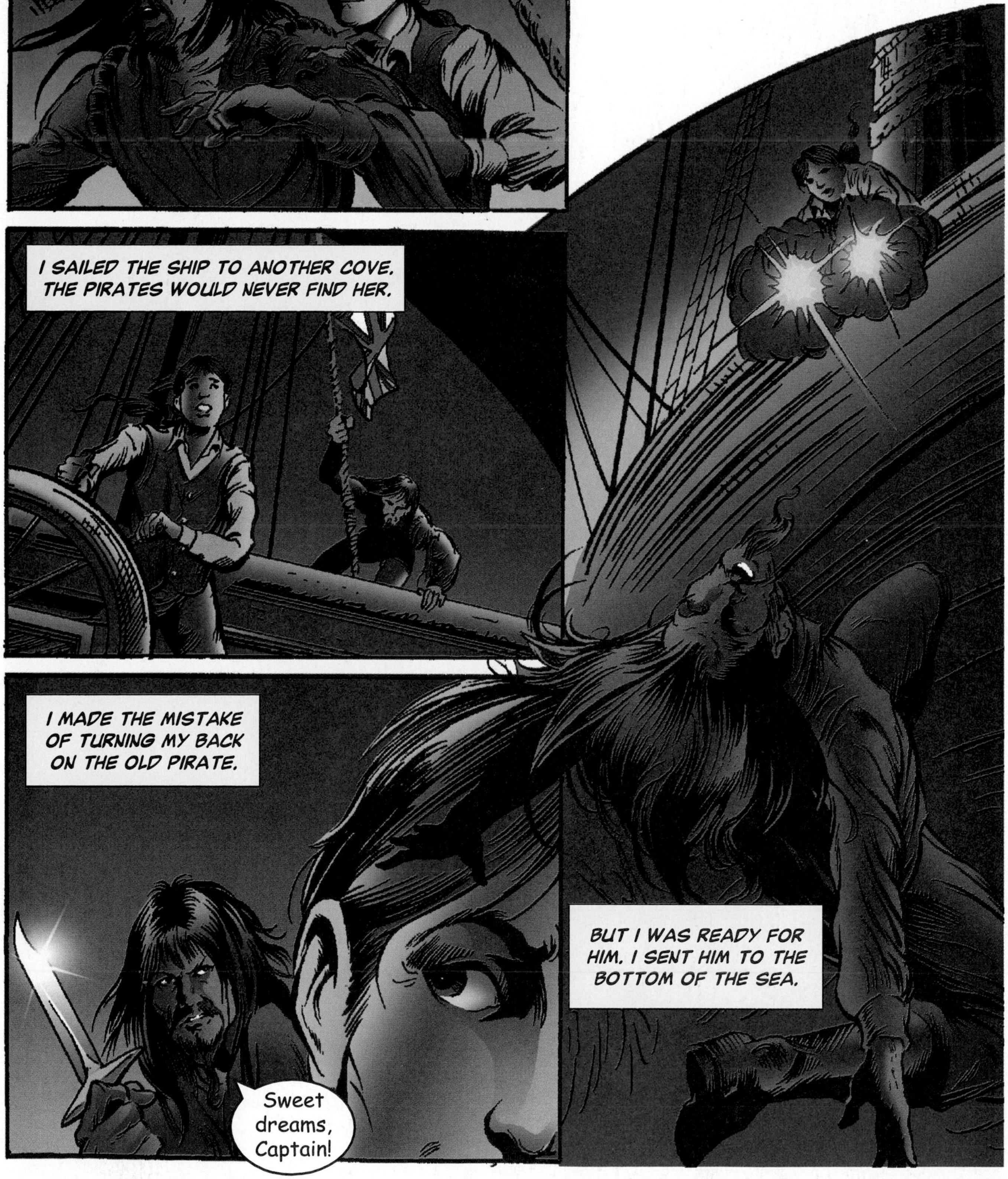
I SAILED THE SHIP TO ANOTHER COVE. THE PIRATES WOULD NEVER FIND HER.
I MADE THE MISTAKE OF TURNING MY BACK ON THE OLD PIRATE.
Sweet dreams, Captain!
BUT I WAS READY FOR HIM. I SENT HIM TO THE BOTTOM OF THE SEA.

I SWAM BACK TO SHORE AND HEADED FOR THE FORT. IT WAS PITCH BLACK IN THERE. I GUESSED THAT MY FRIENDS WERE ALREADY FAST ASLEEP.
I WAS CRAWLING TO MY BUNK WHEN MY FOOT HIT SOMETHING
Pieces of eight! Pieces of eight! BRAAWK!
SOMEHOW, THE PIRATES HAD TAKEN THE FORT. I WAS IN ENEMY CAMP.
Shiver me timbers, here's Jim Hawkins! I always wanted you to join us pirates, and now you've got to!
We ran your friends out of here. They probably think you're dead. So you're either our mate, or our hostage.

SILVER TOLD ME HOW THAT DAY, DR. LIVESEY HAD COME TO THE PIRATE CAMP TO BARGAIN.
The doctor realized that his men couldn't beat us. He gave us the fort in exchange for food and safe passage to the other side of the island.
So you're stuck with us. Why not join us?
There's a thing or two I must tell you, Silver.
You're in a bad situation. Your ship is lost. Your treasure is lost. And you're stuck on this island. And you know who did it? Me! I hid behind the apple barrel and heard your evil scheme. I told it to the captain and the squire. I killed your last man on the *Hispaniola.* And I hid the ship where you'll never find her!

SUDDENLY, A PIRATE JUMPED OUT AT ME.
And it was *you* who stole the map from Billy Bones in the first place! Well, lad, here's my sword!
I WAS RELIEVED—AND VERY SURPRISED—WHEN SILVER CAME TO MY RESCUE.
I'll thank you to shut up till you're spoken to! And that goes for all of you. I'm captain here, and I like the boy. He's more of a man than any *two* of you rats!
Anyway, I've got a surprise for you whining old ladies. It's the treasure map. I got it from the good doctor. So you see, lads, you'll be rich men after all!
Barbecue forever! Hurrah for Captain Barbecue!

IN THE MORNING, WE SET OUT TO COLLECT FLINT'S TREASURE. THE PIRATES WERE TOTALLY EXCITED. I WAS STILL CONFUSED.
Why did Dr. Livesey give up the treasure map?
WE ARRIVED AT THE PLACE MARKED ON THE MAP. BUT ALL WE FOUND WAS A HUGE PIT AND SOME BROKEN BOXES.
SILVER THOUGHT FAST.
Take this, Jim. And get ready for trouble. These men are going to want our heads.
Silver, you told us there was a fortune! And all we find is a hole in the ground!
Mates, let's get them!

JUST THEN, THREE SHOTS RANG OUT. TWO OF THE PIRATES DROPPED DEAD, AND THE OTHER THREE RAN OFF.
BLAM
BLAM
BLAM
MY FRIENDS HAD WAITED IN THE WOODS AND ATTACKED THE PIRATES. I WAS NEVER SO GLAD TO SEE ANYONE IN MY LIFE.
IT SEEMS THAT OVER THE PAST FEW YEARS, BEN GUNN HAD DUG UP MOST OF FLINT'S TREASURE AND HID IT AWAY IN HIS CAVE.
It's not all of it, but it's enough, I reckon.
That's why I traded away the map, Jim. Gunn told us it was worthless. I hated to leave you with those criminals, but I had to look after the others.
I know, sir. I ran off without telling anyone. But I did get the ship back from the pirates and hid her.

SILVER WAS THE ONLY PIRATE LEFT. HE HAD SAVED MY LIFE, SO WE AGREED TO TAKE HIM BACK TO ENGLAND—AND NOT FOR HANGING.
I will not prosecute you, sir. Even though you are a villain and a murderer. Dead men hang about your neck like stones.

WHAT A SUPPER WE HAD IN BEN GUNN'S HOMEY CAVE THAT NIGHT, WITH ALL MY FRIENDS AROUND ME. NEVER WERE PEOPLE HAPPIER.

ASK YOURSELF

- How did Jim's friends trick the pirates?

Stop and think about what's happened before you read on.

WE SPENT THE NEXT THREE DAYS LOADING THE TREASURE ONTO THE *HISPANIOLA*. IT WAS HARD WORK, BUT NOBODY MINDED.
WE SET SAIL FOR THE NEAREST PORT TO BUY FOOD AND HIRE A CREW FOR THE TRIP HOME.

AFTER A FEW DAYS, WE LANDED IN SOUTH AMERICA AND WENT ASHORE.
WHEN WE RETURNED TO THE SHIP, WE HAD A SHOCK. OUR WATCHMAN, BEN GUNN, HAD BEEN KNOCKED OUT. YOU-KNOW-WHO WAS GONE.
SILVER HAD ESCAPED. AND HE HAD STOLEN A SACK OF OUR HARD-WON COINS.
We're lucky to be rid of him. And we're lucky it didn't cost us more.

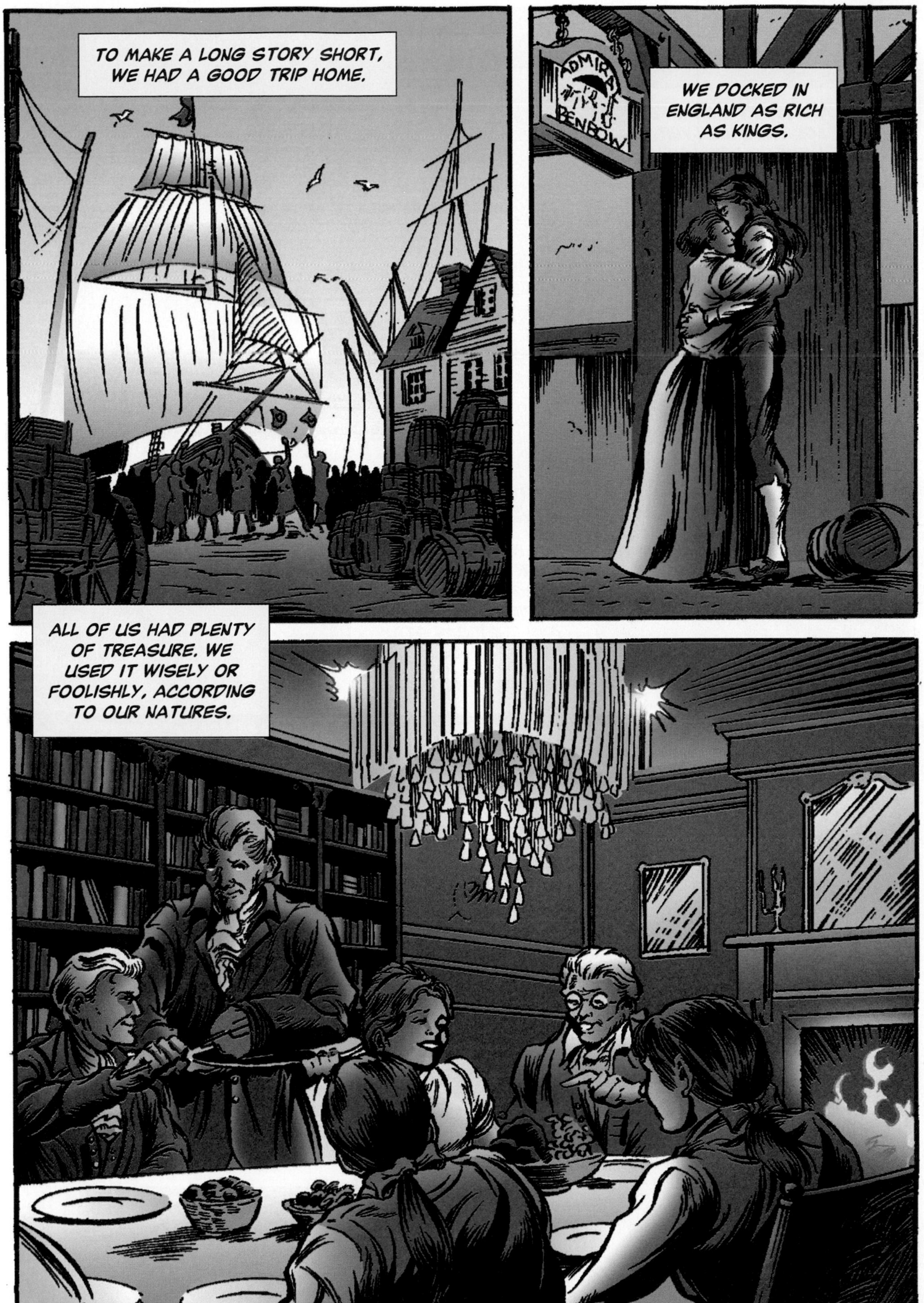
TO MAKE A LONG STORY SHORT, WE HAD A GOOD TRIP HOME.
ADMIRAL BENBOW
WE DOCKED IN ENGLAND AS RICH AS KINGS.
ALL OF US HAD PLENTY OF TREASURE. WE USED IT WISELY OR FOOLISHLY, ACCORDING TO OUR NATURES.

I HAVE HEARD NO MORE OF LONG JOHN SILVER. BUT I GUESS HE'S LIVING SOMEWHERE COMFORTABLY WITH HIS STOLEN TREASURE.
THE REST OF FLINT'S SILVER COINS STILL LIE, I IMAGINE, WHERE THE OLD PIRATE LEFT THEM. AND THEY CAN STAY THERE, FOR ALL I CARE.
WILD HORSES COULD NOT DRAG ME BACK TO THAT ISLAND. THE WORST DREAMS THAT I HAVE EVER HAD ARE WHEN I HEAR THE SURF BOOMING ON THE COAST OR SIT UP IN BED WITH THE SHARP VOICE OF SILVER'S BIRD, FLINT, RINGING IN MY EARS ...

PIECES of EIGHT!
PIECES OF EIGHT!

Wrap-Up

Talk About It

Now that you've read *Treasure Island,* what do you have to say about these questions?

- Would you have risked your life for the treasure? Why or why not?
- Why are adventure stories so exciting? What is one of your favorite adventure books or movies? Explain why you like it.

Comprehension Check

Write your answers to the questions below. Use information from the graphic classic to support your answers.

1. Why does the pirate's treasure map turn out to be useless?
2. How do you think Jim feels when he first learns that his friends have given the treasure map to the pirates?
3. Why do you think all the pirates back at the ship kill each other?
4. How might Jim and his friends have used their money wisely? Foolishly?
5. If you were Jim, would you go back to the island to look for the rest of the treasure? Why or why not?

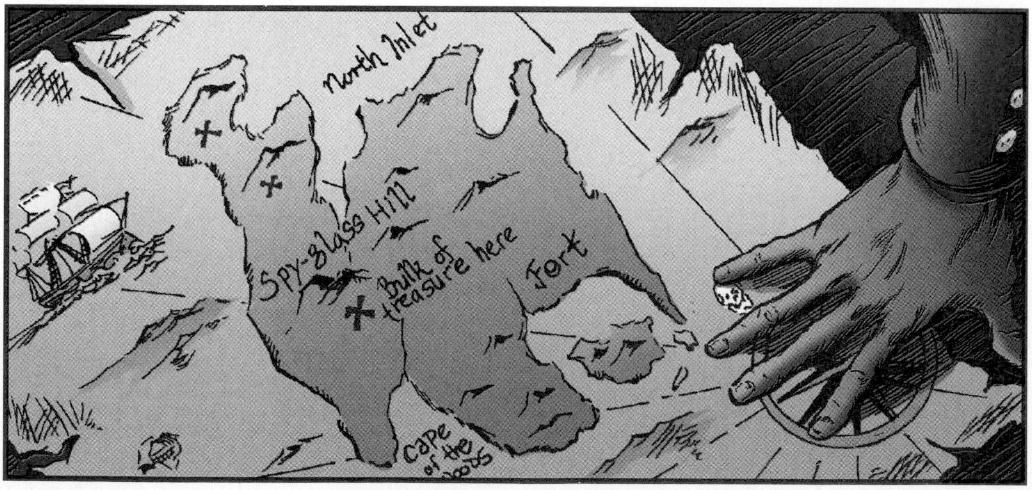
North Inlet
Spy-glass Hill
Bulk of treasure here
Fort
Cape of the Woods

Write About It

Choose one of the writing prompts below.

- If you wanted to hide a treasure, where would you put it? Describe the best hiding place you can think of, and then write out the instructions for finding the loot.
- Write the copy for a "most-wanted poster" for the capture of Long John Silver. Make a list of all Long John Silver's crimes and why it's important to bring him to justice.
- Imagine Jim as an old man with grown children. Write a letter from Jim to his children telling them how to use the money.

About the AUTHOR

In 1881, Robert Louis Stevenson and his 12-year-old stepson were stuck inside their cottage for an entire week of a school holiday because of rainy weather. His stepson liked to draw, and the two of them spent hours doing this together. One day, Stevenson found himself drawing a complex and colorful pirate map. This, says Stevenson, is how the idea for *Treasure Island* was born.

Another famous book written by Stevenson came to him in a dream, actually, a nightmare. That book is *The Strange Case of Dr. Jekyll and Mr. Hyde.* Although Stevenson considered this book the worst he ever wrote, it sold well, and brought him more fame than any of the others.

Reading Movie Reviews

You like to go to the movies. But you don't like to waste your money. How can you find out whether you'd enjoy a new movie? Check out a few reviews. You'll find out what the movie's about and what critics thought about it.

Take a look at these sample movie reviews. Is *New York City Rocks* a must-see film for you?

Three Movie Reviews

A review gives a short summary of the film's plot. But most reviews don't give away the ending.

Reviews tell who stars in the movie and sometimes who plays the smaller roles.

"What would happen if an earthquake hit New York City? Run, don't walk, to see this new movie and find out! *New York City Rocks* is suspenseful and intense. Stars Samantha Stone and Randy Rock are fabulous together. The special effects were totally realistic. A+"
Felicity Flick
Chicago Daily News

"This was a fun movie for the teenage crowd. The plot was weak in moments, but actors Stone and Rock kept me interested. The supporting actors, Lucy Kim and Robert Allstaff, were incredible. Overall, it was a good movie with great special effects. B+"
Gwen Herbert
San Francisco Daily News

Many reviewers give the movie a grade. Don't forget—that's just one person's opinion!

"...This movie was enjoyable, but far-fetched. It strained my imagination. What's more, star Randy Rock needs to take some drama classes! He never changes expression throughout the movie. I'll admit that Samantha Stone is great. And the special effects were incredible. But you should wait till this one comes out on video."
Sam Spellberg
New York City News

"Movie reviewers don't always agree with each other. That's why you might want to read two or three reviews before deciding whether to go a movie."

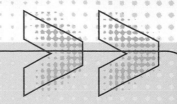

Let's Go to the Movies!

Have you ever ended up at a boring movie—just because the poster looked cool? Movie reviews tell you more than a poster ever could. Reread the reviews and the tips that go with them. Then answer the questions below. Write your answers on your own paper.

1. Which two reviewers liked the movie the most? Which reviewer did not like Randy Rock's performance?

2. What do you think "fun for the teenage crowd" means?
- **a.** You should see this movie with a group of teenagers.
- **b.** This movie helps teenagers improve their study skills.
- **c.** Teenagers will probably enjoy this movie, but adults may not.

3. What did one reviewer mean when he said, "I would wait till this one comes out on video"?
- **a.** He is looking forward to seeing the sequel.
- **b.** Don't pay to see this movie in a theater.
- **c.** See this movie now. You'll never be able to find it at the video store.

4. Which of the following people is most likely to enjoy *New York City Rocks?*
- **a.** Casey likes love stories and movies about sports.
- **b.** Michael dislikes movies in which people get hurt.
- **c.** Sam loves any movie with special effects.

5. What are two reasons to read a review?
- **a.** to find out if the plot interests you
- **b.** to find out how much the movie costs
- **c.** to find out if there are good special effects

Movie Write-Up

Do you think you would enjoy *New York City Rocks*? Using what you read in the reviews, make a list of three reasons you'd go to see the film, or three reasons you'd skip it.

Critical Acclaim

Watch a movie or a TV show. Take notes while you are watching on what you like and dislike about it. When it's over, read through your list. Then write a review.

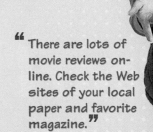

"There are lots of movie reviews on-line. Check the Web sites of your local paper and favorite magazine."

Real-World Words

critics: people who produce reviews of movies or other works
plot: a story
review: an article that gives an opinion about a movie or other work

Real-Life HERO

Pearl Fuyo Gaskins

journalist

Journalist Pearl Fuyo Gaskins has written a powerful book for multiracial young people. She hopes that the book will help kids—of all races—deal with this complex issue.

Even worse than being picked on was being ignored.

Everything will be different now, thought Pearl Fuyo Gaskins.

She was ten years old at the time, and her family was about to move to Japan. Pearl's mother was Japanese. Her father was an American serviceman. They had met in Tokyo and had settled in the United States shortly before the birth of their daughter. Pearl was as American as any of her classmates, but she had often felt the sting of their racism and ignorance.

"I was very young when I first experienced racism," Pearl remembers. "Kids called me names just because I looked Asian."

A Hope for More

So when her father was transferred to Yokohama, a city in Japan, Pearl was not upset. Unlike many kids her age, she liked the idea of moving to a different country. She had Japanese features, so she would fit right in. The insults would stop and she'd feel at home. Or so she believed.

"I thought, 'Great, we're going to Japan. Now they won't call me names anymore,'" Pearl says. "But when we got there, I heard Japanese kids on the streets saying, 'You ugly American!' and 'Americans go home!'"

Even worse than being picked on was being ignored, Pearl would later write. As a mixed-race child, she felt "invisible and alone."

A Reason to Write

Pearl has never forgotten how she felt when she was a young girl. That's one of the main reasons she decided to write her highly-praised first book, *What Are You? Voices of Mixed-Race Young People.*

"Because I'm racially mixed, I wanted to create the kind of book I wish I'd had when I was a teenager," Pearl says. "When I was growing up, there weren't a lot of mixed-race people in my community. There weren't a lot of interracial families."

Pearl, an award-winning journalist who writes articles for an educational magazine for teenagers, spent almost three years researching and writing *What Are You?* She interviewed 80 young multiracial people for the book, and asked them to describe their thoughts and feelings about what it's like to be a mixed-race boy or girl. She combined their responses with essays and poems written by other young multiracial people. She also included comments from experts on race and sociology.

What you'll find is a book that is sometimes funny and sometimes sad, but always thoughtful. There is anger on the pages — after all, it's not easy feeling like an outsider. But there is also joy and hope. The book is a celebration of multicultural life and a challenge to racism and bigotry.

"The book is a forum for mixed-race people to share their experiences," Pearl says. "Readers will get a sense that they're not alone. And, more importantly, if they're having problems because they're racially mixed, they'll understand that it's not because there's something wrong with them. It's because there's something wrong with the way our society puts so much stock in race. And the way people categorize each other by the color of their skin."

A Book for All Kids

Do you have to be a mixed-race person to enjoy this book? "Absolutely not!" says Pearl. "I also hope kids who are not racially mixed will read the book—and maybe they'll start to think, *Gee, what is this race stuff, and why is it*

Sharing food and understanding: Pearl with Nicole Rivera, one of the young people in her book, at a picnic in Central Park.

so important? Why do we notice it? Why do we make ***assumptions*** *about people based on race? And what assumptions do I make?"*

Identity Crisis

In her research, Pearl discovered that mixed-race teens today struggle with many of the same issues she faced while growing up. Because they do not fit neatly into a single racial **category,** they often have to work harder to find their place in the world. People expect them to behave a certain way, or they are expected to embrace a certain culture, simply because of the color of their skin. But to the multiracial teen, it's a much more complicated matter.

"There's a lot of pressure to fit in to a particular group, especially for younger teens," Pearl says. "Often peer groups are organized by race. When you walk into a school cafeteria, the white kids are here, and the black kids are over there. I think if you're racially mixed, it can make it even harder to know where you fit in.

"In our society there's always been an assumption that you can be only one race. A lot of the kids in the book talk about being forced by other people to make a choice: 'Okay, what are you? Black or Latino? Asian or white?'"

Hope for the Future

To her delight, though, Pearl also discovered some very positive changes, too. The number of

Words, Words, Words

assumptions: beliefs taken for granted without knowing that they are true
category: a class or group of things that has something in common
unique: unusual
poignant: emotional and touching
defiant: being bold or standing up to someone or something

interracial marriages in the United States has skyrocketed in the past 30 years. And today's multiracial teens don't have to look far for role models to admire.

Mixed-Race Celebrities

Pop superstar Mariah Carey is multiracial. So is New York Yankees shortstop Derek Jeter. When Tiger Woods won the Masters golf tournament, he was referred to as the first African American to do so. But Tiger quickly pointed out that he wasn't merely African American. His father was a mix of African American, American Indian and Chinese, and his mother was Thai, Chinese, and white. So Tiger decided to make up a word to describe his own **unique** ethnic background. He was *Cablinasian:* Caucasian, Black, Indian, and Asian.

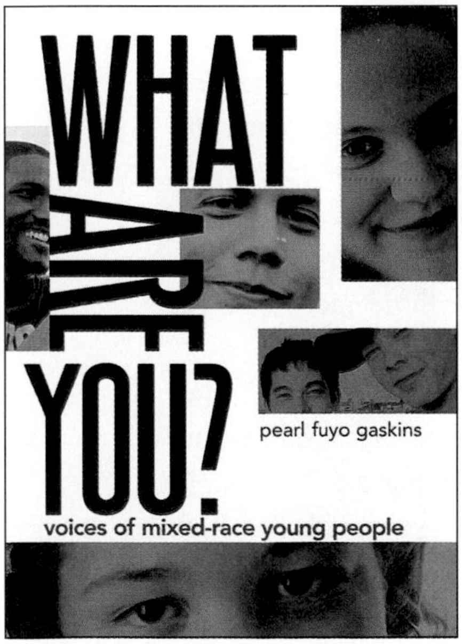
WHAT ARE YOU?
pearl fuyo gaskins
voices of mixed-race young people
***What Are You?* A book that gives mixed-race young people a voice.**

ASK Yourself

- How do you think having role models makes racially mixed teens feel?

Think about what Pearl Fuyo Gaskins says about her childhood.

Proud and Defiant

What Are You? is filled with interesting and **poignant** stories, and powerful voices. Like Tiger Woods, many of the teens interviewed by Pearl are proud . . . but they are also **defiant.** They are searching, experimenting, trying on different racial identities. And in many cases, they seem to be enjoying the journey, even when it's difficult.

"When I was growing up, being racially mixed wasn't really recognized as a unique or positive experience," Pearl says. "I think that's changing. I think there's more of an openness to people of mixed-race backgrounds."

And Pearl is one of the people helping to bring about this change. She has written a book that confronts the issue of race head-on—and gives voice to a generation. ●

RESUMÉ

Name: Pearl Fuyo Gaskins
Born: May 5, 1957, Maryville, Tennessee

Goals:
- to provide a place for mixed-race young people to share their experiences, and to educate others who are not racially mixed
- to write on issues she feels passionate about
- to provide something for a group of people who have been ignored

Education:
- bachelor's degree in sociology, University of California, Berkeley, 1980
- master's degree in journalism, New York University, 1991

Work History:
- ten years as a computer programmer
- eleven years as a writer and editor for *Scholastic Choices* magazine

Major Achievements:
- won three awards from the Educational Press Association of America
- published the highly-praised book *What Are You?*

Voices from
WHAT ARE YOU?
Mixed-Race Young People Share Their Feelings

Genia Linear, 14
Honolulu, Hawaii
Mother: Puerto Rican, Portuguese
Father: African-American, Native-American

You're Special

I like attention. If I'm walking around at a swap meet or something, people just stare at me and my sister, and they stare at my mom, 'cause my mom looks white. I guess they're trying to figure out what I am.

I was born in Hawaii. Practically everyone is biracial here. I'm Puerto Rican, Black, Portuguese, Native American, Caucasian. There's this girl, she's pure Filipino, and she's like, "I wish I had all those races that you have." It's like a person with straight hair wants to have curly hair.

People would ask me, "Oh, what are you?" . . . "Oh, cool, cool." They think it's unique. I never heard anybody say, "You're half black, half white? Eww! What happened to you? What's wrong with your parents?"

I like it when people ask what I am. You get to show your pride and stuff. I'm not saying that being pure is bad or anything. I just think that being mixed is like—you're special.

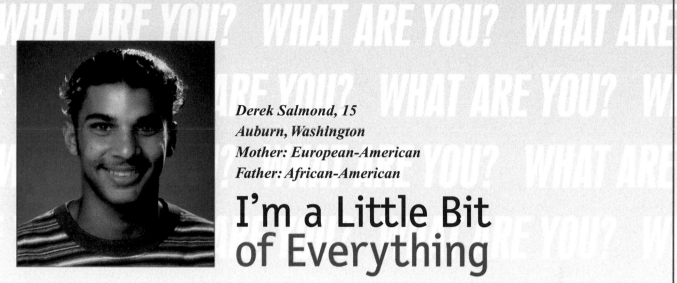

Derek Salmond, 15
Auburn, Washington
Mother: European-American
Father: African-American

I'm a Little Bit of Everything

People often ask me the question, "So what are you anyway?" If I'm having a good day, I won't answer that in a hostile way. But if I'm having a rough day, it gets annoying. You get snappy at people when you realize how often they ask it and how many of them don't really understand.

My answer also depends on how they ask the question. If they ask, "What are you?" I just give them a smart answer. I say, "I'm a human being. Why? What are you?"

Then they go, "Well, what's your nationality?"

I tell them African-American and Caucasian-American. Or I will say, "I'm biracial." There's always that look of surprise when you say, "I'm biracial." Most people look at you for a second. I think they either don't comprehend or don't want to comprehend the expression.

Other people look at you and go, "You are?" because everyone automatically assumes that I'm either black, Puerto Rican, or Mexican. And most people are like, "Oh, so your mom's black and your dad's white."

"No, it's vice versa."

It bugs me that most people also automatically assume that my parents must be split up because it's an interracial marriage. They have this idea that biracial children don't live with both of their parents at the same time.

I can't classify myself as anything, nor do I want to. I play in the jazz band at school. I play in a blues band too. I play classical bass. I play water polo, which is mainly a white-dominated sport. I listen to classical music, occasionally alternative music, and rap and country also. I'm a little bit of everything."

Brian Harris, 14 (when written)
Stanton, California
Mother: European-American
Father: African-American

Half-Breed

I'm told sometimes that I don't fit in,
Told that I'll soon have troubles within.
I'm told to pick either black or white,
I think it over every night.
Should I give in and do as they say?
Or should I stay strong and have it my way?
Race is something you can't pick or choose,
Because if you do you will surely lose.
I know who I am and say it with pride,
As both black and white I experience the best of both sides.
I stand here proud of who I am,
Even if ignored by great Uncle Sam.
All I ask for is two boxes on a form,
Something that allows me not to conform.
Some think of me as the product of a sin,
They wonder what kind of love a black and white could possibly fall in.
There must be something wrong, something can't be right,
When two people are in love, one being black and the other white.
This must be wrong when blacks and whites find love,
This can't be all right with the man up above.
Don't call me an Oreo or a half-breed,
Give me the respect that I deserve and need.
Don't condemn me for the race I just happen to be,
Race is a small part of me.
Remember that people are a lot like books,
The outside shows little more than looks.
Prejudging may cost you a friend for life,
It may even cost you a husband or wife.
So next time you sit and attempt to categorize,
Remember there's more than meets the eyes.

This poem was originally published in *New People* magazine.

Candace Rea, 19
Kaneohe, Hawaii
Mother: European-American
Father: Filipino-American

I Am Not an Other

One thing that has come to bother me more and more in recent years is how to classify myself ethnically or racially on applications and surveys. I have trouble deciding whether to check the "white" box or the "Asian" box, because I don't want to deny either side of my heritage.

But I have even more of a conflict when I check the box marked "other." I am not an other and have never been an other. I am a person of mixed race. I don't belong in some outcast category. I am a person just like everyone else.

I would like to be recognized for the racially mixed person I am. So far, I have only had the chance to check a box marked "biracial" once in my life. ●

Wrap-Up

Talk About It

Now that you've read "Pearl Fuyo Gaskins" and "Voices from *What Are You?*" what do you have to say about these questions?

- How much does your race have to do with who you are?
- How can having more than one race or culture in your background be a good thing?

Comprehension Check

Write your answers to the questions below. Use information from the profile, essays, and poem to support your answers.

1. Why was Pearl Fuyo Gaskins happy to be moving to Japan?
2. Multiracial kids are not picked on now as much as they used to be. Why?
3. Why do you think the kids in some schools tend to stick together according to race?
4. What does Genia Linear mean when she says "It's like when a person with straight hair wants to have curly hair"?
5. Why should kids who are not racially mixed read a book like *What Are You? Voices of Mixed-Race Young People*?

Vocabulary Check

defiant **assumptions** **unique**
category **poignant**

Complete each sentence with the correct vocabulary word.

1. I cried during the movie because I thought it was very _______.
2. I'd rather be _______ than like everyone else.
3. When I refused to go to sleep at 10 o'clock, my mother said I was being _______.
4. I wish people wouldn't make _______ about me just because I dyed my hair blue.
5. I don't think of myself as being part of a _______.

Write About It

Choose one of the writing prompts below.

- How could you explain to people that you'd like them to look past your race? Write an open letter to the world explaining your feelings on the subject.
- Think of a stereotype that you think is untrue. How many examples can you list to disprove it?
- If Pearl Fuyo Gaskins had kept a journal in Japan, what do you think it would say? Write an entry about her experience there.

Fact FILE

THE CENSUS

Have you ever wondered how the U.S. government finds out how many Americans there are, who they are, and what services they need? The government gets this information by taking a census. During the census, people fill out forms that ask questions about age, race, income, and other issues.

In the past, Americans have been allowed to check only one box about their race. This has angered the many multiracial people living in America. So beginning in the year 2000, Americans will be allowed to check more than one box. This will give the government a better idea of how many multiracial people there are in this country. It will also allow multiracial people to proudly represent their identities.

Do you think the government is doing the right thing? What difference might it make for you? For other kids?

Writing a Cover Letter

You see an ad for a great job in the paper. It says applicants must send a resumé and cover letter. In your cover letter, you'll explain why you're qualified for the job.

Check out the cover letter below. It was written in response to the ad next to it. Read the letter and the ad.

Sample Cover Letter

A cover letter should be set up like any other business letter.

May 20, 2005

1722 Russel Circle
Colorado Springs, Colorado 80915

Ms. Pat Dalton
Camp Homesick
P.O. Box 99
Pueblo, Colorado 81009

Dear Ms. Dalton,
I am responding to the ad in last Sunday's *Newstime* for a camp counselor. The position sounds very interesting and I'd love to find out more about it.

I am currently an eighth grader at Bradley Middle School. I am very interested in working with children and have lots of experience. For the past four years I've babysat for several families in my town. Also, last summer I worked at the Bradley Child-Care Center as the arts & crafts director.

I plan to start work as soon as school is finished on June 10. My summer hours are flexible. Please call if you'd like to meet for an interview. You can reach me at 220-555-8320.

Sincerely Yours,

Len O'Brien

Len O'Brien

SUMMER JOB
CAMP COUNSELOR
Camp Homesick is looking for a part-time camp counselor. Ideal applicant will be a student with some work experience. An ability to get along well with people, especially children, is a must. Send cover letter and resumé to Ms. Pat Dalton, P.O. Box 99, Pueblo, Colorado 81009

In the first paragraph, say what job you're applying for and how you found out about it.

Introduce yourself and explain to the employer why you're qualified for the job.

"Before writing a cover letter, look at your resumé. Circle any skills that are mentioned in the ad. Talk about those skills in your letter."

That Covers It!

A cover letter is your first chance to make a good impression. That's why it's important to explain your qualifications for the job. Look over the ad, the cover letter, and the tips. Then use them to answer these questions. Write your answers on your own paper.

1. What are the most important qualifications that an applicant must have for the camp counselor job?

2. What is the main skill or experience that Len describes in his letter?
a. his dislike of arts and crafts
b. his flexible work hours
c. his experience working with children

3. If you were Ms. Dalton, would you call Len in for an interview? Why or why not?

4. What was the tone of Len's letter?
a. polite
b. funny
c. demanding

5. How does Len end his letter?
a. He suggests coming in for an interview.
b. He asks her to call him if he gets the job.
c. He tells her to call as soon as his letter arrives.

Job Hunt

Look at help-wanted ads in a newspaper. Choose three jobs that sound interesting. Make a list of the skills you'd need to get one of those jobs.

Write It

Choose one of the jobs from "Job Hunt." Suppose you had the skills and experiences you'd need to get the job. Write the cover letter you would send to the employer.

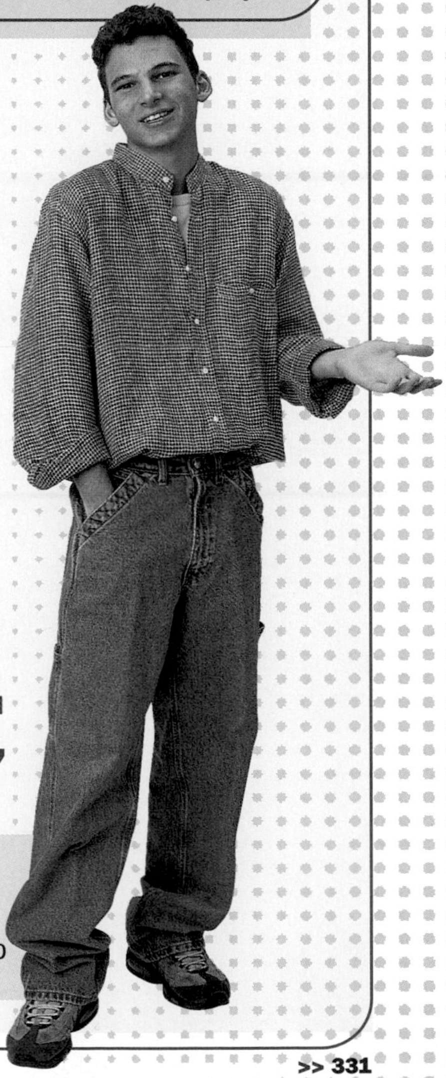

"After you write a cover letter, proofread it carefully. Don't just rely on spellcheck—you could have the *wrong* word with the *right* spelling."

Real-World Words

applicants: people who are applying for a job
employer: a person or company that pays you to work
qualifications: skills or experiences that make someone fit for a job

personal narrative

Cookie

by Gary Paulsen

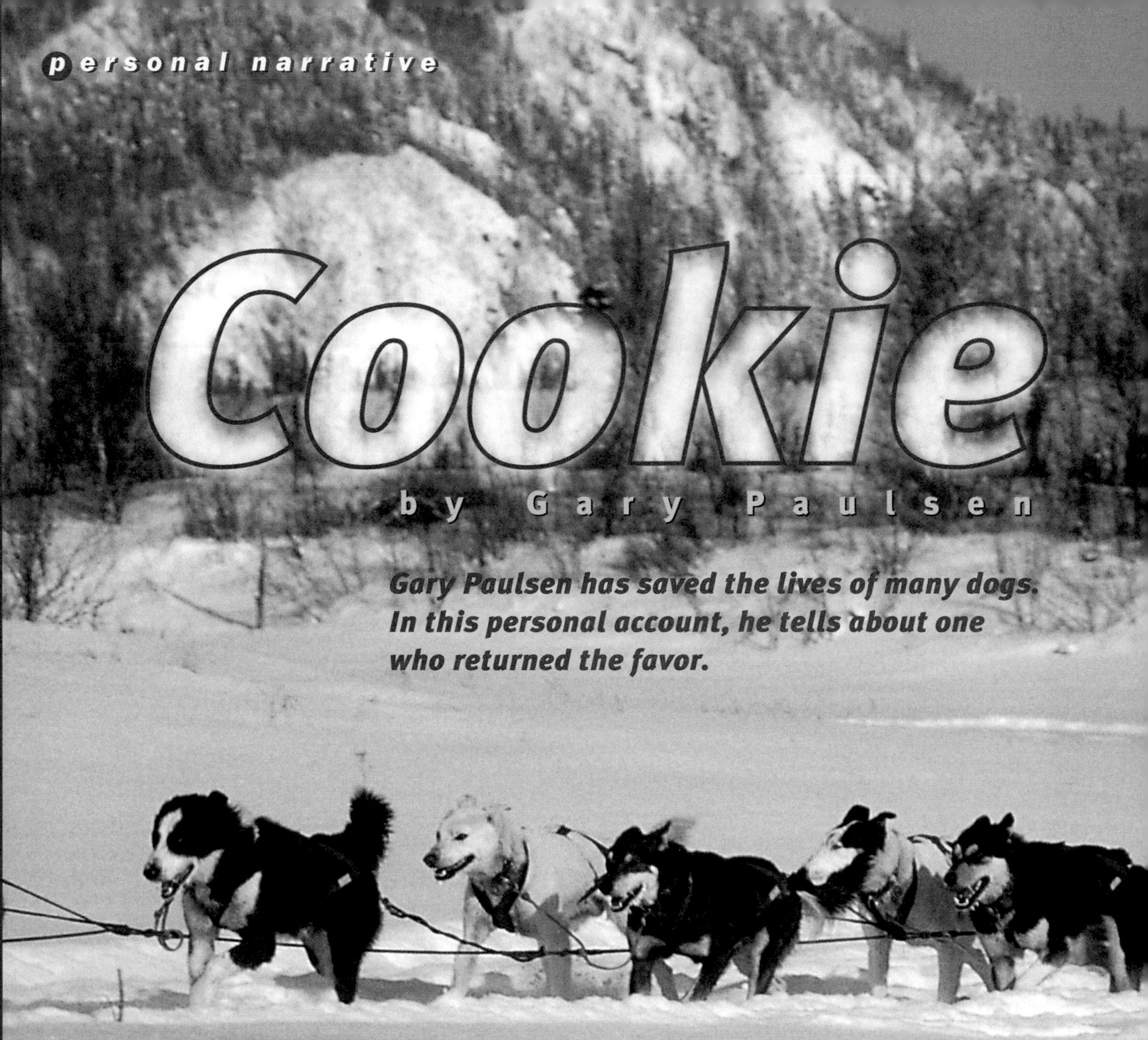

Gary Paulsen has saved the lives of many dogs. In this personal account, he tells about one who returned the favor.

I am—I say this with some pride and not a little wonder—a "dog person." I make no excuses for unabashedly loving them—all of them, even some that have bitten me. I have always had dogs and will have dogs until I die. I have rescued dozens of dogs from pounds, always have five or six of them around me, and cannot imagine living without dogs. They are wonderful and, I think, mandatory for decent human life.

All that said, there are some dogs that are different, special in

amazing ways. Cookie was one of those dogs.

Cookie was my lead dog when I first started to run dogs, and she was also my lead dog in my first Iditarod sled dog race; she took me from Anchorage to Nome, Alaska, when most people—including me—thought I couldn't do it.

But she was more. She was a good friend, a kind of dogsister or dogmother to me, and while I have written much of her in other places, I want to tell her story here.

Man's best friend: Gary with his faithful dog Cookie.

Cookie was given to me by a man who thought she was so sick she couldn't run any longer. She merely had worms, and when I wormed her she became a wonderful sled dog, and then a wonderful lead dog.

I did not set out to race dogs; I used them for work. I brought in wood with them, went to the Laundromat in town with them (it was grand to tie the dogs up to the parking meter and watch people jump as they walked by), and trapped with them.

In January of 1980 I was running a seventy-five-mile line, trapping beaver. I had **previously** trapped with a friend, but this year I was trapping alone, not the wisest thing to do, since there is some risk from bad ice or injuries and it's better to have a **companion.** I was alone when I made a mistake that nearly killed me.

The ice around beaver lodges is very dangerous. Beavers live in their lodges and come out of underwater tunnels to get food they have stored at the bottom of the river or pond through the summer, in the form of branches stuck down in the mud. Each time they come out they let air out of their noses and it goes up to make bubbles under the surface of the ice, and this, along with the beavers' rubbing their backs on the underside of the ice, keeps the ice very thin near a beaver lodge. It can be fifty below with two-foot-thick ice around the whole lake and the ice near the lodge might be less than a quarter inch thick.

I had parked the sled near a lodge and unpacked the gear needed to set a group of snares. Cookie was leading the work team of five dogs and they knew the **procedure** completely by this time. As soon as I stopped the sled and began to unpack they all lay down, curled their tails over their noses and went to sleep. The process could take two or three hours and they used the time to get rest.

A rope tied the **cargo** to the sled. I threw the rope across the ice to get it out of the way. One end was still tied to the sled. I took a step on the ice near the rope and went through and down like a stone.

You think there is time to react, that the ice will give way slowly and you'll be able to hang on to the edge, somehow able to struggle to safety. It's not that way at all. It's as if you were suddenly standing on air. The bottom drops out and you go down.

I was wearing heavy clothing and a parka. It gathered water like a sponge and took me down faster.

Words, Words, Words

previously: earlier
companion: someone you spend time with
procedure: a way of doing something
cargo: a load of supplies
analyzed: examined something carefully

Two things saved me. One, as I went down my hand fell across the rope I had thrown across the ice, which was still tied to the sled.

Two, as I dropped I had time to yell—scream—and the last thing I saw as I went under was Cookie's head swinging up from sleeping and her eyes locking on mine as I went beneath the surface.

The truth is I shouldn't have lived. I have had several friends killed in just this manner—dropping through the ice while running dogs—and there wasn't much of a chance for me. The water was ten or twelve feet deep. I saw all the bubbles from my clothing going up to the surface and I tried to pull myself up on the rope. My hands slipped and I thought in a wild, mental scream of panic that this was how it would end.

Then the rope tightened. There was a large noose-knot on the end and it tightened and started pulling up and when the knot hit I grabbed and held and the dogs pulled me out of the hole and back up onto the ice. There was still very little time. I had a quart of white-gas stove fuel on the sled for emergencies and I threw it on a pine tree nearby and lit a match and set the whole tree on fire and, in the heat, got my clothes off and crawled into a sleeping bag. I stood inside it and held my clothes near the flame to dry them.

I would have died if not for Cookie.

She saw me drop, instantly **analyzed** the situation, got the team up—she must have jerked them to their feet—got them pulling, and they pulled me out.

Everything that has happened in the last seventeen years—everything: Iditarods, published books, love, living, *life*—all of it, I owe to Cookie.

ASK YOURSELF

- Which two things helped save Gary Paulsen's life?

Recall the details of what happened.

What Happened to Cookie?

Gary Paulsen tells this story about Cookie—when she stopped being a sled dog, and became a house dog.

When it was time to retire Cookie, I brought her into the house. She had never been in a house before. And the first thing she did was eat my wife's cat. Yes, it's true. She ate the whole cat. We didn't know it until two days later when we found the cat's collar and some of her stuff. My wife was real upset (as you can imagine). But I said to her, "I don't care. I'll get you another cat." I mean, I owe everything I am to that dog, you know? I mean I'd have been dead, I really would have. ●

Read A BOOK!

Gary Paulsen is an amazing storyteller who's written dozens of great books. Here are three you shouldn't miss.

Puppies, Dogs, and Blue Northers: Reflections on Being Raised by a Pack of Sled Dogs

GARY PAULSEN
Puppies, Dogs, and Blue Northers

Gary Paulsen has spent years training, running, and breeding sled dogs. In this book, he shares stories about his experiences with dogs. Some stories are sad, some happy, and some are just full of information. But all show Paulsen's special relationship with dogs, and people.

Dogsong

GARY PAULSEN
DOGSONG

Russel, a young Inuit boy, takes a dog team and sled to escape the modern ways of his village and to find himself. Is he ready for the wilderness?

Hatchet

GARY PAULSEN
HATCHET

In this novel, Brian's trip to see his father is interrupted when the single-engine plane he's traveling in crashes into the woods. Alone and armed only with a hatchet, Brian must find a way back to civilization before winter.

Two Were Left

Stranded on an island of ice, Noni and his dog Nimuk are slowly starving to death. Will one of them do the unthinkable . . . ?

by Hugh B. Cave

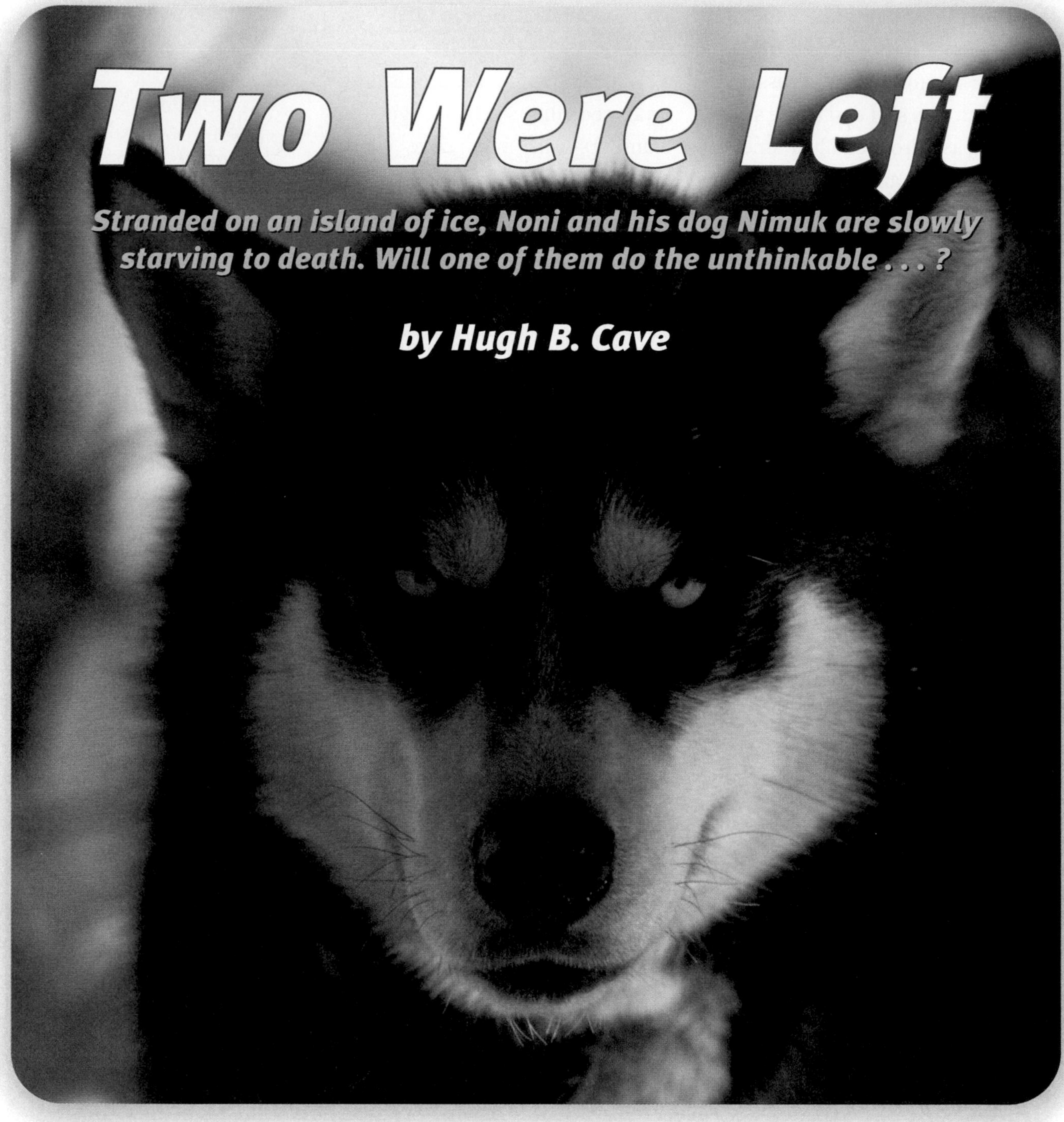

On the third night of hunger, Noni thought of the dog. Nothing of flesh and blood lived upon the floating ice island with its towering berg except those two.

In the breakup, Noni had lost his sled, his food, his furs, even his knife. He had saved only Nimuk, his great devoted husky. And now the two, marooned on the ice, eyed each other warily—each keeping his distance.

Noni's love for Nimuk was real, very real—as

real as hunger and cold nights and the gnawing pain of his injured leg in its homemade brace. But the men of his village killed their dogs when food was scarce, didn't they? And without thinking twice about it.

And Nimuk, he told himself, when hungry enough would seek food. "One of us will soon be eating the other," Noni thought. "So . . ."

He could not kill the dog with his bare hands. Nimuk was powerful, and much fresher than he. A weapon, then, was essential.

Removing his mittens, he unstrapped the brace from his leg. When he had hurt his leg a few weeks before, he had fashioned the brace from bits of harness and two thin strips of iron.

Kneeling now, he wedged one of the iron strips into a crack in the ice, and began to rub the other against it with firm, slow strokes.

Nimuk watched him intently, and it seemed to Noni that the dog's eyes glowed more brightly as night waned.

He worked on, trying not to remember why. The slab of iron had an edge now. It had begun to take shape. Daylight found his task completed.

Noni pulled the finished knife from the ice and thumbed its edge. The sun's glare, reflected from it, stabbed at his eyes and momentarily blinded him.

Noni steeled himself.

"Here, Nimuk!" he called softly.

The dog suspiciously watched him.

"Come here," Noni called.

Nimuk came closer. Noni read fear in the animal's gaze. He read hunger and suffering in the dog's labored breathing and awkward, dragging crouch. His heart wept. He hated himself and fought against it.

Closer Nimuk came, wary of his intentions. Now Noni felt a thickening in his throat. He saw the dog's eyes and they were wells of suffering.

Now! Now was the time to strike!

A great sob shook Noni's kneeling body. He cursed the knife. He swayed blindly, flung the weapon far from him. With empty hands outstretched he stumbled toward the dog, and fell.

The dog growled ominously as he warily circled the boy's body. And now Noni was sick with fear.

In flinging away the knife, he had left himself defenseless. He was too weak to crawl after it now. He was at Nimuk's mercy, and Nimuk was hungry.

The dog had circled him and was creeping up from behind. Noni heard the rattle of saliva in the savage throat.

He shut his eyes, praying that the attack might be swift. He felt the dog's feet against his leg, the hot rush of Nimuk's breath against his neck. A scream gathered in the boy's throat.

Then he felt the dog's hot tongue caressing his face.

Noni's eyes opened, incredulously staring. Crying softly, he thrust out an arm and drew the dog's head down against his own. . . .

The plane came out of the south an hour later. Its pilot, a young man of the coast patrol, looked down and saw the large floating floe, with the berg rising from its center. And he saw something flashing.

It was the sun gleaming on something shiny, which moved. His curiosity aroused, the pilot banked his ship and descended, circling the floe. Now he saw, in the shadow of the peak of ice, a dark, still shape that appeared to be human. Or were there two shapes?

He set his ship down in a water lane and investigated. There were two shapes, boy and dog. The boy was unconscious but alive. The dog whined feebly but was too weak to move.

The gleaming object which had trapped the pilot's attention was a crudely fashioned knife, stuck point first into the ice a little distance away, and quivering in the wind. ●

Wrap-Up

Talk About It

Now that you've read "Cookie" and "Two Were Left," what do you have to say about these questions?

- Why do you think some people say that dogs are man's best friend? Do you agree?
- Have you ever known an animal to act like a person? Describe the experience.

Comprehension Check

Write your answers to the questions below. Use information from the account and the story to support your answers.

1. Why is the ice around a beaver's lodge dangerous?
2. Why is Gary Paulsen still in danger even after Cookie pulls him from the water?
3. Why might it be hard for Cookie to go from being a sled dog to a house dog?
4. Why is Noni afraid of Nimuk?
5. How are Cookie and Nimuk alike?

Vocabulary Check

Complete each sentence starter below. Before you answer, think about the meaning of the vocabulary word in bold.

1. This class period I have lunch; **previously,** I had . . .
2. My normal **procedure** for getting to school is . . .
3. I wouldn't mind if a **cargo** of video games . . .
4. After I **analyzed** the problem, I . . .
5. A dog makes a good **companion** because . . .

Write About It

Choose one of the writing prompts below.

- If Cookie got lost, Gary Paulsen might make a poster to help get her back. Write a paragraph of copy for the poster. In it, describe Cookie and why she means so much to her owner.
- What if dogs could talk? Tell the story of Gary Paulsen's rescue from Cookie's point of view.
- Have you ever had a pet that you considered your "best friend?" Write a short paragraph about that pet, or make up a short story about one.

More to READ

If you enjoyed reading about Gary Paulsen and his faithful friend Cookie, you might also enjoy these books about animal pals.

The Music of Dolphins
by Karen Hesse

Mila is a wild child. Now a teenager, she has been raised by dolphins from the age of four. She is rescued from a deserted island and taken to a lab. There she is studied by researchers, who teach her to speak. But the more Mila learns about what it means to be human, the more deeply she longs for her ocean home.

The Monkey Thief
by Aileen Kilgore Henderson

Steve Hanson is a 12-year-old couch potato. When his parents send him to live with his uncle in Costa Rica for eight months, Steve discovers a new interest—monkeys. His desire for a monkey of his own lands him in the middle of a dangerous plot. To get out of trouble, he'll have to decide who to trust.

information searching

Reading a Field Guide

You're out hiking or biking. Suddenly, you see this really cool animal. You'd love to know what it is. How can you find out?

One way is to look it up in a field guide. That's a book that tells about animals, plants, and other things found in nature. Check out the field-guide entry below.

From a Field Guide

This is the animal's common name. That's the name that most people use. Below the common name is its scientific name.

Green Anole

Anolis carolinensis

Most field guide entries include pictures. They can help you to identify different animals and plants.

This information describes how the green anole looks and behaves and tells you where you might see one.

The green anole is sometimes incorrectly called a chameleon. Like chameleons, anoles are color-change artists. Their skin color depends on body temperature, environment, and mood. When a male is approached by a rival anole, he raises a crest on his neck and turns emerald green with a black patch behind the eye. He bobs his head up and down at the intruder and extends his throat fan. Sometimes rivals chase each other high in trees. Female anoles lay one egg at a time throughout the spring and summer.

Look for: A green to brown lizard with a pink fan-shaped flap of skin on throat. Can quickly change color from green to spotted green and brown to all brown.

Length: 5–9 inches

Habitat: parks, woods, old buildings and lots, palm fronds, thickets

Range:

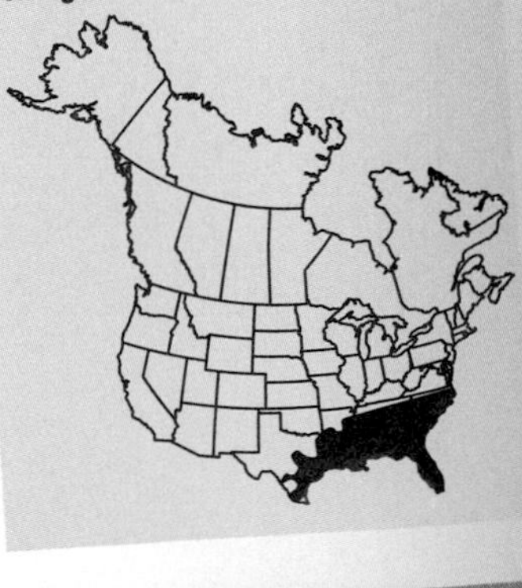

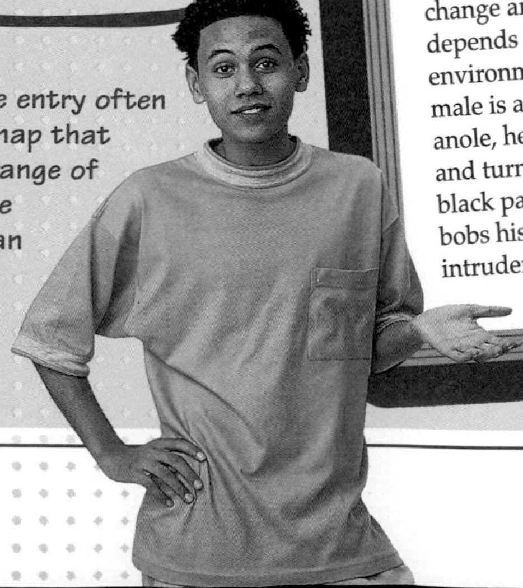

"A field guide entry often includes a map that shows the range of places in the world that an animal or plant can be found."

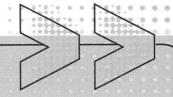

In the Field

Knowing how to use a field guide can help you identify creatures and plants around you. Reread the page and the tips that go with it. Then use them to answer the questions. Write your answers on your own paper.

1. Which of the following statements about green anoles are true? (Pick two.)
a. They are always green.
b. They are the same thing as chameleons.
c. The males puff out their throats when challenged.
d. The females lay eggs only in the spring and summer.

2. **True or false.** You live in California. You just saw a bright green lizard in the park. The lizard is probably a green anole.

3. You might find a green anole in which of the following places? (Pick two.)
a. behind an old building
b. in Florida
c. in the woods of Wisconsin
d. in a snowbank

4. Why might an anole change color?
a. It's afraid.
b. It's cold.
c. It's in new place.
d. All of the above.

Nature Log

You're keeping a nature journal. Last weekend you saw a green anole. Describe the experience. Tell where you were when you saw the green anole, what it looked like, and how it was behaving.

Write About It

Choose a plant or animal that you see all the time. Do some research and write a field-guide entry, telling all about it. Use the entry from this lesson as a model.

"The Web is a great place to find facts about plants and animals. Use a search engine to locate related Web sites."

Real-World Words

entry: a definition or explanation in a reference book
habitat: the environment where an animal or plant lives or grows
range: the region or regions in which a plant or animal is found

Glossary

You will find all your vocabulary words in alphabetical order in the Glossary. Look at the sample entry below to see how to use it.

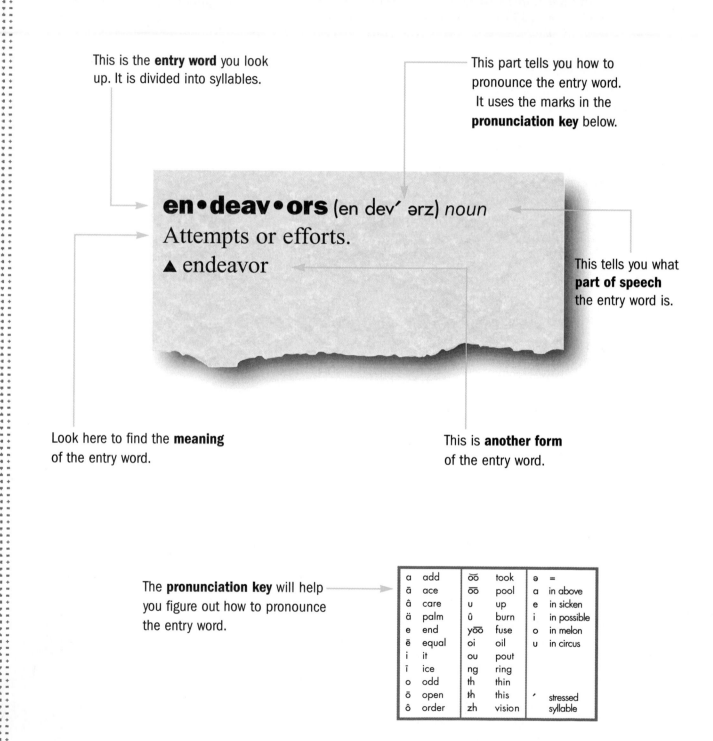

This is the **entry word** you look up. It is divided into syllables.

This part tells you how to pronounce the entry word. It uses the marks in the **pronunciation key** below.

en•deav•ors (en dev′ ərz) *noun*
Attempts or efforts.
▲ endeavor

This tells you what **part of speech** the entry word is.

Look here to find the **meaning** of the entry word.

This is **another form** of the entry word.

The **pronunciation key** will help you figure out how to pronounce the entry word.

a	add	o͝o	took	ə	=
ā	ace	o͞o	pool	a	in above
â	care	u	up	e	in sicken
ä	palm	û	burn	i	in possible
e	end	yo͞o	fuse	o	in melon
ē	equal	oi	oil	u	in circus
i	it	ou	pout		
ī	ice	ng	ring		
o	odd	th	thin		
ō	open	t͟h	this	′	stressed syllable
ô	order	zh	vision		

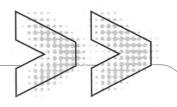

ac•cept•ed
(ak sept´ id) *verb*
Formally admitted into a college or club.
▲ **accept**

ack•now•ledg•ment
(ak nol´ ij mənt) *noun*
Recognition that something exists.

ad•dic•tion
(ə dik´shən) *noun*
The need to use something for comfort or support.

ad•join•ing
(ə joi´ ning) *verb*
Connecting.
▲ **adjoin**

ad•ver•sar•y
(ad´ vər ser´ ē) *noun*
A group of people who want to fight and destroy another group.

al•lies
(al´ īz) *noun*
People who give support to someone.
▲ **ally**

a•lu•mi•num
(ə lo͞o´ mə nəm) *noun*
A light, silver-colored metal.

an•a•lyzed
(an´ l īzd´) *verb*
Examined something carefully.
▲ **analyze**

as•sump•tions
(ə sump´ shenz) *noun*
Beliefs taken for granted without knowing that they are true.
▲ **assumption**

at•ti•tude
(at´ i to͞od´) *noun*
A feeling about someone or something.

au•di•ence
(ô´ dē əns) *noun*
A gathering of people who listen to a performance.

> **Word Origin**
>
> The word **audience** comes from the Latin root **aud,** which means "hear."

awe•struck
(ô´ struk´) *adjective*
Feeling wonder and admiration for someone.

bar•rage
(bə räzh´) *noun*
A large amount of something that all comes at the same time.

be•tray
(bi trā´) *verb*
To be disloyal to someone, especially a friend or family member.

car•go
(kär´ gō) *noun*
A load of supplies.

cat•e•go•ry
(kat´ i gôr´ ē) *noun*
A class or group of things that has something in common.

ca•thar•sis
(kə thär´ sis) *noun*
A process for getting rid of emotional stress.

ca•vort•ing
(kə vôrt´ ing) *verb*
Leaping, skipping, and being playful.
▲ **cavort**

cha•os
(kā´ os) *adjective*
Total confusion.

chauf•feur
(shō´ fər) *noun*
A person who drives a car for someone else.

clique
(klik) *noun*
A small group of people who are very friendly with each other.

a	add	o͝o	took	ə	=
ā	ace	o͞o	pool	a	in above
â	care	u	up	e	in sicken
ä	palm	û	burn	i	in possible
e	end	yo͞o	fuse	o	in melon
ē	equal	oi	oil	u	in circus
i	it	ou	pout		
ī	ice	ng	ring		
o	odd	th	thin		
ō	open	*th*	this	´	stressed syllable
ô	order	zh	vision		

Glossary

co•a•li•tion
(kō´ ə lish ən) *noun*
Two or more groups joining together for a common purpose.

co•in•ci•dence
(kō in´ si dəns) *noun*
A chance happening.

com•menced
(kə menst´) *verb*
Started something.
▲ **commence**

Thesaurus

commenced
began
initiated
started

com•pan•ion
(kəm pan´ yən) *noun*
Someone you spend time with.

com•po•sure
(kəm pō´ zhər) *noun*
Self-control.

con•clude
(kən klōōd´) *verb*
Finish.

con•flict
(kon´ flikt) *noun*
A clash or disagreement.

con•fron•ta•tions
(kon´ frən tā´ shəns) *noun*
Threatening meetings.
▲ **confrontation**

con•scious
(kon´ shəs) *adjective*
Aware of something.

con•serv•a•tive
(kən sûr´ və tiv) *adjective*
Traditional.

con•ven•ient
(kən vēn´ yənt) *adjective*
Useful or easy to use.

cow•ered
(kou´ ərd) *verb*
Crouched in fear.
▲ **cower**

dec•ade
(dek´ ād) *noun*
A period of ten years.

de•feats
(di fēts´) *noun*
The outcome of being beaten by opponents in a war.
▲ **defeat**

de•fen•sive•ly
(di fen´siv lē) *adverb*
Feeling and acting as if you have been criticized.
▲ **defensive**

de•fi•ant
(di fī´ ənt) *adjective*
Being bold or standing up to someone or something.

de•lib•er•ate•ly
(di lib´ ər it lē) *adverb*
Purposely.
▲ **deliberate**

de•mol•ished
(di mol´ isht) *verb*
Destroyed.
▲ **demolish**

dense
(dens) *adjective*
Thick.

de•pen•dent
(di pen´dənt) *adjective*
Relying on something to make a task easier.

de•spair
(di spâr´) *noun*
A loss of hope.

des•per•a•tion
(des´ pə rā´ shən) *noun*
The state of having an urgent need or desire.

de•ter•mined
(di tûr´ mind) *adjective*
Decided or settled on an idea.
▲ **determine**

dev•as•tat•ing
(dev´ ə stā´ting) *adjective*
Shocking and distressing.
▲ **devastate**

di•ag•nosed
(dī´əg nōsd´) *verb*
To have figured out the cause of a medical problem.
▲ **diagnose**

dig•ni•ty
(dig´ ni tē) *noun*
A quality that makes a person worthy of respect.

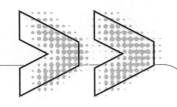

dip•lo•mat•ic
(dip´ lə mat´ ik) *adjective*
Tactful and good at dealing with people.

doubt
(dout) *adjective*
Uncertainty.

dras•tic
(dras´ tik) *adjective*
Extremely sudden and severe.

dread•ing
(dred´ ing) *verb*
Being afraid of doing something.
▲ **dread**

ec•stat•ic
(ek stat´ik) *adjective*
Very happy.

e•lim•i•na•tion
(i lim´ e nā´ shen) *noun*
Removal by being defeated.

e•lude
(i lo͞od´) *verb*
To escape or not be present in.

e•lu•sive
(i lo͞o´siv) *adjective*
Very hard to find or catch.

en•cour•age
(en kûr´ ij) *verb*
To give someone confidence with praise or support.

en•dan•gered
(en dān´ jərd) *adjective*
In danger of not being alive anymore.
▲ **endanger**

en•deav•ors
(en dev´ ərz) *noun*
Attempts or efforts.
▲ **endeavor**

en•dured
(en do͝ord´) *verb*
Put up with something painful or unpleasant.
▲ **endure**

e•rod•ed
(i rōd´ id) *verb*
Worn away over time.
▲ **erode**

es•tab•lish
(i stab´ lish) *verb*
To set up or start something.

e•vac•u•a•tions
(i vak´ yo͞o ā´ shənz) *noun*
The process of leaving a home or area for reasons of safety.
▲ **evacuation**

e•va•sion
(i vā´ zhən) *noun*
The act of avoiding something you should do.

ex•am•ined
(ig zam´ ind) *verb*
Looked at carefully.
▲ **examine**

ex•ot•ic
(ig zot´ ik) *adjective*
Strange and fascinating.

Word Origin

The word **exotic** comes from the Greek word **exoticus,** which means "foreign."

fein•ted
(fān´ tid) *verb*
Moved to fool an opponent.
▲ **feint**

Word Usage

The words **feinted** and **fainted** are **homophones.** Homophones are words that sound the same but are spelled differently. **Feinted** means "moved to fool an opponent" while **fainted** means "to become dizzy and fall."

a	add	o͝o	took	ə	=
ā	ace	o͞o	pool	a	in above
â	care	u	up	e	in sicken
ä	palm	û	burn	i	in possible
e	end	yo͞o	fuse	o	in melon
ē	equal	oi	oil	u	in circus
i	it	ou	pout		
ī	ice	ng	ring		
o	odd	th	thin		
ō	open	t͟h	this	´	stressed
ô	order	zh	vision		syllable

Glossary

flailed
(flăld) *verb*
Swung one's arms wildly.
▲ **flail**

for•bid•den
(fər bid′ n) *adjective*
Not allowed.

for•feit
(fôr′ fit) *verb*
To give up the right to something.

foun•da•tion
(foun dā′ shən) *noun*
An organization that gives money toward helping people.

fric•tion
(frik′ shən) *noun*
What occurs when two objects rub against each other.

fu•tile
(fyo͞ot′ l) *adjective*
Useless.

gen•e•ros•i•ty
(jen′ ə ros′ i tē) *noun*
Unselfish acts.

glared
(glârd) *verb*
Looked at someone in an angry way.
▲ **glare**

gleamed
(glēmd) *verb*
Shined brightly.
▲ **gleam**

grat•i•tude
(grat′ i to͞od′) *noun*
A feeling of being thankful.

grav•i•ty
(grav′ i tē) *noun*
Seriousness.

grim•aced
(grim′ əsd) *verb*
Made a facial expression that shows unhappiness or pain.
▲ **grimace**

ha•rass•ment
(hə ras′ ment) *noun*
The state of pestering or annoying someone.

hec•tic
(hek′ tik) *adjective*
Very busy.

hes•i•ta•ted
(hez′ i tāt id) *verb*
Stopped for a short time before doing something.
▲ **hesitate**

ig•nored
(ig nôrd′) *verb*
Did not pay attention to something on purpose.
▲ **ignore**

il•le•gal
(i lē′ gəl) *adjective*
Against the law.

il•lu•sions
(i lo͞o′ zhenz) *noun*
Things that appear to exist but really do not.
▲ **illusion**

im•i•tat•ed
(im′ i tāt′ id) *verb*
Copied.
▲ **imitate**

im•me•di•ate•ly
(i mē′ dē it lē) *adverb*
Right now or at once.
▲ **immediate**

im•pov•er•ished
(im pov′ ər isht) *adjective*
Very poor.

im•pro•vised
(im′ prə vīzd′) *verb*
Did the best you could on the spur of the moment.
▲ **improvise**

im•pulse
(im′ puls) *noun*
A sudden desire or action.

in•cred•i•ble
(in kred′ ə bəl) *adjective*
Amazing.

Thesaurus

incredible
amazing
extraordinary
unbelievable

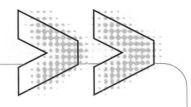

in•di•go
(in′ di gō′) *noun*
A dark violet-blue color.

i•ni•ti•a•tion
(i nish′ ē ā′ shən) *noun*
A task or ceremony that gives admission into a group.

in•spired
(in spī ərd′) *verb*
Influenced by something or someone.
▲ **inspire**

in•stinc•tive•ly
(in stingk′ tiv lē) *adverb*
Thinking or feeling something without being told about it.
▲ **instinctive**

in•tense
(in tens′) *adjective*
Using a lot of effort and energy.

in•ter•rupt
(in tə rupt′) *verb*
To stop for a short time.

in•ter•ven•ing
(in′ tər vēn′ ing) *verb*
Getting involved in a situation to change what is happening.
▲ **intervene**

in•ti•ma•cy
(in′tə mə sē) *noun*
A close personal relationship.

in•ves•ti•ga•ting
(in ves′ ti gāt′ ing) *verb*
Searching or examining something to learn more about it.
▲ **investigate**

in•volves
(in volvz′) *verb*
Includes something.
▲ **involve**

i•ris•es
(ī′ ris iz) *noun*
Round, colored parts of the eyes around the pupils.
▲ **iris**

Word Origin

The word **iris** comes from the Greek goddess of the rainbow, Iris.

i•ron•ic
(ī ron′ ik) *adjective*
When a situation is unexpected and not what you thought it would be.

i•so•la•tion
(ī′ sə lā′ shən) *noun*
The state of being alone or separate from others.

ker•o•sene
(ker′ ə sēn) *noun*
Fuel.

lo•co•mo•tive
(lō kə mō′ tiv) *noun*
An engine.

mar•a•thon
(mar′ə thon′) *noun*
Any long contest or event.

may•hem
(mā′ hem) *noun*
Random or deliberate violence.

mo•not•o•nous
(mə not′ n əs) *adjective*
Dull and boring.

mon•stros•i•ty
(mon stros′ i tē) *noun*
A horrible or frightening thing.

mop•ing
(mōp′ ing) *verb*
Acting sad and depressed.
▲ **mope**

mo•tioned
(mō′ shənd) *verb*
Told someone something through a movement or gesture.
▲ **motion**

mo•ti•vat•ed
(mō′ tə vāt′ id) *verb*
Encouraged someone to do something.
▲ **motivate**

a	add	o͝o	took	ə	=
ā	ace	o͞o	pool	a	in above
â	care	u	up	e	in sicken
ä	palm	û	burn	i	in possible
e	end	yo͞o	fuse	o	in melon
ē	equal	oi	oil	u	in circus
i	it	ou	pout		
ī	ice	ng	ring		
o	odd	th	thin		
ō	open	th	this	′	stressed
ô	order	zh	vision		syllable

Glossary

mus•ter
(mus′ tər) *verb*
To gather something together.

ob•ser•va•tion
(ob′ zûr vā′ shən) *noun*
A comment about something.

oc•ca•sion•al
(ə kā′ zhə nl) *adjective*
Once in a while.

om•i•nous
(om′ ə nəs) *adjective*
Threatening.

op•po•nent
(ə pō′ nənt) *noun*
Someone who is against you in a fight or contest.

op•ti•mis•tic
(op′tə mis′ tik) *adjective*
Always believing that things will turn out for the best.

out•ra•geous
(out rā′ jəs) *adjective*
Shocking and surprising.

pam•pered
(pam′ pərd) *verb*
Treated with special care.
▲ **pamper**

parched
(pärcht) *adjective*
Very dry.

pen•sive•ly
(pen′ siv lē) *adverb*
Thoughtfully.
▲ **pensive**

per•cep•tion
(pər sep′ shən) *noun*
A way of seeing something that may be unfamiliar.

per•spec•tive
(pər spek′ tiv) *noun*
A particular way of looking at a situation.

Word Origin

The word **perspective** comes from the Latin root **spec,** which means "see."

pis•ton
(pis′ tən) *noun*
Something that moves back and forth quickly to create energy.

plac•id
(plas′ id) *adjective*
Calm.

poign•ant
(poin′ yənt) *adjective*
Emotional and touching.

pop•u•lar•i•ty
(pop′ yə lar′ i tē) *noun*
The quality of being liked or admired by many people.

po•ten•tial
(pə ten′ shəl) *noun*
What one is capable of in the future.

pre•cau•tions
(pri kô′ shəns) *noun*
Things you do to prevent something dangerous from happening.
▲ **precaution**

prej•u•diced
(prej′ə dist) *adjective*
To have an unfair opinion of people based on race, religion, or national group.
▲ **prejudice**

pre•ven•tive
(pri ven′ tiv) *adjective*
Created to stop something from occurring.

pre•vi•ous•ly
(prē′ vē əs lē) *adverb*
Earlier.
▲ **previous**

prin•ci•ple
(prin′ sə pəl) *noun*
A rule or law of a certain subject.

Word Usage

The words **principle** and **principal** are **homophones.** Homophones are words that sound the same but are spelled differently. **Principle** means "rule" and **principal** means "main."

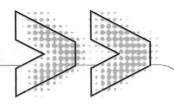

priv•i•leg•es
(priv′ ə lij iz) *noun*
Special rights or advantages given to a person or group of people.
▲ **privilege**

pro•ba•tion
(prō bā′ shən) *noun*
A period of time used to test a person's behavior.

pro•ce•dure
(prə sē′ jər) *noun*
A way of doing something.

pro•ces•sion
(prə sesh′ən) *noun*
A number of persons or things moving in an orderly manner.

prop•a•gan•da
(prop′ ə gan′ də) *noun*
Information that is spread to influence the way people think.

psy•chol•o•gy
(sī kol′ ə jē) *noun*
The study of the mind, emotions, and human behavior.

pum•mel•ing
(pum′ əl ing) *verb*
Punching something over and over.
▲ **pummel**

pur•su•ing
(pər sōō′ ing) *verb*
Working towards a goal.
▲ **pursue**

ral•lied
(ral′ ēd) *verb*
Joined together to help support a person or cause.
▲ **rally**

ramp•ant
(ram′ pənt) *adjective*
Wild and without restraint.

ratch•et•ed
(rach′ it id) *verb*
Moved.
▲ **ratchet**

rau•cous
(rô′ kəs) *adjective*
Wild and noisy.

Thesaurus

raucous
boisterous
harsh
jarring

rav•aged
(rav′ ijd) *verb*
Severely damaged.
▲ **ravage**

razed
(rāzd) *verb*
Tore down.
▲ **raze**

re•coil•ing
(ri koil′ing) *verb*
Shrinking back in horror or disgust.
▲ **recoil**

re•duce
(ri dōōs′) *verb*
To make something smaller or less.

re•flects
(ri flekts′) *verb*
Thinks back on something.
▲ **reflect**

re•in•forced
(rē′ in fôrsd′) *verb*
Strengthened something.
▲ **reinforce**

re•lent•less
(ri lent′ lis) *adjective*
Harsh and endless.

re•nowned
(ri nound′) *adjective*
Famous or well known.

Thesaurus

renowned
acclaimed
celebrated
famous

a	add	ŏŏ	took	ə	=
ā	ace	ōō	pool	a	in above
â	care	u	up	e	in sicken
ä	palm	û	burn	i	in possible
e	end	yōō	fuse	o	in melon
ē	equal	oi	oil	u	in circus
i	it	ou	pout		
ī	ice	ng	ring		
o	odd	th	thin		
ō	open	th	this	′	stressed
ô	order	zh	vision		syllable

Glossary

re•pul•sive
(ri pul′ siv) *adjective*
Distasteful or disgusting.

re•sem•blance
(ri zem′ bləns) *noun*
The state of looking like something else.

re•spect
(ri spekt′) *noun*
A feeling of admiration or consideration for someone.

re•spon•si•ble
(ri spon′ sə bəl) *adjective*
Sensible and trustworthy.

re•veal
(ri vēl′) *verb*
To show or bring into view.

re•vive
(ri vīv′) *verb*
To wake someone up after they collapsed or fainted.

re•ward•ing
(ri wôrd′ ing) *adjective*
Satisfying.

rit•u•al
(rich′o͞o əl) *noun*
Something that is always done in the same way as part of a ceremony or custom.

sa•cred
(sā′ krid) *adjective*
Very important and deserving great respect.

sac•ri•fic•es
(sak′ rə fīs′ iz) *noun*
The giving up of valuable things in order to benefit someone else.
▲ **sacrifice**

sar•cas•tic
(sär kas′ tik) *adjective*
Speaking in an unkind way that is meant to hurt someone.

schol•ar•ships
(skol′ər ships′) *noun*
Grants or prizes that pay for people to go to college.

se•lec•tive
(si lek′ tiv) *adjective*
Having the power to choose carefully.

self-de•struct•ing
(self di struk′ ting) *adjective*
Acting in a way that hurts oneself.
▲ **self-destruct**

sep•a•ra•tion
(sep′ ə rā′ shən) *noun*
An instance of being apart from someone.

shud•dered
(shud′ ərd) *verb*
Shook violently from fear.
▲ **shudder**

sin•cere
(sin sēr′) *adjective*
Honest and truthful.

sit•u•a•tion
(sich′ o͞o ā′ shən) *noun*
The condition that exists at a certain time.

so•lu•tion
(sə lo͞o′ shən) *noun*
The answer to a problem.

sparse
(spärs) *adjective*
Lacking in quality and quantity.

spin•dly
(spind′ lē) *adjective*
Long, thin, and weak.

squad
(skwod) *noun*
A group of people involved in the same activity.

suf•fo•cat•ed
(suf′ə kāt′ id) *verb*
Died from a lack of oxygen.
▲ **suffocate**

sur•veil•lance
(sər vā′ ləns) *noun*
Watching someone or something.

sus•pend•ed
(sə spend′ id) *verb*
Barred from school or another activity as a punishment.
▲ **suspend**

syn•di•cat•ed
(sin′ di kāt′ id) *adjective*
Having work published in many newspapers at the same time.
▲ **syndicate**

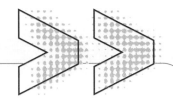

taw•dry
(tô´ drē) *adjective*
Showy and cheap.

tech•ni•cal
(tek´ ni kəl) *adjective*
Having to do with the way an athlete performs certain moves and positions.

tes•ti•fy•ing
(tes´ tə fī´ ing) *verb*
Speaking under oath in a court of law.
▲ **testify**

tex•ture
(teks´ chər) *noun*
The look and feel of something.

threat•ened
(thret´ nd) *verb*
Put in danger.
▲ **threaten**

tor•rent
(tôr´ ənt) *noun*
A flow of violent and swift actions.

trance
(trans) *noun*
Being awake but not aware of what is happening around you.

trans•lat•ing
(trans lāt´ ing) *verb*
Turning words from one language into another language.
▲ **translate**

un•con•scious
(un kon´ shəs) *adjective*
Not awake.

un•em•ployed
(un´ em ploid´) *adjective*
Without a job.

u•nique
(yo͞o nēk´) *adjective*
Unusual.

un•mis•tak•a•ble
(un´ mi stā´ kə bəl) *adjective*
Very obvious.

u•ten•sil
(yo͞o ten´səl) *noun*
A tool that has a special purpose.

Word Origin

The word **utensil** comes from the Latin word **utensilis,** which means "useful."

vi•cious
(vish´əs) *adjective*
Fierce or dangerous.

vi•o•la•tion
(vī´ ə lā´ shən) *noun*
The breaking of a rule.

vol•un•teered
(vol´ ən tērd´) *verb*
Offered to do a job, usually without pay.
▲ **volunteer**

wea•ri•ly
(wēr´ ə lē) *adverb*
In a tired or worn-out way.
▲ **weary**

winced
(winst) *verb*
Made a quick movement because of pain or embarrassment.
▲ **wince**

a	add	o͝o	took	ə	=
ā	ace	o͞o	pool	a	in above
â	care	u	up	e	in sicken
ä	palm	û	burn	i	in possible
e	end	yo͞o	fuse	o	in melon
ē	equal	oi	oil	u	in circus
i	it	ou	pout		
ī	ice	ng	ring		
o	odd	th	thin		
ō	open	t͟h	this	´	stressed
ô	order	zh	vision		syllable

Literary & Reading Terms

author A person who writes a short story, play, poem, novel, article, essay, or book.

autobiography An account of a person's life written by that person. An autobiography is an example of nonfiction.

base word A word from which other words can be made. By adding a prefix to the beginning of a base word or a suffix to the end of a base word, you can change a word's meaning (such as *view/preview/viewing*).

biography An account of a person's life written by another person. A biography is a form of nonfiction.

cause and effect The *cause* is something that makes another thing happen. What happens is called the *effect*. The reader figures out why an event happened or how one event caused another to occur.

characterization The way the author presents the personality of a character. The reader learns about a character through descriptions, actions, speech, and thoughts. *Character traits* are the qualities that a character possesses.

characters People in a story, play, novel, etc. There are *major* and *minor* characters in a story, major characters being more important than minor ones. The *main character* is the most important character.

compare and contrast To compare is to figure out how events, characters, or ideas are similar. To contrast is to find out how they are different.

compound word A word that is made up of two or more smaller words, such as *homework.*

conflict A struggle between characters, between a character and a force of nature, or between opposing views held by different characters. *Internal conflict* lies in the mind of a character who must resolve something.

connotation The implied meaning of a word or phrase as opposed to its exact dictionary meaning or *denotation.* The connotations of a word are the ideas and feelings associated with it.

contraction A word formed by leaving out and combining parts of other words. For example, the word *can't* is made from the words *can* and *not*. The *n* and the *o* in *not* are dropped and are replaced by the apostrophe.

debate A discussion between sides with different opinions or points of view.

denotation The exact dictionary meaning of a word as opposed to its implied meaning, or *connotation.*

dialogue The conversation in a story or play. The exact words the characters say. In a story, quotation marks point out the dialogue.

diphthong Two vowels that spell a sound that is formed by a gliding action in the mouth (such as *oy, oi, ou, ow*).

draw conclusions To make decisions about a story and its characters. To draw conclusions, a reader thinks about events and details in a story and comes to a new understanding.

editorial An article or a statement that reflects the opinions of a newspaper, magazine, or other information source.

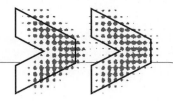

encyclopedia entry Informative article found in an encyclopedia (a set of books with alphabetized entries about many different subjects).

essay A short, nonfiction piece of writing on a subject or theme that expresses a specific point of view.

exaggeration Overstatement of an idea beyond the limits of truth.

fiction An invented story. Although fiction may be based on actual personal experience, it involves invented characters, actions, and settings.

figurative language Words used in a special way to give added meaning. In figurative expressions such as "I'm up to my ears in homework," the words are not intended to be interpreted in a word-for-word, or *literal,* sense. Stories, and especially poems, use figurative language to create images, or mental pictures. (See also **metaphor, personification, simile.**)

flashback A technique that interrupts the present action in a story, play, or novel to tell about something that happened in the past.

foreshadowing A storytelling device that an author uses to give the reader advance warning of events to come.

graphic classic A well-known story told through pictures in a comic-book format.

historical fiction A story or novel whose setting is in some period in the past. Often real people from the past or important historical events are used in works of historical fiction.

homophone A word that sounds like another word but has a different meaning and spelling (such as *hear* and *here*).

humor The quality of being comical or funny.

imagery Words that create mental pictures, or images, that appeal to one or more of the reader's five senses. For example, "The moon floated above the clouds like a ship lost on the stormy seas" appeals to the reader's sense of sight.

irony The contrast, or difference, between what is said and what is meant. For example, if we say in conversation that something feels good when it really feels bad, we are using irony.

lyrics The words of a song. Lyrics often express personal thoughts or feelings. Originally, lyric poems were sung and accompanied by a musical instrument called a lyre.

main idea The most important idea in a paragraph or selection. The reader may find the main idea in a topic sentence or heading and will find details that support the main idea in the rest of the paragraph or selection.

make inferences A reader makes an inference when he or she combines text information with his or her own prior knowledge to figure out something that is not directly stated in a story.

media literacy An understanding of the ways in which mass communication is used in society.

metaphor A figure of speech in which there is an indirect or implied comparison between two things. "Her eyes were stars in the midnight sky" is a metaphor.

mood The general atmosphere or feeling in a work of literature. Mood is created largely through description and setting.

Literary & Reading Terms

motivation The reason a character in a work of literature acts in a particular way. The character's motivation may be stated directly or hinted at by what he or she does, thinks, or says.

myth A story told by people in ancient times to explain life and nature. Many myths, including Greek myths, are about gods and goddesses.

narrative poem A poem that tells a story or relates a sequence of events.

narrator The teller of a story.

nonfiction Writing about real people and factual events. Journal accounts, diaries, essays, interviews, articles, textbooks, biographies, autobiographies, and letters are examples of nonfiction.

novel A book-length piece of fiction that usually has a plot and deals with human experience.

personal narrative A true story about a person's life told in the first person.

personification A figure of speech that describes an object, idea, or animal as if it had human characteristics. For example: "The light spring rain danced upon our heads."

photo essay A collection of photos and words that tells a story or presents information.

play A work written to be performed before an audience. A play may be written in parts called *acts.* Acts may be divided into smaller parts called *scenes. Stage directions* tell the director or actors how the stage is to look and how the characters are to move and speak. The *dialogue,* or *lines,* are the words the characters speak.

plot The sequence of events in a short story, novel, play, or poem. The major element in a plot is the *conflict,* or struggle, between opposing forces. Rising action is the part of the plot in which the action builds and a problem, or conflict, develops. The turning point is the part of the plot in which the struggle between the forces comes to a head in some incident—the crisis, or climax. The resolution is the part of the plot in which the problem is solved.

plot twist A turn of events in the structure of a story, novel, or play that is unexpected, yet logical based on the reader's knowledge of the plot and character.

poetry Literature that uses language chosen for its sound and for its ability to express and evoke emotion. Many poems use images, or mental pictures, which appeal to the senses. Most poetry is written in lines that have a particular rhythm, or pattern of stressed syllables. Poetry can either be rhymed or unrhymed.

point of view The vantage point from which the narrator tells the story. In the *first-person* point of view, the narrator is usually a character in the story. This narrator tells the story by using the pronouns "I" or "we." In the *third-person* point of view—the most common form of telling a story—the narrator may or may not be a character in the story. This narrator uses the pronouns "he," "she," or "they." When the narrator, in the third-person point of view, seems to know what every character is thinking and feeling, this narrator is called *omniscient* or *all-knowing.*

possessive The form of a noun or pronoun that shows possession or ownership.

prefix A word part added to the beginning of a word to change its meaning (such as *view/preview*).

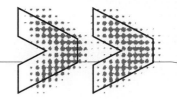

problem and solution A *problem* is a difficult situation that a character in a story has to solve. The *solution* is how the problem is solved.

profile A brief account of someone's life or accomplishments.

read for detail A *detail* is a small piece of information. Details help the reader to better understand the who, what, when, how, where, or why of a part of a story or piece of nonfiction.

root A word or word part from Latin or another language that is the basis of an English word. One example of a root is *port,* which means "to carry" (such as *import/portable*).

science fiction A fantasy story that is often set in the future, on other planets, or in other dimensions in time. Scientific impossibilities may be used in the plot.

sequence of events The order in which events occur. The reader can look for time–order words, such as *first, then* or *next,* and other clues to determine the sequence of events.

setting The time, place, and general environment of a story. The setting tells when and where the story takes place. The reader determines setting by noticing descriptions and events.

short story A brief piece of fiction, usually of 500 to 5,000 words in length.

simile A figure of speech in which two things are compared directly, using *like, as,* or *than.* "Her eyes sparkled like diamonds" is a simile.

stanza A group of two or more lines in a poem that are printed as a unit and held together by length, rhyme scheme, and meter.

style The individual, creative way an author expresses ideas and presents characters, setting, and action.

suffix A word part added to the end of a word to change its meaning (such as *slow/slowly*).

summarize To identify, organize, and combine the most important parts of a story so they can be retold in a brief statement.

suspense The tension readers feel because they are uncertain as to how events are going to turn out.

symbol Something that has meaning in itself and yet stands for something else. For example, in a story, a heart may also stand for love.

theme An important truth about life expressed by the author of a work of literature. It may be the author's thoughts about a certain topic, or the author's view of human nature. The theme is conveyed by the whole story—by the title, the plot, the characters, the setting, and the mood.

Author & Title Index

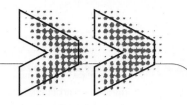

Acknowledgments

Grateful acknowledgment is made to the following sources for permission to reprint from previously published material. The publisher has made diligent efforts to trace the ownership of all copyrighted material in this volume and believes that all necessary permissions have been secured. If any errors or omissions have inadvertently been made, proper corrections will gladly be made in future editions.

Cover: from THE BOOK OF TWINS: A CELEBRATION IN WORDS AND PICTURES by Debra and Lisa Ganz with Alex Tresniowski, photographs by Bill Ballenberg. Copyright © 1998 by Byron Preiss Visual Publications, Inc. and Dream Makers Inc. Photographs copyright © 1998 by Bill Ballenberg. Published by Delacorte Press. Reprinted by permission of Byron Preiss Visual Publications Inc.

"For Pete's Snake" by Ellen Conford. Copyright © 1992 by Ellen Conford. Originally published in SHORT CIRCUITS by Delacorte Press. Reprinted by permission of McIntosh and Otis, Inc.

"Another Extreme: Swimming with the Sharks" and "Muscles on the Move" by Nancy Finton and Carol Sonenklar from *Super Science* magazine, September 1999. Copyright © 1999 by Scholastic Inc. Reprinted by permission of Scholastic Inc.

"Masquerade" by Phyllis Fair Cowell. Copyright © 1989 by Phyllis Fair Cowell. Originally published in *Scholastic Action* magazine, October 20, 1989. Reprinted by permission of the author.

"The Fish Story" by Mary Lou Brooks. Copyright © 1983 by Mary Lou Brooks. Originally published in *Scholastic Action* magazine, May 6, 1983. All rights reserved.

"The Jigsaw Puzzle" from TALES FOR THE MIDNIGHT HOUR by J.B. Stamper. Copyright © 1977 by J.B. Stamper. Reprinted by permission of Scholastic Inc.

"Bearstone" from BEARSTONE by Will Hobbs. Copyright © 1989 by Will Hobbs. Play adaptation originally published in *Scholastic Scope* magazine, January 14, 1994. Reprinted with the permission of Atheneum Books for Young Readers, an imprint of Simon & Schuster Children's Publishing Division.

Cover from BEARSTONE by Will Hobbs. Copyright © 1989 by Will Hobbs. Reprinted with the permission of Atheneum Books for Young Readers, an imprint of Simon & Schuster Children's Publishing Division.

Cover from DOWNRIVER by Will Hobbs. Copyright © 1991 by Will Hobbs. Cover art copyright © 1992 by Robert McGinnis. Used by permission of Random House Children's Books, a division of Random House, Inc.

Cover from SLAM! by Walter Dean Myers. Copyright © 1996 by Walter Dean Myers. Published by Scholastic Inc.

Introduction to "Slam!" from *Scholastic Scope* magazine, January 24, 1997. Copyright © 1997 by Scholastic Inc. Reprinted by permission of Scholastic Inc.

"Slam!" from SLAM! by Walter Dean Myers. Copyright © 1996 by Walter Dean Myers. Reprinted by permission of Scholastic Inc.

Walter Dean Myers interview from "One-on-One with Walter Dean Myers" from *Scholastic Scope* magazine, January 24, 1997. Copyright © 1997 by Scholastic Inc. Reprinted by permission of Scholastic Inc.

Cover from HARLEM by Walter Dean Myers, illustrated by Christopher Myers. Cover illustration copyright ©1997 by Christopher Myers. Published by Scholastic Inc.

Cover from MONSTER by Walter Dean Myers, illustrated by Christopher Myers. Text copyright © 1999 by Walter Dean Myers. Illustrations copyright © 1999 by Christopher Myers. Reprinted by permission of HarperCollins Publishers.

"Finding Your Place in the Crowd" from "Finding Your Place in the Crowd Without Losing Yourself" by Lauren Tarshis from *Scholastic Choices* magazine, September 1998. Copyright © 1998 by Scholastic Inc. Reprinted by permission of Scholastic Inc.

"Nonconformist" from SKIN DEEP AND OTHER TEENAGE REFLECTIONS by Angela Shelf Medearis. Text copyright © 1995 by Angela Shelf Medearis. Reprinted by permission of Diva Productions, Inc.

"Hispanic History-Makers" from "15 Latino Heroes" from *Scholastic Action* magazine, October 4, 1999. Copyright © 1999 by Scholastic Inc. Reprinted by permission of Scholastic Inc.

"Around the River Bend" by Sherry Garland. Text copyright © 1996 by Sherry Garland. Originally published in *Scholastic Scope* magazine, December 13, 1996. Reprinted by permission of the author.

"Dear America" from DEAR AMERICA: LETTERS HOME FROM VIETNAM, edited by Bernard Edelman. Copyright © 1985 by The New York Vietnam Veterans Memorial Commission. Originally published by W.W. Norton & Company, Inc. Reprinted by permission of Bernard Edelman.

"Fighting For My Future" from "I Escaped a Violent Gang" as told to Cate Baily from *Scholastic Scope* magazine, February 8, 1999. Copyright © 1999 by Scholastic Inc. Reprinted by permission of Scholastic Inc.

"The Freedom Writers" from *Scholastic Action* magazine, May 10, 1999. Copyright © 1999 by Scholastic Inc. Reprinted by permission of Scholastic Inc.

"Autobiography in Five Short Chapters" from THERE'S A HOLE IN MY SIDEWALK by Portia Nelson. Copyright © 1993 by Portia Nelson. Reprinted by permission of Beyond Words Publishing, Inc.

"War of the Worlds" adaptation by Mona Koppelman. Based on Orson Welles' WAR OF THE WORLDS broadcast. Copyright © 1940 by Princeton University Press, 1968 Howard Koch. Play adaptation originally published in *Scholastic Scope* magazine, October 20, 1995.

"How Orson Welles Tricked the Nation" and "A Well of Talent" from *Scholastic Scope* magazine, October 20, 1995. Copyright © 1995 by Scholastic Inc. Reprinted by permission of Scholastic Inc.

"Dreaming Aloud" by Rita Williams-Garcia. Copyright © 1993 by Rita Williams-Garcia. Originally published in *Scholastic Scope* magazine, September 3, 1993. Reprinted by permission of the author.

"Growing Up Female" by Amy Miller and Alexandra Hanson-Harding from *Junior Scholastic* magazine, March 8, 1999. Copyright © 1999 by Scholastic Inc. Reprinted by permission of Scholastic Inc.

"Twins: A Celebration in Words and Pictures" from THE BOOK OF TWINS: A CELEBRATION IN WORDS AND PICTURES by Debra and Lisa Ganz with Alex Tresniowski, photographs by Bill Ballenberg. Copyright © 1998 by Byron Preiss Visual Publications, Inc. and Dream Makers Inc. Photographs copyright © 1998 by Bill Ballenberg. Published by Delacorte Press. Reprinted by permission of Byron Preiss Visual Publications Inc.

"Space Exploration" from SCHOLASTIC ENCYCLOPEDIA OF SPACE by Jacqueline Mitton and Simon Mitton. Copyright © 1998 by Marshall Editions Developments Ltd. Reprinted by permission of Scholastic Inc.

"Broken Chain" from BASEBALL IN APRIL. Copyright © 1990 by Gary Soto. Reprinted by permission of Harcourt, Inc.

"Tin Grin" from BECOMING MYSELF: TRUE STORIES ABOUT LEARNING FROM LIFE by Cassandra Walker. Copyright © 1994 by Cassandra Walker. Used with permission from Free Spirit Publishing, Minneapolis, MN. All rights reserved.

"Warriors Don't Cry" from WARRIORS DON'T CRY by Melba Patillo Beals. Original edition copyright © 1994 by Melba Beals. Reprinted with the permission of Atheneum Books for Young Readers, an imprint of Simon & Schuster Children's Publishing Division.

"When the Doors Opened at Central High" by Rodney E. Slater from *The Washington Post*, September 25, 1997. Reprinted by permission.

"Opening Act" by Jane Yolen and Heidi Elizabet Yolen Stemple. Copyright © 1995 by Jane Yolen and Heidi E. Y. Stemple. Originally published in *Scholastic Scope* magazine, February 3, 1995. Reprinted by permission of Curtis Brown, Ltd.

"I'm Sensitive" from PIECES OF YOU by Jewel Kilcher. Copyright © 1994 by Wiggly Tooth/ASCAP. All rights reserved. Used by permission of Warner Bros. Publications U.S. Inc.

"After the Divorce" from A NIGHT WITHOUT ARMOR by Jewel Kilcher. Copyright © 1998 by Jewel Kilcher. Reprinted by permission of HarperCollins Publishers, Inc.

"Out of the Dust Introduction," "Black Blizzard," "A Natural Disaster," "The Soil Blew Away," and "Tough Times" from *Scholastic Scope* magazine, March 23, 1998. Copyright © 1998 by Scholastic Inc. Reprinted by permission of Scholastic Inc.

Dust Bowl map from CHILDREN OF THE DUST BOWL by Jerry Stanley. Copyright © 1992 by Jerry Stanley. Map by Susan Johnston Carlson. Reprinted by permission of Crown Children's Books, a division of Random House, Inc.

"Out of the Dust" from OUT OF THE DUST by Karen Hesse. Copyright © 1997 by Karen Hesse. Reprinted by permission of Scholastic Inc.

Cover from LETTERS FROM RIFKA by Karen Hesse. Copyright © 1992 by Karen Hesse. Jacket illustration copyright © 1992 by Trina Schart Hyman. Reprinted by permission of Henry Holt and Company, LLC.

Cover from THE MUSIC OF DOLPHINS by Karen Hesse. Copyright © 1996 by Karen Hesse. Reprinted by permission of Scholastic Inc.

"Amigo Brothers" adapted from STORIES FROM EL BARRIO by Piri Thomas. Copyright © 1978 by Piri Thomas. Published by Random House, Inc. Reprinted by permission of the author.

"Worst U.S. Natural Disasters" from SCHOLASTIC KID'S ALMANAC FOR THE 21ST CENTURY by Elaine Pascoe and Deborah Kops, illustrated by Bob Italiano and David C. Bell. Copyright © 1999 by Scholastic Inc. Reprinted by permission of Scholastic Inc.

"How a Hurricane Grows" from *Scholastic News Senior Edition*, October 11, 1999. Copyright © 1999 by Scholastic Inc. Reprinted by permission of Scholastic Inc.

"There's a Girl in My Hammerlock" adapted from THERE'S A GIRL IN MY HAMMERLOCK by Jerry Spinelli. Copyright © 1991 by Jerry Spinelli. Play adaptation copyright © 1993 by Scholastic Inc. Play adaptation originally published in *Scholastic Scope* magazine, October 15, 1993. Reprinted with the permission of Simon & Schuster Books for Young Readers, an imprint of Simon & Schuster Children's Publishing Division.

"Alcatraz: The Prison for America's Most Wanted" from ALCATRAZ: PRISON FOR AMERICA'S MOST WANTED by C.J. Henderson. Copyright © 1999 by Scholastic Inc. Reprinted by permission of Scholastic Inc.

"Treasure Island" from TREASURE ISLAND, a graphic classic by Adam Grant based on the novel by Robert Louis Stevenson. Copyright © 1999 by Scholastic Inc. Reprinted by permission of Scholastic Inc.

Cover from WHAT ARE YOU? VOICES OF MIXED-RACE YOUNG PEOPLE by Pearl Fuyo Gaskins. Copyright © 1999 by Pearl Fuyo Gaskins. Reprinted by permission of Henry Holt and Company, LLC.

"What Are You?" from WHAT ARE YOU? VOICES OF MIXED-RACE YOUNG PEOPLE by Pearl Fuyo Gaskins. Copyright © 1999 by Pearl Fuyo Gaskins. The poem "Half-Breed" by Brian Harris was first published in *New People* magazine. Reprinted by permission of Henry Holt and Company, LLC.

"Cookie" from MY LIFE IN DOG YEARS by Gary Paulsen. Copyright © 1998 by Gary Paulsen. Used by permission of Dell Publishing, a division of Random House, Inc.

"What Happened to Cookie?" from "A Dog Saved My Life" by Adam Grant from *Scholastic Scope* magazine, January 26, 1996. Copyright © 1996 by Scholastic Inc. Reprinted by permission of Scholastic Inc.

Cover from PUPPIES, DOGS, AND BLUE NORTHERS by Gary Paulsen. Copyright © 1996 by Gary Paulsen. Reprinted by permission of Harcourt, Inc.

Cover from DOGSONG by Gary Paulsen. Copyright © 1985 by Gary Paulsen. Reprinted with the permission of Simon & Schuster Children's Publishing Division.

Cover from HATCHET by Gary Paulsen. Copyright © 1987 by Gary Paulsen. Reprinted with the permission of Simon & Schuster Children's Publishing Division.

"Two Were Left" by Hugh B. Cave. Copyright © 1942 by the Crowell-Collier Publishing Company. All rights reserved. Reprinted by permission of HarperCollins Publishers.

Photo Credits

pp. 18-19, 34-35, 48-49, 62-63, 74-75, 84-85, 94-95, 108-109, 120-121, 132-133, 148-149, 166-167, 176-177, 188-189, 200-201, 214-215, 228-229, 242-243, 254-255, 270-271, 288-289, 318-319, 330-331, 340-341: Ken Karp for Scholastic Inc.; p. 15tr: ©David Maisel/Tony Stone Images; 15bl: ©David Fox/Oxford Scientific Films/Animals Animals; p. 17: Courtesy of Scholastic Trade Department; pp. 20-21: Courtesy of Burton Snowboards; p. 22: ©Ales Fevzer/CORBIS; p. 23: ©Ken Fisher/Tony Stone Images; pp. 24-25 (all photos): ©Brittain 1995; p. 26: ©Colin Samuels/Photonica; p. 27: ©Todd Gipstein/CORBIS; pp. 28-29: Courtesy of the Maroney Swim Team; p. 37tc: ©Butch Martin/The Image Bank; p. 37tr: ©1999 Comstock, Inc.; pp. 51, 52, 58, 60: ©Chris Roberts; p. 59: ©Jean Hobbs; pp. 64-65: ©Spencer Jones/FPG International; p. 66: ©Anne-Marie Weber/FPG International; pp. 68, 72: ©Telegraph Colour Library/FPG International; p. 70: ©Arthur Tilley/FPG International; p. 71: Courtesy of Scholastic Trade Department; pp. 76-80, 82: ©Silvia Otte; p. 81: ©Will & Deni McIntyre/Photo Researchers, Inc.; p. 81 (background): ©2000 PhotoDisc, Inc.; pp. 86-87: ©Brian Smith/Corbis Outline; pp. 88, 89bl, 92: ©Carrie Muskat; p. 89tr: ©Michael Lavine/Corbis Outline; p. 90ml: ©Archive Photos; p. 90bc: ©Dabre Rotach/CORBIS; p. 90mr: ©Fred R. Conrad/New York Times Co./Archive Photos; p. 91c: ©Bettmann/CORBIS; p. 91br: ©Reuters/CORBIS; p. 91bl: Courtesy of NASA; p. 102br: ©AP/Wide World Photos; p. 102tl: ©Nathan Benn/CORBIS; p. 103: ©CORBIS; p. 104: ©UPI/Bettmann/CORBIS; p. 105: ©Joseph Sohm; ChromoSohm Inc./CORBIS; pp. 110-111: ©Peggy Fox/Tony Stone Images; p. 112: ©Andy Levin/Photo Researchers Inc.; pp. 113, 118: ©Deborah Copaken/Gamma Liaison; p. 115: Courtesy of Doubleday; pp. 116-117: ©Allan McPhail/Tony Stone Images; pp. 122-123, 125, 126, 129tc: Courtesy of Movie Stills Archive/Paramount Pictures; p. 129mr: ©Archive Photos; pp. 142-143: ©Steve McCurry/National Geographic Image Collection; p. 144tl: ©Gamma Liaison; pp. 144-145tc, 145tr: ©Woodfin Camp and Associates; pp. 150-154, 156-161, 164: ©Bill Ballenberg; p. 163 ©Richard G. Rawlins/Custom Medical Stock Photo; p. 168: Courtesy of NASA; p. 168 (background): ©2000 PhotoDisc, Inc.; p. 170: Courtesy of NASA; p. 172ml: Courtesy of NASA; p. 172c: Courtesy of NASA/Science Photo Library; p. 172bc: ©Bettmann/CORBIS; p. 173br: Courtesy of NASA; p. 173 (all other photos): ©Photri, Inc./Microstock; p. 174: Courtesy of NASA; p. 185ml: Courtesy of Odessa Walker; p. 185mr: Courtesy of Free Spirit Publishing; p. 187: Courtesy of Carolyn Soto; p. 190: ©UPI/CORBIS; p. 191: ©AP/Wide World Photos; pp. 192, 197, 198: ©UPI/CORBIS; pp. 193, 195: ©UPI/Bettmann/CORBIS; p. 210: ©Mitchell Gerber/CORBIS; p. 213: ©Erin Grinstead; pp. 216-217: ©CORBIS; pp. 221, 226: Arthur Rothstein/Courtesy of The Library of Congress; p. 222: ©UPI/Bettmann/CORBIS; p. 223: Dorothea Lange/Courtesy of The Library of Congress; p. 225: ©Cheryl Liston; p. 239: ©Nick Dolding/Tony Stone Images; pp. 245, 252: ©Ron Garrison/Zoological Society of San Diego; pp. 246, 247: ©Thaddeus Govan; p. 248: ©John Lei; p. 249, 250: ©Paul S. Howell; p. 267: ©David Creamer/Gamma Liaison; p. 269: John Lei for Scholastic Inc.; 272-273, 282: ©Morton Beebe, S.F./CORBIS; pp. 274, 276 (all photos), 279bc, 279tr, 286: ©Bettmann/CORBIS; p. 279mr: ©American Stock/Archive Photos; p. 279tl: ©Underwood & Underwood/CORBIS; p. 281: ©Robert Holmes/CORBIS; p. 283: ©Bruce Hands/Tony Stone Images; p. 284: ©Andrea Pistolesi/The Image Bank; p. 317: ©Hulton-Deutsch Collection/CORBIS; pp. 320, 323: ©Robin Holland; pp. 322, 324, 326-328: Courtesy of Pearl Fuyo Gaskins; p. 325: ©Yuen Lui; pp. 332-333: ©Jeff Schultz/Alaska Stock; p. 334: ©Ruth Wright Paulsen; p. 336: ©Richard T. Nowitz/CORBIS; p. 338: ©Ruth Wright Paulsen

Illustrations Credits

pp. 6-7, 11, 14, 16: Cathi Mingus; pp. 18, 48, 74, 176, 214, 330: Deb Lofaso; p. 29: Leonard D. Dank; pp. 34, 120, 132, 148, 200, 270, 289: Joe Borzetta; pp. 39, 41, 42-43, 45, 46: Brad Walker; pp. 62, 188, 242, 340: Elliot Kreloff; pp. 84, 94, 166: Elana Goren - Totino; pp. 96-97, 99, 101, 106: Eric Velasquez; p. 108: Bennett/ Christian Science Monitor; pp. 134-135, 138, 146: John Lytle; pp. 140-141, 285: Jim McMahon; p. 156: Courtesy of Byron Press Visual; pp. 179, 180, 183, 186: Matt Archambault; pp. 203, 205, 206, 207, 208, 209, 212: Russell O. Jones; p. 228: Ron Zalme; pp. 230-231, 234, 238, 240: Tom Patrick; p. 251: James Kirkland; pp. 256-257, 260, 261, 263, 266, 268: Don Stewart; p. 318: Glen Davis pp. 291-317: Mike Lilly/ Unstoppable Prod; p. 335: Ruth Wright Paulsen; p. 340: ©CORBIS

Cover Credits

tl (girl), bc (boy), tr (basketball): Ken Karp for Scholastic Inc.; bl (football players): ©Bill Ballenberg; tc (Alcatraz): ©Morton Beebe, S.F./CORBIS; c (basketball players): ©Spencer Jones/FPG International; br (dust storm): ©CORBIS